Creative Drama in the Classroom and Beyond

Nellie McCaslin
New York University

Foreword by Shifra Schonmann

PEARSON

and

Boston   New York   San Francisco
Mexico City   Montreal   Toronto   London   Madrid   Munich   Paris
Hong Kong   Singapore   Tokyo   Cape Town   Sydney

Series Editor: Traci Mueller
Series Editorial Assistant: Janice Hackenberg
Senior Marketing Manager: Krista Groshong
Production Editor: Beth Houston
Composition Buyer: Linda Cox
Manufacturing Buyer: Andrew Turso
Editorial-Production Service and Electronic Composition: Elm Street Publishing Services, Inc.
Cover Administrator: Kristina Mose-Libon

For related titles and support materials, visit our online catalog at www.ablongman.com.

Between the time website information is gathered and then published, it is not unusual for some sites to have closed. Also, the transcription of URLs can result in typographical errors. The publisher would appreciate notification where these errors occur so that they may be corrected in subsequent editions.

Library of Congress Cataloging-in-Publication Data

McCaslin, Nellie
    Creative drama in the classroom and beyond / Nellie McCaslin.—
    8th ed.
        p.   cm.
    Includes bibliographical references (p.) and index.
    ISBN 0-205-45116-0 (alk. paper)
    1. Drama in education.   I. Title.
PN3171.M25   2006
371.39'9—dc22   2004061956

Printed in the United States of America

10 9 8 7 6 5 4 3   09 08 07 06

Arts Education can foster students' independent thinking, enhance their communication and comprehension skills; it can also help to inspire creativity, integrate knowledge and broaden their horizons.

—Hong Kong Arts Development Council

To R. Rex Stephenson, who has enriched the lives of so many in so many different ways.

Contents

7. *Puppetry and Mask Making   109*

8. *Dramatic Structure: The Play Takes Shape   142*

9. *Building Plays from Stories   156*

7. *Puppetry and Mask Making*   109

8. *Dramatic Structure: The Play Takes Shape*   142

9. *Building Plays from Stories*   156

Part II   Programs Beyond The Classroom

Foreword

Nellie McCaslin's seminal book, *Creative Drama in the Classroom and Beyond*, is among the very few in the field of Drama/Theatre Education that have remained relevant for more than three decades. The first edition was published in 1968 and endowed the field with fresh new concepts, methods, and professional standards. Thirty-six years later, its freshness, creativity, and ingenuity remain intact and continue to inspire development in the field.

What makes the book so valuable for educators, researchers, students, and artists alike is its accessibility derived from McCaslin's clear and accurate voice and conscious decision to emphasize practicality backed by theory. It is her personal practical knowledge, broad and deep, that makes the book sincere, authentic, and insightful. Professor McCaslin is a master in the field. Her book is about imagination, dealing with a variety of creative forms in drama and theatre in the classroom and beyond. Her familiarity with the body of literature in the field, old and new, makes this edition a valuable sourcebook for college students and professionals alike.

The field of Drama/Theatre Education has greatly evolved over the years, broadening as new ideas proliferate and as new terms emerge to encapsulate developments. While an assortment of concepts, such as *Applied Theatre* and *Process Drama*, periodically surface, carrying a promise to modernize and reinvent the field, McCaslin preserves the core notions of creativity and imagination, which remain the common denominator of all these new conceptualizations.

In her perception, an ordinary room will become a place in which exciting things can happen only if the leader is sensitive enough to create an atmosphere of mutual trust in which every child is accepted and respected. Nellie McCaslin offers us substantial assertions that continue to sprout debates in the field: *"Imagination is the spark that sets off the creative impulse"; "True play does not know professionalism, for it is a voluntary activity, based on, but different from, the business of everyday life"; "There is no right or wrong order and no prescribed length of time the group should spend on one kind of exercise."*

Her credo is that the sensitive leader *"tries to create an atmosphere of mutual trust. In his or her acceptance of every child and what the child has to offer, the leader has taken the first big step toward helping the child build self-confidence. Freedom will follow, learning will occur."* John Dewey's inspiration is evident in guiding her thinking and adding to her sense of truth and beauty.

Activities and exericses are valued as tools for self-expression and as springboards to other, more extensive, projects. The warning that Professor McCaslin delivers deserves serious attention. She is saying that *"theatre games and warm-ups are fine but they are not ends in themselves. A group needs to advance and will become bored when there is a continued absence of substance with no obvious long-range goals."*

The book is rich with ideas exemplified with thoughtful insight on children and childhood as well as on art and aesthetic education. It leads *"to the challenge to preserve the fun of theatre. A word chosen consciously and with care in our effort to enrich education through drama and to sponsor theatre with greater substance than it has in the past."* She refers to *fun* not in its trivial sense but rather fun as the joy that comes from creating drama or from watching superb performers.

Professor McCaslin thinks about creative drama in terms of education and about education in terms of the arts, which gives creativity and imagination predominance in her own thinking and practice. The book invites us to join an ongoing conversation with past and present changes in the field. We enter classrooms, under Professor McCaslin's guidance, with enthusiasm, care, imagination, and creativity.

SHIFRA SCHONMANN, Haifa, Israel

Preface

In 1968 when the first edition of *Creative Drama in the Classroom* was published, I had no idea that I would be working on an eighth edition 35 years later. The original text contained 168 pages, only ten chapters and no illustrations, but it apparently met the needs of teachers at the time. Four years later a second edition was requested; it was longer and today as I sit at my desk viewing all the succeeding editions I marvel at the expansion of our field, its breadth and depth, and the growth of drama and theatre education.

National and international organizations have been founded during this period; publication has exploded; conferences and conventions are now held from coast to coast; and colleges and universities are offering not only courses but degrees in theatre and child drama.

By the time I began work on the sixth edition, classes were being offered on a regular basis in community centers, churches, libraries, and other nonacademic sites. These venues, though certainly not new, were being funded and administered by professionals and for these reasons I changed the title of the book to *Creative Drama in the Classroom and Beyond*. Photographs of players in these and other settings were added to photographs in schools and colleges. This development obviously called for a new chapter in succeeding editions. Conspicuous areas of interest today are drama in education and drama therapy.

There has been recognition of drama therapy in America since the 1920s, but the distinctions between psychodrama, sociodrama, and drama therapy have not until recently been clarified in the minds of many. Today these disciplines are taught and practiced in a variety of venues, and graduate degrees are awarded in two universities. The Association for Theatre and Disability also meets regularly, focusing on the needs of special populations so often excluded from both theatre and dramatic activities available to the able-bodied.

As for theatre in a multicultural society, its importance today is scarcely news. The first dramatic arts programs in this country were located in social settlement houses for the benefit of immigrant children. The difference between those programs and the ones offered today, however, is that the former were established, in part, to teach children the English language and American ways. Today, in contrast, the goal is to share the cultures of a diverse population by recognizing the rich cultural heritage that the immigrants bring with them. Not that one goal precludes the other, but today's efforts stress inclusion in a larger sense. The settlement houses once provided a place in which parents were welcome to attend programs for their children; today, many theatres are producing and booking plays advertised as suitable for family audiences. The wording may differ, but the goals and results are the same.

Large arts centers with impressive budgets and professional staffs are providing cultural events and arts classes in a field that for the first half of this century—indeed, until the establishment of the National Endowment for the Arts and the state arts councils—was almost entirely nonprofessional and inadequately supported. In reviewing the century in which theatre for young people has grown from a collection of unrelated programs into a recognized and respected movement, we find the same three basic objectives: providing an aesthetic experience for young viewers, promoting the educational values of theatre, and giving opportunities for social growth through attendance and participation in theatre.

Our professional associations have expanded and have undergone major structural changes. The AATE (American Alliance for Theatre and Education), founded in 1987 following the demise of the ATA (American Theatre Association) parent body, now has a large national membership. In July 2003 a joint meeting of AATE and ATHE (Association for Theatre in Higher Education) met in New York City. Support for these organizations comes primarily from dues and advertising, a fact that is astonishing to those of us who held regional conferences in the sixties and remember that we held bake sales to meet expenses. In those days conferences generally took place on college campuses; today they are held in big city hotels. Perhaps we have lost the intimacy we once enjoyed but in becoming larger and better known we can attract nationally known speakers and first-class hotel accommodations.

Advocates for the arts in education have drawn closer to colleagues in other arts organizations, thereby strengthening all of us as we work together toward common goals. Since the publication of the first edition of this book, there has also been an increased awareness of the international scene. ASSITEJ (Association Internationale du Théâtre pour l'Enfance et la Jeunesse) has contributed concepts, research, and professional standards. Creative drama no longer stands alone but is a part of a larger field.

Have these developments made a difference in our philosophy and attitudes? I asked myself. And, if they have, what revision will be required to make this book a stronger and more useful resource? The obvious first step was to go to some of those who use it and ask for their suggestions. This I have done. Their suggestions included the addition of more lesson plans, an expansion of Chapters 14 and 15, an updated bibliography, and a recommendation to keep the basic format and content as it stands. As I believe that a much longer text would work to its disadvantage, I have cut and honed carefully to preserve as much as possible of what readers find valuable as I add the new material.

In the sixth edition I included storytelling; the use of creative drama in the teaching of creative writing; the field of drama therapy; clowning and the circus arts in education; theatre in which puppets and human actors perform together; participatory theatre, in which creative drama and formal theatre merge; and theatre-in-education and drama-in-education, British concepts that have captured the attention of teachers not only in the English-speaking world but in other countries as well. Educational and societal problems are symptomatic of our age, and the theatre arts appear to be effective tools for change. Chapter 20 has been replaced with "The After-School Drama Program," which may be more relevant to the needs of a growing number of instructors.

As in all the previous editions, I have added some new activities, stories, poems, and problems to be solved. A conscious decision was made in the beginning to emphasize practicality rather than theory; the theory is implicit, serving as a guide for activities I have found to be successful. I believe that experience in drama and theatre enhances the quality of life, and it is to this end that I am most deeply committed. To bring satisfaction and joy into the lives of all people and to awaken a respect and concern for all living creatures: these are the ultimate goals of an enlightened society. Clarity, accuracy, and simplicity are the qualities I strive to achieve, with respect for all persons, regardless of age, gender, or social, ethnic, racial, and religious background.

There are many excellent books on drama and theatre education on the market today, and while I include two chapters on this aspect, my focus has been and remains the study of theatre as an art form first and foremost. It is to that end that I am most deeply committed.

As in the earlier editions, I have presented the progression I personally follow, but it may not be the best for everyone. There are many ways of teaching, and I urge every teacher to try different approaches and become familiar with different strategies. This book is intended as a college textbook for students who are preparing to teach in the classroom or to specialize in child drama. It is organized around a point of view rather than along specific age levels, for I believe the philosophy to be the same, regardless of the age of the participants. Indeed, workshops for senior adults have shown that many of the creative drama activities written with children in mind are equally effective with this older population. And, I must add, drama is a form of recreation in the true sense of the word—"to re-create oneself."

Attending plays in the 1980s took on new dimensions as television became the primary form of popular entertainment in America. Producers and sponsors of children's plays, alarmed that live theatre was rapidly being replaced by television and film, recognized their responsibility to provide more than an hour of entertainment if they hoped to survive such formidable competition. This meant new demands on children's theatre: it must have the excitement and aesthetic appeal of the living theatre at its best, yet it must not, in its effort to entertain, be lacking in substance. When content and entertainment are held in balance and the script is well performed, the result is a rich experience to which all children should be exposed.

Although professional theatres employ adult actors, the subject of children's performing does come up. Except for very young children, an occasional performance for a sympathetic audience seems to me a natural culmination of a creative drama project and a highly rewarding experience. I would argue with those who regard all performance by children as undesirable. Their attitude is based on a response that many of us have had to the wooden acting and obvious boredom of children who were forced to endure long rehearsal periods in an attempt to attain a level of perfection that could not and should not have been expected. This goal, unfortunately, often led to another undesirable practice: putting only the so-called talented children on the stage at the expense of their classmates, who may have needed the experience far more than they did. Furthermore, such productions were often put in the hands of teachers who had no background in the theatre arts, yet were required to put on a play or present an assembly program every year. This practice was painful to all involved, rather than being the joyful experience that playmaking should be. Doing away with performance was probably a necessary step in shifting priorities from product to process. An occasional performance under the guidance of a teacher or director with some background in theatre should take place in a familiar setting for a friendly and understanding audience.

I am, however, distressed to see that the old Broadway musical is still a staple for middle schools and high schools. These are too often inappropriate and too demanding of young voices. There is material far better suited to the age and interests of teenagers. Indeed, a growing number of young playwrights are writing scripts that deal with the problems and concerns of adolescents. I urge high school teachers and directors to look into this new material. No longer are fairy tales the only available choices or the Broadway musical the best choice for large group participation. If a shortened version of an appropriate musical is available, I would give a tentative approval but primarily for social goals.

A problem that plagues most teachers of the arts is evaluation of student work. Although many of us would prefer not to give grades at all, we can and should assess both individual and group progress. One tool I have found helpful is a chart listing the criteria for growth and development in skills being taught. If a letter grade is required, making this kind of evaluation first will help the teacher reach a decision. Many elementary schools today use paragraph reports rather than grades, a practice that is particularly appropriate for evaluating students' work in the arts. When teachers review the growth of the participants as individuals and as members of the group, the focus is shifted from product to process. Looking at development of imagination as well as improvement in communication, expression, and cooperation with other players will lead to greater objectivity, although the risk of subjective evaluation can probably never be entirely eliminated. Encouragement, praise when due, and constructive criticism I believe is effective in every case for personal growth and improved skills.

I am aware that few classroom teachers have had much experience in the performing arts and that some directors lack experience with children. If the chapters that follow hasten the learning process by offering a point of view and some practical ways of working, they will have accomplished their purpose. As I have said before, it has never been my intention to provide either a recipe book or simply a collection of exercises. Exercises are valuable in creative drama, as they are in the study of any art, but they are not ends in themselves and should not be used as such. Rather, they should be regarded as warm-ups or as preparation for work in greater depth. Many of the activities I have included are fun, and players enjoy them; all of them strengthen the players in different ways. They help to develop concentration, imagination, and the use of the voice and body. But by repeating them endlessly, as I have seen done, some teachers make the exercises little more than charades, leading administrators to question the validity of drama in the curriculum.

Within the past ten years my travels have taken me to Europe, Asia, and Israel, where I have had the opportunity to lecture and lead workshops with students. We are no longer working in isolation. Theatre has become an important area of interest and is either being taught or promoted vigorously throughout the world. The eighth edition bears witness to the fact.

Multiculturalism is emphasized throughout the text stressing the point that students today must be encouraged to learn about each other's cultures, values, beliefs, and the riches they have brought to our country.

I want to acknowledge the inspiration that has come from my many friends and colleagues in this country and abroad. In the earlier editions I listed the names of persons to whom I felt particularly indebted. That list has grown to the point that it would be impossible to name them all. But their thinking and work continue to shape my views, just as their writing has contributed to the field. I want also to acknowledge the pioneering work that has been done in the area of drama therapy. Teachers of the arts have long recognized the value of drama in special education, but until recently little was done to provide opportunities for participation.

I am most appreciative of the suggestions of the following reviewers, whose observations and insights have contributed to the development of this new edition: Patch Clark, East Carolina University; Leni Dyer, Austin Peay State University; Julie Holston, South Mountain Community College.

My gratitude goes also to the producers and teachers who sent pictures. I cannot thank them enough, for the illustrations add a view of the work that is being done in all parts of the country. Finally, this list would be incomplete without a special word of thanks to my students and colleagues, past and present; their observations and questions stimulate my own thinking and have made me reconsider, clarify, and sometimes modify a point of view.

NELLIE MCCASLIN

Part I

Creative Drama in the Classroom

Part One deals with the uses and techniques of creative drama in the elementary school classroom. Imagination, movement, pantomime, improvisation, story dramatization, puppetry, drama-in-education, and storytelling are among the topics treated. These practical elements are supplemented by the enrichment included in Part Two.

Chapter 1

Creative Drama: An Art, a Socializing Activity, and a Way of Learning

A socializing activity. Back at home after a rehearsal. (Courtesy of Alexandra Plotkin, photograph by Garnet Pennington.)

> Theatre takes the student into many areas of
> human knowledge—literature, art, music, politics,
> economics, philosophy, science, invention—
> practically exploring all of man's activities and
> ideas. The study of the theatre can be, and ideally
> is, the most liberalizing of all the liberal arts.
>   *—Vera Mowry Roberts*

Few adults would deny the importance of the arts in the education of their children. If children are to enjoy the arts and appreciate the richness that the arts can add to human life, however, some preparation is needed. For most children, that preparation is, or should be, given in school. The questions to be addressed, therefore, concern not so much an educational philosophy as practical matters of budget, time, and place in the curriculum; grade-level allocation; and local priorities. Although music and the visual arts have long held tenure in the curriculum of many schools, the theatre arts have not. Now, however, despite budget cuts, drama is being mandated in a number of states. The most valid argument offered in support of this action is the most obvious. Of all the arts, drama involves the participant the most fully: intellectually, emotionally, physically, verbally, and socially. As players, children assume the roles of others, and they learn about and become sensitive to the problems and values of persons different from themselves. At the same time, they are learning to work cooperatively, for drama is a communal art; each person is necessary to the whole.

As spectators, children become involved vicariously in the adventures of characters on the stage. Drama also offers children an opportunity to become acquainted with literature and to enjoy the visual arts through scenery and costumes. Discipline is an important element of the theatre, both on- and offstage, but children readily accept this in much the same way that members of an athletic team are willing to suspend personal wishes and interests for the sake of group goals and interests. Drama is the first art we discover as toddlers and the last we relinquish in old age. Since the advent of television, drama has come into our living rooms, into hospitals, and into nursing homes, making the performing arts available as long as we live. Although we may deplore the number of hours that children spend in front of the screen, for the house-bound and the hospitalized, television provides theatre, music, dance, news, and sports, enabling viewers to escape the physical and geographic boundaries of their beds and chairs.

The child who is given an opportunity to participate in creative drama in a comfortable and nonpressured classroom and to see plays of high quality has advantages that extend into all areas of life. With such an abundance of riches, it is easy to understand why so many believe that drama and theatre constitute an elaborate art form, difficult to implement and expensive to maintain. Actually, creative drama needs no special equipment, no studio, and no stage; time, space, and an enthusiastic, well-prepared leader are the only requirements. As for theatre, most actors can perform anywhere, provided the play does not depend on special effects or sophisticated staging. Professional touring companies perform in all-purpose rooms and cafeterias.

A stage may enhance the production, to be sure, but it is seldom a necessity. There are aesthetic values to be found in beautiful visual effects, but they are not necessary to the majority of plays designed for young audiences. Sincerity, sensitivity, and intelligent planning are the most important components of an effective performance. In many communities, the local university or civic theatre offers plays to which classes are bused during school hours at little or no cost to the children. Many of these productions are excellent, sensitively played, and tastefully staged. In recent years, an educational component has become an important service offered by producers. Workshops for children following a performance, special workshops for teachers, and an effort to relate plays to the curriculum have become common practices and enrich the experience.

The theatre arts, then, are the least expensive of the arts to implement, with the greatest potential for learning. They have a place in our schools on all levels because they constitute a subject in its own right, to be treated seriously, not added only as a frill or an enhancement if the budget permits. Moreover, in the best arts programs, students learn the basic skills through the process of creative drama, for the commonly held objectives of education are remarkably similar to the objectives of creative drama. Let us compare them.

Educational Objectives

One of the most frequently stated aims of education is the maximal growth of the child both as an individual and as a member of society. To achieve this aim, certain educational objectives have been set up. Although these objectives vary somewhat, there is general agreement that knowledge and appreciation as well as skills in the arts are essential. The modern curriculum tries to ensure that each child will achieve these goals:[1]

1. Develop basic skills in which reading, writing, arithmetic, science, social studies, and the arts are stressed.
2. Develop and maintain good physical and mental health.
3. Grow in ability to think.
4. Clarify values and verbalize beliefs and hopes.
5. Develop an understanding of beauty, using many media, including words, color, sound, and movement.
6. Grow creatively and thus experience his or her own creative powers.

Although these objectives were written more than thirty-five years ago, they are still valid for their timelessness and universality. Other objectives are mentioned, but these six are most frequently listed in the development of educational programs designed for today's world and the complex problems that life offers.

---

[1]Robert S. Fleming, *Curriculum for Today's Boys and Girls* (Columbus: Merrill, 1963), p. 10.

The most enthusiastic proponent of creative drama would not go so far as to claim that its inclusion in the curriculum will ensure the meeting of these objectives. But many objectives of modern education and creative drama are unquestionably shared. Among them are these:

1. Creativity and aesthetic development
2. The ability to think critically
3. Social growth and the ability to work cooperatively with others
4. Improved communication skills
5. The development of moral and spiritual values
6. Knowledge of self
7. Understanding and appreciation of the cultural backgrounds and values of others.

In the words of Mary F. Heller, "The children in our classrooms come from diverse backgrounds, when values and beliefs of the family and community influence their thoughts, feelings, and behaviors toward schooling. It is important for teachers to remember that all children bring with them a richness of experience from which to draw upon during the process of becoming literate."[2]

Schoolchildren today represent a rainbow of cultures, each with its own set of traditions and values. They are bringing varied ethnic, racial, linguistic, and cultural backgrounds into classrooms that only fifty or sixty years ago were homogeneous. An influx of immigrants presents a challenge to the teacher, who may have students speaking several different languages. This is a difficult assignment for even the most experienced teacher, yet it brings an unprecedented opportunity to help children learn firsthand about others whose cultural backgrounds are vastly different from their own. There is no better way of sharing life experiences than through drama, which involves both intellect and emotions.

In his *Frames of Mind,* Howard Gardner discusses seven kinds of intelligence, a concept that is relevant to American education: linguistic, musical, logical-mathematical, spatial, bodily-kinesthetic, interpersonal, and intrapersonal. He defines intelligence as the ability to solve problems or to create products that are valued within one or more cultural settings.[3] For example, the Inuit, because of their environment and their way of life, value spatial intelligence, whereas in the Anang society of Nigeria, music and dance are most highly prized. Our society, in contrast, gives high priority to linguistic and mathematical abilities. Were we to reconsider intelligence in Gardner's terms, we could expand our view of language and the arts, thus opening the door to greater understanding and respect for the cultural backgrounds and values of others.

A wealth of possibilities lies inside the door of every classroom: storytelling, improvisation, playmaking, movement and dance, puppetry, creative writing, field trips to the theatre and children's museums, putting on a play.

Before we discuss creative drama in detail, some definitions are in order. The terms *dramatic play, creative drama, playmaking, children's theatre, process drama,*

---

[2]Mary F. Heller, *Reading-Writing Connections* (White Plains, NY: Longman, 1995), p. 23.
[3]Howard Gardner, *Frames of Mind: The Theory of Multiple Intelligences* (New York: Basic Books, 1983).

and *role playing* often are used interchangeably, although they have different meanings. Drama is participant centered, whereas theatre is audience centered. The following definitions will clarify the meanings of these terms as they are used in this book.

Definitions

Dramatic Play

Dramatic play is the free play of very young children, in which they explore their universe, imitating the actions and character traits of those around them. It is their earliest expression in dramatic form but must not be confused with drama or interpreted as performance. Dramatic play is fragmentary, existing only for the moment. It may last for a few minutes or go on for some time. It even may be played repeatedly if the child's interest is sufficiently strong, but when this occurs, the repetition is in no sense a rehearsal. It is, rather, the repetition of a creative experience for the pure joy of doing it. Dramatic play has no beginning and no end and no development in the dramatic sense.

It has been stated that "dramatic play helps the child develop from a purely egocentric being into a person capable of sharing and of give and take."[4] In dramatic play children create a world of their own in which to master reality. They try in this imaginative world to solve real-life problems. They repeat, reenact, and relive these experiences. In the book *Understanding Children's Play,* the authors observed that through this activity children are given an opportunity to imitate adults and are encouraged to play out real-life roles with intensity, to dramatize relationships and experiences, to express their own most pressing needs, to release unacceptable impulses, to reverse the roles usually taken to try to solve problems, and to experiment with solutions. If adults encourage such behavior by providing the place, the equipment, and an atmosphere in which a child feels free, dramatic play is a natural and healthy manifestation of human growth.

Creative Drama and Playmaking

Creative drama is an umbrella term that covers playmaking, process drama, and improvisation; it refers to informal drama that is created by the participants.[5] As the term *playmaking* implies, the activity goes beyond dramatic play in scope and intent. It may make use of a story with a beginning, a middle, and an end. It may also explore, develop, and express ideas and feelings through dramatic enactment. It is, however,

---

[4]Ruth Hartley, Lawrence K. Frank, and Robert M. Goldenson, *Understanding Children's Play* (New York: Columbia University Press, 1964), p. 19.

[5]This definition of the term *creative drama* was accepted by the Children's Theatre Association of America in 1977: "Creative drama is an improvisational, nonexhibitional, process-centered form of drama in which participants are guided by a leader to imagine, enact, and reflect upon human experiences. Although creative drama traditionally has been thought of in relation to children and young people, the process is appropriate to all ages." *Children's Theatre Review,* vol. 27, no. 1, pp. 10–11.

always improvised drama. Dialogue is created by the players, whether the content is taken from a well-known story or is an original plot. Lines are not written down or memorized. With each playing, the story becomes more detailed and better organized, but it remains extemporaneous and is at no time designed for an audience. Participants are guided by a leader rather than a director; the leader's goal is the optimal growth and development of the players.

The replaying of scenes is therefore different from the rehearsal of a formal play in that each member of the group is given an opportunity to play various parts. No matter how many times the story is played, it is for the purpose of deepening understanding and strengthening the performers rather than perfecting a product. Scenery and costumes are not necessary in creative drama, although an occasional property or piece of costume may be included to stimulate the imagination and because players often like to use them. Most groups do not feel the need for properties of any kind and are generally freer without them.

The term *creative drama* is used to describe the improvised drama of children age five or six and older, but it belongs to no particular age level and may be used just as appropriately to describe the improvisation of high school students. The young adult is more likely to label this activity *improvisation,* which indeed it is, but the important distinction is that creative drama has form and is therefore more structured than dramatic play. At the same time, it is participant centered and not intended for sharing, except with the members of the group who are not playing and are therefore observers rather than audience.

The word *drama* is also used to mean "literature." In the present context, however, it is used to mean a play that is developed creatively by a group, as opposed to one that abides by a written script. When dialogue is written by either teacher or students, drama automatically ceases to be spontaneous, although a play may, indeed, be a fine example of creative writing. Whether it is simple or elaborate, if a play is to be properly described as creative drama, it must be improvised rather than written.

Process Drama

Process drama is a term used by Cecily O'Neill to describe the "pre-text" (or what had taken place previously) and the development of a drama created by a group. The teacher begins the session with a situation but, instead of starting to work on it, leads to a discussion about what had led up to the situation. Slowly the group builds a background. The process takes time, but by working in this way, the group expands a body of information, deepens understanding, and develops a richer and more interesting interpretation and enactment. The emphasis is on learning through drama rather than on drama as an art form in its own right.

Children's Theatre

The term *children's theatre* refers to formal productions for child audiences, whether acted by amateurs or professionals, children or adults. Children's theatre is directed rather than guided; dialogue is memorized, and scenery and costumes usually play an important part. Since it is audience centered, children's theatre is essentially different from creative drama and dramatic play. The child in the audience is the spectator, and the benefits derived are aesthetic.

Theatre for Young Audiences

The term *theatre for young audiences* has come into common usage within the past few years. It is a way of saying that the entertainment is appropriate for older children rather than for only the very young.

Family Theatre

The term *family theatre* further states that the play or program will appeal to adults as well as to young people.

What do children gain from attending good children's theatre? They gain much: the thrill of watching a well-loved story come alive on a stage; the opportunity for a strong vicarious experience as they identify with characters who are brave, steadfast, noble, loyal, or intelligent; the release of emotions as the audience shares the adventure and excitement of the plot. Finally, children learn to appreciate the art of the theatre if they see productions that are tasteful and well done.

We are speaking now of children in the audience, not in the play. Although there is much that is creative and of value for the performer, it is generally agreed that participation in creative drama is far more beneficial than public performances for all children up to the age of ten or eleven. Occasionally, children express a desire to put on a play, and when this comes from the young players themselves, it is wise to grant the request. There are times when sharing is a joy and a positive experience, but children's participation in formal play production should be infrequent. Certainly, if it is done, the production should be simple, and all precautions should be taken to guard against the competition and tension that so often characterize the formal presentation of a play. For students in junior and senior high school, however, a play is often the desired culmination of a semester's work. To deprive students of the experience would be to withhold the ultimate satisfaction of communicating an art.

Some leaders in the field believe that any performance in front of an audience is harmful because it interferes with the child's own free expression. I agree up to a point, but the theatre is, after all, a performing art, and when the audience is composed of understanding and sympathetic persons, such as parents or members of another class, performance may be the first step toward communicating a joyful experience. Without question, however, very young children should not perform publicly. Those in the middle and upper grades will not be harmed if their desire and the right occasion indicate that the benefits outweigh the disadvantages. A performance is a disciplined and carefully organized endeavor involving a variety of skills that children in the primary grades cannot be expected to master.

I am not speaking here of the professional child actor, who, most educators agree, is in grave danger of being damaged by exploitation and the pressures of performance. The same dangers, however, are present whenever children are used for ends other than their own growth and development. When children are trained rather than guided, praised extravagantly instead of encouraged, or featured as individuals rather than helped to work cooperatively with others, they risk losing all positive aspects of the experience. Ironically, this leads to poor theatre as well, for ensemble, that most desirable quality of good theatre, is achieved through the process of working together, not by featuring individual players.

Role Playing

The term *role playing* is used most often in connection with therapy or education. It refers to the assuming of a role for the particular value it may have to the participant rather than for the development of an art. Although all art can be considered to have certain curative powers, it is not the primary purpose of either creative drama or theatre to provide therapy or make use of drama to solve social and emotional problems. Role playing is what the young child does in a dramatic play, though it is also a tool used by psychologists and play therapists. (See Chapter 15 for more on this topic.)

Acting is, in a way, an extension of dramatic play. According to Richard Courtney, "play, acting and thought are interrelated. They are mechanisms by which the individual tests reality, gets rid of his anxieties, and masters his environment."[6]

Drama Therapy

Drama therapy is similar to role playing in its stated purpose. Its use assumes a problem for which this type of treatment is indicated. Children who are physically disabled, mentally retarded, emotionally disturbed, or economically disadvantaged may derive great benefit from its use if the therapy is provided by a competent and sensitive therapist. The distinction between role playing and therapy is more of degree than of kind. *Role playing* may be considered preventive in that it provides an opportunity for all members of a group to develop sensitivity toward the feelings of others and encourages changes of attitude through understanding. *Therapy* is the dramatic technique used for its curative power in helping a patient to solve problems that frighten, confuse, or puzzle him or her. "It is in itself both a form of comfort and reassurance, and a way of moving on toward new attitudes about these things."[7]

Participation Theatre

Participation theatre is a technique originated by Brian Way in England. It permits the audience to become vocally, verbally, and physically involved in the production.[8] Children are invited to suggest ideas to the actors from time to time during the enactment of a play. Frequently, the audience, if not too large, is invited to come into

---

[6]Richard Courtney, *Play, Drama, and Thought: The Intellect Education* (New York: Drama Book Specialists, 1974), p. 177.

[7]Peter Slade, *Child Drama* (London: University of London Press, 1954), p. 119.

[8]Brian Way, *Audience Participation* (Boston: Baker's Plays, 1981). In this book Way begins with a description of his study of the child audience. On the basis of his observations, he developed a play structure in which spaces were left open for audience input and actual physical participation. This meant, first, reducing the size of the audience to a manageable group of no more than 250 persons, preferably seated in the round. Next was the training of his actors to handle the technique: how to invite children's responses, how to involve them in the action, and how to get them back into their seats when their part in the play was finished.

the playing area to assist the cast in working out these ideas. Skillfully handled, this can be an exciting technique.

All theatre involves participation the moment the attention is captured. An audience feels, thinks, laughs, applauds, and occasionally speaks out; in our time, unlike the case in earlier periods, adult audiences are expected to sit quietly whether or not the performances please them. The child audience, however, less inhibited and unschooled in these conventions, wants to do more. Children become actively engaged as they suspend all disbelief. They identify with the protagonist and participate in the action to the extent that conditions and authority permit. The younger the audience, the more natural the involvement. The point to be made here is that Brian Way's method offers an approach to children's theatre that combines the formal with the informal in its attempt to establish a closer relationship between actor and audience. The line commonly drawn between creative drama and children's theatre disappears as the spectator becomes a participant.

Developmental Drama

The term *developmental drama* has been used primarily by Richard Courtney in Canada. Although we occasionally find it in the literature here, Courtney's definition is the best and clearest we have:

> Developmental drama is the study of developmental patterns in human enactment. Drama is an active bridge between our inner world and the environment. Thus the developments studied are both personal and cultural, and each is in interaction with the other. These studies overlap with other fields: with psychology and philosophy on a personal level, and with sociology and anthropology on a cultural level. Despite the use of these allied fields, however, the focus of study within developmental drama is always the *dramatic act*.[9]

Drama-in-Education

Drama-in-education (DIE) is the use of drama as a means of teaching other subject areas. It is used to expand children's awareness, to enable them to look at reality through fantasy, to see below the surface of actions to their meanings. The objective is understanding rather than playmaking, although a play may be made in the process. Attitudes rather than characters are the chief concern. Proponents of DIE say that this technique can be used to teach any subject. (See Chapter 14.)

Classroom teachers find drama a valuable tool for involving children in the study of a topic. Rather than dramatizing a story or developing a play, children project themselves into a dramatic moment of the topic at hand (e.g., a mine disaster, a strike, a gold rush, an election); from there they go on to examine and learn more about the topic. They *become* the persons in the situation as they study it. The teacher brings in source materials and guides the study and may even play a role in the enactment. A play may result, but it is not the purpose of this use of drama.

---

[9]Richard Courtney, *Re-Play: Studies of Human Drama in Education* (Toronto: Ontario Institute for Studies in Education, 1982), p. 5.

Theatre-in-Education

Theatre-in-education (TIE) is a British concept that differs from traditional children's theatre in its use of curricular material or social problems as themes. Performed by professional companies of actor-teachers, TIE presents thought-provoking content to young audiences for educational purposes rather than for entertainment. It must entertain to hold their attention, but that is not the primary purpose. The intent is to challenge the spectator and push him or her to further thinking and feeling about the issue. John O'Toole describes TIE as follows:

> TIE (Theatre-in-Education) was conceived as an attempt to bring the techniques of the theatre into the classroom, in the service of specific educational objectives. . . . Its aim was more than to be entertaining and thought-provoking, or to encourage the habit of theatre-going. . . . First, the material is usually specially devised, tailor-made to the needs of the children and the strength of the team. Second, the children are asked to participate; endowed with roles, they learn skills, make decisions, and solve problems, so the programs' structures have to be flexible . . . to respond to the children's contributions within the context of the drama and still to uphold the roles. . . . Third, teams are usually aware of the importance of the teaching context, and try to prepare suggestions for follow-up work, or to hold preliminary workshops for classroom teachers.[10]

See Chapter 17 for more on this topic.

Forum Theatre

Forum theatre participants intervene in the action in order to change the direction. Class members (or audience) will first view a situation involving a social problem that is difficult to solve. After seeing the scene enacted, children are invited to step into the action as protagonists and try another solution. By replacing the original actor, the audience changes the outcome. This solution may not be satisfactory to everyone either, so another group proposes a third solution. This procedure, practiced successfully by Augusto Boal, automatically empowers the spectator to become the protagonist. Forum theatre is an effective way of stimulating thinking and encouraging spectators to take action rather than disagree from their seats.

Special Techniques

The following terms refer to special techniques used by some teachers of creative drama.

> *Side coaching.* This is a technique practiced by some teachers as a way of encouraging and strengthening players. The teacher offers suggestions from the sidelines to keep the improvisation going.

---

[10]John O'Toole, *Theatre in Education: New Objectives for Theatre, New Techniques in Education* (London: Hodder and Stoughton, 1976), p. vii.

Teacher-in-role. The leader assumes a role in order to guide the drama by enactment with the students. Focus, tension, situation, and complication can be stimulated or maintained through mutual participation. Usually the teacher steps in when the group bogs down, assuming a part in order to continue the action and/or get the scene back on track. The leader may continue for several minutes and withdraw as the group moves along on its own.

Parallel work. All students work at the same time, doing the same thing in different groupings (e.g., individual, pairs, two or more groups) to give everyone an equal opportunity for active simultaneous involvement. With all students participating, there are no spectators.

Values in Creative Playing

Television has made us a nation of spectators. Children view it from infancy, and surveys reveal that they spend more hours in front of the screen each week than they spend in school. The current craze for video games has intensified this situation; therefore, it is more important than ever that we make opportunities available for children to experience participation in the arts. Creative drama is an ideal form for this participation, with its inclusion of the physical, mental, emotional, and social abilities of the participant.

There is general agreement among teachers of creative drama that important values can be gained from creative playing. Depending on the age of the children, the particular situation, and the orientation of the leader, these values may be listed in varying order. It is my contention, however, that in spite of these differences, certain values exist in some measure for all, regardless of age, circumstances, or previous experience. To be sure, the activities must be planned with the group in mind and the emphasis placed on the needs and interests of those involved. The five- or six-year-old needs and enjoys the freedom of large movement and much physical activity, but this fact should not deny a similar opportunity to older boys and girls. Adult students in early sessions also gain freedom and pleasure when given an opportunity to move freely in space.

An Opportunity to Develop the Imagination

Imagination is the beginning of our work. To work creatively, it is necessary, first, to push beyond the boundaries of the here and now, to project oneself into another situation or into the life of another person. Few activities have greater potential for developing the imagination than playmaking. Little children move easily into a world of make-believe, but as they grow older, this amazing human capacity is often ignored or even discouraged. The development of the imagination to the point where the student responds spontaneously may take time in some cases, but it is the first step toward satisfying participation.

The sensitive teacher will not demand too much in the beginning but will accept with enthusiasm the first attempts of a beginner to use imagination to solve a problem. After the players have had the fun of seeing, hearing, feeling, touching, tasting, or smelling something that is not there, they will find that their capacity grows quickly. Holding the image until they can do something about it is the next step, but the image must come first. Through drama, the imagination can be stimulated and strengthened to the student's everlasting pleasure and profit.

An Opportunity for Independent Thinking

A particular value of creative playing is the opportunity it offers for independent thinking and planning. Although drama, both informal and formal, is a group art, it is composed of the contributions of each individual, and every contribution is important. As the group plans together, each member is encouraged to express his or her own ideas and thereby contribute to the whole. The leader recognizes the part each child plays and the value that planning has for the child. If the group is not too large, there will be many opportunities for every player before the activity is exhausted. Thinking is involved in forming and answering questions: Who are the characters? What are they like? What parts do they play? Why do they behave as they do? What scenes are important? Why? How can we suggest this action or that place?

The evaluation that follows is as important as the planning. Indeed, it is preparation for a replaying. Children of all ages are remarkably perceptive, and their critical

Dramatic play: Nursery school children at First Presbyterian Church of New York. (Courtesy of Ellen Ziman.)

comments indicate the extent of their involvement. A well-planned session in creative drama provides exercises in critical thinking as well as an opportunity for creativity.

An Opportunity for the Group to Develop Its Own Ideas

Through creative drama an individual has a chance to develop and grow. This is also true of the group, in which ideas are explored, evaluated, changed, and used. As people of any age work together under sensitive and skilled leadership, they learn to accept, appreciate, and stimulate each other. Every teacher has experienced the group dynamic in which all members seem to produce more because of their association. This is not to suggest that creative drama is a magic formula for successful teamwork, but it unquestionably offers a rare opportunity for sharing ideas and solving problems together. The formal play, whatever problems it may pose, cannot offer a group this same challenge. The written script imposes a structure in which free improvisation has no place. There are values in formal production, to be sure, but the major emphasis is on the product rather than on the participants.

An Opportunity for Cooperation

When a group builds something together, members learn a valuable lesson in cooperation. Social differences may be forgotten in the business of sharing ideas and improvising scenes. Teachers who guide children in creative drama cite numerous examples of social acceptance based on respect for a job well done and the bond that develops from the fun of playing together. One boy's story illustrates this process. Jack entered a neighborhood class in drama that several of his third-grade schoolmates attended. It was obvious that he was an outsider, and the leader despaired of his ever becoming a part of the group. For the first three or four sessions, he contributed nothing and was chosen by no one, regardless of activity.

Then one day the children were dramatizing the story of "The Stone in the Road." They wanted a farmer character to drive along the road with a donkey cart. Several boys attempted to pantomime the action, but each time the children insisted, "he doesn't look like he's really driving." Suddenly Jack, who had been sitting on the sidelines, put up his hand and volunteered to try it. The vigorous and convincing pantomime he created as he guided his cart around the stone astonished the class. His position in the group changed at that moment, and although he never became one of the leaders, he was accepted and often sought out. Working together in an atmosphere of give-and-take is an experience in democratic partnership; it provides an opportunity for the Jacks in a group to contribute their skills and have them accepted.

An Opportunity to Build Social Awareness in a Diverse Society

A special effort has been made in this edition to stress the fact that ours is a diverse society. Our immigrants bring untold riches to these shores and we often forget how much we owe them. The best way I know to learn about the customs, values, beliefs, arts, and traditions of others is through theatre. To this end I have included more ethnic material for dramatization and study than in previous editions.

Putting oneself in the shoes of another is a way of developing awareness and understanding. By the time a player has decided who a character is, why she behaves as she does, how she relates to others, and the way in which she handles her problems, the player has come to know a great deal about her. Even the very young or inexperienced player may glimpse insights that help in understanding people and, therefore, in living. Both literature and original stories provide the player with this opportunity to study human nature.

To help young people live in harmony in a society of many ethnic, racial, and religious groups is the most urgent need of the times. There is no better way than through drama, where for the space of an hour they can live in the shoes of another.

An Opportunity for a Healthy Release of Emotion

Control of emotion does not mean suppression of emotion. It means the healthy release of strong feelings through appropriate and acceptable channels. At some time, all people feel anger, fear, anxiety, jealousy, resentment, and negativism. Through the playing of a part in which these emotions are expressed, the player can release them and thus relieve tension. "By permitting the child to play freely in a setting of security and acceptance, we enable him to deal satisfactorily and healthfully with his most urgent problems."[11]

An Opportunity to Develop Better Habits of Speech

To many teachers today, a primary value of creative drama is the opportunity it offers for training in speech. There is a built-in motivation for the player who wishes to be heard and clearly understood. Volume, tempo, and pitch as well as diction are involved in a natural way; no other form of speech exercise captures the player to the same degree or offers so good a reason for working on speech. Being, in turn, a giant, a prince, a king, an old man, and an animal offers further opportunity for developing variation of tone and expression. In creative drama, the concern is less for a standard of speech than for audibility, clarity, and expression.

Not only articulation but also vocabulary is served through this form of oral expression. Conceptual thinking and the cognitive aspect of language are encouraged when words are put into practical use. For young children and students with foreign language backgrounds, vocabulary can be built and distinctions in word meanings made clear through participation in drama. Even abstract learning may come more readily when words are acted or shown.

An Experience with Good Literature

The story one plays makes a lasting impression. Therefore, the opportunity to become well acquainted with good literature, through dramatizing it, is a major value. Not

---

[11]Hartley, Frank, and Goldenson, *Understanding Children's Play*, p. 16.

every story chosen will be of high literary quality, but many will be, and the leader usually discovers that these are the stories that hold interest longest. Both folk tales and modern tales provide fine opportunities for acting. Bruno Bettelheim has advanced powerful arguments for the folk and fairy tale, genres whose relevance for the modern child has in recent years been questioned. In addition to the narrative interest of these tales, there are important psychological reasons why they continue to have value and why they should be used, though not to the exclusion of contemporary literature. A program that includes a variety of material helps to build appreciation and set a standard for original writing. Television shows and comic books attract temporary interest, but put beside a story that has stood the test of time, they rarely sustain attention. Believable characters, a well-constructed plot, and a worthwhile theme make for engrossing drama. What better way of discovering and learning to appreciate literature?

An Introduction to the Theatre Arts

Art is said to represent the human being's interpretation of life expressed in a way that can be universally recognized and understood. The theatre offers many examples. Although creative drama is primarily participant centered, like theatre it deals with the basic conflicts in life and thus offers young players their first taste of magic and make-believe. In the imagination, a chair becomes a throne; a stick, a wand; a change in lighting, a difference in time; and a character, a human being in whom they believe and with whom they can identify. Listening, watching, and becoming involved are required of the theatre audience. Children who are introduced to the theatre first through playing are going to look for more than superficial entertainment when they attend a performance. If we can visualize drama/theatre as a continuum, with dramatic play at one end and formal theatre at the other, we can follow a logical sequence leading from a child's earliest attempts at make-believe to creative drama to the finished product, in which there must also be belief.

Recreation

Implicit in everything that has been said so far, yet different and of value in itself, is the opportunity for recreation, or "re-creation," that drama/theatre affords. Under certain types of circumstances such as camp, community centers, after-school activity programs, and neighborhood clubs, the highest priority of drama may indeed be recreation. Drama is fun. It exists for the pleasure of the players, and it expresses free choice. It may also, in time, lead to serious work or a lifelong avocation. Many universities today have programs in leisure studies, focusing on the constructive use of our increased free time. The human impulse to play makes drama one of the most popular activities in a recreation program.

Creative Drama for the Child with Special Needs

Creative drama offers an opportunity for children with disabilities to participate in a performing art. Because of its flexibility, drama can be a joyful and freeing adventure for groups of all ages. Special needs can be served by adjusting emphases and activities. For these children, the experience of participation in drama often stimulates interest in other subjects and, in so doing, strengthens skills and awakens latent abilities.

Stories are an ideal way to begin work with all children, for the structure is already in place and the characters are clearly delineated, freeing the players to become involved at once in the action. With younger children in particular, the desire to participate is so natural that the teacher is able to move rapidly from the story into pantomime or improvisation. Because immigrant children frequently begin with little or no English, pantomime makes it possible for them to express their ideas and communicate with their classmates. Words come later as they feel the need for them. As the players are usually highly motivated and want to add dialogue, it is suggested that the teacher begin with a simple tale that can first be told in movement. If the story is short, minimal dialogue can be incorporated into the pantomime with results that are often amazing.

In creative drama the teacher's primary objective is to help children grow and succeed, not to rehearse a polished piece. Patience and encouragement are of the greatest importance in building verbal skills for students with limited English. They know what they want to say, but they lack the vocabulary with which to say it. I remember a group of Puerto Rican teachers one summer who spoke little English, but through pantomime and using their own Spanish they were able to enact a tale that the English-speaking members of the class understood perfectly; the audience responded with a round of applause. The players' success enabled them to risk trying English the next time, and by the end of the summer, all had become functional in English. I had a similar experience while teaching a class in Israel in which the students understood English but were freer speaking Hebrew. Suggesting they improvise in their own language resulted in a lively and far more detailed performance.

Values for the Teacher

What do teachers get from creative drama? Probably the most important thing is an expanded perspective on every child in the class. A child's participation in drama reveals his or her imagination, skill in problem solving, and ability to work with others.

What if an exercise fails? Don't be discouraged. No activity is foolproof, and no idea stimulates every class equally well. But we learn as the children do, by doing. Be prepared; then take the risk. The worst thing that can happen is that one lesson will not go as you had hoped it would. You will discover more from your flops than from your successes.

Although I do not suggest that special courses in creative drama are unnecessary to its practice, I believe that the average classroom teacher, because of preparation and experience, is better equipped to teach it than he or she may realize. The reason? Drama does not require mastery of the kinds of technical skills that are required for the teaching of music, dance, or the visual arts. Drama does, however, demand sensitivity to and a knowledge of children, the goals and principles of education, and some child psychology—things the classroom teacher already possesses. To be comfortable and achieve success, however, teachers also need a basic knowledge of theatre and its components: plot, theme, dialogue, character, and structure. If we enjoy the theatre, and I suspect that most of us do, then sharing our interest with children should be a pleasure. Skill comes with experience.

The publication of the *National Standards for Arts Education* (Appendix A) in 1994 marked a historic moment for our profession. Although most of the textbooks in the field list the benefits of drama and theatre and provide methods for practitioners, this document identifies in clear terms what students should know and be able to do at all grade levels. The fact that it was the work of the Consortium of National Arts Education Associations makes it even more valuable as we can now see ourselves in relation to our colleagues in related disciplines.

Summary

Creative drama, whether in the classroom, the camp, or the community program, can be regarded as a way of learning, a means of self-expression, a therapeutic technique, a social activity, or an art form. Children are helped to assume responsibility, accept group decisions, work together cooperatively, develop new interests, and—particularly in a classroom situation—seek new information. Drama is the most completely personal, as well as the most highly socialized, art form we have.

The values of informal play are many, and the leader will discover these and others as the group moves and grows. Not all values listed will be manifested at once, or perhaps ever, for the creative process is slow and takes time to develop. Also, leaders do not all hold the same priorities; they arrange them according to their situations and interests. More will be said on this point later.

The arts help us to develop a humane and enlightened society, for they point out our objectives:

They reflect our values, leading us to question them in time.
They express our feelings and sensitize us to the feelings of others.
They help us to grow.
They give us lifelong pleasure.

I can attest to the value of the arts in my own experience of resuming piano lessons after a hiatus of many years. It was actually done as therapy after I broke both wrists. Today, however, I find an unexpected joy in playing, elementary as it may be, and an enhanced appreciation of concerts, benefits that claim a place equal to, if not greater than, the goal originally sought. The arts are both means and ends, neither exclusively one nor the other.

It is often observed that few persons perform at their highest level. This is true of the beginning player, child or adult, who, because of shyness or actual fear, needs encouragement and acceptance. The sensitive leader recognizes this and tries to create an atmosphere of mutual trust. In his or her acceptance of every child and what the

A creative drama class in Taipei, conducted by Prof. Ren-fu Chung, National Pingtung Teachers College. (Courtesy of Prof. Ren-fu Chung.)

child has to offer, the leader has taken the first big step toward helping the child build self-confidence. Freedom will follow, learning will occur, and an ordinary room will become a place in which exciting things can happen.

Suggested Assignments

1. Visit a nursery school or play group to see what provision the teacher has made for dramatic play. What do the children do? How long does an activity hold their interest? Do the children play alone or with others?
2. Visit a class of older children and observe the attention span and interest in working with others.
3. In your own class, improvise a situation of your choice in groups of two or three. If the class is large, groups may be larger.
4. Repeat the improvisation, but this time have another student play the part of the teacher or leader, who steps in at some point in the action to stop the improvisation and discuss and reflect on what has happened. How does this action (teacher-in-role) affect the plot or outcome?
5. Try image theatre with children, if possible, then with your classmates. Note any differences in their approach and creative work.

Journal Writing

1. Has drama work been meaningful to you as an art form, as a social activity, or a way of learning? Explain.
2. Were any ideas in this chapter new to you? Discuss them.
3. Have you ever seen a play or film that made you think in a different way? Did you change your mind about something as a result? What was the change in your attitude?

Chapter 2

Imagination Is the Beginning

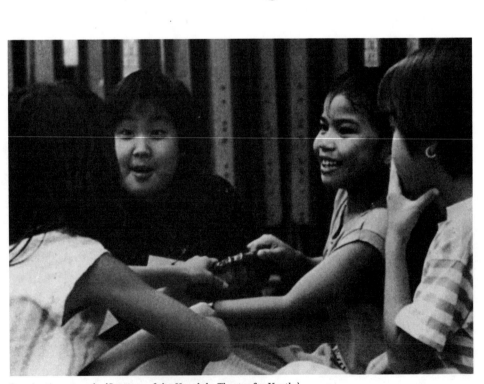

Imagination at work. (Courtesy of the Honolulu Theatre for Youth.)

> Imagination is more important than knowledge.
> Knowledge is limited. Imagination encircles the
> world.
>
> *—Albert Einstein*

Imagination

The *fact* of imagination has long been recognized, but it is only recently that the *value* of imagination has been hailed. Shakespeare described imagination as the spark that makes the human the "paragon of animals." Today, not only the artist but also businesspeople, scientists, military leaders, and educators describe imagination as the magic force that goes beyond the mastery of facts and techniques in the search for new ideas.

Susanne Langer called imagination "probably the oldest mental trait that is typically human—older than discursive reason; it is probably the common source of dream, reason, religion, and all true general observation."[1]

John Allen, in *Drama in Schools,* described imagination as free-flowing, open-ended, transformational. "Artistic discipline is a constraint—but here lies the paradox—only until the discipline has forced the material into its appropriate pattern; then there follows a sense of freedom and exaltation that is the ultimate reward of all artistic creation."[2] Thus can the trivial be transformed into the significant through a creative act, and the ordinary into something unique.

Concentration

If imagination is the beginning, concentration—the capacity to hold an idea long enough to do something about it—must come next. It is not enough to glimpse an idea; the image must be held long enough for action to follow. Inexperienced players of any age may have difficulty here, for self-consciousness and fear of failure are paralyzing and distracting agents. It is now that the teacher needs to encourage every effort, however small, to free the player of self-doubt. This is difficult in some cases: the player may never have excelled at anything and so does not believe that he or she has anything worthwhile to offer. Many children, however, become involved easily. Concentration poses no problems for them because of their freedom from fear and their willingness to experiment.

---

[1]Susanne K. Langer, "The Cultural Importance of the Arts," in *Aesthetic Form and Education,* ed. Michael F. Andrews (Syracuse, NY: Syracuse University Press, 1958), p. 6.
[2]John Allen, *Drama in Schools* (London: Heinemann Educational Books, 1979), p. 70.

Organization

Concentration and organization go hand in hand. When players are able to focus their attention on their material, they can get down to the business of organizing it. They stop thinking about themselves and begin to decide who their characters are, what they are doing, and the overall form the improvisation will take. If the group is working on a story, the organization will more or less follow the plot. The characters are related to a logical sequence of events.

When the group is creating an original situation—pantomime or improvisation—a different kind of planning is involved. More guidance is required because there is no structure to follow, but if children feel free to experiment, they come up with surprising and often delightful results.

Organization does not mean the imposing of a conventional form but rather an arrangement of parts or material to achieve order. Older groups, or groups that have had more exposure to television, movies, and theatre, are less inclined to experiment with organization, but with encouragement they can be helped to find the challenge in "trying it another way." Organization is order, and until it exists in some form, the participants rarely find satisfaction in creative playing.

Creativity

Creativity can be defined in a number of ways. It can be thought of in terms of product or process, depending on whether we are concerned with the solution to a problem or the way in which the problem is solved. Creativity as process may be manifest in a new way of seeing, a different point of view, an original idea, or a new relationship between ideas. Inventiveness and adaptation are often included in the thinking of those who believe creativity to be a way of working. According to pianist Keith Jarrett, "creativity is misunderstood because the result is often given more weight than the process."[3]

If, on the other hand, creativity is defined in terms of product, it is best illustrated by works of art (poems, stories, paintings, music, dance), scientific inventions, and new arrangements or designs. Drama, both informal and formal, is the artistic creation of human beings, based on their observations of human life—selected, arranged, and heightened. There has been great interest in the study and measurement of creativity in recent years, and a considerable body of data has appeared. One assumption accepted by psychologists doing research is that creativity is not a special gift possessed by a fortunate few but, rather, a human capacity possessed to some degree by everyone. It has been found, incidentally, that many individuals learn more if permitted to approach their studies creatively.

According to some authorities, the beginning of creative thinking is found early in the life of the infant, in "manipulative and exploratory activities."[4] In his or her

---

[3]*Utne Reader,* July–August 1997, p. 104.

[4]E. Paul Torrance, *Creativity,* What Research Says series (Washington, DC: National Education Association of the United States, 1963), p. 5.

awareness of human expression, gestures, and sound, the baby is first observer and then investigator. It is but a short step from here to the baby's own experimentation, at which point the infant becomes creator.

Creativity refers both to the cognitive and the affective life and is the result of conscious and unconscious effort. In an anthology titled *Essays on Creativity,* the point is made that "ideas are born from stimulation from within and without, but such stimulation must be grasped, filtered and used."[5] Working together, students and teacher can accomplish this to the satisfaction of all. A creative act does not happen once; it is an ongoing process, which with encouragement and guidance becomes a way of life. Rollo May put the whole thing very simply when he said that creativity is the act of repatterning the known world into meaningful new configurations.

At the moment I must digress to share a delightful anecdote recounted to me by my neighbor this morning. He and a nine-year-old were making their way along a particularly dirty city street. They were commenting on the debris that littered the sidewalk when my neighbor's companion suddenly uttered a sound somewhere between a whistle and a Bronx cheer, waved her arm in the air, and pronounced the dirt gone. Then after a moment she repeated the gesture. "What did you do that time?" asked my neighbor. The young girl was astonished. "Why, Uncle Murray, can't you see the flowers?" Imagine still having the power we had at age nine to transform ugliness into beauty and to be able to see with an inner eye and hear with an inner ear.

Beginning Exercises for Imagination

The first day the class meets, the leader will do well to begin with the simplest exercises in which imagination is involved. Regardless of age level, there must be an opportunity for the participants to go beyond the here and now, but they cannot, and should not, be expected to handle a story or create an improvisation. It is also wise to begin with the entire group, if space permits. This removes all thought of audience, thereby diminishing fear and self-consciousness.

How the leader begins will be determined by the age, experience, and number in the group, as well as the size of the playing space. If the group is fortunate in having a very large room, physical movement is an excellent opening exercise. Music or even a drumbeat will enhance the mood and help to focus the attention. One simple and very effective way of beginning is to have the group walk to the beat of the drum. As the group becomes more comfortable and relaxed, the beat can be changed: rapid, double time, slow, and so on. The participants, in listening for the change in beat, forget themselves and are usually able to use their entire bodies. Galloping, skipping, and hopping are fun for younger children and good exercise for those much older. Adults find freedom and pleasure in physical movement, and when it is over they sit down relaxed and better able to go on to the next assignment.

---

[5]Stanley Rosner and Lawrence Abt, *Essays on Creativity* (Croton-on-Hudson, NY: North River Press, 1974), p. 192.

From the purely physical body movement, the teacher may move on to mood. For example, if the group has been walking to a beat, he or she may suggest that there is green grass underfoot: "How does it feel to you? Your feet are tired. Think what it is like to put them down on soft, cool grass. Take off your shoes. [Some will do so at this suggestion.] Walk on it. Feel it."

Soon the steps will become more flexible as the image of grass grows stronger. The teacher might suggest, next, that there is ice underfoot: "It is hard, slippery, difficult to walk on, dangerous." The movement usually changes perceptibly now as the participants imagine the difficulties of crossing an icy pavement. Muscles are tensed and bodies stiffen. It is here that one or two may act as though they lose their balance or even slip and fall down as they get into the spirit of the situation. The teacher's acknowledgment of their efforts offers encouragement and usually stimulates further invention. As participants imagine that they are running across hot sand, stepping over puddles, crossing a creek, wading through snow, each suggestion stretches the imagination a little more. When the exercise is over, most groups will have moved far from the first stiff, self-conscious steps without realizing when, or how, or even that they have done it.

Inside a bubble bigger than they are, children can pretend they are touching the sky, riding in a spaceship, or looking around the inside of a whale. Indiana University's Children's Theatre director, Professor Dorothy Webb, used a huge plastic bubble to teach creative drama to graduate education students. Once we are inside the bubble, she explains, our imagination is not subjected to the confines of familiar boundaries, and thus we have an environment for creativity.

Games known to all the participants might come next. Tossing a ball is a familiar activity, and the players by this time usually respond eagerly. The teacher may suggest that they are using a tennis ball, then a basketball, and next a beach ball or a ping-pong ball. The players experience little difficulty shifting from one ball to another and have fun showing its size and weight as they throw and catch it. Lively groups sometimes drop the ball, run for it, lose it, or carry the assignment much farther than the leader suggested. Favorite activities such as flying kites, jumping rope, playing hopscotch and stick ball, and playing with jacks provide other opportunities for using the imagination. How long this goes on is best left to the discretion of the teacher, who can tell when interest begins to wane.

A pantomime of seasonal sports might be the culmination of the various exercises and a means of tying them together. If the class is large, this may be the time to subdivide into smaller groups, with each taking a particular game or sport. However the teacher proceeds from here, he or she will find that imagination has been sparked, and the next step will be easier. (Chapter 4 includes a more detailed discussion of ways in which movement, dance, and mime can be used as both means and ends.)

With the first meeting of any group, the leader's goal is to create an atmosphere in which the players feel comfortable; the next step is to stimulate their imagination. There are various ways of doing this, and each of us has his or her own favorite methods, but a good teacher is always looking for fresh ideas. Sometimes a nondramatic, quiet approach is preferable to physical activity. The following game was introduced by a drama teacher from Israel, and I have used it successfully on several occasions with different age levels.

The class is seated in a circle on the floor. After introducing themselves, the students are asked to put some personal object in the center of the circle. The more unusual the object, the better. The teacher then goes around the circle, asking the players to try to remember to whom each object belongs and to return it to its owner. This is followed by each person's selecting another player's object and making up a story about it. Improvisations using the objects or stories told about them may follow, depending on time and interest. If the exercise simply stops with the stories, it will have given the class a chance to get acquainted before moving into active group work.

Another quiet exercise that captures the attention of most groups requires a blackboard and colored chalk. One student after another goes to the board and puts a mark or drawing on it. When everyone has had a turn, second turns are taken; the size of the class determines whether there may be third and fourth turns. The mural created by the class is then described and interpreted. The more abstract it is, the more imaginative the interpretations will probably be. This activity may be a springboard to improvisation or may simply remain a means of drawing a group together. In either case, it is effective with both children and adults in engaging and holding the attention.

Sometimes an idea or activity that stimulates one group won't work with another. Do not be discouraged; try something else. Remember, this is the first time the class has met as a group, and it takes some groups longer than others to become cohesive. Children's games can be used with most groups. Games that any number can play and that are not too complicated, with the players entering at different times, are usually the best.

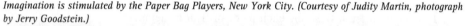

Imagination is stimulated by the Paper Bag Players, New York City. (Courtesy of Judity Martin, photograph by Jerry Goodstein.)

Fruit bowl is a familiar game adaptable to groups of all ages and abilities. It can be used as a warm-up or an activity while waiting for everyone to assemble. Each player who enters the room is assigned the name of a fruit, such as *apple* or *banana*. Players sit in a circle with the leader standing in the center. When the leader calls out "Apple," the players assigned to that group change places; when he or she calls out "Banana," those players change places. When the leader calls out "Fruit bowl," everyone in the circle must get up and exchange places with someone else. The values are obvious: all players must move; there is no winning or losing; concentration is necessary; and the leader can expect total participation. Variations in the game can be made, but however it is played, the leader should always stop and turn to another activity or to the problem of the day before the players become bored.

Games are generally thought of as warm-ups or enjoyable activities, but they also have other values. They provide a framework for communication; they impose rules that develop discipline and self-control in the players; and the social nature of the game is especially important because interpersonal relationships are an integral element of drama.

Deliberate brainstorming for ideas is often a successful way of starting a first session with older or more experienced players. Find out

What interests them
What their concerns are
Whether there is a controversial subject they would like to explore

Imagining something means visualizing it. We already know that the first step is to stimulate thinking. Tell the students to imagine

1. A bowl of fruit. Describe each piece of fruit in detail.
2. A trash can. Imagine everything that is in it.
3. A crack in the wall (or other mark). Look hard and long and imagine what it might be.

Self-Expression

So far we have been talking about exercises that may or may not be expressive. Creative drama implies self-expression, hence the necessity of the participants' involvement beyond merely imitating an action. How do they feel when the kite soars high in the air? Who is winning the ball game? How do we know? How many jacks have they won? Do they enjoy picking flowers in the woods? What are their feelings as they fish or row their boat against a strong current? These are the kinds of questions we may ask as the players grow more confident.

We are not concerned with the quality of the children's performance yet; rather, we are concerned with their developing freedom and the ability to express themselves.

Each child has something to say, something that he or she alone can offer, provided the opportunity and the encouragement are given. No one has put this any better than Hughes Mearns:

> You have something to say. Something of your very own. Try to say it. Don't be ashamed of any real thought or feeling you may have. Don't undervalue it. Don't let the fear of what others may think of it prevent you from saying it. Perhaps not aloud but to yourself. You have something to say, something no one in the world has ever said in just your way of saying it—but the thing itself is not half so important to you as what the saying will be to you.[6]

Communication

Although communication is the responsibility of the formal theatre and therefore not our primary concern, there comes a time when the participants want to share their work in creative drama, and this sharing involves communication skills. (I have already stated that for the younger child, public performance is undesirable; for the older child, under the right conditions, it does no harm.) Unless the class is exceptionally small, there will be periods when some are observers and some are participants. It is to these periods that communication pertains. On the one hand, this audience is not an audience in the usual sense. On the other hand, the observers want to see and hear, and they become deeply involved in the situation. Participants soon learn that they must move on to the next stage of development: that of making themselves clear, of being heard and understood, and of being interesting—in short, of communicating.

Communication comes about naturally in the discussion periods that follow each playing. One procedure used successfully by many teachers is the playing-discussing-replaying method. The teacher begins with the story or situation, which he or she either reads or tells to the group. This is followed by class discussion, in which the characters are enumerated and described, the plot is reviewed, and the scenes are planned. No matter how simple the situation, it is important that it be thoroughly understood before the first playing. The group will decide which characters are necessary to the plot, which ones could be eliminated, or whether others should be added. Often a story that is excellent to read takes considerable adapting to make it good drama.

When the teacher is sure that the group has all details well in mind, he or she is ready to suggest that the group of students play a scene from the story. Asking for volunteers usually brings a show of hands. The teacher will choose the first cast. The players come forward while the rest of the class remains seated. After the scene is finished, the teacher leads a general discussion. This evaluation period covers the plot

---

[6]Hughes Mearns, *Creative Power,* 2nd ed. (New York: Dover, 1958), p. 259.

and the way the children have handled it. The players themselves always have criticisms to offer, but the observers also have reactions to share. Children's criticism is honest and their observations are keen. Because the observers anticipate playing the story themselves, they are as deeply involved as the players. Questions such as these help to guide the discussion:

1. Did the players tell the story as you remember it?
2. Was anything important left out?
3. What did you like about the way the players began the story?
4. Did you understand the ending?
5. When we play it the next time, what might we add, change, or leave out?

The questions are naturally more specific when we have a particular story in mind. There will be further discussion of characters, their relationships, and their motives, but these things usually come after a second or third playing. When the teacher feels that a number of important points have been made and the class is growing eager to resume playing, a second group is given a chance to play the same scene. This group, having the benefit of observation and discussion, will probably succeed in developing more detail and clearer characterizations. This does not necessarily happen, for the first group to volunteer may have been the stronger.

At any rate, when the second cast has finished, a new evaluation period is in order. It is always interesting to hear the different kinds of comments that this second discussion evokes. A third playing, a fourth, even a fifth may follow, depending on the interest of the children and the length of the period. It is a good idea to take the cue from them as to when to move on to the next scene. As long as the scene holds their interest, they will continue to grow in their understanding of it. The teacher will become increasingly sensitive to their involvement as they work together.

When the group works from another source, the questions will be different. The following are general but may be helpful in suggesting how to begin a discussion.

1. Who were the people in the drama?
2. How did their home (occupation, school, way of life, values, etc.) differ from ours?
3. How did they communicate with each other without a telephone (a common language, an automobile, etc.)?
4. What was the problem they faced?
5. Were there other ways of solving it? Shall we try one of them?

If the class has made a study of a particular society, an earlier period in history, or an institution, the questions will be more specific. Often a discussion will take off in another direction; as long as discussion does not continue at too great a length, the teacher will be interested to see where it leads and what the concerns of the class are. If the discussion appears to be tangential and unrelated to the topic, the teacher can guide it back into more productive channels.

As the group gains experience, its members' ability to communicate will increase. Younger children, because of their more limited vocabulary, communicate more easily through body movement and facial expression. Older children are not only better able to express themselves verbally but also enjoy improvising dialogue. Adult students, depending on background and previous experience, will feel more comfortable in one medium or the other, but most are comfortable with oral discussion.

Many stories from other lands have been dramatized for the stage. Older children, working from scripts, enjoy not only rehearsing the play but making props and costumes for it. Scenery need not be elaborate, but it presents another opportunity to study the background of the story and design a setting for it. All the arts can be included in the process of putting on a play. This is one of the best ways I know to study a particular culture, become the characters, and take pride in the creation.

Discipline

As young teachers will tell you, discipline is one of the most difficult problems they face. It scarcely seems necessary to ask why this is so, let alone ask the more basic question of why discipline is necessary. When discipline has been established, both teaching and learning become a far more pleasant and satisfying experience. Part of the problem some teachers have with discipline is a misunderstanding of John Dewey's philosophy, believing that freedom consists of allowing students to do as they please; contrasting this is the traditional approach, again misinterpreted to mean arbitrary authoritarian rule. The dream of most teachers today is a classroom in which freedom reigns within a structure that supports, encourages, and protects the rights of each individual. To achieve this, teachers must establish order, insisting on ground rules to which all adhere. Ideally, self-discipline can be achieved, permitting each member of the group to pursue his or her own interests and goals while respecting the rights of others.

According to C. M. Charles, order in the classroom performs various functions.[7] Order

1. Facilitates learning
2. Fosters socialization
3. Permits democracy
4. Fills a psychological need
5. Promotes a sense of joy

After all, teachers and students are working toward the same end: the best learning, under the most favorable conditions, in the best possible learning environment.

Problems in Creative Playing

Sooner or later, the teacher of creative drama, or the classroom teacher who uses creative drama, is bound to encounter problems. They may be simple problems of time and space: periods that are too short, space that is inadequate, classes that are too large. These problems can be solved, though the solutions are not always easy. They

---

[7] C. M. Charles, *Building Classroom Discipline* (White Plains, NY: Longman, 1992), pp. 7–15.

call for adaptability and ingenuity on the part of the leader and present difficulties that are discouraging and sometimes defeating. Other difficulties confronting the leader, even under ideal circumstances, are the individual problems he or she finds in the group. *Discipline* has come to mean "punishment" in our society. This is not the original meaning of the word, nor is it the sense in which it is used here. Rather, it signifies order or control, preferably control of oneself.

It has been stated many times that self-consciousness is the greatest obstacle to creative playing. Self-consciousness, or fear, takes many forms. The shy child and the show-off are the two forms in which self-consciousness is most frequently encountered in children. The insensitive child is also a problem, for he or she usually lacks friends and so finds it difficult to work cooperatively in a group. Finally, there is the child whose physical, mental, or emotional problems pose special difficulties for the leader.

We must keep in mind that in drama, players are exposing themselves more than in any other art form. Therefore, proper handling of behavior problems requires awareness of their causes. Insensitivity on the leader's part can damage a player whose vulnerability is evidenced by a conspicuous form of behavior. There is great interest in drama as therapy at present, but this is a special field for which the average teacher—even the specialist in creative drama techniques—is not trained. Every teacher is aware of the therapeutic value of the arts, even though their primary purposes are educational, social, and aesthetic. But because there are, in every group, those children (or adults) who experience real difficulty in expressing themselves, consideration must be given to their problems. In many cases, an intelligent, sympathetic effort to build self-respect and bring fun into the lives of the players can go a long way toward solving problems. If the problem is severe, however, it should be handled by a therapist and not the classroom teacher.

Timidity

Timid children present a common problem to the teacher of creative drama. Such children are usually quiet in a class, preferring to sit in the back of the room and let others do the talking. Their fear of making a mistake, or even of being noticed, causes them to withdraw, even though underneath they are eager to express their ideas and take part. They are usually not happy children, for their feeling of inadequacy inhibits both expression and communication.

The little girl who never volunteers will need special encouragement to try doing a part, no matter how simple. The teacher who gives her this opportunity to show her peers what she can do may be taking the first step in helping her build a better self-image. If the child is successful, participation will be less difficult for her a second time. The teacher will be wise to praise her warmly for whatever contribution she makes. Remember that for the little girl, the very act of getting up in front of the class is a big achievement.

Eight-year-old Patty was referred to a Saturday morning play group because of her excessive shyness. At first she took part only when the whole group was moving— simply because it would have been more conspicuous to remain seated than to get up with the others. After five or six sessions, Patty did a pantomime of a child finding a kitten. Her honest joy and tenderness as she fondled its soft body drew spontaneous admiration from the other boys and girls in the class. This was the breakthrough. From that day Patty's eagerness to play was apparent. Her voice was small—inaudible at first—but grew stronger in proportion to her growing self-confidence. She became not only one of the most vocal children in the group but also an unquestioned leader. This was no sudden miracle; in fact, it took three years for the transformation to take place. Patty's feelings of inadequacy had been so deep-seated that many successes were necessary to convince her that she had something to offer that her peers would accept. Whether she would have found her way anyhow no one can say. Creative drama as a technique was deliberately used, and the change during her three years in the class was striking.

Exhibitionism

The show-offs are just as much in need of help as shy children, but they rarely elicit the same kind of sympathetic attention. Their problem is also one of uneasiness, and in trying to prove their importance, they do all the wrong things. Their behavior will range from monopolizing the class discussion to interfering with the work of the other children (pinching, pushing, interrupting). They may deliberately use a wrong word for the sake of a laugh. They are conscious of the effect they are having and so have difficulty concentrating on what they are doing.

An example of this is Arline, a high school student whose weight problem caused her great embarrassment. She expressed this by comic behavior and exhibitionist antics. For years Arline had been the class clown, deliberately tripping, using a wrong word, or misunderstanding a simple question. In this way she made people laugh at what she did before they had a chance to laugh at the way she looked. Successful coping with her problem in this manner had created a behavior pattern that was hard to break. Through improvised drama, in which there was no audience to impress, Arline gradually came to understand something of motivation and, finally, to trust and accept herself. True, the slapstick occasionally took place, but it happened less and less often as the years passed, and Arline was able to get the laughs for the right reasons. Beneath the clowning there was an intelligent, sensitive adolescent who today is a successful educator. Undoubtedly, there were other methods that could have been used effectively, but Arline liked theatre and elected to participate. It was obvious that through the use of creative drama she learned how to believe in herself. Perhaps drama laid the foundation for her future work in special education.

Sometimes the teacher may be forced to ask the disruptive child to go back to his or her seat. Not punishment but the consequences of unacceptable behavior will teach a student that creative drama demands consideration and teamwork.

Isolation

The isolate or loner is often a child who cannot relate to the group. He or she may work hard and have good ideas and the ability to present them effectively, but nevertheless this child is always in isolation. It must be said that isolation is not necessarily a symptom of some problem. Indeed, it may be indicative of superior talent and high motivation. Independence is a desired goal, whereas an inability to relate to others is a problem.

Through movement and dance, all members of a group are drawn together naturally; they discover the meaning of interdependence as well as individual effort. For the person who has real difficulty in relating to his or her peers, joining in movement is a natural way of becoming a part of the group.

Insensitivity

Insensitive players are similar to show-offs in that they are usually rejected by others and do not understand why. They differ in that their clowning brings no laughter, and they have great difficulty in making friends. They tend to reject the ideas of others and criticize others' efforts, often harshly.

Playing a variety of roles may cause them to gain insights and develop an awareness of the feelings of others. Patient attention to their problem in human relations may, in time, help them to listen and learn to accept suggestions from their peers. Theirs is a difficult problem, but once they have begun to feel some small acceptance, these children will prefer belonging to going it alone. Again, we are not talking about an extreme personality disorder but about the human being who is experiencing difficulty in working cooperatively with others.

Distraction

Every teacher has experienced the easily distracted player—the one with imagination, interest, and enthusiasm whose concentration is broken at any unexpected sight or sound. Often but not always this is a hyperactive child. I have taught college students whose ability to remain involved in an exercise was so fragile that the slightest noise in the corridor or the appearance of someone at the door would destroy it. Unfortunately, their reaction stops the other players, making it necessary to build back the situation, but rarely is the same degree or depth of involvement achieved that was present before the interruption. There is no easy solution, but providing short activities may help keep the easily distractible student involved.

Violence

Violence in schools is a disturbing phenomenon of our times. I do not pretend to offer a solution to it, nor do I believe that creative drama can prevent it. I do suggest, however, that techniques for conflict resolution can be introduced into the creative drama class naturally. Such techniques are effective in diffusing emotions. Using the situation that caused the trouble is an excellent way of treating it, although this is easier said than done. Stories about conflicts that students can identify with challenge thinking to see what other possible solutions there may be. Discussion and reflection may help to find alternatives to violent action.

Physical Disabilities

Children with physical disabilities need special attention. Moreover, their teachers need orientation to their special needs, although teachers are not equipped to practice therapy and cannot give time for all the help these special children merit. If the teacher has one or two children in a group who are disabled, he or she will treat them essentially the same as the others—with sympathy, understanding, and encouragement. The teacher must know what can be expected of them and then try to adapt the activities to their capabilities. Often such a child will be in therapy, and if the teacher can work with the therapist, he or she may receive helpful suggestions from the therapist's approach.

It is a common phenomenon that a person who stutters speaks fluently when cast in a play. Although there is no proof that acting ever cured a stutter, children who tend to repeat or whose anxiety causes them to stutter often find relief in speaking as someone else. Regular participation in either informal or formal dramatics may have a therapeutic effect in encouraging successful oral expression.

All people gain in self-respect when their ideas are accepted and put into practice. The child with a problem has a special need for acceptance, and the teacher tries to find the best way to meet it. Creative drama provides an ideal opportunity to help timid children overcome their inhibitions; it provides show-offs with a better way of getting attention; it guides insensitive children to some awareness of the feelings of others; it can help the disabled find an avenue for self-expression; and it broadens the horizons of all participants.

Other Problems

Children today are subjected to pressures and demands that, if not greater than in the past, are certainly new and different. Not only inner-city children but the children of rural, suburban, and affluent communities reflect the changes in values and mores. The pressures they feel often result in bizarre and unpredictable behavior, causing problems for teachers and creating difficulties when freedom is encouraged. The creative drama instructor is particularly vulnerable to these problems, for he or she is dealing with the emotional and social, as well as the intellectual, aspects of human development.

Although freedom is essential to creativity, it is often necessary to impose restraints in the beginning or until children become more comfortable with the group and the leader. Social mobility, broken homes, television programs, the violence in our society, and economic problems are among the causes given for discipline problems. It is not the purpose of this book to explore the causes, but it is important for teachers to be sensitive to unusual behavior and to meet it with understanding, compassion, and firmness. Although we cannot accept certain antisocial behaviors in a child, we must show the child exactly what is being rejected. In other words, we do not reject the *player,* but we do reject behavior that interferes with the freedom of others to express their ideas and feelings. One person cannot be permitted to dominate the group, regardless of his or her needs.

Evaluating Children's Responses

A question that always comes up is how to evaluate children's responses. This is difficult to answer, for progress varies from one child to the next. The teacher has different expectations for each child, and what may be extraordinary growth for one is scarcely an adequate performance for another. (The word *performance* as used here means "work," not "theatre performance.") Let me explain with examples. The shy child may take a long time to come out of his or her shell; therefore, the slightest offering the child makes to the group—idea, vocal or physical expression, ease in working with peers—indicates growth. The overly aggressive child who learns to harness his or her energy in deference to others has also made progress. With the overcoming of individual problems—and every child has them, though they may be less severe than the ones cited earlier—there has been progress. Beyond that, each teacher has social, intellectual, and aesthetic goals he or she hopes will be met:

> Have the individuals in the class become a group, willing and able to work together? Is there easy give-and-take?
>
> Is each child an integral part of the group, sharing without fear or need to impress?
>
> Is there sincerity in the work?
>
> Is physical movement becoming freer, more expressive?
>
> Have verbal skills improved—speech, voice and diction, vocabulary, and the ability to express ideas orally?
>
> Depending on the focus, have other goals been met (e.g., use of resource materials, integration of learnings, involvement in subject matter)?
>
> Is there vitality in the group? eagerness to begin? reluctance to stop at the end of the period?
>
> Does the noise level reflect industry and enthusiasm?

The teacher may want to make "before and after" tapes of the class. These are often more revealing than the teacher's recollections, written notes, or check sheets in showing the progress made from the beginning to the end of the year. My own concern, however, is that no matter how valuable such records are—and there is value—there is also a danger of losing the spirit of creative drama in the quest for proof of its effectiveness. If evaluation can be done quietly, perhaps by student teachers or aides, it is a valuable record for the teacher, to be shared judiciously with staff and administration. The purpose of the class, however, determines the type and use of tests and measurements.

For teachers who may need further help in evaluating growth, a chart is included in Appendix B. Although some sort of rating is usually required and is actually not regarded as unreasonable by most teachers, evaluation remains a difficult task. Teachers do not want to inhibit freedom, nor do we suggest a right or wrong way to perform. As teachers, we see how the arts stretch children. They engage them wholly by challenging their imagination, which calls into operation all the thought processes. By exercising a variety of abilities, the arts draw on human resources and potentials that might otherwise lie idle and perhaps even atrophy. In that process, the arts create bridges between children and other aspects of their lives, including other subjects in the curriculum. Instead of a curriculum of isolated learnings, students begin to make connections that are vital to understanding the relations and interrelations between different areas of the world around them. More important, the arts teach students to expect such connections and to seek them out.

Summary

Imagination is the spark that sets off the creative impulse. Concentration (the capacity to hold an idea long enough to do something about it) and organization (the design or arrangement of the parts) are necessary to self-expression. Communication—the bridge to others—comes last and is less the concern of creative drama than of the formal play.

In all creative work there are obstacles that must be recognized and overcome. They may be problems of time and space or the more difficult ones of human relations. Wise leaders learn to first identify the problems and then look for solutions. They will remember that they are neither therapists nor theatre directors but teachers, guiding players, whatever their age, in the medium of informal drama. Brian Way has described the role of the teacher: "Schools do not exist to develop actors but to develop people, and one of the major factors in developing people is that of preserving and enriching to its fullest the human capacity to give full and undivided attention to any matter in hand at any given moment."[8]

Activities and exercises are suggested not as ends in themselves but as means to self-expression and a springboard to other, more extensive projects. With a point of view and a creative approach, the leader will be able to find additional materials relevant to his or her own and the group's interests and needs.

Suggested Assignments

1. Look out the window at the people in the street. Select one and imagine who he or she might be. Where is the person going? Imagine as many things about that person as you can within a ten-minute period.
2. Imagine a party that you are giving for a friend or a member of your family. Describe the special occasion, the guests, the food, the decorations.
3. You are going on a three-week vacation to another climate. Imagine what clothes you will wear to get there and what clothes you will pack. What kind of place is it? What will you do there?
4. What do you imagine your first (or next) job will be? the location, job description, the "perks"?
5. Create a story about the phrase *trash can*.

---

[8]Brian Way, *Development Through Drama* (New York: Humanities Press, 1967), p. 15.

Journal Writing

1. How do you use your imagination most?
2. What does the word *discipline* mean to you?
3. What problems have you encountered in working with children or with young adults?
4. Evaluation of student work is a problem for most of us. How do you react to the suggestions in this chapter and in Appendix B?

Chapter 3

Play

Play: Are they hiding in a cage or a cave? (Courtesy of Alexandra Plotkin, photograph by Garnet Pennington.)

> The dynamic principle of fantasy is play, which
> belongs also to the child, and as such it appears to
> be inconsistent with the principle of serious work.
> But without this playing with fantasy no creative
> work has ever yet come to birth. The debt we owe
> to play of imagination is incalculable.
>
> *—Carl Jung*

Why a chapter on play in a book on theatre education? I think that Jonathan Levy answers the question most succinctly when he says that "Theatre can teach that quality of controlled playfulness, of invention under pressure . . . for play is the precondition and the matrix of theatre."[1]

To ask the question "What is play?" is to prompt a score of answers. The dictionary definition, though certainly accurate, leaves many questions unanswered: "To engage or join in any game for diversion. Action without special aim or for amusement. Action without specified or special hindrance; freedom of movement. Exercise or action for recreation or diversion."[2] All of us recognize play in the young, but a precise definition of it eludes us, perhaps because play takes many forms and can move in opposing directions, one toward games, sports, and ritual, the other toward drama, in which the players assume the roles of others. The first is structured, whereas the second is free and fluid. Even so, with this distinction in mind, there is no neat separation between them, for the players can shift suddenly from a game with rules to a world of fantasy, in which anything and everything is possible. Moreover, participants in dramatic play will often stop midway to give directions, explain an action, or answer a question.

Although play begins in infancy with a parent, caretaker, or sibling, it is between the ages of two and four that it includes more than one other player at a time. It is at this point that play enters a highly social phase. British educator Donald Baker, in his book *Understanding the Under-Fives,* maintains that play is a form of exploration of self and one's environment.[3] It also, he says, enables the child to create order and give meaning to the chaotic mass of random sense impressions with which he or she is bombarded daily. A third function can be seen in the way that play meets the child's need for security. In the rhythmic stamping or beating of a spoon on a surface, the young child is able to make a predictable noise at predictable intervals; through this pattern of sound and movement, the child's need for security is answered. It is further reinforced by repeating in play events the child has witnessed or experienced in life. In replaying trips to the doctor's office or other disturbing encounters, the child is coming to terms with life; this, according to Baker, is as fundamental a function of play as it is of drama.

---

[1]Jonathan Levy, *Practical Education for the Unimaginable* (Charlottesville: New Plays, Inc., 2002), p. 8.
[2]Funk and Wagnalls *New College Standard Dictionary,* 1947.
[3]Donald Baker, *Understanding the Under-Fives* (London: Evans, 1975), p. 22.

Dressing up is often an element of play, though it is not always included and is not necessary. Children love to dress up but do not need a complete costume; often a hat, shawl, or apron will suggest a wealth of characters. Cheerleaders' uniforms are an example of dressing for a ritual in which the participants are expected to create appropriate actions of their own. Examples of play are found in all countries of the world, at different periods in history, and on every age level. Play is inherent in human beings, and the child early manifests an impulse to engage in it. For to play is to free overselves from restrictions and expand our field of action; in Stephen Nachmanovitch's words, "play makes us flexible."[4]

One of the best examples of play in its earliest stage is seen in the rough-and-tumble of kittens and puppies as they explore the use of their bodies. Clumsy at first, they chase, leap, attack each other, fall down, and scramble up again, learning the skills and controls that will be needed later on. Their need for security is also evident, however, for if the game becomes too rough or the unexpected occurs, they will immediately withdraw to the safety of a familiar corner, even a cage. Every movement they make is preparation for adult life, though at the moment it is a release of energy in play, joyous and free.

Play has yet another dimension, however, according to Sue Jennings in the preface to *Playtherapy with Children*. She wrote, "The play of children is the basis both of drama and of the capacity for human beings to create and recreate." On the basis of this premise, she devised a practical method for working with children as clients. She also wrote that "if as a society we can see that all play is therapeutic as well as educational, it becomes easier to understand its importance as therapy for those children (and adults too) who are deprived, damaged or otherwise cut off from normal play experience. All play, though playful, is also a very serious activity and needs to be taken seriously."[5]

By the age of four most children like to enact their favorite stories and in doing so feel the need of props. Realistic toys flood the market today and although children use them at first, they soon move on to symbolic items, such as a piece of wood standing for a telephone or a scarf standing for an apron, a head covering, or whatever is needed. This use of props is a precursor to the more advanced, symbolic thinking of "let's pretend." In addition to the creativity and learning involved, is the social aspect as players work together.

A Historical Overview of Play

Early societies released the impulse to play through tribal expressions of hope, joy, fear, desire, sorrow, hatred, and worship. What early people felt strongly, they danced or mimed. From their sacred play came ritual; poetry, music, and dance were a part of their play. Philosophy and wisdom found expression in words.

---

[4]Stephen Nachmanovitch, *Free Play* (New York: Putnam, 1990), p. 43.
[5]Sue Jennings, *Playtherapy with Children* (London: Blackwell Scientific Publications, 1993), pp. 37, 182.

In ancient Greece, religious celebration resulted in contests, and these contests gave birth to dramatic forms and plays. As highly organized as they were later to become, these contests could be considered the creative expression of the people from whose ranks individual playwrights emerged. During the Middle Ages, Western drama had its rebirth in the church. Authorship of the scripts is unknown, but there is proof that the performers were amateurs whose participation was voluntary. Professionalism had no part in these plays, which served a religious and educational purpose. The involvement of the audiences was probably great as they responded to the dramatization of the Bible stories and moral tales as enacted by their neighbors.

In more recent periods in the Western world, play became ritualized, as process culminated in product with a conventional form, structure, and rules. Theatre is a typical example of the institutionalization of an art form, with a playhouse; regular times, hours, and lengths of performance; and established rules for the writing and production of plays. Institutionalization does not preclude creativity and brilliance of product, but it does impose order and form; process, however, by its own definition, is fluid and free.

Our modern preoccupation with making big business of play has resulted in its decline among amateurs, and this decline is our loss. True play does not know professionalism, for it is a voluntary activity, based on, but different from, the business of everyday life. Joy and freedom are the hallmarks of play, with the rules and limits established by the players. True play, though free, creates order—indeed, *is* order. Whereas people may sometimes play alone, one of the basic characteristics of play is the teamwork involved; through play, the participants are drawn closely together.

Some Theories of Play

The phenomenon of play has fascinated philosophers, educators, psychologists, and anthropologists through the ages. Studies reveal a persistent search for the meaning of play and its role in life, civilization, and culture. Theories range from its being an expression of surplus energy, a means of relaxation, and an escape from reality to a concern with its importance in the development of higher intelligence and the learning process. Some psychologists have viewed play as a way of working through unconscious pressures; some have discerned a close relationship between play and the creative process, signifying that art is actually one aspect of play. Regardless of theory, however, there is consensus on play as a profoundly important activity in the process of human development. According to Richard Courtney, whose scholarly work on the subject encompasses all areas, "play, initially, and the arts subsequently, develop imaginative constructions whereby people function in the world. The arts are expressions of imagination through which the personality develops, and upon which cognitive and abstract ways of working with the environment are built."[6]

---

[6]Richard Courtney, *Re-Play: Studies of Human Drama in Education* (Toronto: Ontario Institute for Studies in Education, 1982), p. 157.

Playing "feeding the cat." First Presbyterian Church Nursery School, New York City. (Courtesy of Ruth Callahan.)

To Adam Blatner, American psychiatrist and coauthor of *The Art of Play,* the pivotal concept in relation to play is spontaneity or the opposite of habit.[7] Blatner points out the importance of "if" in the study of play. The word is often used by actors in discussing a method of acting. This temporary suspension of reality by the actor is necessary if he or she is to become someone else in a situation created by a playwright. Play does not belong exclusively to the young, as we are prone to think, but is, or should be, a part of our life for as long as we live. Unfortunately, in our modern society it is often discouraged or at least overpowered by structured games and the compulsion to win.

One of the most popular theories of play was advanced by Herbert Spencer, who expressed the idea that play in both animal and human behavior is the result of surplus energy.[8] This theory is illustrated in the physical activities of the young of all species, who are yet to feel the burden of responsibility and whose bodies are young and resilient. Other psychologists explain play as a way of achieving relaxation and rest, not a refutation of the surplus energy theory but a further observation.

Aristotle's theory of catharsis has been interpreted by some philosophers to mean that drama acts as safety valve for pent-up emotions, which are expressed by acts of aggression and play fighting, as well as in laughter. Karl Groos, writing at the end of the nineteenth century, believed play to be a necessary factor in the development of intelligence and the preparation of the young for adult life. It is make-believe,

[7]Adam Blatner and Allee Blatner, *The Art of Play: Helping Adults Reclaim Imagination and Spontaneity* (New York: Human Sciences Press, 1988).
[8]Herbert Spencer, *The Principles of Psychology* (New York: Appleton, 1914).

through which youth gains mastery over its world. Play, in his view, is at a lower stage of development than art, but it is nevertheless a means toward that end, though not an end in itself.[9]

Johan Huizinga, whose work is widely read and admired in America, regards play as a cultural phenomenon. Huizinga is in agreement that it is a form of relaxation and fun, but he also sees in it a serious side, through which art forms are created. Music, poetry, and dance have an affinity with play. "In the turning of a poetic phrase, the development of a motif, the expression of a mood, there is always a play element at work."[10] This theory of play as fundamental to art has been repeated by other philosophers, educators, and psychologists, including Rudolph Laban, and Ruth Hartley and Robert Goldenson, coauthors of *The Complete Book of Children's Play.* Hartley and Goldenson say that through play a child is able to discipline the imagination and thus enter the adult world of the arts and sciences.[11]

Freud's explanation of play as the projection of wishes and the reenactment of conflicts in order to master them is a theory held by many drama therapists. Freud believed that art, like play, offered an escape from the familiar world of reality. Both Erik Erikson and Bruno Bettelheim concurred with this theory, arguing that in externalizing problems and pressures, the player is able to control them. In play an unpleasant experience can be resolved, an enemy beaten, or a problem satisfactorily solved and put to rest. Witness children "playing school" and exorcising a bad experience through repetition of it in play or a reversal of roles, sometimes collapsing in laughter at the outcome. The unpleasant situation is weakened by playing it. For example, if the teacher is perceived as a villain in the drama and is made into the victim, the comedic value of the reversal is therapeutic; moreover, the conflict makes for good drama, over which the players have complete control.

Piaget did not oppose the theories cited, but as an educator, he viewed play primarily as an important aspect of the learning process. A child enjoys play and takes it seriously, a process through which learning takes place. Perhaps it is the word *serious* that gives us trouble. Although play is serious to children, they know they are playing and enjoy it; therein lies their freedom. To Margaret Lowenfeld play is a complex phenomenon that combines diverse strands of thought and experience. Furthermore, she contends that these strands did not disappear as childhood ends. Froebel called play the highest expression of human development, for future life is revealed in the child's freely chosen play.

Similar to the above is the view of Everett Ostrovsky, who believes that what a child hopes for, fears, or wishes is buried in play. The player learns his or her limits and those of the surrounding world through exploration and experimentation, both of which are ingredients of play. Although there is a wide range of speculation as to the meaning of play, the theories cited are among the most commonly known and

---

[9]Karl Groos, *The Play of Animals,* trans. Elizabeth Baldwin (New York: Appleton, 1898).

[10]Johan Huizinga, *Homo Ludens: A Study of the Play-Element in Culture* (Boston: Beacon Press, 1955), p. 132.

[11]Ruth E. Hartley and Robert M. Goldenson, *The Complete Book of Children's Play* (New York: Cromwell, 1975).

accepted. One finds more agreement than argument among the proponents. The fact that today we recognize the value of play is reflected in such events as the conference *The Power of Laughter and Play,* held in Toronto in 1988 at the Institute for the Advancement of Human Behavior. The two-day conference included lectures and workshops on humor as a healing tool, play as a way to alleviate stress, expressive movement, and designing playful experiences; all were conducted by well-known physicians, educators, and psychologists. This is only one of many similar conferences on play as a way to better physical and mental health.

We have only to watch a group of children playing in an empty lot or on a playground to accept the truth of these observations. Children play almost as soon as they move, and through their playing, they learn. In their own dramatic play, three- or four-year-olds try on the roles of those about them; they observe other people's activities and learn by pretending to be and do. They enter the various worlds of their family and neighbors, interpreting and reenacting. First they observe; then they respond, repeating in play what has made a strong impression on them in life. Not unlike primitive people, young children express their feelings through movement and words, creating more complex situations as they grow older, with the boundaries stretched but the rules still clearly established. By the time they are ready for school, they have learned much about the world they live in, and a large part of their learning has come about through their play.

Jon Godden and Rumer Godden, in their recollections of a childhood spent in India, wrote with feeling about play, its magic, and its privacy. When asked, as they often were by their parents, what they were playing, the reply was generally "nothing": "Or if that were too palpable a lie, we would give a camouflage answer like 'Mothers and Fathers,' which we never played or, with us, another improbable play, 'Shops.' . . . Yet if we had told what we were playing no one would have been much the wiser, because our plays were like icebergs, only three-tenths seen, the rest hidden, inside ourselves. It was what we thought into our play that made its spell."[12]

According to Richard Courtney, "play is the principal instrument of growth. Without play there can be no normal adult cognitive life; without play, no healthful development of affective life; without play, no full development of the power of will."[13]

Marie Winn wrote in her book on the effect of television on young viewers, *The Plug-in Drug,* that the child can work out difficulties through play, assuming the roles of adults in his or her life, redressing grievances and reenacting scenes that have caused distress. "In play he can expose, and perhaps, exorcise, fears that he cannot articulate in any other way; more important, perhaps, is the opportunity imaginative play affords the child to become an active user rather than a passive recipient of experience."[14] In our television world, this is an important contribution.

---

[12]Jon Godden and Rumer Godden, *Two Under the Indian Sun* (New York: Knopf, 1966), p. 55.
[13]Richard Courtney, *Play, Drama, and Thought: The Intellectual Background to Education* (New York: Drama Book Specialists, 1974), p. 204.
[14]Marie Winn, *The Plug-in Drug* (New York: Viking, 1977), p. 95.

One of the most delightful and understanding treatments of the subject is found in Virginia Glasgow Koste's *Dramatic Play in Childhood: Rehearsal for Life.* In this book she offers three main reasons for valuing childhood play: "That is the time when most people are most expert and constant in playing; that is the time when they most freely externalize their playing so that it is possible to see and hear it; and that is the time when the power of play as a means of growth and accomplishment can most effectively be nurtured for a stronger rising generation of adults."[15] The text is rich with examples of children at play. Although she purposely eschews the scholarly approach, Koste presents effective evidence of learning, imagination, and social growth. Valuable insights are to be found in this early stage of play, which is preparation for the next—creative drama. That play is also the root of drama and theatre is an obvious conclusion to Peter Slade, whose theory of child drama is based on this premise.[16]

Ritual

Games, sports, and ritual are closely related to play. Whereas sports are like theatre and are designed for an audience, games and drama exist for the participants. A sport is held in a particular place; a game, wherever players may assemble. Ritual can be defined as the observance of a set form or series of rites. We think of the ritual as having religious significance, but the term is more inclusive than that. The repetition of an act or set of acts is also ritual. This is important to remember when working with children, for their games often assume a ritualistic form. Movement and chants play an important part in them. By beginning a creative drama session with the familiar—movement, rhythms, songs, or group games that all know—the leader is using ritual to draw class members together and make them comfortable. Like play, ritual has been defined in different ways. They range from some psychologists' use of the term to describe certain types of compulsive behavior to, in the most general terms, the repetition of a word, phrase, or sign as ritual. A handshake, a salutation or greeting, applause at the end of a play, or familiar repeated action of any kind thus qualifies as ritual. This interpretation is so inclusive that it becomes almost meaningless.

In an article in *Children's Theatre Review,* Lawrence O'Farrell makes a case for ritual as a creative resource for drama. His article clears up some of the confusion that has surrounded ritual, listing the components that distinguish ritual as a special event, different from everyday life. These components are easily recognized by the following characteristics:[17]

1. Tradition
2. Presentational acting, in which the players are conscious of the effects they are creating within their symbolic roles
3. Stylization of both verbal and nonverbal communication

---

[15]Virginia Glasgow Koste, *Dramatic Play in Childhood: Rehearsal for Life* (Portsmouth, NH: Heinemann, 1995), p. 58.
[16]Peter Slade, *Child Drama* (London: University of London Press, 1954).
[17]Lawrence O'Farrell, "Making It Special: Ritual as a Creative Resource for Drama," *Children's Theatre Review* 33, no. 1 (1984): 3–6.

Play leads to drama. (Courtesy of Milton Polsky. Photograph by Roberta Polsky.)

4. Order: any spontaneous actions are framed within a prescribed structure
5. The use of symbols and sensory stimuli to evoke concentration
6. The collective identification of the participants

It is a common belief that with so many prescribed elements, ritual is automatically disqualified as a creative activity. This is not the case, however, as O'Farrell points out, for by providing a supportive setting, participants in a ritual are enabled to express themselves freely and to indulge in divergent thinking, if given the opportunity. When a ritual is extended, it falls into three distinct stages: the first stage detaches the subject from the traditional form, the second offers the opportunity for creative expression, and the third returns the subject to the original structure. In the process, however, a change has taken place. A familiar example is the improvised portion of a hymn; the soloist, secure in the knowledge of the music, and inspired by it, improvises a section of his or her own, then returns to the music as written. So it is in the study of a culture. The teacher brings materials to the class to stimulate interest in the life and customs of a particular people. At some point, if encouraged, the class moves on to another stage in which creative drama, based on some aspect of the subject, takes place. Moving back again, the activity is seen in the context of the study, but change has taken place, for the study has been enriched in the process.

Tradition, presentational acting, stylization, order, appropriate symbols, and unity or collective identification with the subject characterize a play as a ritual drama. Far from discouraging creativity, the structure focuses it and strengthens the players. In concluding his article, O'Farrell says, "Not only can ritual embrace any subject, it can also include any dramatic method. Participants can speak, move, freeze, dance, sing, play, and perform feats of skill. Importantly, they do all of these varied activities in a special way."[18] Myths, originally told by primitive peoples to explain the unknown and allay fears, have been popular through the ages. For myths contain the elements of drama: themes that concern humankind, courageous characters, and plots that hold interest. The simplicity of the stories and the universality of the themes have made them survive as material for artists, musicians, writers, and playwrights. In speaking of myths, philosopher Stephen Nachmanovitch wrote of those who first told them, "Their creative processes are a paradigm for how our own creative processes work, at those especially beautiful moments when the work flows and work is play and the process and the product are one."[19]

Speech Play

Speech play begins in infancy and develops as children grow, experiment with sounds, and learn words. At first babies repeat certain sounds for their own sake. Young children enjoy making the sounds, but at the same time they are forming words. Often they will make up words using the same sounds: *baby, maby, paby,* and so forth. Children's chants are motivated by this interest in rhythm, rhyme, and the repetition of speech patterns. At the same time, they are learning to articulate sounds as they experiment with tongue and lip movements. By the time a child is three or four, what is called speech play becomes social. Children playing together create dialogue, leading into dramatic play. Not yet an art form, speech play is a socializing activity and a way of learning.

The Benefits of Play

It has been implied throughout this chapter that the benefits of play are enormous, ranging from temporal pleasure to lifelong satisfaction. On a practical level, dramatic play in childhood is what Virginia Glasgow Koste calls "a rehearsal for life."[20] And indeed, we can see in the free play of children their perception of adult roles and adult relationships. In her book Koste cites case after case to illustrate the point. Hughes Mearns, in describing his experience as a young teacher in the 1930s, wrote that the creative spirit and creative impulse are found and flourish in children's play.[21] Although Mearns was writing about education, he was committed to the philosophy that only through the spirit of play could creative power be released. A teacher, respecting this power, is able to draw the best from each student, whether it be poetry, exposition, art, dance, or drama.

---

[18]Ibid., p. 6.
[19]Nachmanovitch, *Free Play,* p. 34.
[20]Koste, *Dramatic Play in Childhood.*
[21]Hughes Mearns, *Creative Power,* 2nd ed. (New York: Dover, 1958).

Adam Blatner and Allee Blatner listed the benefits of play as applicable to four important areas of life: the personal-emotional, the social, the educational, and the cultural. These areas are improved, they said, when augmented with the following skills, learned in childhood in play:[22]

Flexibility of mind
Initiative and improvisation
Humility and a sense of humor
Effective communication
Inclusiveness, or the ability to interact and be at ease with others
Questioning, or looking for alternative solutions
Problem solving, or the learning of new techniques and strategies

Many educators regard creativity as the most valuable benefit of play. Whether the teacher approaches play from an art or academic background, the freedom inherent in play is perceived as fertile ground from which the imagination can soar.

Role playing is seen as therapeutic as well as aesthetic. Its cultivation is particularly important when our lives are controlled by the suppression of emotion, which often results in psychic fatigue. Children can express their feelings in play; adults in today's highly competitive and structured world, however, find themselves detached and even alienated from play. When preserved, the ability to play or be playful helps to re-create the spirit and refresh the body. It is a common experience to be tired at the end of a working day and then take part in a favorite activity or play a game with friends and afterward "feel like a new person." "Creativity arises from play, but play is not linked to values. There is not *a* creative process, there are many creative processes, with many layers, many levels of involvement and intent. . . . What we usually call creativity involves intelligence, ability to see connections, fearlessness, playfulness and willingness to experiment."[23]

Ashley Montagu discusses the benefits of play at length in his book *Growing Young.* By keeping spontaneity alive, he contends, adults will find their later years rich and rewarding rather than barren of interest. His thesis is forcefully stated: "In the child's imagination lies the power to know, and to create an environment, his own reality, and so it is with adults—those of us who continue to use our imaginations, for if you will keep your dreams and dream new ones, you will never grow old."[24]

Summary

Play may be the language of the young, but it is not their exclusive property. Play changes as we grow older. It acquires more structure and loses some of its freedom and spontaneity as we assume serious responsibilities, but the spirit of play is within us, ready to be called. Play is also a way of reliving experiences and working out conflicts; it is an important technique of the drama therapist. Therapists working with older groups find that recall of early happy experiences often stimulates creative drama.

---

[22]Blatner and Blatner, *The Art of Play,* p. 37.
[23]Nachmanovitch, *Free Play,* p. 183.
[24]Ashley Montagu, *Growing Young* (New York: McGraw-Hill, 1981), p. 159.

Play has a recognized relationship with the arts, particularly theatre and dance. Socially, play brings us together, for it has a bonding power that contributes to our mental health and satisfaction. I could go on and on, but the major points on which the most diverse theories agree are the value of play in making contact with the environment, in the expression of the child's emotional life, as a means of relaxation, and as a rehearsal for adult life.

Finally, play refreshes and rejuvenates through activities in which the players find satisfaction. To quote Huizinga: "As a regularly recurring relaxation, it becomes the accompaniment, the complement, in fact, an integral part of life in general. It adorns life, amplifies it and is to that extent a necessity both for the individual—as a life function—and for society by reason of the meaning it contains, its significance, its expressive value, its spiritual and social associations, in short, as a cultural function."[25] In every period of history, play has served a significant purpose, interpreting and affecting the lives of the people.

Human beings play when they step out of their everyday lives into a mode of playfulness where they focus on an imagined situation for a sustained period of time. They imagine themselves the characters they are playing, thus erasing the line between their daily lives and play. They participate in these activities for the pure joy of playing, and that joy is its own reward.

Suggested Assignments

1. Observe children at play on the playground, in the street, in school. Note their ages and the kinds of play they engage in.
2. What are the values to you of your own play?
3. Observe and note rituals for one day, wherever you are. Some will be obvious, others so conventional that you may miss them.
4. Ask several people what they consider the difference between games and sport—or do they see a difference?
5. Lead a group of children in a game, if you have an opportunity. Observe their reactions.
6. Study the work of one of the authors quoted in this chapter.

Journal Writing

1. How do you play?
2. How do you distinguish between games and sports? Explain.
3. What rituals do you observe (both ordinary, everyday rituals and more ceremonial ones)? What are your feelings as you go through them?
4. Do you ever or often feel the need to play? What do you do about it?
5. With whom do you play and how?

---

[25]Huizinga, *Homo Ludens*, p. 9.

Chapter 4

Movement, Rhythms, and Dance

Strong movement. Adelphi Children's Centre for the Creative Arts. (Courtesy of Julie Thompson.)

> The first word of the theatrical vocabulary is the
> human body, the main source of sound and
> movement. Therefore, to control the means of
> theatrical production, man must, first of all,
> control his own body, know his own body, in
> order to be capable of making it more expressive.
>   —*Augusto Boal*

Augusto Boal points out that by controlling their own bodies, participants will be able to practice theatrical forms and, in time, free theemselves from the role of spectator to become actors—in other words, to become protagonists in the drama. Movement is a natural response to a stimulus and therefore an important element of drama. Indeed, movement, dance, mime, and drama merge in the expression of feelings and ideas. Theatre began with movement; its origins were closely linked with religious and magical rites. Gradually, the elements of conflict, character, plot, and dialogue were added. When this happened, the theatre as an art form was born.

Early human beings, in attempting to order their universe, explain natural phenomena, and pray to their gods, used rhythmic movement to express themselves; this, in time, became dance. An entire tribe might take part, or perhaps only the young men or the most skilled of the dancers. As the movements were repeated, they became set and took on special meanings. These meanings were understood by both performers and spectators and were taught to the young, thus serving an educative as well as a religious purpose.

Every society has its rituals, and ritual and theatre are never far apart. Traditional garments, body paint, and masks are worn to enhance the performance. Although not theatre in the modern sense, these tribal dancers are nevertheless closely akin to it in the use of body, voice, rhythm, and costume to help express strong feelings and ideas in a form the community understands. As danced movement, therefore, drama is the oldest of the arts. Out of the rites and rituals of dance came myth; and out of myth, story or plot. It was but a short step from plot to play.

Children and Movement

Feelings can be expressed in movement and stories told through mime and body language. Although it is appropriate on any level, younger children particularly enjoy the physical expression of their feelings and ideas. In my own teaching I have found movement the best way to begin work in creative drama with most groups, letting words come when the players are ready. Even with highly verbal students, dialogue is usually limited at first, but as they become more sure of themselves, words and details are added. Younger children often surprise themselves when a word they don't realize they know comes spontaneously as needed.

Folk dancing, taught most often in physical education classes, is more meaningful if accompanied by an explanation of its origin. Again, pictures of costumes and festivals at which the dances take place put the folk dance into a context that makes for understanding beyond the execution of the steps. Many of the folk and fairy tales suggest places in the script for dances and song. When they are integrated into the performance, even if it is only for the class, they add authenticity and enliven the play for both audience and actors.

Creative movement deals with the elements of dance but is more spontaneous. Children move naturally; by encouraging such movement, the teacher can help children to express themselves through physical activity, thereby creating their own styles of movement, gaining confidence in their bodies, and developing spatial awareness. It is easy to move from here to either dance or drama. Drama differs from dance because it involves a linguistic element; the older the players, the greater the dependence on words to communicate meaning. The teacher of creative drama hopes to develop ability and ease in the use of both verbal and nonverbal expression; starting early is an important factor in achieving these goals.

Preschool children use their bodies to express their strongest emotions and communicate their needs and desires. Children's posture, for instance, shows us how they feel, regardless of what they may say. "Body language" is a form of nonverbal communication that includes any posture as well as reflexive or nonreflexive movement of the body that conveys emotion to the observer. Although most of popular writing on body language concerns adults, the attitudes and feelings of children and animals are just as clearly revealed by their movements and expressions. A leader can learn much about the members of a group of any age from the postures they assume, their ability to relax, and the use they make of the various parts of their bodies.

Rhythm classes for young children build on this natural impulse. What happens in the class is well described by an experienced teacher of rhythms and dramatic play. The children remove their shoes and socks as they enter a gym or large, free, unencumbered space. Music is provided by a pianist or a recording, or "if we are lucky, it is music created by the children themselves." Then, as if by signal, the children respond to changing rhythms. If the music is fast, wild, free, so are their movements. If it becomes slower, quieter, softer, so will be their movements. The idea is for the children to listen to what the music says and then to transfer it into bodily activity. "To one child the rhythm may suggest the rhythm of a galloping pony; to another it may mean the branches of a tree buffeted in a wind storm; a third may think of the whirling arms of a threshing machine." The teacher does not suggest what the children should do or ask them questions but, by watching, is usually able to tell what is in the mind of each child. In the middle grades, rhythms can be based on units of study: Native Americans, Greek mythology, the great West, the jungle. "These are samples of the big rhythmic activities that appeal so strongly to growing, energetic youngsters."[1]

Children with language problems tend to find satisfaction in movement. The physicality of dance-movement circumvents their disadvantages in verbal skills, thus

---

[1]All quotations in this paragraph are from *Rhythms by Mary Perrine*, as told to Henrietta O. Rogers (New Canaan, CT: The New Canaan Country School Monograph, Spring 1951).

providing another reason for its inclusion, particularly in the beginning. In addition to these conscious and unconscious expressions, however, there is the physical pleasure a child derives from moving, a pleasure that leads into play, dance, sports, and exercise for its own sake. Today, unfortunately, television constantly bombards the eyes and ears of children, giving information of all kinds but at the expense of their movement experience and natural creative response. In bringing children indoors, we make them passive spectators rather than active participants in games and sports. Most children enjoy moving their bodies and discovering different ways of exploring a space. As they gain physical control, they prefer running to walking, and they enjoy finding new methods of locomotion that are energetic and fast. Running, skipping, galloping, hopping, jumping, leaping, and rolling stretch the muscles and help children to gain a mastery of their bodies as they try out different things they can do. Because movement is so natural an expression, it is the ideal way of beginning work in creative drama.

Teachers and leaders of older groups find that their goals can be reached more easily and quickly if, instead of a verbal approach, they begin with physical activity. Actors call these activities warm-ups and declare them an effective way to relax and tone the muscles of their backs, legs, arms, and necks in preparation for a performance. Through rhythmic exercise a group can be drawn together and released in an objective and pleasurable way.

Rhythm, an element of movement, supplies structure and enjoyment. Rhythm is apparent in many of the games and chants of children and is the basis of music and dance. In fact, music and dance are frequently taught together through the medium of song, rhythm, and the employment of toy or rhythm instruments. This activity is called music-movement and is advocated by many educators. Émile Jaques-Dalcroze, founder of the Dalcroze School of Eurythmics in Switzerland, thought of using the body as a musical instrument by treating rhythm, with its roots in physical movement, as the organizer of musical elements.

Classes in movement are most successful when taught in a large room where students have plenty of space in which to move freely. Too large an area, such as a gymnasium or a playground, presents problems because large, unconfined space can lead to chaos, not freedom, dispersing the group rather than bringing it together. Therefore, boundaries should be established and maintained.

Leotards, pants, sweat suits, or comfortable old clothing of some kind should be worn; rhythm sandals or bare feet prevent slipping on a hardwood floor. When classes in movement are held in the classroom, furniture should be pushed back to create as much space as possible. Piano accompaniment is an asset, if the teacher can play or has an accompanist; if not, a drum is perfectly satisfactory. Later on, recorded music will help suggest mood and possible characterization. In the beginning, however, and for most purposes, percussion instruments are all the leader needs to give the beat and suggest or change rhythms. One advantage of beating a drum is that, unlike playing a piano or changing tapes, it permits the leader to move about freely and watch the group.

In a movement class it is usually a good idea to begin work with the entire group unless the class is so large or the room so small that the participants bump into each other. In that case, the leader should divide the class into two parts, working first with one and then with the other and alternating every few minutes to hold the interest of all. The leader should begin by beating a good rhythm for walking in a large circle. When all are moving easily and without self-consciousness, the beat can be changed to something faster, such as a trot or a run. Shifting the rhythm to a gallop, a skip, a hop, a jump, and then back to a slow-motion walk not only is good exercise, but it holds the participants' attention as they listen for the changes. Depending on the students' ages, more complicated rhythms can be added. The participants themselves can take turns beating the drum or clapping new combinations. Movement classes are often included in programs at senior centers. Instructors work primarily for flexibility and plan exercises not unlike those used with younger groups. Seated at first, the men and women move fingers and hands, then arms and legs, and finally their bodies as they progress. One instructor at a senior center told me that he likes to end a session with jazz.

Why rhythmic movement first? According to Marjorie Dorian, teacher of dance and author of books on the subject, it encourages spontaneous movement within a disciplined framework. This is the goal of the teacher of creative drama as well as the teacher of dance. The arts can best be served through the common denominator of rhythm, by an introduction to rhythmic movement, both disciplined and expressive. Through rhythm the child experiences the dynamic changes of opposites: soft and loud, fast and slow, much and little—qualities that make us sensitive to everything around us. Through the measurement of time and space, the child becomes aware of the limitations that eventually give him or her strength to pursue other disciplines.[2]

As teachers, we have tended to think of creative drama as concerned primarily with developing intellectual and linguistic abilities, whereas we have thought of movement as concerned only with the control and use of the body. Actually, movement and body language are part of creative drama. It is the combined mental, physical, vocal, and emotional involvement that distinguishes creative drama from all other art forms and gives it special value.

Instruments

Although the drum is the most commonly used instrument when working on rhythms, there are other instruments that add variety and are not difficult to obtain. Some of these are triangles, bells, and gongs for metal sounds; sticks and castanets for wood sounds; and shaking instruments like maracas or gourds with pebbles inside. Imaginative leaders and groups will find or invent other instruments of their own. Trying out different objects to discover what sounds they make is an exercise in itself and one most children enjoy.

One of the values of using different instruments is the discovery of the qualities of sound they produce. This in turn helps the student to feel the rhythm in a special

---

[2]This is a summary of the philosophy presented by Marjorie Dorian in *Ethnic Stories for Children to Dance* (San Francisco: BBB Associates, 1978).

way. For example, slow drumbeats might suggest waves washing up on the shore of a lake, whereas the sound of castanets might bring to mind hailstones or raindrops. In telling a story in movement, the use of several percussion instruments will stimulate the imagination, often giving different results from those obtained with the use of a single drum.

Records and tapes are excellent aids, but percussion instruments are recommended primarily because the teacher has complete control over them—stopping, starting, changing the rhythm, and so on, according to the immediate need. The terms *largo, allegro, legato,* and *staccato* can be introduced at this time; they have special meanings that describe rhythms clearly and, incidentally, add to a growing vocabulary.

Remember that you do not have to have real instruments to suggest rhythms or sounds. The following materials work very well and encourage use of the imagination:

For *drumming* try objects found in every classroom or home: wastepaper baskets turned upside down, pans, tabletops or desktops, boxes, coffee cans with plastic covers.

For *sharp noises* use sticks, pencils, rulers, stones, spoons.

For *shaking noises* try cans with pebbles, rice, or beans inside; gourds; anything that can be rattled.

For *thunder* shake a sheet of aluminum.

For *ringing sounds* use bells, water glasses and jars filled with different amounts of water, metal against metal.

For many kinds of sounds the human voice can supply the quality desired. Try having the class hum together, shout, blow, and sing.

Rhythmic Activities

The following activities are designed to help the student discover the drama in movement. In the early stages the leader works within the group, moving out when the participants are secure and able to move without support. The teacher does not *show* the groups what to do but supports, in every way possible, honest effort, involvement, and the development of individual ideas.

1. Take the group on a journey over a desert, across a river, up a hill, over both smooth and rough ground, over slippery rocks, through tall grass, and into an open field. Vivid imaging stimulated by rhythmic accompaniment makes this a favorite game of young children and a challenge to older ones.
2. Have the group listen to different beats and then imagine what gaits or characters they suggest, such as a tall man striding, an old man shuffling, a toddler, a young woman running for a train, a delivery boy with a heavy load, or a night watchman on his rounds. Try moving like these characters.
3. Do the same things with moods. Have the group first listen and then tell whether the beats sound happy, sad, proud, excited, sneaky, angry, or shy. Have the group move together to the same beats, expressing these moods.

4. Rhythms can suggest people working or moving in unison. Try beats that describe an assembly line, a marching band, robots, motorcycles, athletes warming up, workers using picks, joggers, and so on.

5. Not only young children but adult actors enjoy suggesting different animals through rhythmic movement. Try to find rhythms for these animals:

horses	cranes	seagulls
chickens	frogs	snakes
mice	rabbits	monkeys
cats	kangaroos	pigeons

6. Young children enjoy finding rhythms for Mother Goose rhymes; these familiar rhymes are good on any age level as a beginning movement activity. Try "Old King Cole," "Jack, Be Nimble," "Old Mother Hubbard," and "Humpty Dumpty."

7. City children will enjoy the "trash can." A group of ten to twelve children are huddled together as if in a trash can. Suddenly a gust of wind comes along and topples the can, letting all the trash fall on the pavement. When the wind blows, the contents fly in all directions. Suggest that the children decide what they are: cardboard cartons, paper napkins, crusts of pizza, newspapers, and so on. Children who are not in the trash can be the wind, shifting, changing, becoming stronger and then weaker.

8. An imaginative exercise that requires a little more experience is the creation of fantastic creatures. Ask the class to imagine strange or fanciful animals and then to show with their bodies what the animals are like. How do they look? What are they made of? What do they eat? How do they move? breathe? sleep? This exercise can be a source of fun and relaxation as well as a challenge.

9. Students of all ages enjoy moving to jazz rhythms. There is a plentiful supply of recorded music available, and the physical exercise, as well as the concentration needed, is a popular discipline.

10. Quieting exercises can be used after vigorous movement. For example, sitting in a circle on the floor, the group creates different rhythms and sounds. Clapping hands, snapping fingers, tapping knees, and brushing the floor softly with the hands are among the sounds that can be made in this position. Have each child put two and then three of these sounds together in a rhythmic sequence. The group listens carefully and tries to repeat the sequence.

From Rhythms to Dramatic Play

Dramatic play, the child's earliest effort to reproduce life situations and to try out the roles of others, is based on imitation. Through imitating the actions and behavior of others, the young child masters reality and gains self-confidence. Movement thus merges with improvisation as the drama takes shape. Words, the last element to be added, will be scanty at first, for the vocabulary of the preschool child is limited. In fact, much older players in creative drama classes tend to say less than they have planned and feel. In time, however, the need for words is felt: when that moment comes, natural dialogue is born. This is why movement is usually preferred to a verbal beginning for every age level.

Virginia Glasgow Koste, in her book *Dramatic Play in Childhood: Rehearsal for Life,* observes, "Ironically one backlash of the creativity craze has been the neglect, the ignoring of imitation with all of its implications in human learning and art."[3] She urges us to restore imitation to its rightful place, for it is through observation and imitation that children learn. Knowledge of others and their ways of doing things enables children to invent new forms and create dramas and characters of their own. "Holding the mirror up to nature" is a necessary function; imitation is a fault only when it discourages inventiveness and encourages dependency and copying.

Observation and Imitation

Here is an exercise for observation and imitation that younger children enjoy. It is suggesting movement through the "-*ly*" game. The entire class can play it together, or one person can begin and the others follow his or her interpretation. In this way every child is assured of the opportunity to create a movement. Words used might be *lazily, quickly, slowly, curiously, wearily, sleepily, noiselessly, loudly, angrily, happily, joyfully, thankfully,* and *sheepishly.* Incidentally, playing this game is also a way of learning new words.

Similar to this exercise is the beating out of rhythms. Each child beats a rhythm for the others to follow. After each has had several turns, variations of the game can be played: one child can go into the center and begin a rhythm, change it suddenly, and tap the one who will begin the next. This activity has endless possibilities and is an excellent exercise for encouraging close observation and imitation.

Movement Activities

The preceding activities were especially concerned with rhythms and the use of the body. All movement is concerned, however, with *where* and *how* the body is used.

Where the body moves refers to

1. Level (high, low, medium)
2. Direction (forward, backward, left, right, in diagonals)
3. Shape of the movement

How the body moves refers to

1. Energy (much or little)
2. Time (sudden or sustained)
3. Flow (free or tight)

---

[3]Virginia Glasgow Koste, *Dramatic Play in Childhood: Rehearsal for Life* (Portsmouth, NH: Heinemann, 1995), p. 19.

Movement in kindergarten later becomes dance or drama. (Courtesy of Hsiao-Hua Chang, Taiwan.)

The next group of exercises can be used to work on the where or the how of moving. Try the following to show where movement takes place:

Low movement: caterpillar, duck, seal, shallow pool of water, young plant emerging from the earth

High movement: airplane, high cloud, person on stilts, tightrope walker, kite

Horizontal movement: swinging bell, elephant's trunk, lion pacing in a cage, someone paddling a canoe, someone on a swing

Up-and-down movement: seesaw, helicopter, bird, bat, ball bouncing, elevator, falling star, jack-in-the-box, rocket, piece of machinery

Try the following to show how movement takes place:

Fast movement: arrow, fire engine, express train, leaf in a storm, airplane, speedboat, racehorse, top, skateboard, in-line skates

Slow movement: clock, elephant, melting ice, tugboat, turtle, freight train pulling out of the station, movie in slow motion

Turning movement: curling smoke, merry-go-round, revolving door, spool of thread, figure skating, top

Strong, heavy movement: chopping wood, bulldozer, tank, stormy waves, digging in mud

Soft, light movement: balloon, butterfly, flickering candle, soap bubble, kitten, kite, elf, leaf

Sharp movement: bucking bronco, cuckoo clock, cricket, grasshopper, juggler, woodpecker

Floppy, loose movement: clothes on a line, rag doll, mop, loose sail, straw hat blowing down the street, long hair blowing, flag in the breeze

Smooth movement: airplane, cat, fish swimming, syrup pouring, skating, rainbow forming, automobile on a highway

Twisted movement: octopus, pretzel, knot, piece of driftwood, crumpled paper, tangled chain

Change in movement:

A candle standing tall and straight, then burning down to a pool of wax

A piece of elastic stretched and then released

A paper drifting to the sidewalk and then picked up by a sudden gust of wind

A board slowly breaking away from the side of an old building and then falling off

A toy train moving rapidly, running down and stopping, being rewound and, then, repeating the sequence

The following images suggest being, using or doing, and feeling through movement.

WATER

Being: bubbles, rushing water, rain, whirlpool, quiet pool, surf

Using: blowing bubbles, carrying water, watering the lawn, waterskiing, wading in shallow water

Feeling: weightlessness of floating, walking in water, walking against the tide

FIRE

Being: bonfire blazing, forest fire raging, smoke puffing, match being lit

Using: building a fire, putting out a fire, being warmed by a fire

Feeling: hot, warm, sleepy from a fire, choking from the smoke of a fire

AIR

Being: soft summer air with only a slight breeze blowing

Action/reaction. (Photograph by Anne Jackson.)

Using: pumping air into a tire, blowing up a balloon, breathing clean air

Feeling: warm air, cold air, polluted air, pleasant cool air

Try to suggest the following ideas in dance and then in pantomime. They may be expressed differently or they may be much the same, depending on the person moving. Each student must move as he or she feels, for there is no right or wrong way. At this stage sincere movement is the major goal.

1. Visiting a memorial site
   Giving thanks
   Asking for rain in a time of drought
2. Casting a magic spell on someone
   Being under a magic spell
   Trying to throw off a spell
3. Feeling frightened
   Investigating the cause of your fear
   Feeling relief at discovering that your fear was groundless
4. Feeling joyful
   Showing what has made you so happy
   Sharing your joy with others
5. Feeling very angry
   Showing what has made you so angry
   Resolving your anger by doing something about it

Ask students to take one of the ideas above and combine the three parts of it to create a simple story.

Partner Activities

The activities so far have been planned for the whole class. Working in pairs or with partners is more difficult because the movements must be synchronized. Try the following simple exercises as a starter.

1. Have each member of the group take a partner. Have them put their hands on each other's shoulders and then push to see who is the stronger. Working with a partner in this way helps the individual move from group work to individual work without feeling self-conscious.
2. Next try the theatre game of having one person lead another whose eyes are closed. Have the class walk around the room in pairs until all are moving easily together. Reverse roles and try it again.
3. Divide the group into pairs, with one person standing at each end of the room. To the beat of the drum, participants
   a. Walk toward each other, meet, and part.
   b. Walk toward each other, meet, and clash.
   c. Walk toward each other, meet, and go off together.
4. Have one person begin a movement and the partner pick it up and continue it.
5. Have one person begin to make or do something and the partner complete it.

Activities on a Theme

The activities that follow are different from the preceding ones in that they involve group cooperation. Although simple in themselves, they become more complex in their dependency on interaction. Three themes are suggested, but the children as well as the leader will think of others in which the entire class is asked to contribute to a single theme.

1. *The old person's dance.* This is an actors' exercise that most children enjoy. The class is divided in half, and participants stand in two lines facing each other. There may be music with a strong rhythm or a drumbeat as accompaniment. The child at the head of one line invents a step or a movement of some part of the body. The child across from him or her repeats the step and adds another one. The second person in the first line repeats both movements and adds another. This continues until everyone in the class has contributed a step or movement to the dance. The larger the class, the more difficult it becomes to remember all the steps, but the exercise is a good warm-up for a group, as well as a good activity at the end of class, particularly when too little time is left to begin new material.
2. *Building a zoo.* This is fun for younger players. Each child creates a different animal in movement; eventually all the children move into imagined cages around the room. The teacher can be the zookeeper, working in-role with the class.

3. *Making a train, being ants, being boats.* Younger players enjoy this exercise. The problem here is one of precision. The players follow each other in a line, maintaining equal distances between themselves and the children preceding them. The leader (first car, ant, boat, etc.) determines the speed, direction, and rhythm.
4. The popcorn man gave a popcorn ball.
   The popcorn cart was the dancing hall.
   The popcorn dancers hopped and hopped
   And danced until their hats all popped!

   —Anonymous

Telling Stories in Movement

Pure dance has no describable story. Mime, in contrast, uses movement to narrate or describe. Mime can range from the classic form that captures the essence of a person or action to the imitative form that reproduces an action realistically and in detail. All forms of movement and mime demand concentration, practice, and precision. In time, a personal style can be developed that characterizes the work.

Myths and legends lend themselves to mime and mimetic movement. They are generally simple in plot and deal with universal themes and feelings.

The Legend of the Shooting Star

"The Legend of the Shooting Star" is one that I have used on every age level with unqualified success. The story is so simple that children in the primary grades can handle it, yet I have had graduate students with a major in dance create a performance from it. Whatever the group, it is a good idea to experiment with different rhythms, change parts, ask for suggestions, then have participants dance the story several different ways.

When the class is ready, read the story aloud slowly, allowing as much time as needed to perform it. Although any number can participate, I have found twelve or fourteen most satisfactory. Breaking the class into two or three groups gives everyone a chance.

Many moons ago Coyote was a great dancer.
   More than anything else, Coyote loved to dance.
   More than fishing, more than hunting, more than running through the hills, Coyote loved to dance.
   Coyote was a dancer.
   At night Coyote looked up into the sky and watched the stars dancing.
   I should like to dance with the stars, thought Coyote.
   One night Coyote climbed to the top of the highest hill.

"I want to dance with you," Coyote called to the stars, but the stars only laughed.

"But I am a great dancer," called Coyote. The stars laughed again.

"How can we dance with you if we're up in the sky and you are down on earth?"

"Let me dance with you," Coyote cried.

Suddenly the North Star had an idea. "I will throw this rope down to earth and pull Coyote up into the sky."

Coyote caught the rope, and the stars pulled Coyote up into the sky.

They began dancing together.

The stars danced very quickly. Soon Coyote grew tired. "I want to stop," cried Coyote, but the stars danced faster and faster.

Coyote tried to climb onto the back of one of the stars, but his paw slipped and he fell to earth instead . . . and made a great hole in the ground.

To this day, whenever you see a shooting star, it is really Coyote falling to earth.

Anansi and His Six Sons

The Anansi tales of West Africa are wonderful to tell or to act. This particular tale has many possibilities for movement and mime. It can be performed while it is being read or after a reading. Movements can be tried out and different ideas used. If the class is divided into several smaller groups, all can have a chance to perform.

Anansi, the trickster, sometimes got into trouble himself. One time he found himself lost in the forest. But he had six sons: Trouble, Road Builder, River Drinker, Game Skinner, Stone Thrower, and Cushion. Trouble, sensing that his father was in trouble, located him. Road Builder built a road to guide him out of the forest to the river. But when Anansi reached the river, a fish swallowed him. River Drinker came to the rescue and drank all of the water in the river so that Game Skinner could cut the fish open and let Anansi out. Suddenly Falcon swooped down from the sky and carried Anansi off. Seeing this, Stone Thrower threw a rock at the falcon and Anansi fell to the ground, landing on Cushion, where he was safe.

Grateful to his sons, Anansi called upon the great god Nyame to give a prize to the one who deserved it most. Unable to decide, Nyame took the prize, the Globe of Light, to the sky.

The Bat's Choice
A Tale from India

This simple legend lends itself equally well to dance and mime. The birds and animals suggest movement, whereas the plot is so simple that it can be told easily without words. There is plenty of action to make it interesting. If the group prefers to use dialogue, however, the story can be improvised. Another way would be to have a narrator tell it while the group pantomimes the action. In a story of this kind, any number can play. It is included to show the possibilities in a simple tale with a strong conflict and minimal characterization. More specifically, the tale can be told first in movement and then retold with the addition of animal noises. Little children love to tell it in this way, and older students discover they lose all inhibitions when there is no demand for words.

Although many stories that can be expressed in dance can also be dramatized as plays, "The Bat's Choice" is a particularly good example. Indeed, it can be extended into another dimension by comparing the bat's behavior to the behavior of human beings, who shift their positions from one side to another. I have tried this story with all age levels, after first working in movement and then combining movement with animal sounds. Young children usually apply the theme to a playground or school situation, whereas older children see more and deeper implications, from the conflict of loyalties in a broken home to peer pressure and power plays. College students carry the theme much further into areas of personal commitment and political and social issues. Not every story can be extended to this degree, but folk tales often can because they have been preserved for this quality of wisdom and morality.

In India they tell why the bat hides by day and comes out only at night. Many, many years ago there was a war between the birds and the animals. The bat, who had wings like a bird but a body like an animal, watched them fight but could not make up his mind which side to join. Finally, he decided he would go to the winning side. That appeared to be the animals, so he went over to them, declaring his everlasting loyalty.

Then suddenly things changed. With the help of the eagle, the birds began to overcome the animals. Now the bat wondered whether he had made a mistake; perhaps he would be better off with the birds. Until he could be sure, however, he hid in a tree and watched. When peace was finally reached, the bat found himself unpopular with both sides. And so it is to this day that he hides in a tree by day and comes out at night, when the birds and most of the animals are asleep.

The Turnip

The old Russian folk tale of pulling up the turnip can be told completely in movement. Although the tale is about individuals rather than groups, there are so many characters and the tale is so short that everyone in the class can have a turn. It is a very amusing situation but also one that requires skill and control to prevent its becoming a series of pratfalls. Although the story is a simple comedy, there is the basic truth that by pulling together, people can accomplish a difficult task.

It was autumn and time for the turnips to be harvested. Grandfather went out to the garden and bent down to pull the first one. But this turnip was different from any turnips he had ever planted. It refused to come up! So, after trying unsuccessfully with all his might, he called his wife to help him.

When grandmother came out and saw what he wanted, she put her arms around his waist, and together they pulled and pulled. Still the turnip would not budge. Then granddaughter came out to the garden to see what was happening. Putting her arm around grandmother's waist, she pulled grandmother, who pulled grandfather, who pulled the turnip. But the turnip refused to come up.

The story continues in this way with any number of characters included, each one pulling the preceding one. Sometimes it is told with the granddaughter's dog pulling her and a beetle pulling the dog, followed by a second, third, and fourth beetle all pulling at the end of the line.

Finally, when all pull together, the turnip comes up!

The Dancing Tea Kettle

Different rhythms are used throughout this tale. Drum and other percussion can be handled by two children.

   "The Dancing Tea Kettle" is an amusing folk tale from Japan. Although it is short, there is an opportunity to add details and a variety of movements.

There was once a priest who collected rice bowls and tea kettles. He was very proud of his collection, looking at each piece every day. One morning, however, as he began to polish his favorite copper tea kettle, it began to move. He tried to pick it up, but every time he came close to it, it danced off. He was puzzled by this and pondered what to do. Little did he know that there was a goblin inside, who did not wish to have the kettle filled with water. Finally the priest decided that he would take the kettle to the market and try to sell it.

   It was a long trip. He walked quickly at first; then as he became tired, he moved more slowly, occasionally sinking down by the road to rest. He walked uphill and downhill, across streams and through marshes. At length he reached the market. When the people saw the kettle dance, they laughed and clapped their hands. A tinker, seeing his fortune in the tea kettle, bought it for a higher price than the priest had expected to get for it. The priest went home, pleased with the result of his trip. Meanwhile, the tinker surrounded himself with an audience who watched the kettle perform for money.

The Full Moon Festival

Moon cakes are sold in Chinese communities throughout America in the fall of the year. These hard dry cakes can be found, beautifully packaged four to a box, in Chinese stores. The legend told about them is suggested here as one that can be told in movement as well as in words. Like all folk tales and legends, this one also requires that the class be thoroughly familiar with the details before trying to express it in dance.

Percussion accompaniment is all that is needed, although Chinese music helps to establish the mood and stimulate the imagination of the children. The legend can be told and then danced, or it can be performed in movement and mime as the teacher tells it. The mixture of delicacy and violence is typical of Chinese folk tales, and American children usually like performing them.

Once upon a time, there were ten suns in China. The suns were big and bright and they burned houses, so the people were frightened by them. There were also at that time outlaws who stole from people and sometimes even killed them. The people were terrified but could not stop them any more than they could stop the suns' rays. All they could do was to hide in their homes and hope that neither the suns nor the outlaws harmed them.

One day a man who knew how to use a sword skillfully came to the village and killed the outlaws and nine of the suns. The villagers were so grateful that they decided to make the hero their ruler. For years he ruled wisely and well. Then, after a time, he became greedy and foolish. He wanted to live forever and never lose his power. He had heard of a drug that gave the one who took it eternal life, so he sent one of his servants to find it.

His wife, who was kind and generous, realized what would happen if he should live forever; it would be the same as it was before he came and saved the people. So, when the servant returned with the drug, she decided the only way to keep her husband from taking it was to take it herself. Suddenly, she noticed tiny clouds forming at her feet. Then she felt herself becoming very light. Gently, the clouds lifted her to the sky, where she lived all of her life and never grew old.

The day that she went to the moon was September 18, and that is why the people celebrated the Full Moon Festival at that time of the year, for saving them from the evil ruler.

From Tyl Eulenspiegel's Merry Pranks

This is a made-to-order tale for dancing. Moreover, children love the little rascal who can outwit the staid and unimaginative townsfolk. The story can be told easily in movement with music and the beat of a drum. There are many tales of Tyl, and this one may stimulate a class to want to dance or dramatize some of the others.

The adventures of Tyl Eulenspiegel are known throughout the world. This lovable little rascal was always up to some mischief, but he was never found out until after he had gone away. On this particular occasion, Tyl was dancing along the bank of a river. The people so enjoyed his performance that they tossed coins generously in his cap until soon he had quite a collection. In response to their applause, he promised them another performance the following day. Then he hopped on a rope tied to trees on each bank of the river. He did not know, however, that

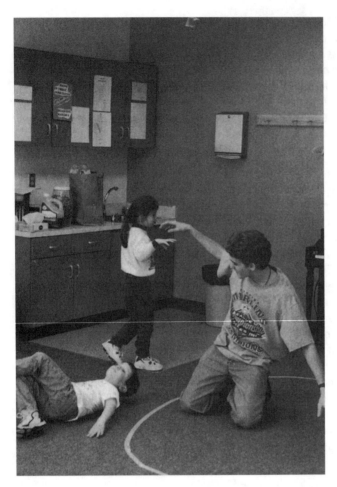

Performers moving like autumn leaves. (The Stage Door Workshop in Allentown, PA. Courtesy of Patty Carlis, director.)

someone had cut the rope on the other side, and when he was halfway across, the rope broke, causing him to fall into the water!

Tyl, not one to be daunted, climbed out, his coins safely packed away in his sack. Suddenly he had an idea. He boasted that he could dance on the rope in anyone's shoes, no matter how small or large, if only they would tie up the rope again. Collecting another sack full of shoes, he danced his way across the river, then tossed the bag of shoes back to the villagers, saying that he had never said he would put on the shoes! Before the people could find their own shoes, Tyl had disappeared off into the woods.

A list of music to evoke mood and stimulate movement is included in the selected bibliography. Most of the titles are readily available. I have found these selections extremely helpful, particularly if the teacher does not play an instrument or needs to give all of his or her attention to the class. There are other occasions when simple percussion is a preferred method; it is an advantage when the leader wants to shift rapidly from one rhythm to another or to talk and beat the drum simultaneously.

Folk Dances

Among the folk dances that many children learn in school are the polka, the jig, the hoedown, the schottische, and the waltz. These can be incorporated in many stories, adding authenticity and enlivening the drama.

For those who see no connection between dance and academic areas, C. R. Fowler in *Dance as Education* reasons that the basic components of dance—pattern, line, form, shape, time, rhythm, and energy—are pivotal concepts in many other curricular areas and can therefore be integrated with and enhance mathematics and the social sciences as well as the language arts.[4]

Summary

Movement—the basis of play, ritual, games, dance, and theatre—is a natural beginning for work in creative drama. Physically, the whole body is involved: torso, arms, legs, head, and neck. Through the use of the body, muscles are stretched and relaxed. Posture and coordination improve with regular exercise. Because the entire group can take part at one time, the possibility of self-consciousness is lessened. Persons of all ages and backgrounds usually find it easier at first to become involved through movement rather than through verbalization. This is particularly true of younger children, those for whom English is a second language, and persons with special problems and needs. Often in the rhythms and patterns of a child's movement the problems in the child's inner life are revealed. This is why movement and dance are recommended as treatment, serving both diagnostic and therapeutic purposes.

Imitation and observation are as much a part of movement as creativity is. The leader encourages imagination but discourages the cliché. Through movement, therefore, children experience both discipline and freedom. By moving into the rituals of the group (and here the word *ritual* is used in its broadest sense), they experience a feeling of belonging. Rhythm, that underlying flow and beat, captures the mover in an experience both objective and pleasurable. Taught together, rhythms and dramatic play provide a sound foundation for acting. Dance-drama encompasses the disciplines of both arts and is therefore a powerful tool for creative expression. "Celebrations, rituals, worship and festivals have historically been part of world culture, focusing the community's attention on common values and traditions. Art, music, dance, drama, storytelling and literature all emanate from these events."[5]

---

[4]C. R. Fowler, *Dance as Education* (Washington, DC: American Alliance for Health, Physical Education, Recreation and Dance, 1978).

[5]Jane M. Gangi, *Encountering Children's Literature, An Arts Approach* (Boston: Allyn and Bacon, 2004), p. 245.

Suggested Assignments

1. Find several verses or stories that can be told or expressed in movement.
2. In groups of five or six, create original stories in movement.
3. Beat different rhythms on the drum for the class to interpret.
4. If you are teaching children, select one of the activities in this chapter to do with them.
5. Give a report to the class on the history of modern or creative dance.

Journal Writing

1. When you hear strong or repeated rhythms, what is your response?
2. Have you a preference for ballet or modern dance? Can you explain why?
3. Why is structure necessary to creativity?
4. Rhythm-improvisation-composition: can you explain the progression?
5. What values do you see in ballroom dance?

Chapter 5

Pantomime: The Next Step

Creative Arts Team Youth Theatre, Director Helen White. (Courtesy of Lynda Zimmerman.)

> What exactly is mime? For the sake of brevity
> Tony Montanaro defines it as physical eloquence.

Pantomime is the art of conveying ideas without words. Many of a child's thoughts are spoken entirely through the body, so the five- or six-year-old finds pantomime a natural means of expression. Group pantomimes of the simplest sort challenge the imagination and sharpen awareness. In kindergarten, basic movements such as walking, running, skipping, and galloping prepare for the creative use of rhythms. Music can set the mood for people marching in a parade, horses galloping on the plains, toads hopping in a field, cars racing on a track, or children skipping on a fine autumn day. In other words, rhythmic movement becomes dramatic when the participants make use of it to become someone or something other than themselves.

During the early years movement becomes more complex, leading to pantomime. While still centered on personal experience and observation, the pantomime of young children may also have elements of fantasy. Pantomime when encouraged helps develop nonverbal communication, concentration, and the ability to put action and thought together.

For older children and adults, pantomime is advocated because it encourages the use of the entire body and relieves the players of having to think of dialogue. Here, also, group pantomime should precede individual work. Familiar activities such as playing ball, flying kites, running for a bus, or hunting for a lost object get the group on its feet and moving freely. If the entire class works at one time, self-consciousness disappears and involvement is hastened. Fifteen or twenty minutes of this sort of activity, changed frequently enough to hold the group's interest, makes for relaxation and readiness to move on to a more challenging assignment.

Others for whom pantomime is especially satisfying are children who do not speak English fluently and those with speech and hearing problems. The child who has an idea but not the words to express it can convey meaning, often very successfully, through body language. I have had students of all ages with speech impediments present characters, stories, and ideas in pantomime with clarity and artistry. Another benefit, in addition to the obvious one of building self-confidence, is motivation for developing skill in the language arts. Having succeeded in pantomime, children are encouraged to express themselves in speech and writing as well.

Classroom Environment

Class Size

Although creative rhythms can be carried on successfully with any number, pantomime requires a group of no more than fifteen to twenty. If a class is very large, the teacher should make every effort to divide it so that half the group is involved with some other activity at that hour. Pantomime demands individual attention, and every child should be assured the opportunity of participation each time the class meets.

This is true whatever the age level, for growth depends on repeated experiences in exercises that increase in complexity.

Length of Class Period

The length and frequency of class meetings depend on the situation (school, club, or camp) and the age of the players. With very young children, daily experiences for ten to fifteen minutes are ideal, whereas for older children, two or three meetings a week for forty-five minutes or an hour work out well. With club groups, the meeting may be only once a week; this is less desirable but may be the only possible arrangement. High school students and young adults can remain absorbed for as long as two hours, but in general, more frequent meetings of shorter length are preferable.

In schools in which creative drama is a definite part of the curriculum, the teacher can look forward to regular meetings throughout the year. Where it is not, it will be up to the classroom teachers to introduce it whenever and however they can. They will probably use pantomime in connection with other subjects that, if imaginatively done, can be of value as a tool for teaching and a creative experience for the class.

Playing Space

A stage is generally used for formal rehearsals, whereas a large room is more desirable for creative drama. Little children enjoy moving all over the room and should be encouraged to do so. The younger the group, therefore, the larger the space required. If a large room is not available, a classroom in which all chairs have been pushed aside will do. Space makes for freedom; a small or cramped area inhibits it. As mentioned in Chapter 4, however, too large an area can present other problems, particularly for a beginning or uncontrolled group. Boundaries are needed, as the leader soon discovers; there is greater freedom when there are clear boundaries of both time and space. An auditorium with a stage and chairs is least desirable as a playing space for a beginning group of any age, since it inevitably leads to a concept of performance with stage techniques before the players are ready for it.

Imagination

Whatever the space, the teacher will try to see that it is kept uncluttered and that the players are seated in a circle or semicircle around it. Having engaged in rhythms and group activities, the players are now ready for pantomime. There are many ways of proceeding, but one that has proved effective is having the class handle a small, nondescript object (such as a small box or blackboard eraser) as if it were several different items. For example, the teacher calls six or seven players to the center, hands one the object, and tells the child that it is a diamond bracelet, the most beautiful piece of jewelry the student has ever seen.

I have found this activity an ideal way of beginning with a new group. It involves several players yet offers each one an opportunity to interpret an action in his or her own way. It is uncomplicated: only one thing is required at a time. Finally, because it is so simple, it does not tempt players to imitate each other; on the contrary, they soon begin to enjoy the different ways they can think of to imagine the object. The teacher will then ask the players to

1. Handle the object.
2. Look at it.
3. React to it.
4. Pass it along to the next person.

When each has had a chance to handle and react to the object, the teacher may say that it is now a kitten with very soft fur. The same group again takes it and reacts to it. The next time it may be a wallet, dirty and torn, with nothing in it. The fourth time it is passed it becomes a knife or a glass of water filled to the brim or perhaps an old, valuable manuscript. Each time it is handed around, the group invests it with more of the qualities of the suggested object. The idea is to stimulate the imagination and help the players realize that it is not the property used but their own imaginations that turn an eraser first into a bracelet, then a kitten, then a wallet, and finally a knife or a glass of water.

The observers are as interested as the players in the growing reality that develops. Depending on the time at their disposal, the teacher may repeat the exercise with another group or move on to a new exercise. The teacher might ask questions of the observers:

1. How did we know the object was a bracelet?
   "One player held it so that the diamonds sparkled in the light." "John held it as if it were very expensive." "Linda tried it on." "Charles looked for the price tag."
2. Why did we know the object was a kitten the second time it was passed?
   "One person stroked its head." "Another girl put it close to her cheek as if it were alive." "Barbara held it carefully when she gave it to Lois." "They all held it as if it were soft and round."

Other questions might be put to the players:

1. What did the wallet look like to you?
   "It was dark green leather." "It was old and torn." "There was a faded snapshot in the front." "It had a hole in the bottom." "It was muddy because it had been lost in the yard."
2. You were careful not to let any of the objects drop, but you handled them differently. Why?
   "The bracelet was valuable." "I didn't want it to get broken." "The kitten was alive, and that made it different from all the others." "When I jiggled the glass, the water almost spilled."

Questions like these push the players to stronger visual images and greater powers of observation.

Another exercise that serves to excite the imagination is the suggestion that a table in the middle of the room is covered with a variety of small objects. Each participant must go up and pick out one thing, showing, by the way he or she handles it, what it is. Although this is an individual exercise, it can be done with several persons at once so that the attention is not focused on a single player. If the rest of the class is seated in a semicircle, some observers will see one player and some another. This exercise is fun for all, and what self-consciousness may have existed in the beginning will soon be gone.

Concentration

Many children will be able to concentrate on pantomime activities; some, for whom this is the first experience of this sort, will not, so the next step is to work on "holding the image." One good exercise is to have the class hunt for a ring that has been lost. A few minutes of searching usually involves them in the assignment. If it does not, the teacher might actually hide a ring and ask them to find it. The reality that comes with the second playing demonstrates clearly the difference between pretending to hunt and really looking. Other good group exercises for developing concentration are

1. Watching a plane come in
2. Watching a funny movie
3. Smelling smoke in the woods
4. Listening for the lunch bell to ring

Sense Images

The class is now ready for some specific exercises involving the five senses. This series might be introduced by a discussion of the ways in which we find out what is going on around us: we see, we hear, we touch, we smell, we taste. Individuals can be asked to do the following exercises, using no props but trying to "see" what is suggested:

1. Enter a large room to look for your sweater.
2. Look for your sweater in a dark closet.
3. Go into your own room to get your sweater.
4. Try to find your sweater among a dozen in the locker room.

These exercises call for the sense of hearing:

1. Hear an explosion.
2. Listen to a small sound and try to decide what it is.
3. Listen to a military band coming down the street.
4. Hear a popular song on the radio.

These exercises involve the sense of smell:

1. Come home from school and smell cookies baking in the kitchen.
2. Walk in the woods and smell a campfire.

*Scott Hanson works with
students at Clinton Middle
School in St. Louis, MO.
(Courtesy of the Metro Theatre
Company, photograph by Kitty
Daly.)*

   3. Smell different perfumes on a counter.
   4. Smell something very unpleasant and try to decide what it is.

Other exercises can evoke the sense of taste:

   1. Eat a piece of delicious chocolate candy.
   2. Try a foreign food that you have never tasted before, and decide that you
      like it.
   3. Bite into a sour apple.

These exercises stimulate the sense of touch:

   1. Touch a piece of velvet.
   2. Touch a hot stove.
   3. Touch or hold an ice cube.
   4. Touch or hold some sharp nails.

   These are only a few suggestions, and the leader will think of many more. Whatever is suggested, however, should always be within the experience of the players.
Practice in actual hearing and observation is good exercise and may be introduced

either beforehand or at any point that the teacher thinks it of value. For instance, the teacher might ask the players to follow these instructions:

1. Close your eyes for one minute and listen to all the sounds you can hear.
2. Go to one corner of the room and describe all the things you see.
3. Touch one object and describe it as completely as possible.

What we are trying to do is to "lead children into experiences that will involve them in touching, seeing, tasting, hearing, and smelling the things in their world. We also want them to become involved in experiences that will lead to imagining, exploring, reasoning, inventing, experimenting, investigating, and selecting, so that these experiences will not only be rich in themselves but lead to personal creative growth."[1]

The following poem suggests familiar reactions to the snow. After miming the action, some groups may find possibilities for original stories. Sharp images stimulate the imagination, leading to characters, situations, and sometimes simple plots.

Definition

J. Barrie Shepherd

Snow is
for stopping to
stomping on
birdwatching in
licking off
looking at
sliding over
and under and through
and throwing
at people who scowl
and curse you
and the snow.

Performing an Activity

There are no right or wrong order and no prescribed length of time the group should spend on one kind of exercise. Generally, the older the players, the longer their attention will be sustained, but this does not always hold true. At any rate, a pantomime guaranteed to capture the interest of every player, regardless of age, is "making or

---

[1]Earl Linderman and Donald W. Herberholz, *Artworks for Elementary Teachers: Developing Artistic and Perceptual Awareness* (Dubuque, IA: Brown, 1990), p. x.

doing something." In the beginning the teacher will offer suggestions, but later the players will have ideas of their own. Some good suggestions are

1. Play a video game.
2. Feed your dog.
3. Get dressed.
4. Turn on and watch a favorite television program.
5. Buy a pizza and take it home.
6. Ride on a crowded bus and go past your stop.
7. Pack your backpack.
8. Choose food in a cafeteria.

Again, let it be stressed that, particularly in working with children, the activities suggested should be ones in their environment. Washing clothes might be more familiar to these children than fishing in a brook and can therefore be easily imagined and acted. Choosing familiar activities also helps children to respect their own ideas and regard their own experiences more positively.

Pantomimes of discrete actions will grow more complicated as the players put them into situations.

1. You are getting ready for a birthday party for your sister and must set the table. What are you going to put on it? Are there decorations, a cake, favors, presents? What dishes and flatware will you use? Is it a surprise? Are you alone?
2. You are baking your first cake. No one is home, so you must read and follow the recipe yourself. What will you put in it? What utensils do you need? Is it a success?
3. You have a new puppy and have come home from school to take care of it. What do you feed it? How much? What kind of dog is it? How big?
4. You are getting up on a Saturday morning. It has begun snowing, so you must dress to go out and play. What do you wear? Is it cold? Are you excited about it? Do you take time to comb your hair or to eat your breakfast?
5. It is after dinner and you have been told to do your homework. There is a television show you would like to see, but you know you should study. What is the assignment? Do you like the subject? Is it hard? easy? boring? What is the show you want to see? Is anyone else in the room? What do you finally do?

Mood and Feelings

Somewhere along the way, feelings have crept into the pantomimes, so a specific assignment on mood will now be appropriate. The teacher may want the group to talk about feelings first, or perhaps this will come about as a result of a particularly good job one of the players has done. The teacher might ask the students what kinds of feelings they have experienced, and their responses will often include many more than the teacher has anticipated. Anger, fear, happiness, excitement, pride, curiosity, vanity, anticipation, sorrow, and hatred are some feelings that seven- and eight-year-olds have suggested.

This might be a time to break the class into groups of four or five, with each group taking one feeling to pantomime. Delightful results are always forthcoming when working on mood. One group showed excitement through a scene taking place on Christmas Eve, when they crept downstairs to look at the tree and presents. Another asked if they could act out the story of Pandora's box because it was such a good example of curiosity. Another group chose fear and set their scene in a dark street.

It soon becomes obvious that more than one emotion is usually involved in a situation of any length. Therefore, the next step will be to show change of mood. Situations like the following help the players to move from one mood to another.

1. You are with a group of friends taking a hike in the woods. It is a beautiful day, and you find strawberries and wildflowers. You stop to have your lunch, but when you are ready to move on, you discover that you have wandered from the path and are lost. Your happy mood changes to panic. Where are you? Should you go on or turn back? Is there any familiar landmark to guide you? Suddenly one of the girls finds a broken flower lying on the ground. As she picks it up, she realizes that she is standing on the path. She must have dropped the flower when she was looking for a picnic spot. Panic turns to relief as the group starts for home.

2. A group of children discovers a cave (or it could be the basement of an empty building). They go in, curious as to what they may find. One of them stumbles over a box. The children open it and find money and jewels. Excitement grows as they realize they have found hidden treasure. Then they hear voices; men are approaching. Terrified, the children hide. The men go past, not seeing them. The children stuff a few coins in their pockets and run, escaping from danger.

3. A group of people get into an elevator in a big downtown building. Suddenly, it stops between floors. Their poise turns to fear as they push one button and then another and nothing happens. Suddenly, the elevator moves again, taking the passengers down to the ground level.

4. You are a group of children who come into your classroom one morning and find a monkey scampering about. You are first startled and then amused by its antics. Finally, the man who has lost the monkey comes in and catches it, taking it away. You are sorry to see the monkey go as it waves good-bye to you from its owner's shoulder.

5. You are going on a field trip you have looked forward to for a long time. You get on the bus, but the bus will not start. After a few minutes, the driver lets you know that your trip must be postponed. Disappointed, you get out. Suddenly, the engine starts. You turn around and see the driver motioning for you to get back in. Your happiness is great because you can now go after all.

6. You are sitting in a movie theatre. First there is a preview of a very dull movie. How do you feel when it seems to be going on forever? Then there is a preview of a hilariously funny movie. How do you react? At last, the feature begins, and you are absorbed.

7. It is three o'clock and you have just come home from school; your mother doesn't get home from work until six o'clock. You decide to do your homework,

but then you hear a noise outside the front door. Someone is trying to open the door. Who is it? What do you do? There are many possibilities.

8. You are invited to dinner at the home of your club advisor. You help yourself liberally to the potato salad, one of your favorite foods, but when you take your first bite, you realize something is wrong with the salad. Should you go on eating it, or should you leave your large serving on your plate? Should you say something to your advisor? You look around the table; what are the others doing?

9. You are on a plane and the flight attendant brings your meal. You enjoy it and eat heartily, finally scooping up the last spoonful of pudding with chocolate sauce. Suddenly the plane gives a lurch, and the sauce spills on your lap. There is a passenger in the aisle seat, and the sauce is rapidly spreading over your clothing. What can you do?

Mood can be created in countless ways, among them through the use of pictures, colors, light, music, and rhythms. The following ideas have been put into practice successfully with widely varying results.

1. The leader selects a picture or photograph that will evoke a strong emotional response. If the picture is realistic, the leader might, after all in the group have had a chance to look at it closely, ask questions such as these: Who is in the picture? Why do you think she is there? What is she doing? What does she seem to be feeling? Why do you think she feels that way?

The discussion that results will lead into possibilities for pantomime or even improvisation, if the group is ready for it. A story can be built from the meanings and mood the children find in the picture. Instead of a composition in which people are represented, however, a picture of a place can be shown. Country roads, city streets, the platform of a railroad station, a deserted house, a stretch of empty beach, woodlands—all are springboards if the mood evoked is one that kindles the emotions and arouses our curiosity. The leader can ask questions about the place: Where do you think this is? Why is no one around? What feelings do you have when you look at the picture? What is there about it that makes you feel this way?

After some discussion the leader will be ready to continue with questions leading to a scene laid in the place portrayed: Who might come along? Where is he going? Does he meet anyone? anyone else? What do they talk about? do? feel? In very little time most groups will fill the canvas with characters, often involving them in an imaginative situation laid in the scene depicted. For example, a deserted house could take the group in several directions. It might be the site of buried treasure (still a favorite theme of eight- to ten-year-olds), important documents, or a fascinating archaeological discovery. Or it might be the home a family has had to leave sorrowfully. Why? What has happened? Perhaps a daughter returns to say a last good-bye. Perhaps she meets a friend and finds something left behind, something meaningful. Or perhaps it is the home of a famous person who has come back after an absence of many years to see his old neighborhood once more. Does anyone see him? Does anyone recognize him?

What happens if they do? How does he feel about his home? What kind of reception is he given? How do his old neighbors react?

2. Instead of a realistic picture, an abstract composition might be shown. Color, dark and light contrasts, design, brush strokes—all will stimulate imaginative response. Not what the artist meant but what it means to the viewer is the object of this exercise. Younger children tend to respond to abstract composition more quickly than older players, perhaps because they do not feel the need for realistic detail. They may appreciate the fact that the artist's expression is direct and free like their own.

3. As noted in Chapter 4, music is a powerful stimulus to creativity. Use of rhythms to suggest kinds of movement, characters, or animals is a popular and highly successful way of working. From this to the heightening of characterization is a natural next step. Actually, only the beat of a drum is necessary, although music, particularly if the leader is able to play the piano, can enrich the activity. Recordings of orchestral music are an extremely effective means of establishing mood and may be used as we used pictures to stimulate the imagination, in a pattern of listening and responding. A leader with no formal background in music can guide the group not in the sense of a lesson in music appreciation but in the sense of encouraging listening and imaginative response. Young children seem to respond more spontaneously to music than older children, who have learned to be concerned with structure, theme, and melody. The procedure is much the same as that followed with the pictures. Ask questions and give directions: How does it make you feel? Show us. Where are you? Who are you? Are there others with you? What might be happening?

To create a story from music takes time, but after several experiences in listening and responding, the group will be ready to proceed with the creation of characters, an original situation suggested by the music, and then some dialogue. Again, music is a way of inducing the flow of creative energy. Because of its abstract quality, music may produce a mood more readily than other stimuli.

Characterization

Until now, we have been pantomiming activities and working to induce mood or feeling. The next step is characterization. Some participants will already have suggested characters different from themselves, but the teacher can use either the same exercises or new ones to start the group thinking in terms of characterization.

Again, situations involving groups are a good way to begin.

1. You are a group of people waiting for a bus on a city street. Each one of you will think of someone special to be: an elderly woman going to see her grandchildren, a businesswoman late for work, a girl on her way to high school, a blind man who needs help getting on the right bus, a young man beginning a new job, and so on.

The Stage Door Workshop pantomime. (Courtesy of Patti Carliss, Director, Allentown, PA; photograph by Cindy Craddock).

2. You are pilgrims who have gone to a shrine where, once a year, one wish is said to be granted. Decide who you are and what it is you want. You might be a disabled man who wants to walk again, a poet who wants very much to have her work published, a young mother who wants her sick baby to be cured. The teacher may choose to play with the group and be the statue at the shrine who indicates which wish is to be granted. This is a good situation to pantomime because it offers an opportunity to work on both characterization and strong motivation.

3. You are people in a bus terminal. Some of you are going on trips, others returning; still others are meeting friends or relatives. There may be a porter, a woman selling tickets, a man selling newspapers and magazines, and so on. By your behavior, let us know who you are and how you feel as you wait for the buses to arrive and depart.

Individual pantomimes like these stress character:

1. You are a thief who is entering a house at night. While you are there, the people return unexpectedly. You listen and finally make your escape, having stolen nothing.
2. You are a neighborhood gossip. You overhear someone else's conversation. You hear some very good news, some bad news, and then some remarks about yourself and your habit of snooping. How do you react? What do you do?
3. You are a child who has wanted a dog for a long time. One day you overhear your parents talking about getting a dog. One parent does not want a dog, but the other thinks it is time you had one. They discuss reasons for and against it. How do you react to their arguments, and what is the final decision?
4. Two of you will be a customer and a storekeeper in a shop in a foreign country. You do not know each other's language. The customer decides, in advance, on three things to buy and tries to convey what they are to the clerk through pantomime. Who are you? What are the three things? How does it turn out? (This is an exercise that the entire class can do in pairs.)

Another exercise is to take one action and do it as three people. Here are some examples:

1. You go into a restaurant to order a meal. Do it as
   a. A teenage boy who is very hungry
   b. A middle-aged woman who has very little appetite and sees nothing on the menu that she wants
   c. A very poor man who is hungry but must limit his choice to what he can afford
2. You are visiting an art museum. First you look at the exhibition as
   a. An artist who knows the painter whose work is on display
   b. A woman who thinks she should go to museums but does not appreciate the pictures
   c. An elderly man who has been ill and is enjoying visiting his favorite museum for the first time in many months
3. You are exercising in a gymnasium. Do the exercises first as
   a. A young woman who loves all athletics
   b. A fat man whose doctor has advised him to exercise to lose weight
   c. A child who has never seen gymnasium equipment before

For each of these exercises, consider what each participant does and how he or she feels about it.

Pantomime Suggested by Other Means

Some exercises are fun to do and stimulate inventiveness, but they have nothing to do with familiar actions, mood, or characters. Exercises like these are good as a change and can be introduced any time the leader feels the group needs a new type of stimulation:

1. Beat a drum and ask the group to move in any way the drumbeat suggests.
2. Ask each person in the class to represent a mechanical appliance. He or she does not operate it, but becomes it. Some very imaginative representations may be expected, such as a pencil sharpener, an egg beater, a lawnmower, a hair drier, or a cassette player. This is a challenging exercise, guaranteed to break down inhibitions.
3. Give each person a color and ask that he or she suggest it by means of movement, attitude, or characterization. This, incidentally, may be followed up with an improvisation in which the color becomes a person—for example, Mr. White, Ms. Black, Ms. Blue, Mr. Green, Mr. Red, and Ms. Yellow might be people at a tea. What are they like? How do they talk? How can we distinguish one from another?
4. Each person selects a property and acts according to what it suggests to him or her. The following items are usually good for stimulating imaginative reactions: a gnarled stick, a ruler, a bracelet, a broken dish, a sponge. Again, the players do not use the properties; they become characters suggested by their qualities.
5. Tell the students to be puppets, trying to imagine what it feels like to be controlled by strings. Ask participants to imagine that they are being controlled and then dropped by the puppeteer. Although there is an element of characterization involved, it is the feeling of the inanimate object being manipulated that interests us.
6. Have the group listen to orchestral music. Suggest that the group try to identify the various instruments. Then have the children be the instruments—not the musicians playing them, but the instruments themselves. If they are enjoying the exercise, suggest that each child select a different instrument to be until a whole orchestra has been assembled. This particular activity will probably not last longer than one session, but it is fun and a means of stretching the imagination.
7. Put up a sheet at one end of the room with a light behind it. Have the children pantomime something behind it. See what happens. The magic quality of a silhouette never fails to stimulate an immediate desire to try out ideas. This particular activity, incidentally, is an excellent one for the timid child, who feels less exposed behind a sheet than out in the open. Practice in acting behind the sheet leads to inventiveness: What happens when the actor is close to the sheet? far from it? approaches or leaves it? How can a figure be exaggerated? enlarged? How is humor obtained? Then try acting out nursery rhymes and stories in shadow.
8. The leader discusses growth and growing. Have the students conceive of themselves as seeds, buried deep in the earth. It is dark and they are quiet. Then spring arrives with rain, sun, and wind. What happens to the seeds? Do they break through the earth? Can we feel them push and grow? As summer comes, the plants grow taller. What are they going to be—flowers or trees? tall, short, bushy, weak, or strong? Tell them to feel the warm rain, the hot sun, the breeze

blowing, the final push to maturity. Poetry written about springtime ties in well with this exercise.

9. Mirror images are popular and great fun for actors of all ages. Two players face each other, one being herself and the other her mirror image. Whatever the person does, her image must reproduce precisely. With practice this can become a skilled performance, challenging to the players and fascinating to those watching. Greater awareness as well as the ability to work together are developed in the process. Older groups may ask to repeat this exercise from time to time, realizing the possibilities for technical improvement.

10. Older players often find the following exercise rewarding: Imagine yourself shut up in a box. How large is it? Can you stand up? move around? get out? Let us see the box—its sides, floor, top. Suppose the box becomes larger. What do you do? It grows smaller. What happens to you then?

As the group progresses, organization improves, and situations often develop into simple plots. The players are learning to use their entire bodies to express ideas and are ready to add dialogue. Although improvisation, or informal dialogue, is the subject of Chapter 6, the teacher will want to alternate exercises in pantomime and improvisation. No matter how old or how advanced the group, pantomime is always good to work on from time to time because of the type of practice it offers.

Starting Places

Situations

The following situations are suggested as starting places to get children thinking. The younger or less experienced the group, the more preliminary work is needed in the form of pantomime and discussion. Group pantomimes related to the situation will stimulate movement, whereas discussing the topic and asking questions about it helps to stir the imagination. When all seem to be ready, divide the class into several small groups to develop simple narratives. Each group will come up with its own ideas as to plot and characters. This can be a one-time activity or the beginning of a creative play done entirely in pantomime. Suggest situations like these:

A beggar at the door
"April Fool!"
A house for sale
A wrong number on the telephone
The tallest sunflower in town
Delivery of a package you didn't order
A magic sandal
A substitute teacher in your classroom one morning
A bracelet found in an alley
Your bus pass missing
A puppy in a box left in a doorway
A new uncle from abroad

Pantomime using an object to foster imagination. (Courtesy of Julia Morris, Imagination Station Project.)

Making a Machine

There are many variations on this exercise, which has great appeal for older students. One way of beginning is for the leader to start a regular beat and ask one person to come into the center of the room and begin a movement. When the movement has been stabilized, a second person comes forward with another movement that relates to the first. This continues until as many as a dozen players become parts of a machine, each one contributing a movement that is coordinated with the rest. The effect can be interesting and dynamic when all players are working together.

This exercise can be made more interesting by adding sounds. Each player makes a noise appropriate to his or her movement. When all parts of the machine are moving rhythmically together, the sounds enhance the effect. This exercise requires imagination, inventiveness, concentration, cooperation, and the ability to sustain both sound and movement until the mechanical quality is established. The machine can run indefinitely or it can break down, either stopping or falling apart.

Summary

Pantomime, while good practice at any time, is usually the most satisfactory way of beginning work in creative drama. Although it is not necessary to follow a prescribed program of exercises, many groups begin with familiar activities and then move on to mood or feeling and finally characterization. By starting with movement and then pantomime, the players learn to express themselves through bodily action, without the additional problem of dialogue. Younger children accept pantomime as a natural means of expression, and older children and adults find it easier to begin with pantomime than with improvisation or formal acting. Pantomime sharpens perception and stimulates the imagination as the players try to remember how actions are done and what objects are really like in terms of their size, weight, and shape. Recalling emotion demands concentration and involvement. Close observation of people is a means of developing believable characters whose bearing, movement, and gestures belong to them and whose behavior seems appropriate. Although pantomime is considered here as a medium of expression, it may become an art form in itself. Mimes like Marcel Marceau have demonstrated its power to communicate with people of all ages and backgrounds when a high level of artistry is achieved.

Suggested Assignments

1. Think of some appropriate pantomimes for very young children. Select a story that has activities children can do as a group (example: "The Elves and the Shoemaker"—making shoes). The leader will probably have to start the action, but little children follow readily and look forward to the next opportunity to mime action.
2. Next, list some ideas for children from age six to eight. The teacher or leader may want to start with a story, but the children are old enough to act parts in pantomime after hearing it told or read.
3. Children from eight to eleven are resourceful and creative if stimulated. Ideas can come from many sources, including ideas and topics that interest them. Discover their interests and make a list for this age level.
4. Finally, make a list of ideas for children from twelve to fifteen. They are capable of building a sequence, telling a story in mime, creating characters, and working both individually and in groups.
5. Take an exercise from this chapter and develop it into a story, told entirely in mine.

Journal Writing

1. Have you ever seen a really gifted mime? If so, do you remember your reaction at the time?
2. Which do you prefer for expressing yourself: mime, improvisation, or acting with a script? Can you explain your preference?
3. Think of the ways we use mime in our daily lives. List them.
4. Have you ever learned something from the body language of another person? Describe it and remember how you felt.
5. How does a dog express itself in body language?

Chapter 6

Improvisation: Characters Move and Speak

Bridge to Terabithia. *Young People's Performing Arts, University of Northern Iowa. (Courtesy of Xan Johnson.)*

> At every moment throughout our lives, we are
> having to adjust to whatever happens around us.
> The more unexpected the happening, the more
> spontaneous and frank the response is likely to be.
> —*John Hodgson*

Improvisation is difficult at first. Dialogue does not flow easily, even when it has been preceded by much work in pantomime and a thorough understanding of the situation or story. With practice, however, words do begin to come, and the players discover the possibilities of character development when oral language is added. Dialogue is apt to be brief and scanty at first but usually begins to flow rapidly after the players become accustomed to it. Players age seven and older enjoy the opportunity to use words to further a story and more fully describe the characters they are portraying. It is a good idea to begin with simple situations so the players get accustomed to using dialogue before attempting more ambitious material.

Many of the situations suggested in Chapter 5 can be used, although they were designed with movement in mind. Frequently, children will begin to add dialogue of their own free will, as they feel the need to express ideas in words. When this happens, the leader accepts it as a natural progression from one step to the next. Younger children, players for whom English is a second language, or older students who lack self-confidence will usually wait until they are urged to try adding dialogue. The teacher will not expect too much and will accept whatever is offered, knowing that more will be forthcoming the next time.

Sounds, incidentally, can stimulate imagination and lead the listener to the creation of an improvisation. For example, the teacher can beat a drum or tambourine, knock, ring bells, or make any other kind of sound. This works particularly well with younger children but is also a good exercise to use from time to time with those who are older.

As mentioned before, the environment for creative playing should be an uncluttered space, with chairs in a circle or semicircle, and no distracting equipment or props. This will get the class off to a good start. Props will be introduced later, but in the beginning we want to focus on the work at hand.

Simple Improvisations Based on Situations

The following improvisations can be done with various age levels, although the backgrounds of the players will determine appropriateness. In some cases, the situations are better for older players.

1. You are a group of people in a subway or train station. It is six o'clock in the evening. In the center is a newsstand at which newspapers, magazines, and candy are sold. It is run by a woman who has been there for many years. She knows the passengers who ride regularly and is interested in them

and all the details of their daily lives. Decide who you are going to be—
a secretary, an actor, a businessperson, a janitor, a shopper, a police officer,
a teenager, a stranger in town, and so on. Then let us know all about you
through your conversation with the proprietor of the newsstand while you
are waiting for your train.

2. Young children enjoy this one: The scene is a toyshop on Christmas Eve. It is
   midnight, and the owner has just closed the door and gone home. At the
   stroke of twelve the toys come alive and talk together. They may include a
   toy soldier, a rag doll, a beautiful doll, a clown, a teddy bear, a jack-in-the-box,
   and so forth. Let us know by your conversation and movements who you are
   and why you were not bought.

3. This improvisation is good on a high school or college level: The scene is a
   meeting of the student council review committee. You have the job of questioning a student who is reported to have stolen the examination questions
   for a history class. What is each one of you like? How do you handle the situation? Is the accused guilty or not? What is your final decision, and what do
   you do about it?

4. The scene is a laundromat. Your mother has told you to take the laundry to
   the operator, but he is very busy and you decide you can do it yourself. You
   manage the clothes, but the coins stick in the slot. Another customer tries to
   help you, but her coins get stuck, too. She calls the operator, who tries to dis-
   lodge them, but he also fails. How is the situation solved?

5. The scene is a popular pizza parlor. You order a large pizza to take out, but
   the other customers and the delivery drivers keep pushing in ahead of you.
   Finally your order is filled, but it costs more money than you have with you.
   There are three solutions; try each one.
   a. The manager lets you take the pizza and says you can pay the rest tomorrow.
   b. The cashier refuses to let you have it, but another customer helps you out.
   c. The cashier refuses to let you have it, and no one helps. You change
      your order to a cheaper one, and the people behind you in the line are
      impatient.

6. This is another improvisation for older students: You are a group of young
   women in a suburban community. One of you has invited the new neighbor
   in to meet the rest of the group. Coffee is served, and you talk together. All
   seems to be going well until the hostess notices that an expensive silver dish
   is missing from her coffee table. One by one, you begin to suspect the newcomer. Why do you suspect her? Did she take it? Is it found? Where? If she
   took it, why did she? Let us know what each of you is like by your reaction to
   this situation. How does it turn out?

7. This improvisation is good with younger children: You are a group of children in an apartment house. It is Valentine's Day, and you are gathered in the
   front hall to look at and count your valentines. You see one child in the
   building going to her mailbox, and you notice that she did not receive any
   cards. How do you feel about this? What is each of you like? Do you decide
   to do anything about it? If so, what do you do?

8. You are a group of children who live near a very cross, elderly woman. She chases you away from her property whenever you come near. This particular morning, you see that someone has broken her fence and ruined many of her flowers. For the first time you feel sorry for her. What do you do? How does she react to you? Do you all agree as to whether you should help her? Do your actions change her attitude toward children?

9. A new child has entered your class at school. He does not speak English, and some of the children laugh at him. When recess comes, you all go out to the playground. How does each of you treat him? How does he react to you? You are all different, so you will each feel differently toward him. Do you finally take him in, or do you exclude him? Try changing roles so that different players have the experience of trying the part of the new child. Does the improvisation change as you all think more about the situation?

10. The scene is a small bakery. One of you is the owner, one of you is a boy or girl who helps on Saturdays, and another is a beggar. It is not busy this particular morning, so the owner goes out for coffee. While he or she is gone, the beggar comes into the shop and asks for some bread. The student knows that he or she should not give away the bread but feels sorry for the beggar. What do you say to each other? What does the owner say when he or she comes back? Try changing parts in this improvisation to see whether it will turn out differently.

Improvisations Suggested by Objects

Not only situations and stories motivate improvisation; some very imaginative results can be obtained by the use of objects or properties. Try some of the following suggestions as springboards.

1. Put an object (any object) in the center of a circle where all the players can see it. Tell them to look at it, without speaking, for three or four minutes, and think of a story about it. Where might it have come from? How did it get here? What else does it bring to mind? Each player will have an original story to tell; have the students tell their stories.

2. This time, divide the class into groups of three or four. Present an object and ask each group to make up an improvisation about it. Perhaps the property is a wooden spoon. When used with one class, the following ideas were suggested and these situations improvised:

   a. The scene was a settler's cabin more than a hundred years ago. The family had very few household items and so they prized each one. Among them was a wooden spoon. In this scene it was used to stir batter for cornbread and then was washed and put carefully away.

   b. The scene was a museum and the spoon a relic from the Native Americans who once inhabited the region. The characters were the curator of the museum and two children who were visiting it. The curator answered their questions by telling the history of the spoon.

Improvisation in the classroom. (Courtesy of Milton Polsky, photograph by Roberta Polsky.)

    c. The scene was a cave. Three children were hiking and found the spoon. They used it to dig and discovered an old box of coins that had been buried there. They took the old spoon home with them for good luck.

    d. The scene was an industrial arts class. The students were making things of wood, and a blind child carved the spoon. It was so well done that the teacher said she would display it as one of the best things made in her class that year.

    e. The scene was a dump. The old wooden spoon was the speaker, and it told the other discarded items how it had been used and handed down from one generation to the next. Finally, its owners became rich and threw it away because they considered it too old and ugly to be of further use to them.

Any object can function as a springboard, and no two groups will see it in exactly the same way. Many kinds of properties like these will suggest ideas:

a velvet jewelry box	an old hat	a headset radio
an artificial rose	a cane	a pair of athletic shoes
a foreign coin	a quill pen	a pair of in-line skates
a feather duster	a bell	an old dog leash

An improvisation with unusual interest was developed from a whistle by a very imaginative group of ten-year-olds. They decided that it was a police officer's whistle, made of silver and bearing an inscription. They laid the scene in the officer's home on the day of retirement from the force; the characters were the police officer, the officer's spouse, and their grandchild. The police officer came in that evening, took off the whistle, looked at it nostalgically a long time, and then laid it on the supper table. The grandchild, coming into the room at that point, begged for the story again of how the officer had received it. As the story began, there was a flashback scene in which the police officer was rescuing a child from burning in a bonfire many years before. Honored for bravery and given the inscribed silver whistle, the officer had treasured it ever since. At the finish of the story, the flashback scene faded, and some neighbors came in with a cake and presents. The improvisation was effective both in its good dramatic structure and the reality of the characterizations.

Not every group is able to develop improvisations to this degree, but occasionally one will, and when it happens, it is an inspiration to the rest of the class. Incidentally, it is nearly always the result of the play's having been based on familiar material so that the players are sure of the dialogue and can identify easily with the characters. Again, respect for their background and acceptance of the ideas that come out of it not only make for comfort but also bring forth ideas that the teacher probably would not have thought of. Children of foreign background have a wealth of material on which to draw, but too often it remains an untapped source because they have been made to feel that it is unworthy of consideration. Both the stories they have been told and the details of their everyday lives contain the basic ingredients of drama. For example, one group of boys who lived in a housing project played a scene in an elevator. The situation was simple but had reality. Two boys, having nothing to do, decided to ride up and down in the elevator, angering the tenants and almost causing a tragedy because one man on a high floor was ill and waiting for the doctor. The teacher did not know whether this had been an actual experience, but the situation contained reality, humor, and drama, with characters who were believable.

One final example of the use of properties was an improvisation done by a group of high school girls. They had been asked by the teacher to search their purses and select the six most unusual or interesting objects. The objects they finally chose were a newspaper clipping, a snapshot, a lipstick in a Japanese case, a key ring with a red charm, a pocketknife, and a purse flashlight. Within minutes they had created a mystery, prompted by and making use of every one of the properties they selected. There were six players, and their preparation time was approximately ten minutes.

Improvisations from Costumes

Similar to the use of objects or props, and equally effective in stimulating ideas, are pieces of costume. Garments such as hats, capes, aprons, shawls, tailcoats, and jewelry will suggest different kinds of characters. Innumerable examples could be given of situations that grew from characters developed this way. For example, to one boy, a tailcoat suggested a musician, down on his luck and playing his violin on a street corner for pennies. A feathered hat helped a little girl create a woman of fashionable pretensions and become a comic character in her extravagant dress and poor taste. A shawl suggested witches, grandmothers, people in disguise, or a scene laid in very cold weather.

It is wise for the teacher on any level, working anywhere, to keep a supply of simple and sturdy costumes available for this kind of use. If children experience difficulty in getting into character, a piece of a costume may sometimes be all that is needed to provide the necessary incentive. Costume used in this way is not dressing the part but is an aid to more imaginative thinking.

Improvisations from Characters

In Chapter 5, an illustration was given of an improvisation created from a character. This is a successful method of starting and encouraging observation. If the group is small and has had some experience, original monologues are good practice and fun for the players. If the class is large, however, this is probably not a wise assignment unless the monologues are kept short.

To help students create from a character, the teacher can ask each member of the class to think of a particularly interesting person he or she has noticed that day or sometime during the week. This is followed by questions:

> Who was this person?
> What was he or she doing?
> Did he or she have anything to say?
> How did he or she dress?
> How old was the person?
> What special thing about this person attracted your attention?

One girl offered as a character a woman who served the hot vegetables in her school cafeteria. Although the woman was bad tempered, she was always extremely generous in her servings and did her job more efficiently than the other workers. The group that chose her as a heroine for their story decided that the woman had been a refugee. Because she had experienced hunger during that period in her life, she was determined that all plates would be generously filled now that food was available. Her irritability they attributed to the woman's unhappy experiences and her separation from her family. The scene that the children improvised, using this particular character as an inspiration, was thoughtful, sympathetic, and interesting to the class.

Another improvisation based on an actual person was the story of an elderly woman whom one child noticed every day sitting on the front porch of her house. The group that chose her for a heroine decided that she was really very rich but miserly and was saving her money for the day when her son would come home. They agreed that he had gone into the army several years before and had not returned. Although he had been reported missing, his mother clung to the hope that he would come back

Improvising "The Tortoise and the Hare." (Courtesy of the New Canaan Country School, photograph by Mary Perrine.)

some day, and so she sat on the porch waiting by day and counting her money by night. The group decided to have him return, so the story had a happy ending.

Improvisations from Clues

Older players enjoy creating improvisations from clues found in strange places. The following exercises can be done to build characters.

1. With these clues, what kinds of people do you imagine? In an improvisation, create a character who is suggested by two of these items:

raw vegetables	a hair dryer	a checkbook
a cane	a television	a belt
a book	a hat	a stick
Coca-Cola	a fur piece	a bag

2. This exercise is good for experienced players: Select a place where a number of strangers might gather. This could be an airport, a bus stop, outside a grocery store in the morning before it opens, a parking lot, a picket line. One person enters and is soon joined by another. They get into a conversation.

Another comes in and then another, until a large group has assembled. The class can decide in advance who each will be or, what is harder, will come into the group as the character, making those already there decide who he or she is. This exercise has wonderful possibilities for character study and simple plot development.

Biography

This exercise is suggested for older players: The leader chooses a character (real or fictional) and describes him or her briefly. After some general discussion, the class is divided into five or six small groups, each representing a period in the character's life. Each group then plans its interpretation of the character at a given time. The periods could be

birth to age six	the thirties or forties
six to twelve years	later life
the teens	old age
the twenties	

The persons in the first scene would have to be members of the family, neighbors, or others. The character about whom the scenes are built need not actually appear in each one, but the scenes must be related in some way to the person's life. This is an excellent way to study a character; if a historical person is used, the exercise will lead to research. If the character is not a real person, the exercise is a challenge to the imagination. "Biography" implies representing not only the character but other significant persons in the character's life. This exercise can be extended to several sessions to acquire greater depth.

Improvisations for Two

Have pairs of students try to imagine themselves in the following situations:

1. You receive a letter in the mail telling you that you have won first prize in a poster contest. Tell your mother the good news.
2. Your dog has been hit by a car. When you come home from school, your father meets you and tells you what has happened.
3. You have been warned not to go down a dark street by yourself at night. This evening, however, you are in a hurry and decide to go anyway because it is a shortcut. When you are about halfway down the block, you hear footsteps behind you. You look over your, shoulder and see someone hurrying after you. You speed up; so does the other person. You decide to slow down; so does the person who is following you. By this time you are frightened, but it is too late to turn back. You start to run, and so does the other person. You run faster; so

does your follower. Finally, you reach the corner, but there is a lot of traffic and the light has turned red. As you stand there alone waiting for it to change, a friend comes up. It was the friend who was following you, but neither of you recognized the other, and both of you had been running to get to the brightly lit corner. You have a good laugh when you recognize each other.

4. You are moving to a new neighborhood today. Your best friend comes around to say good-bye to you. Although you are looking forward to your new home, you are sad to leave the old neighborhood. What do you say?

5. Your aunt, whom you have never met, has come for a visit. You answer the door. What is she like? What do you say to each other?

6. You have been wanting ice skates for your birthday. Your grandfather, who always selects the right presents, comes to the door with a box in his hands. When you open it, you find it contains stationery. What do you say to each other?

7. You wore your sister's bracelet on a picnic, and when you get home, you discover you have lost it. Now you must tell her what happened.

Improvisations for Three

These situations can be used as springboards for groups of three:

1. You are delivering papers. You throw one toward a house, but instead of landing on the porch, it breaks a window. The owners come out to see what has happened.

2. You and your friend find a $5 bill on the sidewalk. You want to keep it, but at this moment a woman comes down the street looking for something. You are certain she has lost the money. What do you do?

3. Your mother has just given your old rag doll to your younger cousin, who is visiting you. Neither of them knows how much the doll means to you. You try to pretend it is all right.

4. You saw the student across the aisle cheat on a test when the teacher stepped out of the room. The teacher suspects that there has been cheating and asks you and the other student to stay after class. What does each one of you say and do?

5. You are delivering flowers for a neighborhood florist. On this particular day you are carrying a very large plant, but you have lost the delivery address. You think you remember it, however, so you go to what you hope is the right door. It is the wrong address, but the person who answers the door accepts the plant, then discovers the mistake. You have left by that time. How do you, the florist, and the resident work things out?

6. Three of you are getting refreshments ready for a party. It is said that too many cooks spoil the broth. This happens when all of you put salt in the chocolate pudding, thinking that it is sugar and needs sweetening. This can be a very funny situation. How do you handle it?

The Tea Party. *First Presbyterian Church Nursery School, New York City. (Courtesy of Ruth Callahan.)*

7. You are falsely accused of cheating on an examination. You are angry and upset. The three persons involved are your teacher, the principal of the school, and you.

8. You are at the checkout counter of a supermarket. The cashier is checking off your items when you realize that you forgot to get milk. You run back for it. This annoys the person behind you. Then you discover that you don't have enough money to pay the bill, so you have to return some items. By this time the cashier and two people behind you are annoyed. You push the items to a corner of the counter, but when you pick up your shopping bag, which the cashier has packed for you, it splits open. Now you are angry too. This makes everyone laugh, including you; suddenly the annoying situation becomes funny.

"You End It!" Improvisations

Unfinished stories can also be used to stimulate thinking. If the teacher introduces a character and sets the scene, the group is given the problem of completing the story. Although this is more an exercise in plotting than in character, the action is motivated by the character: an interesting character makes for an interesting plot.

1. The personnel officer in a store is faced with a difficult decision. Business has been poor lately, and the president of the company has said that two employees

must be let go. The personnel officer calls in the last three people hired and discusses the problem with them. After they leave, he or she must decide which two will go and which one to keep. The three are then called back into the office and told. The decision has been made on the basis of what has been said, the quality of the employees' work, and what was expected of them.

2. The scene is a courtroom. A street vendor has been apprehended for selling what police suspect is stolen jewelry. Two or three witnesses are called to tell what they have seen or know. Then the vendor is called to give her explanation of how she came by the articles she was offering for sale. The judge decides whether or not she is guilty of possessing stolen property.

3. Take a well-known story, but instead of ending it in the usual way, stop before the final action and end it differently. For example, take "Rumplestiltskin." Imagine that the straw is not spun into gold. How would you end the story?

4. A small group of people are hiking in a national park on a beautiful day. They go farther into the forest than they had intended. Suddenly, they realize that it is growing dark. They turn to go back but discover there are two paths, and they are not sure which one they had been following. A decision must be made quickly: one path will lead them back to their campsite; the other may be fraught with danger, and they will be hopelessly lost. What will they decide to do? Why do they make this decision?

5. The scene is a country fair. A raffle is being held, and the person calling the winning numbers announces the number for the grand prize. Two people rush forward and claim to be the winners. They both show their tickets, which are identical. The person in charge calls a stranger from the crowd (in this case, from the class) and asks him or her to make the decision. This is to be done by pulling one of the tickets from a hat.

All of the above situations are open-ended. They are to be played as regular improvisations until the end, when someone or the group itself must make an important decision. Players may use details they observe, information they gather, or intuition in arriving at the decision; there is no right answer because each time the situation is improvised, it will be done differently and the variations will affect the decision.

Here are some other ideas:

1. Arrange furniture and props to create an environment or setting. What does it suggest to the players? Create an improvisation that might take place in this setting.

2. Divide the group into two subgroups representing opposite sides of an idea or issue. Improvise in individual groups first; then bring the two groups together with the aim of reaching a solution.

3. Create a plot from one of the following phrases:
   a. Can you spare some change?
   b. Where's the bus station?
   c. May I have a cup of coffee?
   d. Do you have the time?
   e. Which way to Main Street? (or any familiar street)

4. Tell or read the group a short story. Then have them improvise it. Next, create a scene that might take place after the ending of the original story.
5. Two friends meet after many years. One, who was once very attractive, is now greatly changed; she is obviously down on her luck. The other, who had been plain, has been successful.

Improvisations with Problems for Discussion

Television, films, and open discussion of heretofore taboo topics have affected the subject matter that has come into creative drama sessions in recent years. While most children still enjoy working on the material the teacher brings in, their own experiences and problems often surface when they are given a chance to express their own ideas. Broken homes, divorce, racial discrimination, illness and death, values, and social issues of all kinds can be disturbing to children, and the leader must be prepared to deal with problems if or when they come up.

The following open-ended situations involve problems. Older players may enjoy first improvising them and then discussing the options with the rest of the class.

1. You are in a gift shop in an airport. Over the glass and china counter there is a sign that says, "You break it, you pay for it." Your sweater sleeve accidentally catches a glass dish, which falls to the floor and breaks. The airport is so noisy that no one hears the dish break. What are you going to do?
   a. Go to the clerk with the broken pieces and explain what happened.
   b. Decide to do nothing, hoping you can get away without paying for the damage.
2. Your class is competing in a play festival. The group about to go on is very good. Suddenly, you see this group's most important prop lying on the floor outside the stage door. You realize that if the players lose their prop they won't be able to replace it, and any substitute prop will probably upset them. What are you going to do?
   a. Pick up the prop and give it to the stage manager.
   b. Hide the prop in a trash basket in an effort to make the other group do less than their best.
3. You are invited to a party in a very beautiful home. Your mother says you should dress up, but your friends say they are going to wear jeans. One of them says she has no dress clothes. What will you do?
   a. Try to persuade your friends to dress up.
   b. Dress up; then change into jeans at the last minute.
   c. Wear your best clothes and find that everyone else is dressed casually.
   d. Loan some clothes to your friend who has nothing dressy to wear.
4. You are buying a birthday present for your sister or brother. You know exactly what she or he wants. You find two different gifts, one cheap and the other

expensive. You also see something you want for yourself. If you buy the expensive item, it will take all your money. If you buy the cheap item, there will be enough money left for you to get what you want too.

a. You decide on the expensive gift.

b. You decide on the cheap gift and get yourself what you want as well.

5. You live with your mother, who has planned to take you to the circus next weekend. Your father, however, with whom you usually spend the weekend, has tickets to a baseball game. You have been wanting to go to both. It is up to you to reach a decision.

6. There has been a bad flood in your neighborhood, and many families have had to leave their homes quickly. Your mother invites some people to stay in your house till the crisis is over.

a. One of them is a boy or girl you dislike.

b. You have to give up your room to a family.

c. You decide to help in any way you can.

Improvisations for Older Players

The following situations are suggested for older students, who are faced with similar problems. Having several groups work on them at the same time and then enact them for the entire class gives an opportunity for good discussion. Rarely will two groups come up with identical reactions and solutions. The problems make for good drama, perhaps because they have reality for the players, and they combine imagination and emotional and intellectual involvement in the situations.

1. A young girl answers the telephone. The caller is a boy in her class who asks her to go to a movie with him on Saturday night. Although she does not like him particularly, she has nothing else planned, and she does want to see that film. So she agrees to go and hangs up. A few minutes later the telephone rings again; this time it is one of her girl friends, inviting her to a party. She really wants to go and accepts, but after she hangs up the phone, she realizes that she will have to get out of the first invitation or call her friend back and explain why she must decline after all.

    (Stop for discussion.) What should she do? Discuss all solutions suggested. Then try them all out. What was the best decision and why?

2. A young person has a part-time volunteer job in an animal shelter. Not only does he or she love working with the animals, but the job gives school credit for learning outside the classroom. The student has been doing very well and on occasion is left alone to fill water bowls, clean cages, and so on. One day the student opens a cage door too far, and a cat leaps out and is suddenly gone. The student knows it is in the kennel, but finding a gray cat among all the cages and supplies seems impossible. Should the student call a staff member and explain what happened? Will the confession jeopardize this volunteer

job? Or is it better to say nothing, hoping that the animal's absence won't be noticed right away?

(Stop for discussion.) What does he or she do? What was the best solution?

3. A girl is home alone. Her parents are out for the evening and have told her not to let anyone in and to call them if a problem arises. She is watching television when the doorbell rings. She hears the voices of some of her friends. She opens the door, and her friends burst into the room. She tries to explain that her parents are out, but the friends take this as an invitation to stay. They order from the deli, play tapes, and have a party. As time goes on, the party gets out of hand, and a valuable piece of pottery is accidentally broken. There is silence as the young people realize that the situation has gone too far.

(Stop for discussion.) What should be done? What can be done? What will happen when the adults find out about the party and the broken pottery? Try out the various solutions. What was the right thing to do?

In situations in which both adults and young people are involved, their reactions differ. An interesting thing to do with these problems is to have the students shift from child to adult roles to get a better understanding of the whole situation. If they respond very positively to the activities, perhaps they would like to suggest some of their own, either problems they have had to face or some they can imagine. This is an exceptionally effective activity for high school students.

In working on the following improvisations, students should ask the following questions:

- Who am I?
- Where does the scene take place?
- What has preceded it both recently and earlier in the life of the character?
- Where does the action take place?

Students won't have all the answers, so to start they will have to think the situation through carefully. Next come these questions:

- What is the action?
- What is the problem?
- What is the conflict that follows?
- How is the conflict resolved?

1. Staying Out Too Late

CHARACTERS:
Mother
Father
Daughter
Grandmother

TIME: *Midnight on a school night*

PLACE: *The family's living room*

The daughter, who is in high school, has repeatedly stayed out too late at night. This particular evening she agreed to be home by eleven o'clock, but it is now approaching midnight. The other members of the family are waiting for her, each reacting to the situation in his or her own way. Think through each character, deciding on the motivation for attitude and action.

2. The Shopping Center

CHARACTERS:

Several residents of the town opposed to a shopping center
Several residents in favor of it
Developer, who is eager to start the project
Owner of the meadow, who sees two sides to the situation

TIME: *8:00 P.M.*

PLACE: *Town hall of a very small town*

A developer wants to buy a beautiful meadow on the edge of a small town and put up a shopping center and parking lot. Some of the residents think it a good idea, but others are violently opposed to the plan. For one thing, it will mean destroying a lovely meadow and razing three nineteenth-century farmhouses that are the pride of the town. The owner of the land is not sure which way to go. Decide who you are and how you feel. Then, considering the questions asked above and the information you have about the situation, you will find your motivation and will act on the proposal.

3. The Playground or a Gym?

CHARACTERS:

Group of neighborhood children
Playground Director
Community Leader

TIME: *A summer morning*

PLACE: *The playground*

A new gymnasium is being proposed on the site of a children's playground. The children have just heard about it, and most of them are upset. The playground director is not sure where he or she stands but tries to comfort them by talking about it. The community leader comes along and is very enthusiastic about the idea. He or she offers strong arguments in favor of it. Decide who you are, how you feel about the proposal, and why you feel as you do. Knowledge about yourself, your past use of the playground, and your fear of or interest in the new gym will help you discuss the proposal.

Make up other situations in which there are conflicts and characters caught up in them. A strong situation could become the plot for a play. Situations such as these offer excellent opportunities for developing dialogue. Arguments must be clear, well presented, and motivated by the interests, needs, and values of the characters stating them. Most players like the challenge of controversial real-life situations.

4. The Sweep-In

CHARACTERS:
Any number of players engaged in the cleanup of the block
First Helper
Second Helper
A boy or girl who vandalizes and refuses to cooperate

The block is engaged in a project to clean up the neighborhood and plant a street-corner garden. Most of the neighbors are busy sweeping, picking up paper and bottles, and cleaning the proposed garden space. There is one family who refuses to cooperate and continues to throw trash in the street. Two young people try to persuade the son or daughter to join the sweep-in. Try to resolve the conflict.

5. The Soup Kitchen

CHARACTERS:
Boy or girl helper
Best Friend
Supervisor of the soup kitchen
Other boys and girls, if wanted

The community center operates a soup kitchen, and Friday night is the boy's or girl's night to help. At the last minute he or she is invited to a game and wants very much to attend. The kitchen is short of help, which creates a greater conflict. How is the problem finally resolved?

6. The Job Interview

CHARACTERS:
Personnel Manager
You
A friend or parent, if desired

You are being interviewed for your first job. The salary sounds good but you would be working for a large pharmaceutical company that tests its products on animals. You oppose this practice so how do you feel about working there? What questions do you ask? How does the personnel manager respond? You are in conflict because you had planned to use the money for education. What will be your decision?

7. Another Point of View

One way to change an improvisation would be to tell the story from the viewpoint of another character (e.g., to tell the story of Hansel and Gretel from the witch's point of view or "Humpty Dumpty" from the standpoint of the king's men). This is a challenging assignment, which can be used in the teaching of language arts as well as serving as an exercise in creative drama.

Improvisations Based on Holidays

One club group showed an unusual interest in holidays, so the teacher used this interest as a springboard for the entire year. She brought in stories about Halloween, Thanksgiving, Christmas, New Year's Day, Valentine's Day, St. Patrick's Day, April Fools' Day, Memorial Day, and the Fourth of July. Sometimes the group acted out the stories she read to them; sometimes the players made up stories of their own, suggested by the occasion. One day they observed that there was no holiday in August. The result was an original play, which they called *A Holiday for August*. It was to be a festival of children's games, and it developed into a particularly attractive summer pageant. August was the narrator, who began by telling of his disappointment that no one had ever thought to put a holiday in his month. At the conclusion, he expressed his joy that the children had made him special with a festival of games played in his honor.

Improvisations Based on Stories

The most popular and, in many ways, most satisfactory form of improvisation is based on good stories. Although making up original stories is a creative exercise, a group endeavor rarely achieves the excellence of a story that has stood the test of time or has been written by a fine author. Improvising from a story is a way of introducing literature, and when a story is well chosen it offers good opportunities for acting. Chapters 8 and 9 illustrate the ways in which both simple and more complicated stories have been approached.

Good stories on any level should have literary quality, worthwhile ideas, correct information, and dramatic values. Children up to the age of ten and eleven like fairy tales and legends. Older children may still enjoy them but tend to prefer adventure, biography, and stories of real life. Frequently, the real-life stories, because of their length, will have to be cut or the incidents rearranged. This is a learning experience that, if the group has had some experience, should not be too difficult.

To present the right story, the leader must, first, know the group well. One leader, who was later to achieve remarkable success, told of her first experience as a young teacher at a settlement house in an inner-city neighborhood. Nothing she brought to the children in her drama group captured their interest. Improvisation seemed an impossible goal, though the children were alert and lively when she saw them on the street. Finally, she hit upon the idea of asking them to tell her stories they knew. Hesitantly at first, then willingly, family anecdotes came. She tried using them as springboards for improvisation. Not only was the material a success—the group doubled in size. Parents began to look in. Before the end of the year, an activity that had seemed doomed to failure became the most popular. Some years later, the drama department was to achieve nationwide recognition as an arts center. The search for material had led to the children themselves. Their cultural heritage, and their creative use of it under intelligent and sensitive guidance, was the first step.

Role Playing

As noted in Chapter 1, role playing as therapy is not the job of the creative drama teacher or the classroom teacher using creative drama techniques, although some teachers have tried it with an educative rather than a therapeutic purpose. Human conflicts and the ways in which problems are solved can promote social growth. Family scenes, school situations, and playground incidents give opportunity for interaction and group discussion. Discussion is the most important aspect of role playing, according to some teachers, for it is during these periods that various points of view are presented and attitudes clarified. The teacher must accept all ideas, giving the boys and girls a chance to express themselves without fear of disapproval. The teacher poses questions: How do you think the father felt? the brother? the mother? What did the man next door think when you broke his window? How do you think he felt the third time it happened? If you were he, how would you feel?

Exchanging roles is a good way to put oneself in the shoes of another in order to understand that person. One teacher gave a demonstration of role playing done with her group of junior high school girls, who lived in a neighborhood with a growing Puerto Rican population. The girls had had difficulty in accepting the newcomers, and the teacher's introduction of role playing as a way of helping them understand the problem led to the following improvisation. The scene was the planning of a school dance by a small clique. The committee wished to exclude the newcomers but could accomplish the exclusion only by making them feel unwelcome. This led to a serious breakdown in group relations. The period spent in playing the situation reportedly did much to restore peace and communication. The problem was faced squarely, and the girls were able to discuss their own attitudes and feelings. Later, when the improvisation was done as a demonstration for a university class, it made a tremendous impression. The insights expressed through the honesty of the players proved the value of the experiment. The leader did not claim to be a therapist but was an intelligent and experienced classroom teacher who was deeply troubled about a condition that was interfering with the work of the class.

Peter Slade, an early British educator, in *Child Drama* summarizes the use of role playing: "I would go so far as to say that one of the most important reasons for developing child drama in schools generally is not actually a therapeutic one but the even more constructive one of prevention."[1]

It must be pointed out that playing the part of fictional characters also demands identification with the characters and their problems. Exchange of parts gives all of

---

[1]Peter Slade, *Child Drama* (London: University of London Press, 1954), p. 119.

the players a chance to experience both sides of a conflict. The real-life conflict that the group itself experiences is stronger than the fictional one, and the solution, if found, is of practical benefit.

The Mysteries of Harris Burdick[2] makes an exceptional springboard for improvisation. The haunting illustrations and accompanying captions stimulate the imagination without giving a clue as to what the illustrator had in mind.

Summary

Improvisation is the creation of a situation in which characters speak spontaneously. There are many ways of introducing improvisation, but some groundwork in pantomime is the best preparation. Once the players have achieved a sense of security in movement, they are ready to add dialogue. Dialogue does not come easily at first, but continued practice with familiar material usually induces the flow. There are many points of departure, and some of the most successful are those described in this chapter: improvisation from situations, objects or properties, sounds, characters, ideas, and stories. A good program is one that makes use of all, though the teacher will be flexible in his or her approach, using those methods that lead to the greatest success for the group. Stories should be chosen with care and should include both familiar and new material. Although I have recommended improvising from literature, I want also to urge the building of original scripts: stories, situations, documentaries. Here the teacher must guide the class carefully to assure understanding, development, plotting, and solution or climax. Without a plot from which to work, progress will be slow but the results can be exciting and always worthwhile.

As the student progresses, improvisation generally moves in the direction of product or theatre art. The beginning level is creative drama, with an emphasis on personal and group development. The second level, as described by Margaret Faulkes-Jendyk, is an awareness of the dramatic art form. It is still process, and "personal development continues with special emphasis on expansion of experiences."[3] The final level is improvisational theatre art and is achieved by only the few. There is a natural progression from one level to the next, though not all students are equally interested in going on to develop the skills demanded of the serious theatre artist.

A word of warning: theatre games and warm-ups are fine, but they are not ends in themselves. A group needs to advance and will become bored when there is a continued absence of substance with no obvious long-range goals. A perceptive graduate student, after observing four different groups of children for several months, recently remarked: "On a physical level the work was good, but the mental content was lacking. They did nothing for the entire semester but movement and games."

---

[2]Chris Van Allsburg, *The Mysteries of Harris Burdick*. (See the Bibliography.)
[3]Margaret Faulkes-Jendyk, "Creative Drama–Improvisation–Theatre," in *Children and Drama*, 2nd ed., ed. Nellie McCaslin (Studio City, CA: Players Press, 1996), p. 19.

Suggested Assignments

1. Plan an improvisation with two other students in the class and present it.
2. If you are student teaching, do some improvisations with the children in the class, basing the subject matter on their interests or studies. Describe the results to your classmates.
3. Make a list of five or six situations in which a conflict must be resolved. Discuss them in class or, if time permits, improvise possible solutions.
4. Role playing can be very revealing. Select a situation, political or social, and play it, exchanging roles in your college class.
5. Using a serious conflict, have groups of three or more discuss and resolve it.

Journal Writing

1. What do you consider of greatest value in improvisation?
2. Was it easy for you to improvise a scene with your classmates? If not, can you explain the reason for your discomfort?
3. Do you see, or can you think of, any negative aspects of improvisation? What are they?
4. If you have seen improvisational theatre, what special quality did it have for you? If it did not make a positive impression, do you know why?

Chapter 7

Puppetry and Mask Making

Puppeteer and friends. (Courtesy of Penny Jones' Early Childhood Puppet Theatre.)

Anything can be a puppet. It's the puppeteer who
gives it life.

Puppets and masks are an important part of theatre history, predating the play as we
know it by centuries. In many countries of the world, puppetry enjoys the status of a
fine art, designed and performed for adults, whereas in our country it is generally regarded as children's entertainment. In recent years, however, there has been an interest in puppetry as an art form, resulting in a new popularity, and as a teaching tool.

By the 1990s American audiences were seeing productions in which human actors and puppets were performing together. The international puppet festival, sponsored by the Jim Henson Foundation and the Public Theatre of New York, introduced
a galaxy of companies that demonstrated new and imaginative ways in which mari-
onettes, puppets of all sizes, human actors, objects, and masks could be combined
with extraordinary effectiveness. Children have known and done this kind of thing all
along; it took a festival of this magnitude to awaken adults to the possibilities for the
classroom.

One could say that puppetry starts with dramatic play, when dolls and toys are
manipulated to perform various roles and actions. The young child's game of peek-a-
boo, with the hands hiding the face, illustrates an early concept of the mask. As children
grow older, they assign both mask and puppet more specific functions and handle
them with greater dexterity. A child's first awareness of the mask as a mask, however,
probably occurs about the age of four or five, when the child wears a mask as part of
a Halloween costume. Children of that age who put on masks are confident that they
are hidden from view and disguised as ghosts, witches, or monsters. Puppets and
masks have much in common; in fact, at times they are indistinguishable from each
other. This chapter discusses some of the ways both can be made and combined with
creative drama. Although each form merits a book in itself, the limitations of space
and content preclude more than the most elementary discussion. There are, however,
a number of excellent books on the market concerning both forms, and teachers interested in incorporating puppets and masks into the curriculum should investigate those
sources listed in the bibliography.

Puppetry, like creative drama, is another way of introducing students to the arts
and literature of different ethnic groups. Because the puppet has been so popular
throughout history in all parts of the world, children need no introduction to it as an
art form and thus eagerly respond to its magic. Whether attending a puppet show in
assembly or creating one in the classroom, children are absorbed in the adventures of
these little actors. Children believe in and care about their puppet characters. For less
secure children, puppets are the actors behind whom they can hide.

Masks also have a fascination for many children, who enjoy making and wearing
them. For older students a study of the uses and symbolism of masks can be a particularly interesting way of learning about the people who created them. It is probable
that every society has its masks; although they are different from one another, they illustrate our commonality.

Puppets

With the popularity of the Muppets and other puppet characters on television, children learn about puppets at an early age and become acquainted with some of the techniques of handling them. This familiarity suggests to teachers ways in which they can include puppets either as special craft projects or as tools for teaching other subjects. A further, and particularly valuable, use is a social or therapeutic one: through the puppet, shy or troubled children are often able to express what they cannot state as themselves. Best of all, perhaps, because these engaging little creatures are such fun to make and manipulate, puppets capture children's attention and hold it in a variety of situations.

What is a puppet? Contrary to what many think, puppets are not dolls, although they often resemble them. Puppets are "actors" who come to life with the help of a puppeteer. Almost any object can be a puppet: a toy, a tool, a hairbrush, a lollipop, a spoon, a broom. Even the hand can be a puppet, if you move it and speak so that the hand appears to be doing the walking and talking. Just to prove it, try out a few things. Kneel behind a table and move an object along the edge of it. Keep moving. Here are a few things that can be used:

A wooden spoon. Make it walk, run, jump, disappear.

A toy. A teddy bear or a rag doll will do; these items are soft and move in different ways from the spoon. Sometimes toys make fine puppets, but it is not a good idea to depend on them. Puppets you make yourself will almost always be better.

A pencil, a ruler, a lollipop, an artificial flower. They will all become different characters when you start moving them. Now try holding one in each hand. What happens when a pencil and a ruler meet?

Your hands. What can they do that the other things couldn't do? Hands make wonderful movements. Let them walk, dance, jump, fight, bow, march off.

Look around for some other objects that have not been mentioned. Invent actions for them and decide what kinds of characters they seem to be. Remember that you make the puppet. It is not alive until you move it.

Puppets are also versatile. Although we think of them in the theatre and in schools, they are equally at home in the sickroom or hospital bed where a bedridden child can play with his or her puppets on a pillow stage.

Making Puppets

There are many different kinds of puppets. Some hang from strings; some are fastened to sticks called rods. Others slip over the hand like gloves. Some puppets are as tall as a person and must be pushed or moved from inside. Because the string puppet is the most complicated to make and manipulate, it is not recommended for the beginner or for the elementary school classroom. The hand puppet with its many variations is the most satisfactory for any age level, and the classroom teacher will find it within his or

Monkey King *produced by Chinese Theatreworks,*
using overhead projector. (Courtesy of Kuang-Yu
Fong.)

her capabilities, regardless of previous experience. The hand puppet includes the bandanna puppet, the finger puppet, the paper bag puppet, the flat puppet, the shadow puppet, the sock puppet, and the glove puppet.

Materials Just as a costume closet or box is handy to have for creative drama, so is a supply of scrap materials necessary for making puppets. You probably will not have to purchase anything because most of what you need will be in your own or the children's homes or in the school. Scraps of paper and fabrics, boxes of all sizes, sticks, Styrofoam, lollipops, apples, balls, and paper bags are all usable. Ribbons, yarns, sewing materials, paper cups, paper napkins, discarded decorations, old socks, and gloves will all find a use as somebody's puppet.

Bandanna Puppets The easiest one to begin with is the bandanna puppet. Put a bandanna or cloth over the hand. Let the first and middle fingers be the head of the puppet, and put a rubber band around them for the neck. The thumb and little finger are the arms. Put rubber bands around them in order to hold the cloth in place. Imagine that the hand is the actor. Have the puppet you have made clap its hands, shake its head, and fall down.

There are many more things you can do in making a bandanna puppet. For instance, try cutting a hole in the middle of the bandanna and poking the first finger through it. Next, take a Styrofoam ball with a hole scooped out for your finger, and use the ball for a head. Heads can be made out of many different things: a small paper cup, an apple (after cutting out the core), a ball, and so on. The bandanna puppet can be quickly made by the teacher, but making one is also within the capability of young children.

Finger Puppets Finger puppets are the smallest of all puppets. They slip on the fingers and can be played with as they are or used with larger hand puppets to show different-sized characters. For instance, a finger puppet might be an elf, with a hand puppet as a human being. One way to make a finger puppet is with felt. First, make a pattern. Put the hand down flat on a piece of paper and draw around the fingers with a pencil. Be sure to add a little extra material all around to allow for the sewing. Next, cut out the paper patterns and pin them on a piece of felt. You will have to cut two shapes for each puppet. Put the two shapes together and sew around the edges. Leave the bottom open for your fingers. Another way to make finger puppets is to cut the fingers off an old glove. Light-colored or white gloves are the best because you can draw faces on them. Slip the glove fingers over your own and you will have five little puppets! Using other material or remnants of the glove, you can cut circles and paint faces on them; when the paint is dry, the faces can be pasted on the puppets.

Paper Bag Puppets The paper bag puppet is one of the best puppets to begin with because bags come in all sizes and are easily obtained. Also, if you happen to tear the bag, there are many more around. Adults, children, giants, and elves can all be suggested with different-sized paper bags. Small bags fit on the hands, whereas big bags will go over the head. If a bag is worn on the head, holes will have to be cut out for the eyes and mouth. Next, paint or draw a face on the bag. You can use your hands, your head, or even your feet for puppets. Hands work best, however, because you can do so many more things with them. You can paint and paste on paper bags, and if the paper is strong enough, you can sew through it. A bag can be just a head or a whole puppet.

Flat Puppets Flat puppets are also often called rod puppets. They are easy to handle and can be used with other kinds of puppets. Flat puppets are a little like paper dolls. They can be cut out of lightweight cardboard, colored, and pasted on tongue depressors or sticks. Hold the stick just below the edge of the stage or tabletop. As the puppet is moved, it will seem to be walking by itself. Animal characters make good flat puppets because you have to draw only the side view. Incidentally, if you would like to show your puppet moving in both directions, you can cut out two shapes and paste them together with the stick in between. Color both sides so your animal can be moved from left or right. One more advantage to flat puppets: they are easy to keep in good condition because they don't take up much space when put away in neat piles.

Shadow Puppets Flat puppets can be used for shadow shows also. To give a shadow show, all you need are some flat puppets, a sheet, and a lamp placed behind the sheet. When you move the puppets behind the sheet, they cast shadows on it. The closer they are to the sheet, the stronger the shadow, or silhouette, will be. Shadow puppets can be made more exciting if pieces within the outside boundaries are cut out and backed by colored gels or plastic sheets. Stores that handle stage lighting equipment carry relatively inexpensive gels in a variety of colors. Older students love the challenge of making these puppets, which in some ways resemble stained-glass windows. The strong light shining through the gel brings out the richness of the color and creates a magical effect. In the Oriental theatre, where shadow plays originated, one can still see performances using puppets made of wood or hide decorated with elaborate open-work patterns. The stylized result can be beautiful and effective.

Sock Puppets A sock makes a very good puppet because it stretches yet won't slip off the hand. You can do many things with a sock puppet, such as making it into a mouth. Take one of your own old socks and put your hand inside it. Put your fingers in the toe and your thumb in the heel. You now have the upper and lower jaws of a mouth. Bring them together in a big bite. By adding eyes and other markings, you can create a bird, a wolf, a crocodile, or a dragon. You can make a puppet mouth more exciting by sewing a piece of red felt inside it and adding another piece for a tongue. Many children's stories have animal characters, so the "mouth" is a useful puppet to have on hand.

Glove Puppets The glove puppet needs more sewing than the other types. It has to be cut out of two pieces of sturdy cloth sewn together. It may also have a separate head. First, take a piece of strong cotton cloth and double it. Felt is good, if you have it, because it won't fray. Other fabrics will do, however, so use what you have on hand.

Cut a pattern out of paper for your puppet. There should be a head and two arms, and the pattern must be large enough to fit the hand. Pin the pattern to the material and trace around it. Then remove the pattern and cut out the puppet. Keep the two pieces of cloth together and sew around the edges, remembering to leave the bottom open for your hand to go through. A felt puppet is ready to use as it is. A puppet made of softer material should be turned inside out to keep it from unraveling.

Children will want to put a face on the puppet. Eyes, nose, and mouth can be drawn or embroidered on it. Buttons make excellent eyes, and yarn makes good hair. A little stuffing makes the head rounder. If you want to make a separate head, a lightweight material such as Styrofoam or papier-mâché works well. Decorate the head first, then slip it over one or two fingers. Although it is harder to handle a puppet with a separate head than a puppet that is all in one piece, most children can learn how to manage it.

Giant Puppets Some puppeteers use puppets as tall as they are or even taller. These giant puppets must be made of lightweight material so they can be carried or pushed from behind or inside. Unless you have a large area in which to perform, you probably will not be making life-sized puppets; for those who want to try, however, here are some suggestions. An easy way is to put a paper bag or papier-mâché head on a broomstick or pole. Then hang a blanket or cape on the broomstick and have the manipulator hide inside the covering. He or she can then carry the stick to "merge" with the puppet.

Another way to make a giant puppet is to use a tall, narrow cardboard box. A face and clothes can be painted on the box, which the puppeteer pushes from behind. A variation of this, and one that can be very effective, is to take a piece of cardboard decorated on one side and manipulate it from behind.

The inspiration for giant puppets has probably come from two main sources: the Japanese puppet theatre, with life-sized puppets requiring two or three persons to manipulate them, and the Bread and Puppet Theatre of Glover, Vermont. Some of the puppets are eighteen to twenty feet tall; in a production they are combined with smaller puppets, thus adding to the effectiveness of each one. For one thing, the variation in size aids in suggesting not only difference in character but also difference in importance.

Water Puppet

A unique form of puppetry is the water puppet of China and Korea. The puppet is manipulated from below, either in water or behind water, so that it appears to be swimming or performing. Wings are an important appendage and, of course, the wings must be made of plastic. The water puppet could be handled by older children, working behind a large basin of water.

Body Puppets

Body puppets are similar to giant puppets in stature. The difference, however, is that the puppets are actually human beings who wear huge masks covering the entire head. Because speaking may be difficult, narration by another student or the teacher, or even a taped recording, can tell the story as it is being enacted.

Toy Theatre

Toy theatre, akin to puppetry, was popular as family entertainment in the nineteenth century. It was interactive and was enjoyed much as television is today. A stage placed on a table in the living room was the setting for plays performed informally by family members and friends, who often made the little figures and props, although commercial kits were available. Players pushed the characters on stage by hand, improvising the dialogue. This obscure form of theater has enormous educational possibilities for older children.

Tabletop Theatre

Tabletop theatre is an old yet new form of puppetry that can be enjoyed in both a living room and a classroom. It is an inexpensive and simple way to give plays on the smallest of stages, such as a desk or dining room table. Children enjoy creating their own plays and then manipulating the little actors themselves. Use of an overhead projector, when one is available, adds to the effectiveness. This form of puppetry is an ideal teaching tool since it does not require a stage and puts no strain on the voices of the young puppeteers.

Holding the Puppet

There are different ways of holding puppets, partly depending on the kind of puppet you have, so use the one that works best for you. Because younger children have short fingers, they will have to experiment to find a comfortable way to hold the bandanna and glove puppets. Some puppeteers put their first and second fingers in the neck, their fourth and fifth fingers in one arm, and their thumb in the other arm. Puppets can be held either in front of you or over your head. Again, use whichever way is easier for you. If you are playing for a long time, it is usually more comfortable to work the puppet in front of your face.

If you decide to hold your puppet that way, you will be seen by the audience. This doesn't matter. The audience, if you have one, will soon forget you are there. If you want to hang a curtain between you and your puppets, you will need a stage. A dark, lightweight piece of cloth at the back of the stage will hide you and make your puppets stand out. If the cloth is semitransparent, you can see through it without being seen by the audience.

Some Basic Actions

Moving the puppet's head up and down means "yes." Shaking it from side to side means "no." When the puppet's hands point to itself, it means "me" or "mine." Moving one of its hands toward its body means "come here." Waving its hand may mean either "hello" or "good-bye." Walking, running, and jumping can be suggested by the way you move the puppet across the stage. Try not to lift it up in the air. You will soon get the knack of holding it down so that it seems to be doing all the moving.

When two persons are puppeteering together, the chances are they will each be holding a puppet. This is more difficult than playing alone, but it is also more fun. The puppeteers have to watch out that the puppets don't bump into each other. Also, when one puppet is speaking, the other one should remember to listen. Occasionally, there will be a scene for three puppets. This takes some doing, for three people will have to work together backstage, or one person will have to handle two puppets. It is a good idea at first to use stories that have no more than two characters on the stage at one time.

The Puppet Stage

It is not necessary to have a stage, for puppets can act anywhere. All you need is a smooth surface about three feet long. A table, a bench, or a box will do. In a setting with windows opening on a porch, one group of children used the windowsill for the stage. Another idea for a stage is a cardboard or wooden box with the front and back cut off and a curtain across the back. Making such a stage takes some work, as well as requiring a place to store it when not in use. But a stage with a lamp placed in front of the box to light it adds a professional touch.

Scenery

You do not need scenery any more than you need a stage, but sometimes you may want it. If you do, make it of cardboard or stiff paper, and be sure to fasten it securely so that it won't fall down. Doll furniture can be used if it is the right size, but a simple background is usually all you will want. You don't even need that if the puppets tell the audience where the story takes place.

Nursery school children are fascinated with puppets. (Courtesy of Ellen Ziman, Director of First Presbyterian Church Nursery School.)

Stories for Puppet Plays

It is a good idea to work without scripts because you have your hands full just moving the puppets. If you know the story you are presenting very well, you can make up the dialogue as you go along, just as you do in creative drama. Besides, it will sound more natural if you do. Although many stories that are good for creative playing are also good for puppets, not all work well. One thing must be kept in mind: there is very little room backstage. Therefore, stick to stories in which no more than two or three characters are onstage at the same time. Often you can arrange the scenes to have no more than two, but some stories will lend themselves to the puppet theatre better than others. Here are three examples.

The Bird and the Girl

Written and Illustrated by Judith Martin

The following story by Judith Martin, founder and producer of the Paper Bag Players, is delightful in its utter simplicity. While the book has illustrations, the story can be adapted to puppet presentation by very young players. It can be done with or without a narrator and without scenery. Little children accept the fantasy and the relationship between human beings and animals.

Narrator: This story is about a girl named Rose.

She lived in a very small house with her mother.

She spent whole days making wishes.

She had a favorite wish.

Rose: I wish more than anything else that I would have an adventure.

Narrator: One   day Rose went for a walk.

She didn't plan where to go.

She would follow her feet.

And then her feet stopped.

They couldn't go any further and they didn't know the way back and neither did Rose.

She looked up and saw a Bird.

The Bird seemed to be looking at her.

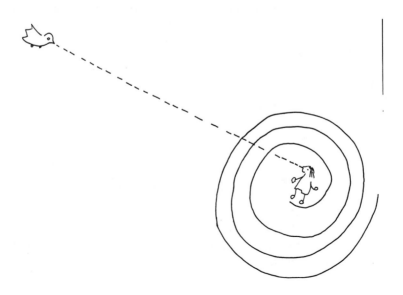

And sure enough, he swooped down to the ground and stood right in front of the little girl.

Bird: I can see you're lost.

I can help you.

Narrator: Just then the Bird's flock could be seen flying in the sky.

They never noticed the Bird talking to the girl.

Bird: My family just went by.

I've got to catch up with them.

Rose: First get me out of here!

Don't just leave.

Narrator: Then the Bird had an idea.

Bird: I'll take you with me.

Hold on.

We'll need a run and a jump to get in the air.

Narrator: Soon they were in the sky.

The Bird flew as fast as he could to catch up with his flock.

But as hard as he tried, his flock seemed to get further away and began to look like little spots in the distance.

The Bird realized that Rose was heavy and was slowing him down.

Just then Rose looked down and spotted her very own house on the ground.

Rose: I see my house.

Set me down, set me down.

Narrator: And the Bird put Rose on the ground.

Rose: Oh, Bird, thank you.

I'm so glad to be home.

Bird: Now I'm lost.

Rose: Have some water and a
few bread crumbs.

It will make you feel better.

Narrator: Then tears fell from the Bird's eyes.

Rose: Don't be sad.

You can stay with us.

You'll be happy here.

Bird: No! No! No! I want to be
with my flock, my friends
and family.

There's my
family.

They came back
for me.

Narrator: Just then a flock of birds could
be seen making a circle in the sky.

Rose: Goodbye, Bird. Goodbye, Bird.

Narrator: The Bird joined his friends and
his whole flock flew out of sight.

Rose realized her mother was in the house.

She wanted to tell her about all the things that had happened to her that day.

She called to her.

Rose: Ma, guess what? I had an adventure today!

A discussion after playing the story leads to the relationship between human beings and animals: understanding, kindness, and sharing.

The Talking Cat
A French Canadian Folk Tale

This French Canadian folk tale works better for puppets than for human actors. One of the characters is a ventriloquist, so this story is ideal for the puppet stage.

CHARACTERS
> Tante Odette, an old woman
> Chouchou, her cat
> Pierre, a workman
> Georges, his friend

There is an old woman who is fooled into believing that her cat can speak. Tante Odette lives alone on her farm, deep in the Canadian woods. She is careful and thrifty, always keeping a pot of soup on the stove for herself and her old gray cat, Chouchou. She takes good care of her small farm. But as the years go by, she sometimes complains that the work is becoming too much for her. She talks to Chouchou about the chores that have to be done and how she must save her money for later. Often she says to him, "How I wish you could talk, Chouchou. Then I should not be so lonely."

One evening as Tante Odette is sitting by the fire, there is a knock at the door. When she opens it, she sees a man in workman's clothes with a red sash tied around his waist.

"I am looking for work," he says politely. "If you can give me some chores, all I ask is a bowl of soup and a night's sleep in your barn."

"Go away," says Tante Odette. "I do not need anyone to help me. Besides, I have only enough soup for myself."

Just as she is about to close the door in his face, an amazing thing happens. Chouchou speaks! "Wait a minute," he says. "You are getting older, and it would be a good idea to have a strong young man on the place."

Tante Odette can't believe her ears. She looks at the man, then she looks at the cat. "Well, if you think so, Chouchou."

"I certainly do," says the cat. "Ask him to come in and join us in a bowl of soup."

The old woman invites the man in and asks him to supper. "It's only cabbage soup and bread, but we like it."

The man thanks her. When he has finished his supper, he tells her tales of his travels and the different places he has worked. But he says that now he would rather stay in one place, even though he wouldn't make any money. He tells her his name is Pierre. As time goes on both the old woman and Chouchou become very fond of him.

One day Chouchou says to Tante Odette, "Why don't you give Pierre meat and cakes? He works hard. I'm sure he gets very hungry."

"But we have no meat," she replies.

"Then let him go to the store in the town and buy some meat. He will not waste your money."

Pierre appears in the doorway. "I heard what your cat said just now. He's very wise. Let me strike a good bargain."

The old woman goes to a chest of drawers and takes out some money. "Mind you don't waste it," she tells Pierre.

When Pierre has gone, she turns to Chouchou. "How is it that you never spoke in all the years that I've had you and now you are giving me advice?"

But as always, when they are alone, Chouchou says nothing.

The next day when they finish their dinner of meat and cakes, Pierre is in a very good mood and Tante Odette says that she has never enjoyed a meal so much! "Why don't you let Pierre move into the house?" asks the cat.

"What?" says the old woman.

"Winter is coming and it will soon be cold in the barn. We have plenty of room inside."

Pierre says that he would like this very much. And so he moves in.

A few weeks later when the old woman is alone in the house, there is a knock at the door. She opens it and to her surprise, she sees a working man standing there. He is wearing a red sash just like Pierre's.

"Have you seen a workman who calls himself Pierre?" the newcomer asks.

"A man by that name works for me," the old woman says.

"Is he a good worker?"

"A very good worker," she says; and she tells of all the things Pierre can do.

"It certainly sounds like the same man. One more thing, can he throw his voice? Is he a ventriloquist?"

"Throw his voice? Oh, no! I could not stand having anyone around who did that."

"Then it can't be the same person," says the man, as he turns to go.

At this moment Pierre comes to the door. "Georges!" he shouts. "My old friend!"

"Pierre! I've been searching for you everywhere. I want you to go with me to get furs. You know they pay good money for furs in the city. How about it?"

Pierre thinks for a moment. "If I go with you, I'll make money, but it will be cold. If I stay here, I have a good job, food, and a warm place to sleep. What shall I do, Chouchou? You're a wise cat."

"Stay here," the cat answers. Then the cat turns to the old woman. "Why don't we pay him some wages? You have money in the chest. Surely he's worth a few pieces of gold."

The old woman doesn't know what to do. Finally she says, "Very well. I can give you a small wage, if you'll stay."

"Good!" says Pierre. "Then I'll stay." He says good-bye to his friend and walks with him down the road.

The old woman looks at Chouchou. "I don't believe he throws his voice, do you?"

There was no answer. She stares at Chouchou, who says nothing as usual.

Just then Pierre returns. "It will be a much better winter for me here than in the north woods. And I can earn money at the same time, thanks to your cat."

The cat bows and speaks.

"That's all right, Pierre. Fair is fair." Then Chouchou looks at the old woman. "Well, we may as well sit down at the table and celebrate the way it has all worked out."

The Fisherman and His Wife

This is another good story for puppets to play. You don't need any scenery. If you want to show the different houses, you can draw pictures of them and put them up behind the puppets.

CHARACTERS
The Fisherman
His Wife
The Flounder

A poor Fisherman lives with his wife in a Japanese village in a cottage by the sea. Every day he goes down to the shore to catch a fish for their supper. When his luck is good, he has enough fish to sell to their neighbors. One morning the Fisherman goes out as usual and sits down in his favorite fishing spot. Suddenly there is a tug on his line. He pulls and he pulls.

"What have I caught?" asks the Fisherman. He gives another tug on his line, and up comes the biggest flounder he has ever seen.

Then, to his amazement, the fish speaks. "Please let me go. I have done you no harm."

The Fisherman can't believe his ears. "You can talk? I have never heard of a fish that could talk."

"I was once a prince," says the Flounder sadly. "An evil spell was put on me, and I am doomed to spend the rest of my life as a fish."

"I am sorry if I've hurt you," says the Fisherman, taking the hook from the fish. "Go back to your home in the sea."

"Oh, thank you," the Flounder says. "You have saved my life. If I can ever do anything for you, call on me. I'm never far away."

The Fisherman promises the Flounder that he will do so. Then, eager to tell his wife about his strange adventure, he packs up and goes home. When he has finished his tale, his wife scolds him for his stupidity.

Making puppets in a Hong Kong primary school; Kannie Chung, teacher. (Courtesy of Simon Wong.)

"That's just like you! Why didn't you ask him for a nice house and some food for our dinner? He was a magic fish, and you let him go."

"I'm sorry, wife," says the Fisherman. "I didn't think of it."

"Well, go back down to the sea and ask for a house like our neighbor's, with enough food to last us a year."

"Very well," replies the Fisherman. So he goes down to the place where he had caught the Flounder and calls out:

For my wife, my wife, the plague of my life,
Oh, fish of the sea,
come listen to me.
For my wife, my wife, the plague of my life,
Has sent me to ask a boon of thee.

Scarcely does he finish when the Flounder appears.

"What can I do for you?" the fish asks politely.

The Fisherman tells him.

"No sooner asked than granted," says the fish. "Go home and you will find a house like your neighbor's."

The Fisherman hurries home, and there is a beautiful stone house where his little cottage had been. His wife appears at the door, delighted with their good fortune.

For a time the Fisherman and his wife live happily. Then one morning his wife, who is always discontented, says, "I don't know why you asked for this house. I should like a castle with servants to wait on me."

"This house is plenty good enough," says her husband.

"No," she replies. "Go back and tell the fish I must have a castle." The Fisherman doesn't want to do her bidding, but at last he agrees. He goes down to the sea and again calls out:

For my wife, my wife, the plague of my life,
Oh, fish of the sea,
come listen to me.
For my wife, my wife, the plague of my life,
Has sent me to ask a boon of thee.

In a flash the Flounder appears. "Nothing easier," he says, after the Fisherman explains the matter to him. "Go home to your castle."

Then the Flounder disappears and the Fisherman returns home. Instead of the stone house, there is a great castle with towers and walls surrounding it. His wife is overjoyed. But after a time, she again becomes discontented.

She sends her husband back to the Flounder many times. She wants to be the richest woman in the world. Then a Queen. Next, an Empress. And finally, Goddess of the Universe. Each time her husband begs her to be content with what they have, but she will not listen. And each time the fish grants her wish—until the last one.

"What is it now?" the Flounder asks the Fisherman.

"Oh, gracious Flounder," replies the Fisherman, "my wife wants to be Goddess of the Universe."

"Never!" declares the Flounder angrily. "I will grant no more wishes. Your wife can return to her cottage."

There is a loud noise like a clap of thunder and the fish disappears. Then the Fisherman goes home, where he finds his wife in the doorway of their humble cottage.

Puppets as Teaching Aids

Puppets also make excellent teaching aids because of their power to hold and sustain the attention of a class. Unlike some curricular materials, puppets are not limited to any one area of study. They can be used to teach any subject, ranging from the language arts to science and math. They can be combined with other teaching materials or used alone. Moreover, puppets cost little or nothing to make. As has already been stated, their value lies in their mobility, not in their beauty or complicated construction. Puppets made by teachers and children are usually more satisfactory than commercial puppets. If puppets are purchased, however—and there are many on the market—they should be selected for durability. Avoid nonwashable or perishable materials.

The degree of sophistication of puppets that students create depends on the age and previous experience of the students. Although the simple puppets of young children can be wonderfully effective, experienced older groups find a challenge in making more elaborate ones. It cannot be repeated often enough, however, that a good puppet is one that can be manipulated easily; the most beautiful puppet in the world is a failure if it does not move easily and well. Another consideration, and an important one, is the child's perception of his or her work. In other words, "it is not what the puppet looks like that counts but rather how the child feels about the puppet. . . . A rabbit puppet made by a child does not have to look like a real rabbit—the child needs only to believe in it."[1]

Probably the most extensive use made of puppets as a teaching tool is in the area of the language arts. According to John Warren Stewig, "Children generate more verbal language during dramatic play than in any other situation."[2] In both creative drama and puppetry, extemporaneous speaking is involved; use of the puppet has the added advantage, however, of shielding the speaker who may be shy or weak in verbal skills, thus enabling him or her to communicate through the puppet. A skillful teacher makes use of the opportunity afforded by this communication to open up new areas of learning and tune in to a student's thinking. Telling stories with puppets is not only fun but a valuable activity on all levels. The move from storytelling to story dramatization is a natural next step, involving dialogue, character study, play structure, and growth in language competency. The use of puppets in the teaching of poetry has also proved successful in promoting the appreciation and writing of this form of literature.

Some teachers have found puppets invaluable aids in the study of elementary science and environmental education, two areas that are difficult for many children; writing original skits on these subjects, to be enacted by puppets, is strong motivation. Social studies provides a wealth of puppetry opportunities for the study of other people, other countries, historical events, and current problems.

The Story of Noah's Ark

A puppeteer who works with the New York City Board of Education has a number of scripts that can be adapted for a hands-on experience in the primary grades.[3] One delightful script, which works very effectively, is The Story of Noah's Ark. *I have included it here because it can be expanded to include as many animals as needed and is simple enough for even the youngest children to perform.*

The Story of Noah's Ark *is a puppet pageant with parts for up to three classes. The roles of Noah and his family and the technical stage business (the flood and sound effects, etc.) should be handled by an older class (third or fourth grade), while the younger children "march" the animals and "dance" the fish. One advantage of having three classes share responsibilities is the presence*

[1]Tamara Hunt and Nancy Renfro, *Puppetry in Early Childhood Education* (Austin, TX: Nancy Renfro Studios, 1982), p. 24.

[2]John Warren Stewig, *Teaching Language Arts in Early Childhood* (New York: Holt, Rinehart and Winston, 1980), p. 123.

[3]Penny Jones's Early Childhood Puppet Theatre, Ltd.

of three teachers to help organize the children during the performance. The younger classes can sit out front and watch the show until it is time for them to come onstage.

Teacher A concentrates on helping his or her class make the fish and rehearse dancelike movements for them when it is time for them to appear onstage. Teacher B has his or her class study animals, collects pictures, perhaps takes the class to the zoo, and helps the children make stick puppet animals. Once the puppets are made, all that the class has to do is march its animals on and off the stage in the performance. Teacher C's class makes people puppets, the ark, the two doves, the rain, and so on. He or she assigns parts and rehearses the children in their parts.

Teacher A remains backstage to help throughout, while Teacher B sends the children up from the auditorium when it is time for them to perform. Teacher C narrates the story and cues in the children. He or she may insert dialogue if the children miss their cues.

It is desirable for the children to perform at least twice, with discussion between performances about how the show might be improved. It is also a good idea to have two casts as insurance against absence and also because children learn from watching each other. Four performances in two days will serve most schools, at the same time enabling both casts to perform twice. In general, the fewer combined rehearsals and the more performances, the better for all.

How to Stage *The Story of Noah's Ark*

Noah and his family stand behind a low screen, holding their puppets above their heads or above the top of the table or desk while kneeling behind it. All the other children sit in the audience until they are called onstage or to the playing space. To avoid congestion the children cross from one side of the stage to the other and then go back to their seats in a continuous clocklike circle of movement. The animals march on and off to marching music. Slow waltz-time music is good for the movement of the fish.

Space is left in the script for dancing and music, if desired. The ark entertainment is optional, but it is an excellent opportunity to include songs the children know and want to sing. Animal songs are particularly appropriate, as are water and rain songs.

If the pageant is given in a classroom, a table or desk is satisfactory for the puppet stage. If it is given on a platform or stage in an auditorium, then a large table with a screen behind it is better.

CHARACTERS
>Narrator
>Noah
>Noah's Wife Esther
>Ham
>Shem
>Japheth
>Rachael
>Sarah
>Ruth
>Animals—any number

Properties and Scenery

Scenery is unnecessary, but props are essential to this play. All props can and should be made by the children as part of the experience.

The ark—a flat cutout of cardboard, shaped like an ark and attached to a long stick. It is large enough for several puppets to appear behind it at one time and should be moved by a child with a steady hand so that it can rise and fall with the floodwaters.

Rainbow—a cardboard cutout painted in bright colors.

Mountain—a cardboard cutout.

Fish and animals—cardboard cutouts taped to sticks and decorated in the colors of the animals they represent. The fish should be made of flexible paper and painted on both sides so that they can turn while swimming.

Doves—two identical paper birds, one with a leaf in its beak, on long wires.

Noah's family—cardboard cutout puppets taped to sticks.

Sound Effects

Rain—plastic bags that make a noise when rustled.

Thunder—a sheet of thin metal or an aluminum pan that rumbles when shaken.

Hammering

Apples, corn, and honey—cardboard cutouts of bags taped to sticks.

Flood—a long piece of light blue fabric raised and lowered by two children, one at each side of stage.

The Script of *The Story of Noah's Ark*

The cast members playing Noah's family sit backstage waiting for their turns, while the rest of the children sit out front, watching and waiting to be sent backstage. The Narrator sits at one side of the stage to be able to monitor both backstage and the audience area.

Five children holding signs that spell out *The Story of Noah's Ark* walk across the stage, stopping center long enough for the audience to read the words.

Narrator: This is *The Story of Noah's Ark.* Once there lived a good man named Noah. (*Noah pops up, looks around, and leaves. As each member of his family is introduced, that puppet pops up, then leaves.*) He had a wife named Esther. They had three sons, Ham, Shem, and Japheth. But the rest of the world was very bad, so God decided to have a flood to wash it clean and start all over again. He wanted to save the animals, and he liked Noah. So he told Noah to build an ark—a boat big enough to hold his family and two of every animal in the world. Then, when the flood came, they could all just float away in the ark. Noah called his sons.

Noah: (*Appears, looks around, and calls loudly.*) Shem, Ham, Japheth, come here! We have to build a boat. I'll make the design and you get the wood. (*The sons appear.*)

Shem: What, father?

Noah: There's no time to talk now. I'll tell you later. Just get the wood.

Ham: All right. (*They leave.*)

Narrator: And so they began to build. They hammered and they sawed. (*Sounds of hammering.*)

Shem: I'm tired. It's hard working day and night like this.

Ham: (*Offstage.*) Ow! Watch out for my fingers!

Japheth: (*Offstage.*) I'm sorry, the hammer slipped. I'm very tired. I need sleep.

Narrator: Finally the ark was finished. (*The ark slowly rises to the stage on the right side but remains partially hidden. Rachael, Sarah, and Ruth appear and admire it. Shem, Ham, and Japheth are at the other side of the stage.*)

Rachael: That's a fine-looking boat you made.

Shem: Thank you.

Sarah: It looks strong, too.

Ham: It is.

Ruth: It better be. I can't swim! (*They leave.*)

Narrator: Then the women filled the ark with food—bags and bags of it. (*Rachael enters carrying a bag of apples.*)

Rachael: Here's another bag of apples. (*Disappears behind the ark.*)

Sarah: Here's the last of the grain. (*Disappears behind the ark.*)

Ruth: Someone help me with the honey. It's heavy. (*Disappears.*)

Esther: Don't drop it! (*Disappears behind the ark.*)

Narrator: Finally the storerooms were filled with food. Suddenly Japheth saw something on the other side of the hill.

Japheth: Look, look what's coming! (*The whole family crowds center stage.*)

Rachael: Animals!

Sarah: They're coming here!

Ruth: You mean they're going to be on the boat, too? Oh, no!

Esther: Now, Ruth, there's plenty of room for *all* the animals, for the universe includes the beasts and birds as well as human beings. Get on the boat, everyone, so we can show the animals where to go. Come on!

(The following lines should be divided among the family members and spoken rapidly so as to suggest the general hubbub.)

All: I want to be upstairs! I want to be downstairs! I want to be in front. I like the back. Don't push. Who's going to show the animals where to go? Me! Me! I'll help. We'll all help.

Narrator: (*By this time the family have all gone behind the ark.*)

Cats, bats, and rats; dogs, frogs, and hedgehogs.
And so the animals came.
In a long, long line, two by two,
The elephant and the kangaroo.

Cows and baboons, camels and raccoons;
Cats, bats, and rats; dogs, frogs, and hedgehogs.
All these and many more came to the door.
Even the aardvarks came to the ark.

(While the Narrator speaks, the children in the audience are lining up their animals, ready to go backstage and march them on the ark. Marching music accompanies the procession, which can be of any length, depending on the number of animals crossing, two by two. One cat turns around when it reaches the ark and scampers off stage left.)

Narrator: Finally, they were ready for the flood. But before he closed the door, Noah told his family to check one more time to see if all the animals were safely inside.
Rachael: We have only one cat!
Sarah: Where's the other one?
Ruth: There he goes—running away!
Esther: Go, catch him. We need two cats. Hurry!

(The entire family disappears behind the ark; the cat runs out, then turns around and runs the other way. They all chase it except Japheth, who waits and catches him.)

Japheth: Got him!
Noah: (*As Japheth goes behind the ark.*) All right, everybody inside. I feel the first drop of rain.
Narrator: The rain began to fall. It rained and it rained. (*Sound effects of rain.*) Thunder cracked! (*Sound effects.*) Lightning flashed. (*Lights are clicked on and off.*) It was a terrible storm. (*Repeat sound effects.*) Pretty soon there was a lake. (*Floorcloth is lifted up by two children.*) The lake got deeper. The water rose higher and higher until it reached the ark. (*The cloth is lifted up to the ark.*) The ark began to rock and then to float. It rained for forty days and forty nights. And the wind blew. (*Children in the audience blow.*) And the lightning flashed. The thunder cracked. And the waves rose and fell. (*Sound effects are louder and cloth lashes the ark.*) At last it stopped. (*Sound effects gradually stop.*) The fish came out to play. (*Slow music as children glide their fish back and forth. They glide in a pattern, perhaps one at first, then two, and finally all together.*) For a time Noah and his family looked at the fish. Then they grew tired of watching and wanted to do something themselves.
Rachael: I'm tired.
Sarah: Me, too.
Ruth: I'm tired of just sailing around with nothing to see but water. Why don't we make our own entertainment?
Esther: Good idea. Let's sing!
Narrator: (*This is an open place in the script where the children may sing songs if they want to.*) Well, they sang until they were tired of singing.
Rachael: I'm tired of singing.
Sarah: Me, too.
Ruth: I'm sick of this ark and the animals and the same old faces. Won't we ever get somewhere?
Esther: I have a dove. Maybe he can find some dry land now that the rain has stopped. Come, little dove. Spread your wings. Fly over the water to see what you can see. Bring us something from the land.

Narrator: (*The dove comes up and flies off stage right.*) The dove flew east but he came back with nothing.

Esther: Oh, dear. Try again, little dove. This time go west. (*The dove flies off stage left.*)

Narrator: This time he came back with an olive leaf. (*This is the second dove, who has the leaf in its mouth.*)

Noah: Look, everybody, the dove has found land! The water must be going down.

All: Hooray! (*All appear, then go back down again.*)

Narrator: They drifted for a few more days. Then suddenly the ark bumped into the side of a mountain.

All: (*Ad lib lines like:*) What was that? It must be a rock. It's land!

Narrator: The water kept going down. (*Flood cloth begins to go down.*) And down. And down. At last they were able to leave the ark, but they were not sure they wanted to. After all, what if there was another flood?

Rachael: I'm scared of leaving the ark.

Sarah: Me, too.

Shem: I don't think we should take a chance.

Ham: I don't either.

Ruth: I can't swim.

Narrator: Just then there was a clap of thunder. (*Sound effect.*) But it wasn't a storm this time. It was a rainbow. (*The rainbow is held up.*)

Japheth: Look! Isn't it beautiful!

Noah: I think this is a sign that everything is going to be all right now. We can leave the ark and start the world all over again.

All: (*Divide up the lines.*) I'll go north. I'll go south. I'll see you in the spring. I'll take the cows and start a herd. I'll take the sheep. Good-bye, good-bye!

Narrator: And they did.

The children march off the animals, two by two. If desired, they can go around the audience. Next go the family, the fish, and the sound effects children behind them. The parade circles the audience, returns, and takes a bow on the stage; then they march out, with monitors collecting the puppets at the door.

Puppets as Therapeutic Tools

Puppets have been used effectively as both diagnostic and therapeutic instruments. It is understood that neither the classroom teacher nor the creative drama specialist is a therapist; nevertheless, the puppet offers insights often indiscernible in other situations, and the sensitive teacher will take note of them. For the puppet becomes a nonthreatening little friend in whom a child can confide, entrusting his or her most private thoughts and feelings without fear of censure. This friend has access to the child's inner world and is also able to speak to the outer world as an intermediary.[4]

---

[4]*Puppets—Art and Entertainment* (Washington, DC: Puppeteers of America, 1980), p. 9.

Thus, the teacher will find puppetry an exceptionally effective way of drawing out children who are reluctant to participate in creative drama. Here are a few exercises to stimulate expression of strong feelings.

1. Try to find ways of showing that the puppet feels

angry	happy
excited	curious
shy	scared
tired	hungry

2. Next, see if you can put actions together with a feeling:
   Curious—and looks into a box
   Angry—and hits someone
   Happy—and claps its hands for joy
   Thoughtful—and comes up with an idea
3. Most of us get into trouble at one time or another. Do you remember a particular time when you got into trouble? Was it your fault? Did you think you were punished unfairly? How did you feel about it? Let your glove puppet be the other person in this story, and you be the finger puppet. Act out the situation.
4. Talking with your puppet is fun. Like a conversation with a person, it builds as it goes along.
   a. Imagine that your puppet is mischievous. You ask it to do something, and it refuses. It thinks of reasons why it won't do what you ask. How do you handle the puppet? Who wins in the end?
   b. Imagine that your puppet is angry. Try to find out what is wrong.
   c. Imagine that your puppet can't speak English. Try to make it understand you.
   d. Imagine that your puppet's feelings are hurt. Can you say or do anything to make it feel better?
5. The puppet is you. Talk to it, imagining that you are one of the following: your mother, your best friend, the owner of a candy store in your neighborhood, your teacher, a new child on the block.
6. Begin with a discussion of behavior. The following questions usually elicit good responses.
   a. Do you ever act one way when you feel another (for example, polite when you are really angry, rude when you are unhappy, quiet when you want to talk, or loud when you are afraid)?
   b. Why do you think you behave this way?
   c. After the discussion, have students work in pairs: one is the "inside" and the other is the "outside." Ask them questions and see how they answer.

This exercise is valuable in gaining more understanding of behavior, and it is also fun.

Try out the following verse as you look into your own inner world. Some children are amazingly perceptive in comparing their inner and outer selves.

I have two Selves or so I'm told.
  My Outside and my In.
And if I take a thoughtful look
  I'll see myself within.

Although I know my Outside Self,
I see it every day,
My Inside Self seems hidden,
So neatly tucked away.
It seems so strange I cannot touch
Or taste or hear or see . . .
I only *feel* all those things
That are inside of me.
Both my Selves are special
That's what I'm about.
Feeling on the *Inside*,
Showing on the *Out*.
—*Tamara Hunt*

7. It is fun to make up stories. Here are a few ideas for starters, but soon all members of the class will be coming up with ideas of their own.

A Mistake

CHARACTERS
You
Your Family (they talk offstage)

You come to breakfast early one morning, and no one is up yet. You call your mother, but she tells you to be quiet; she is trying to sleep. You find some food to eat; then you get your books and pack a lunch. You call to your family and say they are all going to be late. You run out of the house, but a minute later you come back in. Your father calls to ask who it is. You tell him that the school bus isn't there. He laughs and says, "Of course, not. Did you forget? Daylight saving time is over!"

Space Traveler

CHARACTERS
You
A Person from Another Planet

Imagine you are walking in the country when you meet a person from another planet. The spaceship has landed in a field nearby. He or she wants to know who you are, where you live, what you do, and what you eat. Then the space traveler tells you all about himself or herself. Can you understand each other's language? How do you communicate?

George, The Timid Ghost

CHARACTERS
Father Ghost
George

There was once a timid ghost named George. He lived with his parents at the edge of a ceme-
tery not far from town. He wanted very much to be able to scare people like a proper ghost, but
every time someone approached him, he ran away. "Someday," he often said to himself, "I'll be
as spooky as the rest of my family. Someday, but not today."

One night George's father decided that it was time to teach his son a lesson. When it was
quite dark, George's father showed him how to sneak up behind someone without being
heard, and to say "Boo." "Never hurt anyone," his father warned him. "Just give them a little
scare."

George was eager to learn all of his father's tricks, so he practiced saying "Boo" in different
tones of voice. He jumped out from behind trees and he ran back and forth, waving his arms in
the air.

"Good," said his father approvingly. "You're going to be the scariest ghost in town."

George strutted back and forth after his father went into the house. "I'm going to be the
scariest ghost in town."

Suddenly he heard the sound of somebody running behind him. He froze in his tracks, determined this time not to run away.

This is an unfinished story. What happened next? You make up the ending.

Masks

Closely related to the art of puppetry is the art of mask making. A brief section on
masks is included in this chapter because masks can be either part of a puppet project
or an extension of creative drama. Interesting experimental work with mixed media
is being done these days in which the human actor, often masked, and the puppet are
used in the same production. In the case of life-sized puppets, the human body actually merges with that of the puppet in order to move it. It is difficult to say which
one is the performer, the human being or the puppet. Young children have no problem with this, for in their own play they assume both animate and inanimate roles
simultaneously. Older students and adults, however, faced with an inanimate or
grotesque character to act, often find that the wearing of a mask helps to stimulate
the imagination and free them of their inhibitions. A mask is not necessary to performance, but the teacher who enjoys arts and crafts may find mask making a relevant
activity.

Many persons link the mask with theatre, even though its functions go far beyond costume and performance. The mask is used in a variety of ways, but its four major functions are

To act as a protective covering for the head or face (ski and fencing masks)
To function as a disguise or concealment
To describe or identify a character (in a play)
To serve as a symbol (religious and ritualistic rites)

In children's theatre the mask is commonly used in costuming an animal or a fantastic creature, though stage makeup is preferred by many directors and costumers today.

Background

Historically, masks and makeup have enjoyed wide popularity throughout the world. Tribal societies have worn them in performing religious rites and rituals. Early human beings thought that by putting on the faces of others, one gained power over them. For example, if the hunter wore the skin and mask of an animal, he believed it would bring him a good day of hunting. In time, the mask or facial paint became stylized and more elaborate as it was embellished by generations of wearers. Tribal masks were thought to be potent in other ways as well. They could release the wearer's personality by concealing it, and they became symbols of a universal awareness of gods or a creative force in the universe.

In the ancient Greek theatre, the mask served the practical purpose of projecting the actor's features and amplifying his voice. The mask was larger than the human face and was made with protruding lips that created resonance. Thus the masks of comedy and tragedy gave the actor in the huge ampitheatres, where the performance took place, an objective reality larger than life.

The Keepers of Harmony *with masks created by members of the Zona Gale Youth Theatre in Portage, WI. (Courtesy of Xan Johnson.)*

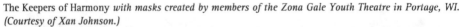

In the Asian theatre, on the other hand, the mask was part of an elaborate costume, designed primarily for its aesthetic appeal rather than its practical use. Japanese masks, familiar to audiences today, are colorful, decorative, and smaller than the human face. Although they suggest the characters in a play, they make no attempt at realistic representation. The audience, knowing the story, recognizes the symbolism in the mask and the actor's movements and is appreciative of the skill of the highly trained performers.

In the commedia dell'arte, the Italian traveling theatre of the sixteenth and seventeenth centuries, the mask was an essential part of the actor's costume. Special masks represented stock characters and were always associated with them. A character's actions and appearance were thus closely connected; in fact, the covering of the face seemed to have an effect on the actor's body, making it freer and more expressive. An example of this connection is found in Punch, a descendent of the commedia character, whose flesh-colored face with its great red nose and bulging eyes is as familiar to us as his outrageous behavior. His face and his actions go together in more ways than one.

Clowns, who prefer greasepaint to the mask, observe a unique tradition relating to the mask. Each clown creates his or her own face and is careful never to copy that of another. A clown's face is thus an individual creation to be respected as long as he or she lives.

Most children are fascinated with these various uses of masks and attitudes toward them and enjoy inventing masks of their own. One of the most creative projects I have ever seen involved puppets and children wearing paper bag masks, both made by a class studying a unit on Native Americans. Because the mask has been used by so many people at so many different periods in history, it is a valuable resource for the teacher and a magic prop for the student who makes and wears it.

Types of Masks

The mask may cover the entire head, the face, or the upper part of the face only, leaving the lower part exposed. The simple half-mask, worn on Halloween or at masked parties, is a well-known example. The obvious advantage of the half-mask is its comfort. It is cooler than the mask that covers the entire face, and it makes speaking easier. Speaking through the mouth of a mask is difficult and distracting for the inexperienced performer.

Masks may be simple, elaborate, beautiful, or grotesque, but except for the representation of animals, they are rarely realistic. The values of mask making are many and are implicit in this brief discussion. Masks provide an extension of the drama lesson; they reveal aspects of a culture in which the mask is an important artifact; and they release the wearer from his or her inhibitions. Many children feel freer when they are shielded from view by even a partial face covering. Children project their feelings and ideas through a mask, while they themselves remain hidden. The mask serves the same purpose as the puppet in this respect. In fact, some interesting research has been done on the use of masks and makeup in therapy.

The teacher will be wise to avoid using the commercial masks sold in stores around Halloween, just as he or she should avoid commercial puppets. One of the values of including the mask in a classroom is the opportunity it offers for imaginative construction and design. This is particularly valuable for a child who is shy about acting but who has interest and ability in arts and crafts. In using a commercial mask or puppet, the teacher misses a rich opportunity for teaching.

Makeup is another form of mask. It is not the purpose of this text to go into its application for the stage; however, the makeup that persons create themselves provides valuable insights for the leader and drama therapist. Nancy Breitenbach, a therapist working in Paris, described her innovative work with makeup as "a form of free association," helping children through its use to discover who they are, what they want others to believe they are, and who they would like to be. In an article published in England, she described the response of children of different ages to makeup and how it released them into drama.[5] In her opinion, the eventual removal of makeup, resulting in the reappearance of the child's familiar face, brings an affirmation of personal strength; strong feelings can be expressed, and yet the individual will return to his or her normal state with a greater degree of confidence and social well-being.

Greasepaint applied to a child's face by an adult, on the contrary, tends to place the emphasis on the outer rather than the inner aspects of character. This is not to say that the formal, scripted play produced with costume and makeup is without value. It is simply not germane to a book on creative drama, and the art of makeup is therefore left until later, when the student is ready for formal play production.

Materials Like puppets, masks can be made of a variety of materials. The older the student, the more complicated the techniques one can introduce, and the more experimentation one can anticipate. Students who are particularly interested in the craft of mask making will bring in many materials, often combining them in interesting and original ways. Myths and animals are always good sources of inspiration, for they remove the possibility of using the human face as a model, thus releasing the imagination to create new and wonderful designs.

Paper Bag Masks For very young children the paper bag mask is by far the easiest and cheapest to make. It is also the most satisfying because it can be completed in a single class period. The brown paper bag from the grocery store slips comfortably over the head, and holes can be cut in it for the eyes and mouth. Younger children need help in locating the right places. After the holes are cut out, the mask is ready for decoration. Strips of colored paper can be pasted on the bags for hair, moustaches, and even eyelashes. Paint, chalk, and crayons can be used to color masks. Older children, studying a particular culture or tribal society, may paste or sew on feathers, cloth, jewelry, buttons, and so on.

Cardboard boxes can be used effectively to suggest robots and stylized characters. These are more difficult to work on than bags, and it is often hard to find boxes of the right size and shape. Because both bags and boxes cover the entire head, they muffle speech and limit freedom of movement. In a follow-up activity, however, after a class has worked on material dramatically, masks have value in extending the learnings. When masks are incorporated in a project that is further developed for an audience, they offer an added dimension for the observers.

Paper Plate Masks Because of their shape, toughness, and availability, masks made of plain white paper plates are recommended for the middle grades. To make

---

[5]Nancy Breitenbach, "Secret Faces," *British Journal of Drama Therapy* 3, no. 2 (Autumn 1979): 18–23.

the mask appear three-dimensional, cut two slits about two inches deep and two inches apart on the edge of the plate. Overlap the edges adjacent to each slit and staple them back together again, forming a chin and making the mask fit on the child's face. As with the paper bag mask, holes for eyes, mouth, and nose must be cut in the appropriate places. A nose that protrudes from the face can be made of construction paper and pasted on the plate, further adding to the three-dimensional quality. From here on experimentation with other materials is fun and will make each mask unique.

Papier-Mâché Masks Papier-mâché is a substance made of pulped paper or paper strips moistened with thin wheat paste (wallpaper paste). The paper used may be newspaper, tissues, napkins, or toweling. Wheat paste is available at any hardware store (follow directions on the package).

You will need a form or mold to work on. This may be made of modeling clay, or you may use a wig form or a large round balloon as a foundation. Be sure the mold is lightly greased with oil or cold cream. Cover it with strips of torn paper (approximately one by ten inches) dipped in paste. Apply the strips to the form diagonally, bandage fashion, and overlap them. Two layers of paper are usually enough. Paper pulp (soft paper torn into small pieces and soaked in paste and then squeezed out) can be added to build a nose, eyebrows, lips, and so on. Allow the mask to dry for two to three days before removing it from the form.

When dry, the mask will be firm and brittle. Use a razor blade or a sharp knife to cut holes for the eyes, nose, and mouth. If you use a balloon blown to larger than head size, you can make a whole-head mask (e.g., for an animal). Leave it open at the base and trim it so that the form will slip over the head and rest on the shoulders.

Basic forms for whole headcoverings can be made from chicken wire covered with cheesecloth and then layers of papier-mâché. Use tin snips to cut the wire; be careful that all wire ends are bent under and covered with papier-mâché. The dry head or face mask can then be painted or decorated with cut paper. Feathers, yarn, or paper strips can be added for whatever effect you want. Spraying the mask with a lacquer or plastic finish (such as Krylon) will add to its durability.

Unless you want to cover the entire head, which is uncomfortable for the wearer, let the mask cover just the face, and fasten it with elastic across the back of the head. A scarf, hat, or wig will complete the disguise.

Activities for Masks

Although just making masks is fun, they are even more fun and more satisfying when they serve a purpose: for instance, when they are worn in a play or creative drama class or when they carry out a theme. Sometimes the mask will suggest an idea to the wearer.

1. *Pandora's box.* Pandora's box contains a variety of evil spirits. Try making masks to represent them. Players who have created movements for the spirits will love adding masks; this is a perfect example of the relationship that exists between mask and movement.

2. *A circus.* A circus calls for clowns, animals, a ringmaster, and any number of sideshow characters. Every person in the class can invent a different mask for a circus parade.

3. *Holidays.* Although Halloween comes to mind first as an occasion for mask making, every holiday contains possibilities. Take Valentine's Day, the Fourth of July, or St. Patrick's Day. What about your birthday? Every child in the class might try making a mask of himself or herself. It may look like its model, or it may be simply an invention.

Summary

Puppetry and mask making provide an added dimension to creative drama as well as being arts in their own right. Although the types of puppets and masks described are simple, requiring no previous experience or special course work, it is always wise to try out an assignment before giving it to a class so you can foresee any problems that might arise and solve them yourself in advance. Gathering materials and providing enough space for construction is important. As in creative drama, the encouragement of original ideas will help to prevent imitation of familiar television characters.

The teacher who includes puppets and masks in the curriculum will find them a rich resource. Regardless of the reasons for including them, the possibilities they offer are limitless. The major values can be summarized as follows:

1. Puppets and masks provide opportunities for developing motor skills. Tools and materials must be handled with care in order to construct puppets and masks that are sturdy and functional.

2. Puppets require control. It takes controlled fingers to manipulate a puppet to perform as the operator wishes.

3. Dressing and decorating puppets require imagination. Each puppet must become a character, first through its costume and then in the way in which it is decorated and painted.

4. Puppets and masks offer an avenue of expression as the operator acts out the thoughts and feelings of characters.

5. Both puppets and masks have therapeutic power. Through them, timid or withdrawn children can find release, whereas aggressive children learn to subordinate themselves to the personality of the characters they present.

6. Puppetry demands cooperation from students, who learn to take turns and work together for a successful performance.

7. Puppetry and mask making are inexpensive arts. Delightful results can be obtained within the most limited budget.

8. Puppets and masks may be ends in themselves or the means by which other ends are reached.

Given half a chance, the puppet engages the student as performer, playmate, teacher, and alter ego. The mask, though less versatile, is closely related, serving many of the same purposes.

Suggested Assignments

1. Make a hand puppet for a particular story.
2. Make a mask of your own choice.
3. If you are teaching, have the children create puppets appropriate to their age.
4. With another student, create and perform a short story or situation with your puppets.
5. Make a study of the puppet theatre of another country such as China, Japan, Italy, or France.

Journal Writing

1. Why is the puppet such a valuable therapeutic tool?
2. Think of the word *mask*. Relate the mask we wear to the use of the word in regard to human behavior.
3. As you watch a puppet show, are you able to forget that the characters are puppets and believe in them as actors? How is this possible?
4. Think of the word *puppet* as it is used to describe a person. Have you ever felt like a puppet?
5. Do you remember your first puppet show? Describe your reaction to it.

Chapter 8

Dramatic Structure: The Play Takes Shape

Trelawny of the Wells. *(Courtesy of Jennifer Fell-Hayes, Drama Director at the Friends Seminary, New York City.)*

> All theories of what a good play is, or how a good
> play should be written, are futile. A good play is a
> play which when acted upon the boards makes an
> audience interested and pleased.
>
> —*Maurice Baring*

If creative drama teachers are going to help students create a play, they must know something of the structure and fundamental dramatic elements that distinguish the play from other forms of literature. They will not be expected to become expert at playwriting or drama criticism, but teachers' enjoyment will be greater and their guidance more helpful if they have a basic understanding of the art form with which they are working. Although there is no rigid formula for writing a play, particularly in this period of experimentation, there are certain elements that are necessary to its existence. First, a play is to be played. Until it finds life on a stage, it is not a play. It is born through the process of interpretation by actors and the mounting by costume and scenic designers, and it will live or die according to the communication it has for an audience.

We are not concerned with formal production or the printed script at this point; we are, however, concerned with the knowledge of drama that older students sometimes want to carry beyond the classroom. It is here where process and product merge and where knowledge of play structure and elementary theatre techniques are necessary. For this reason some attention is given to terminology and definition in this chapter.

Younger children are rarely concerned with linear structure. Their dramas may move backward or forward in time, absent characters may appear without explanation, and action in different times and places may take place simultaneously. This occurs not because children lack a sense of order but because they do not know the conventions of playwriting until they experience them in the theatre or until they are pointed out. Children have a logic of their own but need some help in communicating. Indeed, some of our modern playwrights, in creating new forms, are doing what children do naturally: letting form follow function instead of traditional rules.

The teacher, therefore, should not change children's work; in giving them a concept of structure, he or she will be helping them to express, improvise, and perhaps write plays of their own. When they do this, they will want to communicate with an audience. Far from stifling their creativity, this knowledge will help to stimulate and focus it. Given boundaries, children are freer to express themselves than they are with no boundaries or form to follow.

Elements of a Play

Aristotle said that there were six elements in every tragedy. Although styles of playwriting have changed radically throughout the ages, we can still find these six elements in all plays, comedy and tragedy: fable (or plot), characters, thought (or underlying theme), language (dialogue), melody (mood, including cadence and sound of words),

Teacher-in-role. (Courtesy of Lee Elementary School, Austin Independent School District. Creative drama leader: Coleman A. Jennings, Department of Theatre and Dance, University of Texas at Austin. Photography by Ramona Cearley.)

and spectacle (in our terminology, mounting). Although teachers will not burden children with the list or its origin, they will find these elements useful to keep in mind when questioning and guiding children in need of structure.

In addition to Aristotle's six elements, there are other terms used in discussing the theatre that children in the intermediate and upper grades should know. In fact, older children like knowing and using them; some of the following are the most common.

Plot

The *plot* is the story. It may be simple or complex, internal or external, but what happens between the opening scene and the final curtain is the action we call story or plot. Although tastes differ and styles change, a good plot holds the interest of the audience and is consistent. The most bizarre events must belong to it, and the outcome, whatever it may be, must seem logical. Plot involves exposition, complication, climax, and dénouement.

Theme or Thought

The *theme* is the underlying thought or basic idea upon which the play rests. Not every play has a well-defined theme; it may, however, be the most important element. If there is a theme, the story both springs from and expresses it.

Conflict

Conflict is the basis of drama, whether comic or tragic. Without conflict, there is no resolution; with conflict, the interest is sustained to the end. The successful play-wright resolves the conflict in a way that is satisfying and acceptable.

Climax

The *climax* is the high point of the play. A three- or five-act play will have more than one climax, but there will always be a point at which the interest is highest. This scene usually comes somewhere near the end, after which there is an untangling, or dénouement.

Dénouement

Dénouement is the portion of the play that follows the climax. It may be long or short, depending on the number of situations that need straightening out. In a children's play, the dénouement and climax are often one; children are satisfied when the con-flict is settled, and long explanations at this point do not interest them.

Characters

A play involves *characters*. It is their conflict that holds our attention, and it is through them that the playwright delivers the message. Whether tragic or comic, lovable or despised, a character must be believable and belong to the play. Even in fantasy, a character must have reality; a witch or a ghost, for example, though unrealistic in itself, must compel our belief through the consistency of its behavior.

The *hero* or *heroine* should be someone with whom the audience can identify. Whatever his or her faults or human weaknesses, our sympathy must be aroused, mak-ing us care what happens. Whether this person should be more good than bad is de-batable, but we must accept the hero or heroine as real and his or her actions as true.

Characters respond to each other in a natural way. Although the major characters are clearly established, there are other characters in the play who help to advance the plot through their involvement with it and their relationship to the hero, or *protago-nist*. A skillful playwright develops character and situation through this interaction. Sometimes many characters are needed to tell a story; sometimes it is done better with one or two. The fewer there are, the greater the responsibility they have for telling the story, and the more the audience learns about them. The actor, however, must find in the most minor characters the answers or clues to many questions about them.

age
education and cultural background
interests
occupation or profession
religion
relationship to family members
other social relationships
physical appearance and health
dominant mood
qualities of personality

Good characterizations are at all times consistent. If they are not, either through the writing or the actor's interpretation, we cannot believe in them. A believable character, in contrast, has a reality that exists for the audience long after the final curtain has been drawn. Even when a character is fantastic, he or she must be credible.

Dialogue

Dialogue is the term given to the lines of the play. Good dialogue should belong to the characters, both in content and manner of speech. A noblewoman will not talk like a peasant, nor will a country boy talk like a prince. Although dialogue must be understood, the speech patterns of the characters must not be sacrificed. For example, a character of little education who comes from a particular region will use colloquial speech or appropriate dialect. Poetic dialogue has been employed in the drama during certain periods of history, but even this convention does not obscure the speech patterns and individuality of the characters. Unlike the novelist, who can explain actions and motives, the playwright must incorporate explanations into the speech of the characters. Although writing dialogue appears easy, it can be very difficult, and this is why improvising dialogue before attempting to write it is extremely helpful to the fledgling playwright, child or adult.

Dialogue also advances the plot. The playwright's job is to tell the story as economically as possible through the words of the characters. A *soliloquy,* in which only one person speaks, is a device used occasionally, but in general it is through conversation between two or more persons that characters are revealed and the plot is unfolded.

Action

Action is the physical movement of the actor on the stage. It involves both movement and gestures that are used in developing a role.

Business

Business is the appropriate activity for the actor: knitting, sweeping, raking leaves, eating. It helps define the character by what it is and the way it is done.

Planning the action for Big Mary, City Lights Theatre for Youth. *(Courtesy of Jennifer Fell Hayes, photograph by Dorothy Napp Schindel.)*

Mood Created by Sound: Melody

During the time Aristotle was writing, musical instruments were used as accompaniment to dialogue. Music enhanced the mood of the drama, and, as we know, it is a very effective means of evoking emotion in the audience. The American musical is the most obvious example, although musical backgrounds in certain scenes of plays perform the same function. Sound effects, both on- and offstage, are used in many plays to add credibility as well as mood.

The human voice is also a musical instrument. A trained voice can lift dialogue from a practical to a poetic level. Pitch, rhythm, tempo, emphasis, and tone are all qualities of voice that a good actor acquires to move the audience and express the feelings of the character. Although the term *melody* is not used in this book, music and sound effects are necessary elements of some productions described.

Acts

Acts are the major divisions in a play. Short plays are generally written in one act. Longer plays may be divided into two, three, or even five acts, depending on the plot and the need to break it into parts. Although three acts are most often used, there is no right or wrong number. Many playwrights today use the two-act form with one in-termission between them.

Scenes

Scenes are divisions within acts and are most often used to indicate a different time or place. A play does not have to have any particular number of scenes; the time covered and the locations in which the action takes place determine them. Many one-act plays are written in a single scene because they are concerned with a single plot and no subplots.

Mounting

We use the word *mounting* to embrace all the visual aspects of a production: direction, scenery, costumes, lighting, makeup, and properties. In the contemporary theatre, these things vary enormously in importance; some plays are given elaborate produc-tion, whereas others are produced with minimal scenic effects. Plays using modern costumes and little or no scenery are familiar to audiences, although with less sce-nery, more lighting is usually required to highlight a scene or change it. Color, line, and design also enter into the picture, particularly in producing plays for young audi-ences. The trend now is toward simplicity, even to the point of uniform costumes in some types of plays, enabling the players to move quickly from skit to skit and to use props rather than take the time to change costumes between scenes. Children do, however, enjoy a full-scale production despite their ability to imagine colorful sce-nery and costumes, and most producers are sensitive to which plays are best served by spectacle.

Subplots

Sometimes longer plays tell two stories: the story of the major characters and another story of the minor characters, the *subplot*. One-act plays rarely have subplots. Full-length plays frequently do.

Flashback Scenes

Flashback scenes are sometimes used to show an important event that happened at an earlier time, before the play began. The flashback is a device that helps to explain the behavior or attitudes of characters more dramatically than merely telling about them.

Unity

Unity is the overall term applied to the integration of the various parts of the drama, making a smooth and consistent whole. Unity can be achieved in a number of ways, such as the creation of a single hero, a single action, a single idea, a single mood. A good play, no matter how many characters or episodes, can also be unified through the sensitive arrangement and organization of the various parts.

Dramatic Irony

Dramatic irony is the term used for letting the audience in on a secret. Suspense is usually greater when irony is employed, and many comedy scenes are funnier because of it.

Comedy

Comedy is defined as a play that ends satisfactorily for the hero or heroine. Comedy may be funny, but humor is not essential according to this definition. Many comedies are serious or satiric.

Tragedy

A *tragedy* is a play that ends with the death or defeat of the leading character. Although fashions in playwriting change according to the times and public taste, the downfall of the protagonist places a play in the category of tragedy.

Prologue and Epilogue

Prologue is the portion of the play placed at the beginning to introduce the play or to establish atmosphere. The *epilogue* includes the play and usually summarizes the plot or emphasizes the theme. Such scenes are not an integral part of the play, although a narrator may appear in them and also be involved in the play. Many children's plays employ narrators or are written with prologues as a means of imparting necessary information to an audience composed of different age levels and theatre experience.

Narrator

The *narrator* is a person who tells or reads an exposition that ties the incidents together. Narration is a useful device when an extended period or a variety of scenes are included and is also a way of bridging the distance between actors and audience. A narrator is often used in children's plays.

Theatre for Young Audiences

Children's theatre is above all good theatre. In this respect, it does not differ from theatre for adults. There are, however, special requirements that must be met if the children's play is to hold their interest as well as be worthy of their time and attention. The script contains the same basic elements—characters, dialogue, plot—but not all material appropriate for adult audiences is suitable for children. Action, for example, is particularly important: the playwright writing for children must remember that it is more important to "show" than to "tell." Speeches should be short; long, "talky" dialogue is lost on the audience. Although vocabulary is necessarily adapted to the age level of the audience, it should not be oversimplified but rather should add enrichment and an opportunity for learning new words.

In writing an adaptation of a classic or well-known story, the playwright must make every effort to retain the essential elements of the source material so as not to disappoint or offend the audience. Characters must be believable. Fantasy and fairy stories make up a large segment of plays written for children; nevertheless, the characters in such plays must be endowed with credibility, exhibiting a pattern of behavior that is consistent.

If the story calls for difficult technical problems, the playwright must decide whether they can be carried out successfully or whether any modification of the effect will damage the play. *Technical problems* include events such as blackouts; characters who fly, disappear, or change into birds or other animals; or unusual lighting and sound effects. What might be easily solved in the professional theatre can often pose an insoluble problem on the school stage, where equipment, budget, and technical assistance are limited.

Children's theatre, like adult theatre, should not depend on extravagant effects or gimmicks to stimulate interest; if such scenes are essential to the plot, however, and can be executed artistically, they will certainly add to the effectiveness of the play. Children do not demand theatricality, but there is no question that their enjoyment is enhanced by scenes that offer excitement and color. Many children's plays call for music and dance; therefore, the actor in children's theatre should study both so as to be able to sing, dance, fence, and master any other performance skills demanded by the play. More will be said of this, however, in Chapter 18.

The following script illustrates a story that contains the basic elements of a play:

A worthwhile theme
A plot that holds interest
Characters who motivate the action
Believable dialogue
Melody
Spectacle or appropriate scenery and costumes

Mr. Hare Takes Mr. Leopard for a Ride[1]

Carol Korty

In this play we find the major element of a play: character, dialogue, plot, theme, climax, and mood (in this case, humor). Because the play is so short, it is not divided into acts or scenes.

CHARACTERS:
   Mr. Hare
   Mr. Leopard
   Mrs. Leopard

Narrator: One day Mr. Hare was sitting out in front of his house.
Mr. Hare: (*Sitting, twiddling his foot with a very nonchalant, ho-hum air.*)

>   Hey, ho, what do you know,
>   Hey, ho, what do you know,
>   What will I do today, today?
>   What will I do today, I say;
>   Oh, what shall I do today?

(*Mr. Leopard rushes by carrying something. It could be a bucket, which he brings back filled or emptied on the return trip, or any other object to show he is taking care of business.*)

Mr. Hare: (*Leaps up delighted.*) Good morning, Mr. Leopard! How are you?
Mr. Leopard: Grrrr . . . (*Throws a glance over his shoulder as he hurries off.*)
Mr. Hare: Very nice friend! (*Calls after him.*) You can't even stop long enough to say, "Hello." I don't know why I'm surprised. The only time you are ever friendly to me is when you think you might be able to trick me and catch me for your next meal. Well, it hasn't worked yet. I'm too fast for you. (*Returns to sitting and twiddling.*) Hey, ho, what do you . . .

(*Mr. Leopard hurries back again.*)

Mr. Hare: (*Leaping up.*) Hey! What do you know! Greetings, again, Mr. Leopard!
Mr. Leopard: (*Charges across to exit without pausing to notice Mr. Hare*). Grrr . . .
Mr. Hare: Right in front of my door he passes, and not even a nod! He knows I'm safe on my own territory, so he won't bother with me at all. Not even a nod. (*Calls after Mr. Leopard.*) That's not right! Just because you're big, you should not be rude. At least you can say, "Hello," even if you don't chase me.

(*Mr. Leopard again rushes past, barely missing knocking over Mr. Hare.*)

Mr. Hare: (*Brightly.*) Hello! (*Looks after him; realizes it's too late and shrugs, sitting down again.*)

>   Hey, ho, what do you know?
>   Hey, ho, what do you know?
>   What will I do today?

Today! (*He jumps up.*) I know exactly what I'll do today. I'll do something to make that leopard notice me, (*looking at audience*) and I don't mean as something to eat! (*He stops and continues to think aloud.*) If his house is that way (*points to Mr. Leopard's first entrance*) and he ran that way (*points to Mr. Leopard's exit, then looks at audience*), it means he's not at home. I think I'll just take a little walk over to his house and leave a little message.
Mr. Hare: Hello there, Mrs. Leopard.
Mrs. Leopard: (*Very attentive and very polite.*) Greetings, Mr. Hare.
Mr. Hare: How are you today?
Mrs. Leopard: Fine, just fine, thank you. How are you?

Mr. Hare: To tell you the truth, I'm not very well.

Mrs. Leopard: (*Concerned.*) Oh, I'm sorry to hear that, Mr. Hare.

Mr. Hare: Is Mr. Leopard home by any chance?

Mrs. Leopard: No, he left this morning to go hunting.

Mr. Hare: Oh, that's too bad. I needed to use him.

Mrs. Leopard: Needed to use him? (*Not understanding.*) What do you mean by that?

Mr. Hare: I'm not feeling well, and I want to go to a doctor. It's too far a walk for me feeling this poorly. I thought Mr. Leopard could give me a ride.

Mrs. Leopard: (*More perplexed.*) What do you mean, "Give you a ride"?

Mr. Hare: Well, I don't have a horse to ride, so I thought I would ride Mr. Leopard instead.

Mrs. Leopard: (*Shocked.*) Ride Mr. Leopard! Are you crazy, you little rabbit?

Mr. Hare: Hmmmmmm, no. I'm sure I could do it.

Mrs. Leopard: (*Very worried.*) It's a good thing for you he isn't around to hear you say that. He'd eat you up in a minute for being so insolent.

Mr. Hare: (*Reassuring.*) Oh, I doubt that. (*Very pointedly.*) Besides, I know I could ride him, and I'll bet you I will ride him before the day is over. You can tell him that for me, if you will.

Mrs. Leopard: I just can't believe I'm hearing you right.

Mr. Hare: (*Mimicking her voice.*) Oh, you're hearing me right. (*Mrs. Leopard looks at him, almost realizing he is mocking her. Mr. Hare stops the mimicking and continues in his own voice.*) Guess I'll go home again and lie down. Good-bye, Mrs. Leopard.

Mrs. Leopard: Good-bye, Mr. Hare. (*Calling after him.*) And you'd better be more careful.

Mr. Hare: (*To audience.*) Leopards might be big, but they aren't very bright. It's time they learned their lesson. I'd better get the bridle and whip ready for my ride.

Mr. Leopard: (*Rushing on in terrible anger.*) Mr. Hare! Mr. Hare!

Mr. Hare: (*Jumping up bright and hoppity.*) Greetings, Mr. Leopard. How are you?

Mr. Leopard: (*Confused.*) Ah . . . Greetings. (*Refocusing his anger.*) Mr. Hare . . .

Mr. Hare: I saw you several times earlier. Sorry you didn't have time to say hello.

Mr. Leopard: I was in a hurry. (*Angrily.*) Mr. Hare . . .

Mr. Hare: How are you, by the way?

Mr. Leopard: Fine. (*Exasperated, he grabs Mr. Hare and leans on him to stop his jumping around.*) Listen, Mr. Hare. My wife said you were by my house earlier and boasted you would ride me like a horse.

Mr. Hare: (*Slipping out from his grip.*) Heavens, that's ridiculous, Mr. Leopard!

Mr. Leopard: It's worse than ridiculous. It's insulting.

Mr. Hare: It is very insulting!

Mr. Leopard: I'm absolutely furious.

Mr. Hare: I would be, too!

Mr. Leopard: (*Stops.*) Wait, now you're the one who said that. (*Mr. Hare gives innocent shrug.*) My wife said so!

Mr. Hare: Maybe your wife was mistaken.

Mr. Leopard: (*Circling him and speaking slowly and deliberately.*) My wife told me very clearly that you told her to give me the message that you would ride me like a horse.

Mr. Hare: There must be some mistake.

Mr. Leopard: Now, wait a minute. (*Reflects.*) My wife wouldn't just make up a story like that. There is no mistake. (*To Mr. Hare with anger.*) And no one is going to make a fool out of me.

Mr. Hare: Certainly not, Mr. Leopard.

Mr. Leopard: (*Very sure of himself.*) I want to hear the two of you straighten this out. Come on home with me. (*He starts to leave, assuming Mr. Hare will follow.*) I'll ask my wife to repeat the message in front of you.

Mr. Hare: (*Brightly.*) I'd really like to come with you, Mr. Leopard (*changes instantly to sick act*), but I'm sick today. Didn't Mrs. Leopard tell you? I barely made it home myself.

Mr. Leopard: (*Exasperated.*) Come on! You know I live nearby.

Mr. Hare: (*Collapsing.*) That's true, but I'm feeling weaker every minute. I know I'd never be able to walk that far today.

Mr. Leopard: (*Furious.*) I have been insulted today, and the matter is going to be settled today! Do you hear?

Mr. Hare: (*Weakly.*) I don't see why it can't wait until I'm feeling stronger.

Mr. Leopard: You're coming with me today, even if I have to carry you! (*Grabs his arm and pulls him to his feet.*)

Mr. Hare: (*Weakly.*) All right, then. You'll have to carry me; I'm too weak to walk. (*He sinks down again.*)

Mr. Leopard: (*Thoroughly exasperated and frustrated.*) Hurry up. Get on my back. (*Bends over.*)

Mr. Hare: I'm afraid I'll fall off your back while you're running. Do you mind if I get a little rope?

Mr. Leopard: (*Considers and is unable to think of any objection.*) Nope.

Mr. Hare: I'll just put this through your mouth so I'll have something to hang on to.

Mr. Hare: Now I need a little stick.

Mr. Leopard: (*Speaking through clenched teeth.*) What for?

Mr. Hare: (*Directly to Mr. Leopard's face.*) To push aside the low branches so they won't knock me off your back while you're running.

Mr. Leopard: (*Considers briefly.*) All right.

(Mr. Hare gets stick.)

Mr. Hare: (*Runs around to mount.*) I'm ready now. (*He thinks of one more thing.*) Could you get a little lower?

(As Mr. Leopard continues to respond, Mr. Hare skips around with increasing delight at the situation.)

Lower, lower, lower, lower . . . (*Mr. Leopard looks around at him.*) . . . Ah, steady! (*With mock seriousness.*) Now let me get hold of the rope . . . and my stick.

(Jumps on Mr. Leopard's back.)

. . . We're off!

Mr. Hare: Faster, Mr. Leopard, faster. (*Using the stick.*)

Mr. Hare: (*As they pull up in front of house.*) Hello, there, Mrs. Leopard!

Mr. Leopard: (*Very authoritatively.*) We just came by to check up on the boast that Mr. Hare would ride me like a horse.

(Mrs. Leopard looks alarmed as Mr. Leopard slowly straightens up. It almost dawns on Mr. Leopard what has happened. Mr. Hare slowly slides off his back and steps aside.)

Mr. Hare: Well, guess I'll be going now. I feel lots better. (*Starts moving off.*) Thanks for the ride.
Mr. Leopard: Like a horse!

(Both exit in chase. Mrs. Leopard exits slowly shaking her head.)

Summary

Although the study of dramatic structure belongs to the upper rather than the lower grades, it is a part of playmaking on any level. The advancement of plot and the development of character depend on a structure of some sort. Younger players, unfamiliar with theatre conventions, often invent highly imaginative forms, and this is not to be discouraged. The main thing to keep in mind is that structure is necessary to create order out of the profusion of ideas that a lively group offers. Breaking a story into scenes, finding the climax, listing the necessary characters, seeing where additional characters can be added or where extraneous material can be cut—all develop critical judgment and a sense of organization in young players.

Whether performing or writing, the student needs boundaries within which to work. Too rigid a boundary stifles creativity, whereas its lack often causes good ideas to become dissipated. Form and content are of equal importance; creative drama offers a superb opportunity to shape material into a form that communicates with the spectator as well as expresses the thoughts and feelings of the players.

The dramatization of a story is, in many respects, much easier to write than an original play. First, there is a plot that supplies the basic structure. Characters are clearly defined but must be given appropriate dialogue. In a play, dialogue serves three major functions: to describe the characters, to further the plot, and to help show the time, place, and circumstances in which the story takes place. Because the players do not have to create an original narrative, they can focus their attention on characterization and believable dialogue. Time spent on improvisation before the actual writing is time well spent; then, when the group is ready to write the play, it will have a much clearer idea of what to include in each scene and how the characters would respond in light of their circumstances, interpersonal relationships, and the period in which they lived. Often new characters have to be added to flesh out parts of the story that the author has told through simple exposition. Sometimes characters and scenes need to be cut if the plot is too long or too complicated for dramatic presentation. When such additions or deletions have to be made, young players need our help. Children are usually quick to find solutions, however, when a discussion is held as to how best to solve the problems. Questions such as "How do we know that . . . ?" or "What can we do to show . . . ?" or "Can we think of a way to explain . . . ?" will elicit suggestions.

Whereas there are many values in the writing of an original script, most teachers find it more satisfactory to start with an adaptation of a well-known story. The players have the experience of working with a good piece of literature and from it will be better able to handle the additional problems that a totally original project presents, if or when they want to try one. Again, it must be emphasized that creative drama is participant centered. Product can never be totally separated from process, however; therefore, when a class is ready for the next step—the writing of a play or dramatization of a story for an audience—some knowledge of dramatic structure is necessary. This knowledge can be learned through improvisation, through the development of a script or, ideally, through a combination of both.

Suggested Assignments

1. Write a short scene for a play adapted from a well-known children's story or folk tale.
2. Read a play written by a children's playwright.
3. What children's classics or modern stories do you think would translate into plays? List three or four and explain why.

Journal Writing

1. Have you ever been disappointed with a dramatization of a book you liked very much? Why?
2. Has there been any adaptation for either stage or film that you consider highly successful? Analyze why you think so.
3. In your mind, what would be the procedure for writing a play from a favorite book? Think through the steps you would take.
4. Should a play for children teach a lesson?
5. What is a "worthwhile play or theme"?

Chapter 9

Building Plays from Stories

Improvising The Boxcar Children *(book by Gertrude C. Warner, adaptation by Barbara Field). (Courtesy of Xan Johnson, Director, Zona Gale Youth Theatre, Portage, WI.)*

> He cometh unto you with a tale that could holdeth
> children from play and old men from the chimney
> corner.
>
> *—Sir Philip Sidney*

Although creative drama includes many techniques and practices, probably the most popular practice involves "acting stories." This may be the reason that many persons, unfamiliar with creative drama, think that is all we do. Because of the popularity and importance of stories, I am including this chapter on playmaking. Incidentally, it is also an excellent way of familiarizing children with stories from many cultures.

There is a wealth of good literature readily available that both group and leader can enjoy and will find worthy of their efforts. The stories and poems included in this and following chapters illustrate the kinds of material that groups of all ages have used successfully. Suggestions are offered on ways in which material can be presented and handled. It should not be inferred that these are the only or even the best ways of using the material; they are merely illustrations of the thinking done by some groups.

Folk tales, legends, and fables are recommended for use on all levels, though different age groups will view them according to their own maturity and experience. For younger children, stories should be simplified in the telling, whereas in working with older children, greater emphasis can be given to characterization. Meanings and insights come with experience as well as age; hence, a really good story spans many age levels.

When the teacher has decided on an appropriate story, he or she must decide whether it is better told or read. In general, telling the story is preferable because it establishes a closer rapport with the class and gives the teacher a chance to observe the listeners' responses and to clarify, as he or she goes along, any points that appear to puzzle the listeners. This means that the teacher must be thoroughly familiar with the material; in fact, the beginning teacher will do well to practice telling the story aloud before presenting it to the group. This will add to the teacher's own self-confidence and help to develop greater variety and color in the presentation.

After the story has been told and all questions have been answered, the children are ready to begin planning how they will handle it. A discussion should include a review of the plot and descriptions of the characters. When the leader feels that the children have the details well in mind, he or she will suggest that they try playing it. Asking for volunteers is a good way of starting: this gives the stronger ones a chance to try it first and the more timid ones an opportunity to become better acquainted with it before taking their turns. Casting is done on a voluntary basis the first two or three times. Later, the leader may suggest that other children try various parts: "Lynne hasn't had a chance yet. How would you like to try the princess this time, Lynne?" or "John has been the cobbler. Let's give Alan a chance to play it. And you, John, be one of the townsfolk." or "I know David has a strong voice. How about letting him be the giant?"

In other words, it is the development of each participant that concerns us. Later, when the group is ready to play the story for the last time, the leader might suggest those children who have brought the greatest reality to each part, but this is as close as we come to typecasting.

The situation may be played any number of times, but the replaying should not be interpreted as rehearsal. It is hoped that with each playing the story will gain in substance and depth, that there will be deeper insights, and that the participants will develop greater freedom and self-confidence. The discussions preceding and following each playing are important aspects of creative dramatics, for it is during these periods that some of the most creative thinking takes place. Questions like these might precede the first playing:

1. What do we want to tell?
2. Who are the characters?
3. What are these people really like?
4. What are they doing when we first meet them?
5. Where does the first scene take place?
6. What kind of house do they live in?

After the scene has been played once, more specific questions can guide the discussion:

1. Did the players tell the story?
2. What did you like about the opening scene?
3. Did the people show that they were excited (angry, unhappy, etc.)?
4. Can you think of anything that would improve it when we play it again?
5. Was anything important left out?

Throughout a year, there are often delightful results, and both the leader and group may honestly wish to share them with others. There is no reason why this should not be done, provided public performance was not the original intention. More often, however, the initial results will be crude and superficial. Dialogue will be scanty, despite the most careful planning. To the experienced leader, this does not represent failure. It is an early stage in the development of the group and may, at that point, indicate real progress. Acceptance of the effort does not mean that the leader is satisfied to remain at this level; rather, it means that he or she recognizes the efforts that have been made and is aware of the values to those who have taken part. As the leader works with the group, he or she will become more selective. In the beginning, however, the teacher will accept all ideas simply because they have been offered. It is important for every member to feel that his or her ideas are worthy of consideration. In time, even eight- and nine-year-olds will learn to distinguish between contributions that advance the play and those that distract or have little to do with it.

The following stories have been chosen because of their simplicity. Most children are familiar with them and like them and need only to be refreshed as to the details. The first one, "The Little Scarecrow Boy," makes a good transition from pantomime to improvisation, with the teacher reading the story and encouraging both physical and oral participation.

The Little Scarecrow Boy

Margaret Wise Brown[1]
Arranged for creative playing by Aurand Harris

Once upon a time, in a cornfield, there lived a scarecrow (*he enters and takes his place*), and his scarecrow wife (*she enters and takes her place beside him*), and their little scarecrow boy (*he enters and joins his mother and father*).

Every day of the world old man scarecrow would go out into the cornfield to make faces at the crows. (*He crosses the room and takes up his position in the cornfield.*) And every day of the world little scarecrow boy would want to come, too. (*He goes to his father and pulls at his coat.*) And every day of the world, old man scarecrow would say:

You're not fierce enough to scare a crow.
No!
No, little boy,
You can't go.
You're not fierce enough to scare a crow.
Wait until you grow.

(*He shows how high little scarecrow boy will have to grow. The little boy is discouraged and returns to his mother.*)

So, little scarecrow boy would have to stay home all day and just grow. (*His mother holds up her hand to the height he will have to grow. First he stretches his neck, then he stands on his toes and finally he jumps but he does not reach her hand.*)

Every morning when the sun came up (*the sun crosses the room*) old man scarecrow went out to the cornfield. He waved his arms and made terrible faces.

Every day the crows cried, "Caw! Caw! Caw!" (*The crows fly in and circle around the corn, then one by one each crow sees old man scarecrow, screams, and flies away.*) He made such terrible faces that the crows would fly far, far away.

Every night, when the sun went down (*the sun walks back across the playing space, smiling happily*) old man scarecrow would go home (*he goes to the mother and the little boy*), and there he would teach little scarecrow boy how to make fierce faces. (*He makes a face and the little boy imitates it.*) One—two—three—four—five—six. Old lady scarecrow would clap her hands and whistle through her teeth at the looks of them.

One day after the little boy knew all six of his father's terrible faces so that he could make them one after the other, he decided to go out into the cornfield by himself and frighten a crow. (*The scarecrows have closed their eyes in sleep.*) So the next morning, before the sun was

---

[1]Margaret Wise Brown, *Fun and Frolic* (New York: Heath, 1955).

up, or old man scarecrow was up, or old lady scarecrow was up, little scarecrow boy got out of bed. *(He steps forward cautiously.)* He dressed and went quietly ... *(he takes one step)* ... quietly ... quietly ... quietly out of the house and over to the cornfield. He stood in his father's place. *(He takes his father's position in the cornfield.)*

It was a fine morning and the sun came up. *(The sun crosses the stage, smiling.)* Far away over the trees, crows flew around and around. Little scarecrow boy waved his arms through the air. He had never felt fiercer in all his life. *(The little boy waves his arms and makes faces.)* In the distance the "caws" of the crows were heard. *(The leader enters and all of the crows fly in, circling the corn. One crow at a time sees the little boy, screams and flies off. Only the leader is left and he is not afraid. He starts toward the little scarecrow boy.)*

"Oh!" said little scarecrow boy, and he made his first fierce face. Still came flying the big crow.

"Oh, oh!" said little scarecrow boy, and he made his second fierce face. Still came flying the big crow. He made his third fierce face. "Oh, oh, oh!" It was time to go. *(He jumps down and runs in a circle, covering very little ground but running hard. The crow flies after him.)*

So, little scarecrow boy ran and ran. Then he stopped. He made his fourth fierce face. Still came flying the big old crow. He ran and he ran and he made his fifth fierce face. Still came flying the big old crow. Little scarecrow boy had only one face left now. So he stopped. He held his arms wide above his head and he made his sixth fierce face. *(As he makes his sixth face, the old crow stops, backs up, then turns and flies off.)*

Whoa! The old crow stopped and then backwards flew through the air, feathers flying everywhere, until there wasn't even the shadow of a crow in the cornfield. A scarecrow at last!

(Meanwhile, old man scarecrow walks to his side.) Then little scarecrow boy saw a shadow in front of him and he looked around. There beside him stood his father. Old man scarecrow was proud of his little boy and shook his scarecrow hand. *(They shake hands.)* Old lady scarecrow was proud of her little boy, who could make all six fierce faces. *(She pats him fondly.)* And when little scarecrow boy grew up, he was the fiercest scarecrow in all the cornfields in all the world.

This is a somewhat shortened version of the story. Stories read while acted help the more timid or inexperienced children to follow the plot and feel the sense of accomplishment that comes from successful dramatization.

Caps For Sale

"Caps for Sale" is popular with younger children but equally interesting to older children, and even adults, because of the underlying theme. Very young children enjoy being monkeys and like to take turns acting the Peddler. Older children, however, quickly see a parallel between human behavior and the behavior of monkeys and hence find in this simple tale a meaning worthy of their thought and effort. Although "Caps for Sale," or "The Peddler and His Caps," is very well known, a brief synopsis of the story is included.

There was once a little old man who made caps. All year long he worked at them: red caps, pink caps, yellow caps, blue, green, and purple caps, caps with feathers and caps without. Every so

Children in Hokulani School playing the story of "Caps for Sale." (Courtesy of Prof. Tamara Hunt, University of Hawaii at Manoa.)

often, when he had made a large enough number of caps to sell, he would put them in his pack and take them around to the villages. This particular morning he decided that he had plenty of caps to peddle, and since it was a very fine summer day, he took himself off. His cries of "Caps for sale" roused the townsfolk, and soon many of them were trying on caps and selecting the ones they wanted to buy. Butchers, bakers, shoemakers, mothers, children, and even the mayor himself gathered around the little Peddler, trying on caps and admiring their appearances. Finally, the mayor, who had found nothing to his liking, took off his cap and tossed it back to the Peddler, suggesting that he come again some other day. "Not today, Peddler. Come back another time."

Reluctantly, all of the townsfolk followed his example, echoing the mayor's words that he would return another day. Realizing that he could sell no caps in this village, the little Peddler departed. Before long, he passed by the edge of a woods and, feeling very sleepy, decided to lie down and rest. Soon, however, he fell fast asleep, his hats lying on the grass beside him. Now it happened that this part of the woods was inhabited by a band of monkeys. Monkeys are curious little fellows, and finding the Peddler asleep under a tree, they decided to investigate the contents of his pack. First one, then another, cautiously approached. When they saw that the Peddler was wearing a cap on his head, the monkeys tried the caps on their own little heads. Then they scampered a distance away, chattering excitedly, for they were very much pleased with themselves. The sound of the chattering soon awakened the Peddler. He reached for his pack and was astonished to find it empty. Greatly puzzled, he looked about him to see where the caps might have gone. Suddenly he saw the monkeys. He called to them, pleasantly at first, and asked them to give back his caps. They only chattered, "Chee, chee, chee," pleasantly, in reply.

Then he shook his fist at them and demanded his caps, but they just shook their fists back. Angrily he stamped his foot at them, but they only stamped their little monkey feet at him in return. He begged, and they begged; he moved a few steps away, and they moved a few steps away. Suddenly it occurred to him that the monkeys were doing everything he did. With a sweeping gesture, he removed his own cap and tossed it to the ground at his feet. Immediately all of the monkeys removed their caps and threw them down to the Peddler. He gathered his caps up as quickly as possible, then made a low bow and thanked the monkeys for returning them. Chattering happily, the monkeys also bowed; each was pleased with the trick he thought he had played on the other.

After telling the story, the leader will be wise to review the plot to make certain that it is clearly understood. From here on, there are many ways of proceeding. The leader may ask where the story begins and how many scenes the group sees in it. The children may suggest two, three, four, or even five, although they usually come to the conclusion that three main scenes are necessary:

1. The Peddler starts out on his travels.
2. He arrives in the village.
3. He stops to rest in the forest.

Some groups imagine a road running all around the room, with the three scenes laid in different areas. This arrangement enables the Peddler to move from one place to another and gives him an opportunity to talk to himself as he walks along. Since no scenery is used in creative drama, such an arrangement is perfectly feasible. Incidentally, one advantage of a large room in dramatizing this story is the amount of freedom it provides the players: they are not limited by rows of seats or a traditional stage area. When playing in an auditorium, however, the succession of scenes will follow a more conventional pattern, unless there is an apron (area in front of the curtain) to accommodate some of the action.

In discussing how the Peddler's occupation might be introduced, one group may suggest that he have a wife with whom he can talk over his plans for the day at breakfast. Another group may give him a helper; another, a son; and still another may insist that he lives alone and thus have him talk to himself.

Whether or not his trip down the road is considered a separate scene depends on the importance the group attaches to it, but the next major scene is certainly the village in which the Peddler attempts to sell his caps. One of the advantages of a story of this sort is the opportunity for characterization afforded by the villagers. As any number of villagers may be included, many children can take part. The mayor is always a favorite, though other delightful characters may be created; a shoemaker, a mother, a farmer, a young girl or boy, and a milliner are examples. The playing of this scene may be long or short, depending on the characterizations and the fun the children have with it. Again, if a road is used to suggest the Peddler's travels, he will move along to a place designated as part of the forest. If the group is small, the same children who were villagers can be monkeys. If the group is large, however, there is ample opportunity for others to play the monkeys. One of the best features of this particular story is the flexibility of the cast: whatever its size, the entire group can take part in the playings.

Regardless of age, children always respond to the monkeys, and the activity demanded by their antics is conducive to bodily freedom. There is such great opportunity for pantomime in the final scene that the leader might do well to begin with it, as a means of relaxing the group. By the time all have been monkeys, they are better prepared to begin on the story.

In this—indeed, in any story selected for dramatization—it is a good idea to work on small portions first rather than to attempt the entire story at once. No matter how well the children may know the material, it is another thing to improvise the scenes. Therefore, working on short bits, not necessarily in sequence, makes for more successful playing. In this respect, creative drama is similar to rehearsing a play: the director does not attempt to run through the complete script until he or she has rehearsed each individual scene.

A word is in order here regarding the use of folk and fairy tales in creative drama. At one time they were the exclusive fare for dramatization and children's theatre. The reaction against them was based in part on a need for more diversified material and contemporary themes and in part on a question of whether modern children were interested in fantasy. Bruno Bettelheim's *The Uses of Enchantment* has caused us to take a second look at traditional material. Yes, we do want to introduce new stories, but in seeking them we must take care not to discard the rich resources of the past. The psychological values of the fairy tale and the cultural insights offered by folk tales are important aspects of a child's experience. For this reason, as well as for the imaginative possibilities they offer, a number of folk and fairy tales are included in this chapter and the next. It is further hoped that the leader, in planning a unit or season, will offer material from both the old and the new, the fantastic and the real, the amusing and the serious. Variety and quality capture and hold the interest. Fantasy is not necessarily escape from reality; it can also be an instrument for the analysis of reality.

Fables are popular with some groups, though the obvious moral does not appeal to others. One advantage of a fable is its brevity. There is action as well as a quick and satisfying ending. Although there is little opportunity for character development, some groups will fill in the plot with delightful and imaginative dialogue.

The Woodcutters and the Mermaid

Aesop

There was once an honest woodcutter who had been hard at work all day when he accidentally dropped his axe in a deep pool of water. "Oh, how could I have done such a thing," he cried. "Without my axe I cannot cut down another tree and I haven't the money to buy a new one."

A mermaid overheard his cries and asked him what had happened. "Let me see if I can find it for you," said the mermaid and with that she dived down into the pool. In a few minutes she came back up with a beautiful golden axe in her hand. "Is this the one you dropped?" she asked, but he replied that it was not. "Then let me look again," she said. This time she brought up a shining silver axe. Again the woodcutter shook his head and again the mermaid dived down in the water. She came up with an old iron axe. The woodcutter was overjoyed. "Yes, that is my faithful old axe," he said. "How can I ever thank you?"

"Take all three home with you," replied the mermaid. "For your honesty your family will never go hungry."

Now the woodcutter had a brother, who, hearing the story, said, "Why should my foolish brother have all the luck?" And so the next morning early he went to the pool and threw his axe into the deepest part. Once again the mermaid appeared and asked him what had happened. When he told her, she dived down into the water and brought up a golden axe. "Is this the one you lost?" she asked but he answered before she had finished speaking. "Oh, yes, that is it!" This time, however, the mermaid threw the axe back into the water, saying, "Because you have not told the truth, you will not recover the axe you intentionally threw into the water. Let this be a lesson to you." And with that, the mermaid disappeared.

"The Sun and the Wind," "The Country Mouse and the City Mouse," and "The Tortoise and the Hare" are favorite fables with many children. They also provide excellent opportunities for pantomime, as well as ideas for discussion. A group of fables, incidentally, makes a good program without taxing either teacher or players.

The stories that follow are longer than the Aesop fables, but they have the same advantages of a simple story line based on an amusing or intriguing idea. When a group has mastered the fable, it is ready to take on a longer and more detailed story. The following stories were selected for characterization, theme, ethnic background, and opportunities offered for group discussion.

The Two Foolish Cats

This fable comes from Japan. It can be enjoyed by all ages, although I have found it to have particular appeal for younger children. The idea of fair play is well understood by even the youngest, and the trickster is always a popular character. The simplicity of the story precludes depth so far as character study is concerned, but there is a lesson in it if the leader wants to pursue it. "The Two Foolish Cats" is fun and, for that reason alone, worth doing.

There were once two cats who lived together in peace and harmony. They were good friends, sharing food and shelter. One day, however, each of them came upon a fresh, sweet rice cake on a path leading into a woods. Delighted with their discoveries, they showed their cakes to each other, comparing them for size and freshness. Now it happened that the larger of the two cats had picked up the smaller rice cake. "This is not fair," he said. "I am larger than you and therefore I should have the larger cake. Come, let us trade."

But the smaller cat refused. "No, I am smaller than you and I need more food so I can grow to your size. I wouldn't think of trading."

Well, this led to an argument, each cat insisting that he should have the larger of the two cakes. They accused each other of greediness, and as they grew angrier they began to growl and spit. The argument went on for some time, neither one willing to give in to the other. Finally the bigger cat said, "Let us stop. We will get nowhere fighting like this. Let us go find the wise monkey who lives in the forest. If we ask him to divide our cakes equally, we shall each have our fair share and our argument will be over."

The smaller cat agreed, for he was hungry and wanted to eat his cake. So the two took themselves off to the forest to find the wise monkey. They looked in the bushes and treetops, around rocks and behind the trunks of the trees, until at last they found him. They explained what they wanted, but the old monkey replied that he needed to hear each side of the argument. The bigger cat began. Then the wise monkey said, "Stop. Let me hear the other."

The smaller cat spoke up. When he had finished, the old monkey nodded his head gravely. "I think I can solve your problem. Give me the rice cakes."

The cats handed them over eagerly. The monkey took one in each hand and weighed them with care. "Yes," he said, "this one is heavier. Let me take a bite out of it. Then they will be the same size."

But he took a very big bite and what had been the larger cake now became the smaller. "Dear, dear," said the monkey, "I shall have to take a bite out of this cake to even things up."

As you can imagine, he again took a large bite and the first cake became the larger. Paying no attention to the cats, who were anxiously watching their cakes disappear, the old monkey went from one to the other until both cakes were gone.

"Well," he said, "you asked me to solve your problem, and I have done it. Without the cakes you have nothing to quarrel about." Whereupon he went off, leaving the two cats hungry and feeling very foolish indeed. But never did they quarrel again!

A discussion of greed and fair play is bound to follow. Each child in a small group will be able to play all three parts because of the brevity of the story. After playing and replaying the monkey, most children are ready to talk about his way of handling the problem. The humor must not be sacrificed for the moral, however; the value of the fable is its ability to convey a lesson in a humorous anecdote, usually told through animals.

Darby and Joan

This story about a barometer is from England and appeals to both boys and girls. It is easy to play in a small area. There are only three characters, but the story is so short that, unless a group is large, every boy and girl will have a chance to try one of the parts.

Have you ever seen a little house about the size of a birdhouse, with two doors in front marked "Fair" and "Rain"? And have you ever noticed that a little woman stands in the doorway marked "Fair," and a little man in the doorway marked "Rain"? And, depending on the weather, that one is always out while the other is in? Well, this little man and woman are known as Darby and Joan, and the following story is told of how they came to be there.

Many years ago Darby and Joan lived happily in a little cottage together. As time went on, however, they began to quarrel. Regardless of how peaceably the day had begun, before long they were disagreeing and finding fault with one another. And so a spell was put on them: from that day forth, one must be out while the other was in, depending on the weather. Our story begins many years later. The day has been fair but the weather is beginning to change, and Darby is about to come out, allowing Joan to go inside. As they talk together, not seeing each other, they regret the quarreling that led to their punishment.

"How I wish I could see you, Joan. Do you realize it has been ten years since we sat down at the table together?"

"I know, Darby. I'm sure if we could be released from this spell, we should never quarrel again."

"Imagine not seeing one's own wife for ten years. It is too cruel a punishment."

As they are talking together, Darby notices someone approaching the cottage. He calls out, "It's beginning to rain. Won't you stop and rest here for a bit?"

The stranger, who is a Fairy in disguise, comes to the doorway and asks Darby why he is standing out in the rain while his wife stays in the house. He explains and sighs over their misfortune. The Fairy then tells him who she is and offers to release them from their spell, but only on one condition: that they never quarrel again. They agree joyfully and the Fairy goes off, but not without warning them that if they do quarrel, they will be put under the spell again, and this time it will be forever.

The old couple can scarcely believe their good fortune as they move their arms and legs stiffly and venture outside together. The rain is clearing, and they decide to have supper in front of the cottage. Darby brings out the table and chairs while Joan gets the food. Scarcely have they sat down to eat, however, when Darby criticizes the way Joan slices the bread. Joan replies with annoyance that if he objects, he can cut it himself. Furthermore, she notices that he is wearing his hat at the table. Before they know it, they are quarreling furiously. Suddenly, the Fairy appears. The old people are stricken. They beg the Fairy for one more chance to try getting along, but she replies, "It is too late. You knew the condition and should have thought of the consequences."

Darby and Joan feel the spell coming on, and slowly move back into their old positions. The Fairy disappears, with the old couple once more back in their doorways marked "Fair" and "Rain."

Children of all ages enjoy this story and have a grand time with the quarrel. First, playing the puppet-like figures while under a spell is a good pantomime for the entire group. Release from the spell gives practice in making the transition from a stiff, controlled stance to free movement. After all have tried it in pantomime, they will be ready to add dialogue. "Darby and Joan" is a delightful little story that calls for strong feeling and changes of mood.

The Peasant Who Dined with a Lord
A Ukrainian Folk Tale

Once in a small Ukrainian village there was a rich lord who would have nothing to do with the common folk. As a matter of fact, he was so proud and so greedy that he had little to do with anyone, save his servants. He had no family, and this gave rise to curiosity on the part of the villagers. Whenever a group of them gathered, their conversation was apt to be about the great lord: who had seen him pass by in his carriage, what he looked like, what clothing he wore. Some, who had never seen him, wondered what his servants had bought in the market that day.

One afternoon a poor peasant, overhearing one of these conversations, said laughingly, "Why spend time asking questions? You can find out by simply climbing over the wall and looking into the kitchen."

"When have you done that?" demanded one of the old men, who had dwelt in the village longer than any of the rest of them.

"Yes," said the others, "have you been inside those gates? Has the master asked you to dinner?"

The group laughed uproariously at the young peasant in his ragged clothes, but he answered impudently, "I could dine with him before the week is out, if I wished."

"Dine with a lord? You?" said one of them, then they all laughed again. "Why, if you so much as put one foot inside the courtyard in those clothes, he would have you thrown off the place!"

"Will you make a bargain with me?" asked the young peasant.

All nodded vigorously in agreement.

"Very well. If I dine with him, then will you each give me a sack of your best wheat and a bullock? If I do not dine with him, I will be your servant and do everything that you ask for one month." All agreed to the bargain, certain that they would get the better of it. Whereupon the young man walked boldly into the courtyard of the great lord. As had been predicted, he was met at the gate by two servants, who started to chase him out. "Wait a minute," said the peasant. "I have good news for your master, but I can tell it only to him."

The lord, being told of the promised message, was curious about it, and asked that the bearer of good news be shown into the house. The peasant said that what he had to say must be said in private, so the lord ordered his servants to leave. "Now, what is it that is meant for my ears alone?"

"What," whispered the young man, looking cautiously about, "is the cost of a piece of gold the size of a horse's head?" The lord could not believe his ears and asked that the question be repeated. He was sure that the peasant must have found a great treasure. He tried to discover why such a poor man would want to know the value of so much gold. But the peasant, who was far more clever than he appeared, simply said that if the lord did not wish to tell him, he would be on his way and find someone else who would. The lord, afraid that a great treasure was about to slip out of reach, said, "Why not stay and have dinner with me? We can talk while we eat." He called his servants and ordered them to bring bread, fruit, meat, and cheese as quickly as possible. Then the two sat down at the table together. When they had eaten their fill, the lord said, "And now, tell me, where is your gold the size of a horse's head?"

"I have no gold," replied the young man.

"You have no gold?" the lord repeated after him. "Then why did you ask what it was worth?"

"I just wanted to know, my lord. And it was a kind of bet." The lord was very angry when he heard this, and he ordered the peasant out of the house.

"I am not as stupid as you think me," said the young man, courteously. "I have had a very good dinner and I have won a bet besides. Now I must go and claim my sacks of wheat and my bullocks."

And bowing low, the clever peasant left, chuckling all the while at the way he had outwitted both the villagers and the lord.

Folk tales telling of cleverness, especially on the part of ones who are young and poor, are popular with most people. Children love the double trick played in this story and are always eager to take turns being the peasant. Although there are only two major roles as the story is told, there is no reason why the villagers cannot be fleshed out, giving each of them his or her own motives and personal qualities. The story can be played just as it is, or additional scenes can be added. It can lead to deeper character analysis or a study of the kind of society that is represented by the master and the peasants. Children are quick to detect greed, vanity, arrogance, and scorn, and they like to participate in a discussion of what these attitudes are and how they are found in our lives today. The humor amuses children because it functions on two levels.

Little Burnt-Face
Native American—Micmac

Retold by Frances J. Olcott

This folk tale is a Native American version of "Cinderella," but it is also a fascinating study of masks, or appearances. The Great Chief, who is a god, wears the mask of invisibility to everyone but Little Burnt-Face, who is pure of heart. Scarred and beaten by her envious sisters, she wears the mask of ugliness. When the god becomes visible to her, she is restored to her original beauty. In one version of this story, the girl is called Little Scar-Face. Through the healing power of love, she is so transformed that she becomes known as Little Star-Face.

Once upon a time, in a large Micmac village on the border of a lake, there lived an old man who was a widower. He had three daughters. The eldest was jealous, cruel, and ugly; the second was vain; but the youngest of all was very gentle and lovely.

Now, when the father was out hunting in the forest, the eldest daughter used to beat the youngest girl, and burn her face with hot coals; yes, and even scar her pretty body. So the people called her "Little Burnt-Face."

When the father came home from hunting he would ask why she was so scarred, and the eldest would answer quickly: "She is a good-for-nothing! She was forbidden to go near the fire, and she disobeyed and fell in." Then the father would scold Little Burnt-Face and she would creep away crying to bed.

By the lake, at the end of the village, there was a beautiful wigwam. And in that wigwam lived a Great Chief and his sister. The Great Chief was invisible; no one had ever seen him but his sister. He brought her many deer and supplied her with good things to eat from the forest and lake and with the finest blankets and garments. And when visitors came all they ever saw of the Chief were his moccasins; for when he took them off they became visible, and his sister hung them up.

Now, one spring, his sister made known that her brother, the Great Chief, would marry any girl who could see him.

Then all the girls from the village—except Little Burnt-Face and her sisters—and all the girls for miles around hastened to the wigwam and walked along the shore of the lake with his sister.

And his sister asked the girls, "Do you see my brother?"

And some of them said, "No"; but most of them answered, "Yes."

Then his sister asked, "Of what is his shoulder-strap made?"

And the girls said, "Of a strip of rawhide."

"And with what does he draw his sled?" asked his sister.

And they replied, "With a green branch."

Then she knew that they had not seen him at all, and she said quietly, "Let us go to the wigwam."

So to the wigwam they went, and when they entered, his sister told them not to take the seat next to the door, for that was where her brother sat.

Then they helped his sister to cook the supper, for they were very curious to see the Great Chief eat. When all was ready, the food disappeared, and the brother took off his moccasins, and his sister hung them up. But they never saw the Chief, though many of them stayed all night.

One day Little Burnt-Face's two sisters put on their finest blankets and brightest strings of beads, and plaited their hair beautifully, and slipped embroidered moccasins on their feet. Then they started out to see the Great Chief.

As soon as they were gone, Little Burnt-Face made herself a dress of white birch-bark and a cap and leggings of the same. She threw off her ragged garments and dressed herself in her birch-bark clothes. She put her father's moccasins on her bare feet, and the moccasins were so big that they came up to her knees. Then she, too, started out to visit the beautiful wigwam at the end of the village.

Poor Little Burnt-Face! She was a sorry sight! For her hair was singed off, and her little face was as full of burns and scars as a sieve is full of holes; and she shuffled along in her birch-bark clothes and big moccasins. And as she passed through the village, the boys and girls hissed, yelled, and hooted.

And when she reached the lake, her sisters saw her coming, and they tried to shame her and told her to go home. But the Great Chief's sister received her kindly and bade her stay, for she saw how sweet and gentle Little Burnt-Face really was.

Then as evening was coming on, the Great Chief's sister took all three girls walking beside the lake, and the sky grew dark, and they knew the Great Chief had come.

And his sister asked the two elder girls, "Do you see my brother?"

And they said, "Yes."

"Of what is his shoulder-strap made?" asked his sister.

"Of a strip of rawhide," they replied.

"And with what does he draw his sled?" asked she.

And they said, "With a green withe."

Then his sister turned to Little Burnt-Face and asked, "Do you see him?"

"I do! I do!" said Little Burnt-Face with awe. "And he is wonderful!"

"And of what is his sled-string made?" asked his sister gently.

"It is a beautiful Rainbow!" cried Little Burnt-Face.

"But, my sister," said the other, "of what is his bow-string made?"

"His bow-string," replied Little Burnt-Face, "is the Milky Way!"

Then the Great Chief's sister smiled with delight, and taking Little Burnt-Face by the hand, she said, "You have surely seen him."

She led the little girl to the wigwam and bathed her with dew until the burns and scars all disappeared from her body and face. Her skin became soft and lovely again. Her hair grew long and dark like the Blackbird's wing. Her eyes were like stars. Then his sister brought from her treasures a wedding garment, and she dressed Little Burnt-Face in it. And she was most beautiful to behold.

After all this was done, his sister led the little girl to the seat next to the door, saying, "This is the Bride's seat," and made her sit down. And then the Great Chief, no longer invisible, entered, terrible and beautiful. And when he saw Little Burnt-Face, he smiled and said gently, "So we have found each other!"

And she answered, "Yes."

Then Little Burnt-Face was married to the Great Chief, and the wedding feast lasted for days, and to it came all the people of the village. As for the two bad sisters, they went back to their wigwam in disgrace, weeping with shame.

Although this tale has been compared to "Cinderella," there is an element that the European story lacks. Both have as heroine an uncomplaining household drudge, but Cinderella's presence at the ball is made possible through the intervention of a fairy godmother; in the Native American story, Little Burnt-Face goes to the Chief's wigwam on her own, and there, because of her sheer goodness, she can see him. Thus it is not her outer beauty that attracts him but rather the beauty that lies inside. The thesis makes for discussion, and even young children see the reason for the transformation from the ugly younger sister to the beautiful maiden that she is.

Jack and His Animals
An Irish Tale

"Jack and His Animals" is another tale of poetic justice, but it is told with humor that children love. It is less familiar than "The Musicians of Bremen," but there is a similarity, and children respond to both of them. Playing the parts of animals is appealing, but the underlying motive is one of compassion and a sense of responsibility, giving the tale two levels rather than one.

Years and years ago there lived in that part of Ireland which is now County Tyrone a man named Lorcan with Brid his wife and Jack their only child, a boy in his teens.

They had been happy and fairly comfortable till the father lost his health. He had worked very hard to provide a good home for his wife and child, but his health broke down under the strain of the hard labor.

Jack was a kind, loving boy. As he grew older he felt he should find some means of helping to make life easier and happier for his parents.

He was very fond of animals and had wonderful power in training them and winning their affection.

"Mother," he said one day, "I have thought of a plan to make life easier and more comfortable for you and my father. We have four animals here, the ass, the dog, the cat, and the goat."

"Well, Jack, what do you mean to do?"

"You know, Mother, I have trained the animals to play tricks and I have thought that perhaps I could earn money by amusing the people who would see them performing."

"Certainly, Jack, you have done extraordinary work in teaching the beasts. Not only do they perform wonderfully, but they also enjoy the play."

"Well, Mother, I will start on my travels at once, and I promise you I will return home as soon as possible."

Jack made all things ready and set off. He took his fife with him.

The parents stood side by side at the window of the room where the poor invalid passed his days. They waved a loving farewell to their good son.

He, with the four animals, traveled on till they reached a field near a small town.

Jack placed the animals in a row, took out his fife, and began to play. Immediately the four responded to the music. The ass began to bray, the dog to bark, the cat to mew, and the goat to bleat.

In a little while most of the people in the neighborhood assembled in the field to listen to the "band."

After a short time Jack stopped playing. Immediately the animals followed his example.

One old lady, a lover of animals who had been brought out to witness the performance, gave orders to have a good meal prepared at her house for Jack and his animals. Both man and beasts thoroughly enjoyed the food. She also gave Jack a good sum of money.

Jack wished to derive as much profit as possible from the long day.

He gathered his band together and started off to go to another town. When they reached it he arranged the animals in order on a patch of waste ground.

The music started. In a short time it seemed as if all the people of the town were gathered together to hear and see the strange band. The animals themselves seemed to enjoy the game.

Among the crowd was a rich man named Feilim, with Finola his wife and Maeve their seven-year-old daughter.

"Father, where are the man and the animals going now?" Maeve asked.

Jack himself answered the question. "We will travel a bit farther and reach a wood. We can sleep under the trees."

"Oh!" said Feilim, "rain might come on and you would have no shelter."

"There is a big empty shed near the back of our house," said Finola. "The animals could sleep there. You yourself can find a bed in the house."

Both Jack and his animals slept comfortably that night. They started off early next morning after having a good breakfast.

Feilim with his wife and daughter stood at the gate of the house to say good-bye. Maeve had been given a purse of money to put into Jack's hand. He was delighted to think of the joy the money would bring to his parents.

He traveled on till he came to a splendid mansion surrounded by trees. It was the home of a wealthy chieftain named Angus, Anna his wife, and their daughter, Eva.

They had been for years a very happy family but were now a sad one.

Eva was a beautiful girl and was as good as she was beautiful. A marriage had been arranged between her and a fine young chieftain named Oscar.

All preparations had been made when a sad occurrence put an end to the joyful anticipation.

One lovely spring day Eva and two of her companions, Brid and Siobhan, went for a walk along a winding road known as the Witch's Lane.

It was so called because a wicked witch had her home there among the bushes and brambles.

The witch was feared by the people of the neighborhood.

It was said she put cruel spells on anyone who dared to go near her dwelling place.

When the three girls came toward it, Siobhan and Brid turned back but Eva went on. "I am not afraid of the ugly old creature," she said.

She had gone only a very short distance when the hideous old hag rushed out from among the bushes.

She had a crooked stick in her hand.

With it she struck Eva on the mouth as she said:

Till strange, quaint music greets your ear
Power of speech you'll ne'er regain
All help and cures will be in vain
Till strange, quaint music greets your ear
And drives away all doubt and fear.

Laughing and cackling, the witch rushed back toward her den.

In her savage delight she forgot the deep lake near her home. She stumbled over a large stone. In vain she tried to reach the brambles. The water seemed to drag her down, down. She was never heard of more.

Her wicked power had put poor Eva under a cruel spell. She was deprived of the power of speech.

Oscar wished the marriage to take place as arranged, but Eva herself would not consent to such an arrangement.

Jack happened to select for his next performance a field near Eva's house.

The day was bright and sunny. The birds were singing and the blossoms were sprouting on the trees. Scenes of beauty and renewed life appeared on all sides.

Angus, his wife, daughter, and Oscar were seated at the midday meal when they heard the sound of extraordinary music.

Eva loved music. She rushed without ceremony from the table and hurried to the place from whence the sound had come.

The parents and Oscar followed her. All four were amazed to see Jack and his band.

The sight was a fantastic and funny one.

The poor donkey was getting tired, but he kept on bravely with his part so as to hold his place in the orchestra.

The dog kept on changing the key from threatening growls to barks of joy and welcome.

The cat mewed loudly but now and again softened the tone to a gentle purr.

The "meg geg geg" of the goat was somewhat nasal but was constant and well sustained.

The parents and Oscar listened for a moment to the "choir," but what was their joy when they turned toward Eva and saw that she was laughing heartily.

"Oh! Father, Mother, Oscar," she cried, "the cruel spell is broken. The witch's prophecy has come true. Strange, quaint music has been my cure."

All the listeners came forward with generous money gifts.

Angus asked Jack what were his plans for the future. "I will go home now to my parents," was his reply.

"Is your home far from here?"

"Well, it is a good distance."

"Oh! Then we must find some means of sending you back."

"Do you remember, Father," said Eva, "there are wagons in the stables that would take more than twice the number of animals? And Jack himself could be sent home on one of the side-cars."

The triumphant march home began. Jack received a tumultuous welcome from all his neighbors and friends.

With great care and good food the father regained his health, and both people and animals lived happily ever after.

An aspect of this tale that sets it apart is that Jack and Eva do not marry and live happily ever afterward but, rather, go their separate ways, having achieved the goals they sought.

Jack and the Hainted House

R. Rex Stephenson

Most children love ghost stories. The following tale from the Blue Ridge Mountains is simple in structure, yet it has all the elements of a good ghost story for creative playing: a hero with whom children can identify, a scary situation that is resolved in the end, and strong dramatic action.[2] It is told here in the dialect of the region.

This is a story about a boy named Jack. Now Jack is a boy who lives up in the Blue Ridge Mountains of Virginia. Old Jack, why, he is always getting himself into a fix. This tale is called "Jack and the Hainted House." "Hainted" is what mountain folks say when they mean haunted. So this tale is gonna find Jack meetin' some ghosts and the like.

Well, one day Jack was walkin' in the woods, and it commenced to get dark. Jack was lookin' for a good place to spend the night. Finally he came upon this house with a light in the window, and he went up and knocked on the door.

When the door opened, an old man stepped out carryin' a candle. He had about the wildest bunch of hair that Jack had ever seen on anybody's head.

"What can I do for ya, boy?" the old man asked.

---

[2]Published for the first time in this book.

"I'm lookin' for a place to spend the night and maybe get somethin' to eat," answered Jack.

"Afraid I have no room here. Too crowded," the old man said, all the time studyin' Jack real careful with his candle.

"I'm awful hungry, too," Jack said.

"Well, I have a goose that I'll give ya. But you'll have to cook hit. Now then, a place to sleep. I got a little house over there you can stay in . . . iffen you want to." With that the old man handed Jack the goose and slammed the door in his face.

Jack took that goose and moved purty slow to the house. When he got there, Jack opened the door and went inside. But before he knew what was happenin' that door shut fast and he was trapped. Try as he would, Jack couldn't get that door open.

Well, all that work tryin' to get that door opened left Jack plumb tuckered out, so he looked around for a place to sleep. He spied a bed over in the corner, picked up a quilt, spread it over himself, and before a cat could of blinked twice, he was fast asleep.

Jack was just beginnin' to dream about bein' home and eatin' ash cakes and sorghum, when he felt this tuggin'-pull on that quilt. Well, the harder Jack pulled, the harder that tuggin'-pull was from the other end. Finally old Jack gave up and tore that quilt half-in-two and said, "I don't know who you are or what you are, but I guess I'll have to give ye half of this quilt iffen I'm gonna get any sleep tonight."

After Jack tore that quilt half-in-two, he went right back to sleep, but it wasn't long before he felt that tuggin'-pull on the quilt again. Jack pulled, but the other thing pulled harder and finally Jack fell on the floor. So Jack just gave that quilt to whatever it was and went someplace else to sleep.

Well, it wasn't long before Jack was fast asleep again, dreamin' of his maw's ash cakes and sorghum, when he heard these strange sounds. When Jack looked up, he saw these seven witches comin' in the room! Well, they surrounded Jack, but when they went to grab him, Jack jumped out of the way and all them witches bumped into one another. Well, old Jack, he jumped up and started yellin', "Get out of here, 'fore I beat the Devil out of ye!"

Well, to old Jack's surprise, those witches left. Jack went over to another corner of the room and decided he'd stay awake, to see if there was any other strange critters in that hainted house.

Hit wasn't long till these seven witches returned, not only makin' those scary sounds but carryin' a dead body. The witches left the body and disappeared again.

Well, Jack remembered something his grandpaw had told him. If you speak to a haint using the lord's name, hit will talk back to you.

So Jack walked over to that haint and said, "What in the lord's name are you doin' here?" That haint told Jack that he had been killed in this house many years ago by a robber, who was after his gold. The haint told Jack to go find the gold, which was hid in the fireplace, and to give one-third each to the haint's two sons, and, for doin' that, Jack could keep one-third for himself.

Well, Jack did just what that haint said, and you know Jack took the money and bought him a little piece of ground up on the mountain, and today he's got seven sons, jist as ornery as he was. And that's the story of Jack and the Hainted House.

The leader might begin by having all the children be witches. How do witches move, speak, carry the body, disappear? What makes them scary? Many children will want to try the parts of Jack, the old man, and the haint. When all have had a chance to try their favorite parts, the group will be thoroughly familiar with the story. The mountain dialect provides a special quality of authenticity and distinguishes it from other ghost stories that may be more familiar. Older children will appreciate the humor.

The preceding stories were selected for this book because of their simplicity. All can be used successfully with beginning groups of any age. Each age group brings its own insights, meanings, and humor to the playing of the stories. There are many excellent stories just as suitable for beginning creative playing, and the interested leader will have no difficulty finding them. Tastes and interests of the group will guide the selection, though one of the values in creative drama is the opportunity it offers for introducing new material and good literature. One thing the leader will discover is that no two groups ever handle a story in the same way; if he or she is able to present the story without a preconceived plan as to how it should be done, the leader will find that every group brings original ideas to its playing.

The procedures suggested are essentially the same, regardless of age level:

1. Presentation of the story
2. Organization of the material
3. Improvisation
4. Evaluation
5. Replaying

Evaluation is an important aspect of creative drama and leads into the replaying, which should acquire new depth and richer detail. Changing parts with each playing may not always make for a better performance, but it does give each participant a chance to play the part of his or her choice at least once. When the leader feels that the group has gone as far as it can with the story, he or she may suggest that the group cast it for final playing. This usually makes for a successful conclusion: the group has created something of its own and has found the last playing to be the most rewarding.

The older the participants, the more preliminary planning the leader can expect. Children, in contrast, tend to move quickly into improvisation. Their dialogue is brief and the scenes are shorter than planned, but their attack is direct. Children, less conditioned to the conventions of the proscenium stage, are likewise freer in their use of space, planning scenes in various parts of the room simultaneously. When class members are held in a room with a stage at one end, they are likely to use it as a particular place—perhaps a mountaintop or a distant land—rather than consider it the central playing area. For every age group there are fewer inhibitions if a large room, instead of a stage, is used. Playing in the round reduces self-consciousness and is conducive to freer movement, since the scattered observers do not seem so much like an audience.

When the group has shown that it can handle the problems of simple fables and stories, it is ready to move on to more demanding material. The following stories illustrate the possibilities offered for characterization and multiple-scene planning.

Building a play. (Courtesy of Lynda Zimmerman, Artistic Director, Creative Arts Team, New York City.)

Prometheus

Greek mythology is a rich source of material that can be successfully dramatized. One myth, which has been used many times with success, is the story of Prometheus, who stole fire from the gods. Basic human emotions and a dramatic story make it particularly appealing to children from ages seven to twelve. The idea of a formless earth stirs their imagination and provides an unusual opportunity for creativity. The story must be told carefully and in considerable detail, since not all children will be familiar with it. Although Greek myths are readily available, a brief synopsis of "Prometheus" is given here, with suggestions as to ways in which the leader may handle it.

The Greek gods and goddesses were believed to have dwelt on Mount Olympus, high above the earth. Ruling over them was the mighty Zeus. Among the young gods, most in favor with Zeus for his bravery in helping defeat the Titans, was Prometheus. One day Zeus and Athena, Goddess of Wisdom, were walking in the garden. They caught sight of Prometheus in the distance, looking down toward the earth. Zeus called to him and asked him what interested him, for he had often seen the young god staring down at the forests and mountains below.

Prometheus replied that he was troubled because the earth was so empty and silent, with no one moving about its surface. Zeus smiled and said that for some time he had been considering a reward for the young god. "Prometheus," he suggested, "perhaps you would like to descend to the earth and fashion human beings out of soil." Prometheus was overjoyed.

"You are wise and kind," added Athena. "When you create them, remember to give them strong bodies, keen minds, and tender hearts. Let them also see that there is a need for beauty as well as for the necessities of life."

"You may give them any gifts you wish except the gift of fire," continued Zeus. "That alone belongs to the gods and must remain on Olympus. When you have fashioned them and are satisfied with your work, I will come down to earth and blow the breath of life into their bodies."

Prometheus was eager to begin and went off swiftly. Working with power and skill, he modeled his first human being upright and powerful and called him "the Builder." Then he took more soil and made a second person, who was likewise tall and strong. Putting a few grains of corn in his hand, he named him "the Sower and Reaper." The third he pronounced "the Hunter," and to that one he gave a stone. The fourth he called "the Musician." Finally, he finished his fifth, whom he proclaimed "the Thinker."

Scarcely had he stepped back to admire his efforts when the deep voice of Zeus was heard from Olympus. "We are pleased with your people, Prometheus. I shall now come down to blow life into them."

Miraculously, each statue came to life and breathed and moved and walked. As the days passed, Prometheus cared for his people and worked with them, teaching them to do the special jobs for which they had been created. They learned quickly and worked happily. One day, however, the seasons changed. The warm air was replaced by cold winds and snowy weather. The people were cold, and Prometheus was deeply disturbed as he watched them huddling together, trying to keep warm. Finally, he could bear it no longer. He knew he must give them fire.

When he called to Athena for help, she asked, "Do you care so much about your people, Prometheus?"

Prometheus declared that he did.

"Enough to risk the wrath of Zeus?" continued Athena. "He will surely punish you. The one thing he has forbidden them is fire."

"I have made my people, and I must help them, even though I suffer for it," replied Prometheus.

"Very well, then," said Athena. "I will help you find the fire to give them."

As swiftly as he had gone down to earth, Prometheus returned to Olympus to get the fire that he was determined his people should have. Then he called the five together and told them not to be frightened, but to learn to use their new gift. Just as he had taught them other things, he taught them how to use a fire for warmth and for the cooking of food. He warned them never to let the fire go out. The people were fascinated with the many possibilities of fire, and they were soon warm and comfortable again.

It was not long, however, before Zeus learned what had happened. Angrily he told Prometheus that he had disobeyed and must be punished for his act. "I am ready to accept my punishment, great Zeus," Prometheus replied, "for I cannot let my people suffer from the wind and cold."

"A gift that has been given cannot be recalled," continued the god. "Human beings now possess fire, but you must pay the price. I shall have you bound by chains to yonder mountain.

There you must remain forever and serve as an example to those who dare to disobey my laws."

So saying, Zeus sent his messenger, Hephaestus, down to seize Prometheus and put him in chains. The people were grieved when they saw the dreadful thing that had happened to their creator and teacher, but their hearts were filled with gratitude for his great gift to humankind.

The discussion preceding the story can take many directions. It may begin with a consideration of human qualities and feelings. It may begin with occupations and some pantomime suggesting them. It may begin with an analysis of the characters in the story and their conflicts. Eventually, no matter how the story is introduced, there must be a focus on the characters, their behavior, and the consequences of Prometheus' act. Like the other stories, the myth should be broken down into scenes before it is acted. Work in pantomime can easily be done with the whole group, for there is rich opportunity here. Together, the children can do the following actions: build a hut, hunt for food, plant a field, make a musical instrument (drum or pipe) and discover how to play it, suggest the beginning of human thought processes. Each activity gives scope for imaginative pantomime. Though music is not necessary, it may be helpful in stimulating movement. Children love playing the statues who come to life and learn to do the things for which they were intended. One whole period can easily be given over to these activities.

When the players are ready to begin the story, they may wish to take turns playing gods and people. If playing in a large room, the children may conceive of one end of it as Olympus and the other end as earth. Or if there is a platform, they may decide to locate Olympus on a higher level. The plot calls for at least three scenes, though some groups may see it in five or six. More than one group has played it with simultaneous settings, with Zeus and Athena observing and commenting while Prometheus works. When this approach is used, the scenes may move back and forth without a break or scene division.

"Prometheus" is a story strong enough to hold the children's interest for three or four class sessions, with constructive discussion preceding and following each playing. If the group enjoys the story, other myths may be introduced, for there are many with fine dramatic action and values that children comprehend. Like the other stories in this chapter, "Prometheus" gains depth and detail with each new playing. The young god's sense of responsibility and compassion for his people begins to emerge, adding another dimension to the character. The conflict between the law of Zeus and Prometheus' moral courage as he begins to feel for his people makes for powerful drama. The final playing can be most rewarding as theme, story, character, and action are unified. The group that has become really involved in Prometheus' dilemma will have had a rich experience. This is a story better suited to an older group, although even seven- and eight-year-olds can understand and play a simplified version.

Bluebonnets

This Comanche legend, telling how the first bluebonnet flowers appeared on the earth, is a story that appeals to children of middle and upper grades. Many Native American legends are excellent for improvisation, but this one has a special appeal because it is the story of a child and her sacrifice.

Yellow Star is a little Native American girl who lives with her father and mother in a village belonging to the Comanche tribe. As the story begins, the Chief calls his people together. He describes the trouble that has come to their village after many weeks without rain. The long drought has caused the brooks to dry up, vegetation is dying, and animals have left the parched plains in search of food. The people sit quietly in a circle around the campfire as they listen to their leader. Then they beat the drums and dance, praying to the Great Spirit for rain. At first, nothing happens. Then, suddenly, they hear the voice of the Great Spirit far in the distance. They stop, put down the drums, and listen: "You are being punished for your selfishness and greed. You have lived in a land of plenty for many years, but your people have not shared with their brothers."

The Chief begs for mercy, but the Great Spirit replies, "I will forgive your tribe and send you the water you need only when one among you sacrifices on the campfire that which is dearest to his heart."

Excitedly, the braves talk together. They suggest that one give his horse, another his jewelry, and still another offer his strongest bow to the Great Spirit. No one, however, is willing to make a sacrifice for the sake of his brothers, and so they move from the campfire and start slowly off toward their homes. The Chief calls them. "Come to this place again in the morning. By that time, one among you may have found the gift that will bring us all forgiveness."

The people slowly disappear, each hoping that someone will think of a way to save them. Only little Yellow Star remains. In her arms she carries her fawn-skin doll with its bonnet of blue jay feathers. The doll is her dearest possession. She realizes that she must throw it into the fire to please the Great Spirit, but it is not easy to part with her only toy. Finally, she reaches her decision as night falls on the village, and she tells the Great Spirit that she is ready to give that which is dearest to her heart. She watches the doll burn slowly; then, seeing the blue feather bonnet lying in the ashes, she picks it up and throws it into the flames. To her amazement, the feathers do not burn but become small blue flowers. Yellow Star knows, then, that the Great Spirit has accepted her gift, and with a light heart she runs home.

The next morning, all of the people gather together as their Chief has commanded, but where only last night there was a campfire, there is now a huge bed of blue flowers. The people are mystified, for they cannot understand how flowers could have sprung up from the hard, dry earth.

Yellow Star's mother tells the Chief about the doll. "Surely," she says, "it must be a sign. Hundreds of flowers now grow on ground that was trampled and dry."

The people, however, are unwilling to believe her story, for why should the Great Spirit be satisfied with so small a gift as a child's fawn-skin doll? At that moment, there is a roll of thunder in the distance. The Chief knows now that the Great Spirit has accepted Yellow Star's offering. Again, he asks his people to beat their drums and give thanks that they have at last been forgiven. The first raindrops fall.

This charming legend gives an opportunity for total group participation. Since movement is an important element, a good beginning can be made with a dance around the campfire. The use of a drum aids enormously as the Comanches move and dance and pray. The leader can begin with the story, but before dialogue is attempted, practice in rhythmic movement helps the players to become involved.

Discussion of the story and its theme should precede the playing, inasmuch as this will deepen the understanding of a people different in custom, yet like us in their human strengths and weaknesses. When the group is ready to begin, short scenes, rather than the whole story, should be played first. For example, the opening scene, in which the Chief calls his people together and explains the seriousness of their situation, is enough for one sequence. Yellow Star's sacrifice is another. The players may conceive of the story as taking place in one act, with a break to indicate passage of time, or they may see it as a play in two or three scenes. Because it is a story in which any number may participate, playing it in the round is desirable. Players and observers are one and are therefore involved to an unusual degree.

The part of Yellow Star is a favorite, but the Chief, the mother, and the selfish men and women can all be built into characters who are believable and interesting. If this story finds favor, the leader may wish to bring other Native American legends to class. Most of them require little more than space for playing, since they are concerned with human beings in conflict with nature and with human weaknesses familiar to all.

Bimi
Kitty Kirby

Stories and legends of the Bahamas are almost unknown in this country. Yet, like all places where people have lived, worked, played, and worshiped, it has a rich supply of folklore that waits only to be discovered. The following tale makes wonderful material for creative playing. An entire class can take part, with different players taking turns as Bimi. This tale also gives information about the islands in its description of plants, foods, and the life of the people, including the legends told by one generation to the next.[3]

Long ago in Andros Island in the Bahamas, where the blue-green waters roared and the palm trees nodded in the sun, stood a mighty forest. It was there that the wild horses and donkeys roamed, there that the green parrots and whistling ducks flocked, and there where the magical Chickcharnie elves were said to make their home.

Not far from this forest lived a little boy named Bimi. His name, in fact, wasn't Bimi at all . . . but his grandma, who was born in Bimini, called him "Bimi" after her beloved Island.

When Bimi was five, he wanted to be a giant. At seven, he wanted to be a fisherman and go out to sea. Now that he was nine, he wanted to be a pirate. Several times Bimi wandered off into the nearby woods, even though his grandmother warned him not to. But Bimi's thoughts were always full of adventure.

Every night after supper, Mama Ellen would tell him stories full of mystery and adventure. Bimi listened with excitement when she told him of the pot of gold hidden under the Bay Cedar Tree.

---

[3]Published for the first time in this book.

"Pot of gold, left under the Bay Cedar Tree?" said Bimi.

"Yes, Bimi, a pot of gold left by pirates long ago, deep in the Green Pine Forest. Never wander near the forest, for many have gone in search of the treasure, but no one has ever returned."

At the end of the story one night, Bimi saw tears on his grandmother's cheek. "Why are you crying, grandma?" asked Bimi.

"Oh, Bimi, we have enough shillings to last us for only a little while."

"Don't worry, Grandma, I will take care of you," said Bimi as he gave her a big hug.

Grandma went off to bed smiling at Bimi's thoughtfulness.

Bimi spent the night tossing and turning, unable to sleep, thinking about the buried treasure under the Bay Cedar Tree. Very early the next morning, Bimi slid out of bed, picked up his pail and shovel, and tiptoed out of the house, making his way to the Great Pine Forest.

First, he had to pass Aunt Julia's house. She was in the backyard, picking up mangos that had fallen to the ground.

"Good morning, Bimi!"

"Good morning, Aunt Julia," said Bimi, as he hurried on, for he did not want to be questioned by her.

"Want a mango, Bimi?" called Aunt Julia, but he was already too far away to hear her.

Next Bimi met the old man with the wheelbarrow, Mr. Sweeting, who sold bananas and coconuts down at the marketplace.

"Good morning, little Bimi. What are you doing out so early?" said Mr. Sweeting.

"Good morning, Mr. Sweeting . . . ummm . . . ummm . . . ," Bimi hesitated, because he did not want the old man to know where he was going.

At that moment, a large coconut rolled off the wheelbarrow onto the ground.

"Watch out for your barrow so it doesn't turn over," said Bimi, as he quickly caught the coconut and put it back in the wheelbarrow.

"Why, thank you, Bimi," said Mr. Sweeting as he hurried on down to the marketplace. Bimi was happy that he had been able to help him and, at the same time, not be asked any more questions. He continued on his way to the forest.

In the distance, Bimi could see the tall palm trees swaying in the breeze and the spikey tops of the great pines standing high against the sky. As Bimi entered the pine forest, he heard the sound of the hummingbirds. He saw long green and gold lizards scuttling from rock to rock, seeking shade from the sun. He had stopped short and crouched down behind a large brown rock when suddenly he heard the sound of hooves coming toward him. Peeping through the tall grasses, he saw a herd of wild horses galloping by on their way to adventure.

"Wish I could run like them," thought Bimi as he continued on his way into the forest.

Further along were water wells, where tall banana trees grew. Great bunches of green and yellow bananas reached out from within the leaves like large waving hands. Bimi waved back and hurried on his way.

Then he came to a turn in the forest where Bimi could see beds of pink, purple, and white orchids soaking up the richness of the soil. He stopped to pick a big pink orchid for Grandma, then continued on his way.

As he pushed deeper into the forest, he saw giant soursop trees, their branches laden with fruit that also seemed a good present to take home. But the soursops were much too high off the ground for him to pick them. He jumped and jumped, then gave up and decided on some sea-grapes from a sea-grape tree within arm's reach. He grabbed a handful of sea-grapes and was about to settle down and eat them when suddenly he heard singing!

I'm a speckled green frog,
Happy as can be,
Hopping through the woods
Is so much fun for me!

Bimi was amazed to hear the little green frog sing. "What a curious thing," Bimi said. "Whoever heard of a singing frog? Did I really hear you sing?"

"Of course you did," answered the speckled green frog. "Here in this forest all the animals talk and sing! I've been hopping around all morning without a thing to eat," continued the frog. "May I have some of your grapes? They are too high up in the tree for me to hop and reach."

"Of course," said Bimi. He picked up the frog and held him in the palm of his hand. "I'll share some of my sea-grapes with you."

"Thank you," said the frog. "But where are you going so early in the morning?"

"Oh," said Bimi, "I'm looking for the Bay Cedar Tree. You see, I'm a pirate and I'm searching for the buried treasure."

"The buried treasure? You are brave, my friend," said the frog. "But you'd better beware of the Chickcharnies."

"The Chickcharnies? What are they? Grandma never told me about the Chickcharnies," said Bimi.

"They are little elves who make mischief for people who lie or laugh at them," said the frog. "They are the guardians of this forest. You must be careful. Do not speak ill of the Chickcharnies. And now, I must be on my way. I have a lot of hopping to do today."

"How far is it to the Bay Cedar Tree?" asked Bimi.

"It is much farther," answered the frog. "It is difficult to find. You should go back, my friend."

"But I'm a pirate!" replied Bimi. "Pirates don't turn back. I must go on."

So he said goodbye to his little friend and went on his way.

After walking for some time, Bimi heard mysterious noises. Looking up, he saw tall pine trees with green vines wrapped around them. Suddenly, he heard voices. As Bimi stepped on the pine needles, they whispered his name: "Bimi! Bimi! Why are you in the forest? Go back!"

Bimi was astonished at trees talking to him. They seemed to know him! But then he thought of what the little frog had told him. "I had to come. I'm looking for the buried treasure, the pirates' gold buried under the Bay Cedar Tree!" said Bimi.

"The Bay Cedar Tree! Buried Treasure! It doesn't belong to you. It belongs to the animals of the forest," said the pine trees. "Do not go further into the forest! We have warned you, Bimi!" said the pine needles.

"I'm not afraid of anything. I'm a pirate! And the treasure belongs to whoever finds it," said Bimi.

"Remember, we warned you, Bimi," said the pine needles, crackling under his toes.

Bimi walked on until he came to a clearing where large coconut trees grew. Among the coconuts he saw flocks of beautiful blue parrots with swooping tails of yellow and red. With their pointed beaks turned toward one another, they all were chattering together. "A little boy is in our forest! A little boy is in our forest!"

The branches swayed, and a large round coconut fell nearby. Bimi heard a shrill peal of laughter. Just above him, sitting on a coconut limb, was the most beautiful parrot Bimi had ever seen. As it flapped its wings, all the colors of the rainbow covered the branch of the tree. It was a mother parrot protecting her young. At that moment Bimi saw the bird preparing to push another large coconut on him.

Bimi laughed. "You want to knock me on my head again?"

The parrot answered, "Yes, I do! Yes, I do! Why are you in our forest, silly Bimi? Silly Bimi!"

"How do you know my name?" asked Bimi.

"The wind tells us all secrets, and we hear things with sharp ears," said the parrot.

"Then you should know why I'm here in the forest," said Bimi. "I'm here to find the buried treasure."

"Does your Grandma know you're here?" asked the parrot. "Don't let the Chickcharnie elves hear you say that you're looking for the buried treasure, or they will turn your head backwards on your shoulders. You don't want your head turned backwards, do you? Do you?"

Bimi laughed. "Head turned backwards? Never heard of such a thing! Anyway, I don't believe you. Just tell me which way to the Bay Cedar Tree."

"If you must go, follow the path of the white stone, where the pine needles fade away. There you will find the purple Bay Cedar Tree and the treasure you seek." The parrot suddenly flew over and behind the palms. "The base of the Cedar Tree is not too far away," screeched the parrot. "Silly Bimi! Silly Bimi!" The screech turned into a shrill peal of laughter.

"Not too far away!" Bimi repeated. "Thanks, parrot! 'Brave little Bimi,' Grandma will say when I bring home all that gold and silver."

Behind the parrot's palm tree was a path of white stones shining in the sunlight. Bimi followed it past the sharp-bladed palmetto grove. Here the ground rose up suddenly. Bimi saw a large dark cave.

"It looks just like Grandma's coal stove in her backyard, only ten times larger and wider," said Bimi aloud. "I wonder what those markings and bones decorating the front of the door mean."

Bimi was about to look when suddenly a roar came from the cave. Bimi stood still. He couldn't move. His heart was beating wildly. Birds flew from their hidden nests in the trees, and the leaves tingled with alarm. Another roar! This time even louder. Flocks of wild ducks and a group of grunting hogs burst through the clearing and dashed off into the dense undergrowth. Bimi didn't know which way to run. Suddenly, something caught him from behind! Claws, scaly and green, closed in around his waist, raising him off the ground in one sudden swoop. Bimi was too frightened to turn his head. He could only feel squeezed more and more tightly and his heart filled with fear. A blaze of smoke burst in front of him and a flame of fire pierced the air.

"What are you doing in my forest?" boomed an angry voice. "Answer me, little boy! Why are you here?"

"I-I-I-Ah-h-h!" Bimi couldn't speak, couldn't look, could barely breathe. "I-I-I'm I-looking f-f-for the B-B-Bay Cedar Tree!"

"BAY CEDARRRR-RRRR," announced the voice. And Bimi felt himself being turned around in the claws of the monster. Bimi dropped his pail and shovel. For there in front of him stood a large green creature with blazing eyes and a piercing glare. Its long green neck was covered with coral seashells, and his body was covered with green scales. His teeth sparkled and glinted in the sunlight, while a long red tongue slithered in and out of his mouth.

"DO YOU KNOW WHO I AM?" thundered the monster.

"N-n-no," stammered Bimi, fearfully.

"I am the Dragon King of this forest!" bellowed the monster. His tail flapped and curled snakelike in the air.

"P-p-p-please, Mr. Dragon!" cried Bimi. "Please let me go!"

"NO-O-O-O-O, I'm going to take you into my cave! I'm going to keep you there!" said the Dragon, as Bimi struggled to get out of his grasp.

Suddenly, the forest grew dark and cold. A flash of lightning streaked across the sky. Thunder clapped overhead, and a large pine tree cracked and fell to the ground on the dragon's tail.

"AHHH . . . AARRRGGHHH" screamed the dragon, with fire and smoke coming out of his mouth as he tried to free himself from the heavy tree. Bimi felt himself falling to the ground, freed from the tight claws. Picking up his pail and shovel, he scrambled through the tall grass and ran as fast as he could, forgetting the orchid for his Grandma. He scarcely knew where he was running, except that it was away from the mighty Dragon.

Finally, Bimi felt that he could go no further, and, panting with exhaustion, he collapsed, his body scratched by the sharp blades of the palmetto leaves. The grass beneath him felt like a velvet carpet. At that moment, Bimi looked up and saw a huge purple tree. "It's the Bay Cedar Tree! It's the Bay Cedar Tree! Just what the parrot said!" Bimi jumped up and quickly gathered his pail and shovel, and he began to dig.

He was so excited he didn't notice the hole becoming larger. He was being swallowed into it! Suddenly his shovel hit something shiny. "I've found the buried treasure!" Bimi cried in delight. But he couldn't move; he couldn't believe what he was seeing. Above him were little people with white feathery beards and popping green eyes. Bimi rubbed his eyes. To his amazement, the little people began to sing:

Chickcharnie elves of the Bay Cedar Tree;
Three fingers, three toes, are all that you see!
We hang by our tails from morning till night;
Singing and dancing is our delight!

"Chickcharnie elves! Chickcharnie elves!" shouted Bimi. Suddenly Bimi remembered what the little frog had told him. Their high-pitched singing stopped as they danced in and out of the trees and somersaulted around little Bimi.

"Please don't hurt me!" cried Bimi. "I can't even move!"

"Why did you come here, Bimi? Why did you come here? You were warned. We are the Chickcharnie Elves!"

Bimi hesitated. "I was looking for the buried treasure," cried Bimi. "Please help me! The Dragon was after me."

"The Dragon will not harm you here," said the elves in unison.

"The Bay Cedar Tree is our home."

"Your HOME?" said Bimi

"Yip! Yip! Yip!" answered the little people, peering out at Bimi.

"Why aren't you home, Bimi? Does your Grandma know you are here in the forest? Does she know?"

"Yes," said Bimi. "My Grandma sent me here to bring home the treasure!"

"That's not true! You lie to Chickcharnies!" shouted the elves. "Your grandma warned you never to come near this forest!"

And with that, Bimi felt his head turning backwards on his shoulders. Bimi screamed, "Please, please do not turn my head backwards!" His arms grew stiff, and he couldn't speak.

"The little frog warned you, the pine needles warned you—even the parrot warned you! But you wouldn't listen to them," said the Chickcharnies. "There are many kinds of treasure, little Bimi," continued the elves. "But the buried treasure under the Bay Cedar Tree belongs to us and the animals of the forest. Here in the forest, the treasure is magical. If you were to take it away from the Bay Cedar Tree, it would vanish into thin air. Now do you understand?"

Bimi blinked his eyes. His jaw began to relax and his head slowly turned back. His arms were no longer stiff. The elves lifted Bimi out of the hole and wiped the dirt off him. With tears still in his eyes, Bimi said, "Yes I understand. But oh, we are so poor I had to come; our roof doesn't keep out the rain, and we have only a little food to eat. I wanted to bring my Grandma some of the buried treasure so that she would never cry again."

"Because your heart is good," said the Chickcharnies, "we'll give you our most precious coin. But you must not let anyone hear of this, or ever return to the forest, or the treasure will disappear. Take this gold coin, and place it under your Grandma's pillow; she will find it when she wakes up."

Bimi was overjoyed. "I promise! I promise! Thank you! Oh, thank you!" He cried in delight.

"Come, we will show you the way back," said the Chickcharnies. "And our little Elfy will guide you all the way to see that you get home safely."

Bimi was overwhelmed by the Chickcharnies' kindness. As he said goodbye to the elves, he could hear their high-pitched voices singing as they danced around the Bay Cedar Tree.

Hesitantly, Bimi started back through the pine forest, looking carefully about him. When he spotted the cave of the Dragon, He cried out, "Oh, save me, someone, PLEASE!"

From out of nowhere the little Elfy appeared. "Don't be frightened, Bimi. I'm always at your side." And with that, the Elfy disappeared. Bimi did not look back.

He ran past the palmetto grove, down the white stone path and the carpet of needles. He didn't stop to hear the parrot chatter or talk with the little speckled frog. He kept running until he came to the edge of the forest.

Once more Elfy appeared, and he said, "Goodbye, Bimi." But just as he was about to thank his little friend, Elfy was gone. All that Bimi could see was a white feathery beard flying in and out through the trees.

Bimi felt a thrill of joy as Aunt Julia's house came into view. He grinned at Aunt Julia, who was still in her garden, and kept on until he reached his house. He tiptoed in and silently slipped the coin under his Grandma's pillow. Soon she awoke and began to fluff her pillow.

"Bimi!" she said, surprise and joy in her voice. "Bimi, come look! It must be magic—a gold coin for us!"

"See, Grandma, I told you everything would be all right!" said Bimi, his chest puffed out with pride.

The tale of "Bimi" gives information about the Bahamas in its description of the country: the trees, plants, birds, and animals and the occupations of the people. It could therefore be used in connection with a social studies unit on the islands of the Caribbean. It could also be played purely for the exciting story. Although it features just one character, the things that frighten Bimi arouse the imagination and are fun to create. Every student who wants to try the part of

Bimi should be given a chance to do it. Sound effects are also important to the story and provide another kind of participation. This tale could be done with puppets if the class is interested in them or if the space is too limited for the physical action. It was written by Bahamian kitty kirby; the story comes out of her own background.

The Wise Old Woman
Yoshiko Uchida

This version of the Japanese folk tale "The Wise Old Woman" is included for several reasons.[4] It is a good story. The narrative holds the interest of the players and provides complications that make demands on them. Also, the characters can be interpreted in considerable depth. The situation, though extreme, can be discussed in relation to our attitudes toward older people: How do we feel about them? How do we treat them? What value do older people have in our society? What have we to learn from them? Why do you think we react to them as we do? What has caused our attitude? What are the implications in this story for our own old age?

Many long years ago, there lived an arrogant and cruel young lord who ruled over a small village in the western hills of Japan.

"I have no use for old people in my village," he said haughtily. "They are neither useful nor able to work for a living. I therefore decree that anyone over seventy-one must be banished from the village and left in the mountains to die."

"What a dreadful decree! What a cruel and unreasonable lord we have," the people of the village murmured. But the lord punished anyone who disobeyed him, and so villagers who turned seventy-one were tearfully carried into the mountains, never to return.

Gradually there were fewer and fewer old people in the village, and soon they disappeared altogether. Then the young lord was pleased.

"What a fine village of young, healthy, and hardworking people I have," he bragged. "Soon it will be the finest village in all of Japan."

Now there lived in this village a kind young farmer and his aged mother. They were poor, but the farmer was good to his mother, and the two of them lived happily together. However, as the years went by, the mother grew older, and before long she reached the terrible age of seventy-one.

"If only I could somehow deceive the cruel lord," the farmer thought. But there were records in the village books, and everyone knew that his mother had turned seventy-one.

Each day the son put off telling his mother that he must take her into the mountains to die, but the people of the village began to talk. The farmer knew that if he did not take his mother away soon, the lord would send his soldiers and throw them both into a dark dungeon to die a terrible death.

---

[4]From Yoshiko Uchida, *The Sea of Gold and Other Tales from Japan* (New York: Scribner's, 1965), pp. 61–71.

"Mother—" he would begin, as he tried to tell her what he must do, but he could not go on. Then one day the mother herself spoke of the lord's dread decree. "Well, my son," she said, "the time has come for you to take me to the mountains. We must hurry before the lord sends his soldiers for you." And she did not seem worried at all that she must go to the mountains to die.

"Forgive me, dear mother, for what I must do," the farmer said sadly, and the next morning he lifted his mother to his shoulders and set off on the steep path toward the mountains. Up and up he climbed, until the trees clustered close and the path was gone. There was no longer even the sound of birds, and they heard only the soft wail of the wind in the trees. The son walked slowly, for he could not bear to think of leaving his old mother in the mountains. On and on he climbed, not wanting to stop and leave her behind. Soon, he heard his mother breaking off small twigs from the trees that they passed.

"Mother, what are you doing?" he asked.

"Do not worry, my son," she answered gently. "I am just marking the way so you will not get lost returning to the village."

The son stopped. "Even now you are thinking of me?" he asked, wonderingly.

The mother nodded. "Of course, my son," she replied. "You will always be in my thoughts. How could it be otherwise?"

At that, the young farmer could bear it no longer. "Mother, I cannot leave you in the mountains to die all alone," he said. "We are going home, and no matter what the lord does to punish me, I will never desert you again."

So they waited until the sun had set and a lone star crept into the silent sky. Then in the dark shadows of night, the farmer carried his mother down the hill, and they returned quietly to their little house. The farmer dug a deep hole in the floor of his kitchen and made a small room where he could hide his mother. From that day, she spent all her time in the secret room, and the farmer carried meals to her there. The rest of the time, he was careful to work in the fields and act as though he lived alone. In this way, for almost two years, he kept his mother safely hidden and no one in the village knew that she was there.

Then one day there was a terrible commotion among the villagers, for Lord Higa of the town beyond the hills threatened to conquer their village and make it his own.

"Only one thing can spare you," Lord Higa announced. "Bring me a box containing one thousand ropes of ash and I will spare your village."

The cruel young lord quickly gathered together all the wise men of his village. "You are men of wisdom," he said. "Surely you can tell me how to meet Lord Higa's demands so our village can be spared."

But the wise men shook their heads. "It is impossible to make even one rope of ash, sire," they answered. "How can we ever make one thousand?"

"Fools!" the lord cried angrily. "What good is your wisdom if you cannot help me now?"

And he posted a notice in the village square offering a great reward of gold to any villager who could help him save their village.

But all the people in the village whispered, "Surely, it is an impossible thing, for ash crumbles at the touch of the finger. How could anyone ever make a rope of ash?" They shook their heads and sighed, "Alas, alas, we must be conquered by yet another cruel lord."

The young farmer, too, supposed that this must be, and he wondered what would happen to his mother if a new lord even more terrible than their own came to rule over them.

When his mother saw the troubled look on his face, she asked, "Why are you so worried, my son?"

So the farmer told her of the impossible demand made by Lord Higa if the village was to be spared, but his mother did not seem troubled at all. Instead she laughed softly and said, "Why, that is not such an impossible task. All one has to do is soak ordinary rope in salt water and dry it well. When it is burned, it will hold its shape and there is your rope of ash! Tell the villagers to hurry and find one thousand pieces of rope."

The farmer shook his head in amazement. "Mother, you are wonderfully wise," he said, and he rushed to tell the young lord what he must do.

"You are wiser than all the wise men of the village," the lord said when he heard the farmer's solution, and he rewarded him with many pieces of gold. The thousand ropes of ash were quickly made and the village was spared.

In a few days, however, there was another great commotion in the village as Lord Higa sent another threat. This time he sent a log with a small hole that curved and bent seven times through its length, and he demanded that a single piece of silk thread be threaded through the hole. "If you cannot perform this task," the lord threatened, "I shall come to conquer your village." The young lord hurried once more to his wise men, but they all shook their heads in bewilderment. "A needle cannot bend its way through such curves," they moaned. "Again we are faced with an impossible demand."

"And again you are stupid fools!" the lord said, stamping his foot impatiently. He then posted a second notice in the village square asking the villagers for their help.

Once more the young farmer hurried with the problem to his mother in her secret room.

"Why, that is not so difficult," his mother said with a quick smile. "Put some sugar at one end of the hole. Then tie an ant to a piece of silk thread and put it in at the other end. He will weave his way in and out of the curves to get to the sugar, and he will take the silk thread with him."

"Mother, you are remarkable!" the son cried, and he hurried off to the lord with the solution to the second problem. Once more the lord commended the young farmer and rewarded him with many pieces of gold. "You are a brilliant man and you have saved our village again," he said gratefully.

But the lord's troubles were not over even then, for a few days later Lord Higa sent still another demand. "This time you will undoubtedly fail, and then I shall conquer your village," he threatened. "Bring me a drum that sounds without being beaten."

"But that is not possible," sighed the people of the village. "How can anyone make a drum sound without beating it?"

This time the wise men held their heads in their hands and moaned, "It is hopeless. It is hopeless. This time Lord Higa will conquer us all."

The young farmer hurried home breathlessly. "Mother, Mother, we must solve another terrible problem or Lord Higa will conquer our village!" And he quickly told his mother about the impossible drum.

His mother, however, smiled and answered, "Why, this is the easiest of them all. Make a drum with sides of paper and put a bumblebee inside. As it tries to escape, it will buzz and beat itself against the paper, and you will have a drum that sounds without being beaten."

The young farmer was amazed at his mother's wisdom. "You are far wiser than any of the wise men of the village," he said, and he hurried to tell the young lord how to meet Lord Higa's third demand.

When the lord heard the answer, he was greatly impressed. "Surely a young man like you cannot be wiser than all my wise men," he said. "Tell me honestly, who has helped you solve all these difficult problems?"

The young farmer could not lie. "My lord," he began slowly, "for the past two years I have broken the law of the land. I have kept my aged mother hidden beneath the floor of my house, and it is she who solved each of your problems and saved the village from Lord Higa."

He trembled as he spoke, for he feared the lord's displeasure and rage. Surely now the soldiers would be summoned to throw him into the dark dungeon. But when he glanced fearfully at the lord, he saw that the young ruler was not angry at all. Instead, he was silent and thoughtful, for at last he realized how much wisdom and knowledge old people possess.

"I have been very wrong," he said finally. "And I must ask the forgiveness of your mother and of all my people. Never again will I demand that the old people of our village be sent to the mountains to die. Rather, they will be treated with the respect and honor they deserve and share with us the wisdom of their years."

And so it was. From that day, the villagers were no longer forced to abandon their parents in the mountains, and the village became once more a happy, cheerful place in which to live. The terrible Lord Higa stopped sending his impossible demands and no longer threatened to conquer them, for he too was impressed. "Even in such a small village there is much wisdom," he declared, "and its people should be allowed to live in peace."

And that is exactly what the farmer and his mother and all the people of the village did for all the years thereafter.

It is suggested that the major discussion of "The Wise Old Woman" be held after several playings. By that time the story will have had an impact on the group, and the players will be ready to discuss the theme and its modern implications. This can lead into a discussion of stereotyping of age, the meaning of wisdom, and the social values in our society. The depth of perception will affect the playing of the story, for as the students discover its meaning, they will find their playing enriched, more serious.

Kalilah and Dimnah

The ancient fables of Kalilah and Dimnah were translated from the Arabic into Persian in the twelfth century but may have originated in India. They are similar to Aesop's fables in that animals and human beings have personalities and are at the mercy of their own and each other's passions. Kalilah and Dimnah are clever jackals.

In the first tale Dimnah, who is ambitious and greedy, asks Kalilah why the Lion King never leaves the palace these days. Kalilah replies that it is not their business to question the king's habits. They are rich enough to live comfortably. But Dimnah persists, suggesting that perhaps he can advise the king if something is troubling him. Kalilah tells him to mind his own business, for, if you try to do something you know nothing about, you will end up like the monkey.

"How is that?" asks Dimnah.

"Well," explained the other jackal, "once a monkey saw a carpenter sawing a piece of wood."

Kalilah tells how the carpenter used two nails to keep the wood balanced as he worked. He would pound one nail, then the other. For some reason, after a while he went away, leaving the monkey alone. The monkey was curious and, thinking he could do the job just as well as the carpenter, pulled out one of the nails. Suddenly the wood broke into two pieces, catching the monkey's tail and holding him fast. Hearing the commotion, the carpenter rushed back to see what had happened. In his anger he beat the monkey and said, "Carpentry is not a monkey's job!"

"That," said Kalilah, "is where the saying 'Carpentry is not a monkey's job' came from."

The story is best played by four characters so as to "show" rather than "tell" the exciting part. The animals possess the human traits of ambition, greed, wisdom, and curiosity. For young players or players with limited language, the brevity of the narrative is a plus, and the point can lead to a good class discussion.

Another "Kalilah and Dimnah" fable goes like this. Dimnah thought about Kalilah's advice, then decided to approach the king anyhow. The king explained that there was a wild thing with a terrible roar in the forest, and he feared to leave the palace. Dimnah told him that not every powerful voice or huge body was dangerous. "Just ask the fox."

"What do you mean?" asked the king.

"Well," said Dimnah, "there was once a fox who saw a large drum lying by the trunk of a tree. When the wind blew, it caused a lower branch to beat against the drum, making a loud roar. The fox was impressed by the sound and thought that surely such a round fat body must contain lots of good meat. Whereupon he tore the drum apart, only to find a thin skin and nothing inside it. Then the fox said to himself, 'I should have known that the bigger the body and the louder the voice, the less substance there would be.'"

Again, here is a good opportunity for mime. The two fables can be played together, as the first leads into the second. Some groups may want to make up fables of their own, either using the jackals or creating new characters. The fact that the stories are so short makes them less intimidating.

300 Ounces of Silver Not Buried Here

The following fable comes from China, and like most fables, it offers an explanation for a well-known saying. Because it is so short, it can be played by the entire class at one time working in pairs, space permitting. When the children have finished, each pair can play the story for the class. At this point the teacher or a narrator is needed to introduce it. The only props required are a large bag for the silver and a shovel. The action can be done in pantomime if a shovel is not available.

Long, long ago in China there lived a man named Chang San. He worked hard and managed to save 300 ounces of silver. But he didn't want to keep the sliver in his house for fear his hard-earned nest egg might be stolen.

After thinking long and hard, under cover of darkness Chang San dug a hole at the foot of an earthen wall to bury his silver. But he still wasn't sure the money was safe, so he pasted up a sign saying, "300 ounces of sliver not buried here." When Chang San had finished, he marched away with an easy mind.

Meanwhile Chang San's neighbor Wang Erh waited until he thought Chang was fast asleep and then made off with all the silver. Wang Erh was pleased with himself for being so clever, but suddenly he became afraid that Chang would find him out. So Wang Erh also pasted up a sheet of paper on the wall, writing on it "Wang Erh next door didn't steal it."

Ever since that day people have used the expression "300 ounces of silver not buried here" to refer to people giving themselves away in the very act of trying to hide something.

The children may want to add to the story. Was Wang Erh found out? If he was, what happened? Were any other people involved? Did Chang San recover his silver, or did Wang Erh spend it? There are all sorts of possibilities, and the class will have fun imagining what they might be.

Summary

Because of the greater plot complications and length, all of the stories in this chapter will demand more time in planning than the selections for younger players. There is sufficient content to absorb the interest of the average class for several sessions, depending on the length of the periods and the age of the participants. Characters are presented in greater depth; hence, much more time must be spent on their development. Most groups like to consider such questions as these:

1. What is the character really like?
2. Why does the character behave as he or she does?
3. What do others think of him or her? Why?
4. If the character is not like that, why do others think so?
5. How is the character changed, or what has he or she learned as a result of his or her actions?

As the participants grow in experience, they will find new ways of telling the story. Some groups will want to use narrators; others, many scenes; and some may rearrange the sequence of events altogether. Every group is unique, and the leader learns to expect an endless variety of ways in which the same material can be handled and interpreted. The growing self-confidence of the players releases ideas that lead to further thinking and experimentation. Each group, regardless of age, becomes more critical of its efforts as, with the help of the leader, it strives for a higher level of accomplishment.

Suggested Assignments

1. If you are teaching or student teaching, try dramatizing a story with your class. If you are not, then try it with your classmates and demonstrate it to the rest of the class.

2. Describe your method and cite any problems you had.
3. Make a list of stories you think could be successfully made into plays with six- to eight-year-olds; with nine- to eleven-year-olds.
4. Take a story from a different culture and make a lesson plan for it, including any customs, words, attitudes, or values that you think should be understood by the class in order to appreciate it. This will deepen the experience and provide a guide for future work with stories.

Journal Writing

1. What ideas did you get from this chapter that you think will be most useful to you?
2. Books and stories differ in emphasis. Can you think of a book or story that requires a focus on character to be effective as a play? one that is primarily dependent on plot? another that is theme- or issue-oriented?
3. Is there a story you remember from your childhood that would make a good plot for a play? Why would it work well? Try to compose a scenario.
4. Recall a story from your own background. Why do you remember it so clearly?

Chapter 10

Creating Plays from Other Sources

Iskender, *narrative theatre production based on mythology. (Courtesy of Angela Waldegg, Artistic Director and performer, photograph by Bettina Freuzel, Vienna.)*

Oh, gentle reader, you would find a tale in
everything.

—Simon Lee

Where does one go to find good material for creative playing? There are many sources
other than stories, and the longer we teach creative drama, the more we find. The children's room of the public library is the best source for literature: stories, biography,
science, history, and other areas of interest. The creative drama teacher as well as the
classroom teacher will be wise to investigate its shelves. What are the children's interests? Do any of them have special interests they would like to share and pursue?
There are also family anecdotes, family recollections with ethnic backgrounds, stories
no one else knows. Consider them current events. They might make very good plays.

For example, Stories My Grandparents Told Me, a creative writing contest held
every year now in New York City, is a rich resource for dramatization.[1] Lively characters, amusing and touching anecdotes, customs of other lands, and experiences of
immigrants in America are all fodder for the adult playwright and actor, but they are
equally good for the classroom, and children love sharing them. In addition, family
tales help to build respect for the cultural backgrounds of both self and others. I have
been one of the judges of this contest for several years, and I am always amazed at
the variety of stories that are submitted. Children from eight to eighteen write their
stories, which are first read by the classroom teacher. He or she then selects the six or
eight best ones from each class and sends them to the sponsoring agency of the city,
which in this case is the Police Athletic League (PAL). PAL next distributes the manuscripts among the judges, who read and rate them first, second, or third. More than
one judge reads each story to ensure careful, professional evaluation. Finally, ten
winners in each of the three ratings on the several grade levels are announced at a
simple but moving ceremony and reception. I have often suggested at the ceremony
that many of these stories would make wonderful plays. I hope some are used in
this way.

Dramatizing Legendary Material

Myths, legends, and folk tales are particularly good for creative playing. First, these
stories have been told and retold over the years so that the story line is clear and easily
followed. Characters are generally well defined, they have complete relevance to the
plot, and, even in the case of the supernatural, they have credibility. The theme is
usually strong, for one generation has passed the tale along to the next, carefully if
unconsciously preserving the values of the culture. Creation myths, explaining natural phenomena, are particularly good today in the face of our expanding body of
information about the universe and the new kinds of questions we are asking.

---

[1]Conducted by the Police Athletic League of New York; Kitty Kirby, director of the Performing Arts Program.

Lower East Side Story, *a City Lights Youth Theatre collaboration with the Lower East Side Tenement Museum, directed by Deborah Nitzberg. (Photograph by Susan Lerner.)*

A group might dramatize a well-known myth or legend, or, through the study of legendary material, develop a play of its own. A holiday, for instance, often has an interesting origin that would make good material for a play.

Halloween

Of all of the holidays, Halloween must certainly be one of the favorites of children. Their fascination with the supernatural, the dressing up in fanciful and grotesque costumes, the parties, the games, the treats and tricks (all to be forgiven in the spirit of the occasion) make for a holiday with appeal for every age. (Collecting money for UNICEF has replaced the traditional treats in many communities.) Even the commercialization of Halloween in the form of ready-made costumes, masks, crepe paper decorations, and packages of candy corn in the supermarket have not spoiled the holiday's appeal, though it has perhaps shifted the emphasis. At any rate, Halloween as a suggestion for dramatizing is guaranteed to elicit an enthusiastic response from the most resistant group. Let's take a look at Halloween to see what some of the possibilities are.

Its roots date from antiquity, thus providing a rich source of information for playmaking as well as the fun and the social activities associated with its celebration. As a holiday, Halloween enjoys great popularity because it offers interesting content, action, and an opportunity for dressing up. Fifth and sixth graders, with the help of the teacher, can learn about play structure through the process of building a creative drama from source material concerning this holiday.

The customs associated with Halloween spring mostly from three distinct sources: Druid, Roman, and Christian. The strongest influence was probably the pagan. Each year the Druids of northern and western Europe celebrated two feasts: Beltane, on the first of May, and Samhain, on the thirty-first of October. The latter was a fall festival, held after the harvest had been gathered, thus marking the end of summer and the beginning of winter. Their new year began on November first, so Halloween was actually the new year's eve. Fortune-telling was a popular custom on this holiday, as people were eager to learn what the new year held.

The Druids believed that the spirits of persons who had died the previous year walked the earth on this night. They lighted bonfires to frighten away the evil spirits. It is thought that the candle in a pumpkin is a descendent of this custom. One legend has it that a rogue named Jack was caught playing tricks on the devil. As punishment, Jack was doomed to walk the earth forever, carrying a pumpkin lantern to light his way.

To ward off evil spirits and also to imitate them and so frighten others, many persons took to wearing costumes and masks. This led to playing tricks, mixing fun with fear and superstition.

In Rome the festivities were mainly in the form of feasts honoring the Goddess of Fruits, Pomona. When the Romans invaded Britain, they took their customs with them. The traditional use of fruits and vegetables (apples, corn, nuts) may be derived from this intermingling of celebrations.

During the Middle Ages the Christians observed All Saints' Day, which fell on November first. The eve of that day was October thirty-first, which became known as Halloween, or hallowed evening. There is little, if any, Christian significance left in the United States; for most people it is a secular celebration, retaining only the outward trappings of ancient customs and rituals. Witches, ghosts, goblins, cats, bats, and pumpkins come to mind when we hear the word *Halloween*.

Because so much information is available and much of it is not generally known, Halloween is a good choice for a program that can be researched, improvised, written, and, if desired, performed for the enjoyment of others. Several tasks would be involved:

1. Looking up information about Halloween (the amount dependent on the age of the group and the time that can be devoted to research)
2. Improvising legendary material with the greatest appeal for the children
3. Developing a program or play by the group based on the information found
4. Writing a script that has come out of the research and improvisation (optional)

Should this prove to be something the children want to perform for others, it will lead naturally into the next stage: a play for an audience. What we are concerned with here, however, is an understanding of dramatic structure, obtained through the process of creating an original play or group project. Later, if the group desires, it might try creating a myth of its own. Children enjoy thinking of ways to explain phenomena, sayings, or characters for which they have no ready answers. Because an activity of this sort involves creative writing as well as creative playing, it is a way in which drama can be integrated naturally into the curriculum. Younger children might want to find their own explanations for characters and customs such as the man in the moon, Groundhog Day, Jack Frost, candles on a birthday cake, or perhaps local jokes and customs. Older children find intellectual stimulation in the research and dramatization of myths and legends. The study of dramatic structure, through the creation of an original plot, is a sound and rewarding experience.

Class Projects

Sometimes a class interest will evolve into a project that can be dramatized. This can happen on any level, from preschool through high school.

Threads

Ann V. Klotz

An unusual theme was developed by older girls through an interest in women living in America a hundred years ago. Although the following account describes the work of a high school class, the subject could easily be pursued on the junior high school level. I learned of the project from the drama teacher, who helped her students develop the project. They went through the following steps: a study of the role of American women in the nineteenth century, including their occupations, arts and crafts, family life, and community service. Next the students did improvisations based on the study. This was followed by playwriting using the dramatic elements of the material and, finally, a performance of the play for the rest of the school and their families. The project was an entire semester's work, which was made possible by the enthusiasm of the students and the skilled leadership of the teacher.

"The Making of Threads,*" a full and detailed report of the project, is too long to include, but excerpts from it give a picture of the steps taken in creating and producing a play from a theme that captured the imagination of the students and teacher. What follows is taken directly from the writer's own words.[2]*

In the fall of 1986, a colleague lent me a lovely book entitled *Anonymous Was a Woman*, a collection of words and photographs about women and the works of art they regularly and anonymously created as part of their daily lives. The book was filled with journal entries and diaries of extraordinary women, and as I sat reading parts of it to my American literature class, I was struck by how dramatic this material was. Several months later, I approached the members of the Drama Club with the suggestion that we create a script of our own. The idea was not greeted with enthusiasm. Some complained that they wanted to do a *real* play, that they could *not* write their own script, and that they didn't want to, anyhow. I had envisioned enthusiasm

---

[2]Ann Klotz's report on "The Making of *Threads*" by her students at the Chapin School, New York City.

and inspiration, yet, against my better judgment, I set about trying to convince them that they *could* write a play, that other students had done it, that it would be a great experience. . . . They were unconvinced, but a few, probably to humor me, agreed to meet several times to brainstorm with me about subject possibilities. . . .

In our first session, I suggested they list all the topics about women that they could think of, no matter how bizarre. They listed topics which included everything from the lives of Greek goddesses to a show about women in different professions. Ironically, they also mentioned wanting to explore several generations in a family and/or looking at a day in the life of a village—topics which we ended up including in *Threads.* Throughout these early conversations (and indeed, throughout the entire process) I had to fight my own instinct to impose my ideas upon them or to force them into directions I wished them to take; yet, at the same time, I had to provide enough guidance so that they did not feel abandoned and completely overwhelmed. Finally, I suggested that we narrow our focus to American women for the purposes of ease in researching material. When I had shared *Anonymous Was a Woman* with them, some liked it, but what I sometimes think really convinced them that the lives of rural women could be interesting was their realization that this kind of production would allow them to wear long dresses on the stage!

They shared my desire to focus not on the few famous women whose personalities and accomplishments have been preserved, but rather to explore the lives and feelings of the average women who lived and worked in the nineteenth century. Although my students are all city girls, they were interested in looking at rural women—perhaps because their lives are so different, or so they thought at first. We titled the production *Threads* since we were planning to explore the feelings that the women had about their handiwork and because we were interested in looking at the ways in which lives entwined and connected.

In June the girls left for the summer, full of plans for research and interviews with ancient family members, eccentric relatives, and friends. Several of the girls planned to visit the historical societies and libraries in their summer communities. I spent one sweltering morning in the library in Muncy, Pennsylvania, where the library staff and the Historical Society gave me full run of the Pennsylvania Room, a collection of documents and articles about the area in which I spend my summers. I discovered no crumbling love letters or journals. I began to realize that one of the difficulties in documenting the lives of rural women of the nineteenth century was that most of them were too busy to spend time writing down how they felt. And the materials available in print tended to be too impersonal for our purposes. . . .

Later in the summer, I drove to the Laporte Historical Society. One of the members of the society accompanied me through the crowded little building. Crammed full of clothing, farm implements, scrapbooks, and family histories, the collection was fascinating. In seeing real objects that had been used, I had caught a glimpse of the women we were looking for. . . .

In September we returned to New York and our playwriting group reassembled to share information. Our February production dates seemed unreal and far off to them. I, however, was feeling more than a little nervous about how little time we had to write, cast, and rehearse a play. Once again, I encouraged them to explore more primary sources now published about women. The idea of having to do formal research was another hurdle. "Research," they exclaimed. "This is worse than history class!" Many wanted to set about creating characters out of their heads, but I suggested that they browse through some of the books our own library had to offer. Again, I wanted them to understand the value of research that was needed to enrich their work. Our school librarian was wonderful and increased the collection of appropriate materials. Some writers went to the library and copied down bibliographical information and potential quotations. Others were caught up in the process of researching trivia. One heard from her American history teacher that nineteenth-century women did not wear underclothes and she immediately came to report the news to the Drama Club. English and history teachers commented on the drama girls' fascination with the life of the nineteenth-century woman. I was pleased that they were learning because they wanted to find out information in order to bring specific characters to life.

Our writing committee had several conversations about how to begin, how to create characters. The script was slow going. . . .

As a metaphor for the production, I suggested that we create a quilt to hang at the back of the stage. I felt that making a quilt of their own would help the girls to understand the type of creative work the women they were writing about found so important. I also thought that the group effort would be another way to reinforce the ensemble spirit which is important to create with a cast. I had never made a quilt myself and neither had any of the girls, but the club president and I examined several books on quilting and decided to go ahead with it. Each member was to design a 12" by 12" square and we would put them all together. It sounded simple! The girls were later awed when they learned that the sewing skills of a nineteenth-century five-year-old far exceeded their own humble abilities.

As our writing sessions continued, we decided to name the protagonist Grace. Naming her helped clarify her character. . . .

[What followed was a detailed description of the elements that the group selected to include in the script. The plot was interspersed with poems, music, narration, and a collage based on a woman's day.]

Gradually Grace's story took shape as we gathered more and more material. One student came across family letters from the Civil War and another brought into school the cameo her great-grandmother had worn across the Oregon trail. . . .

Early in January, our costume designer came to work on costumes. We were lucky to have a number of simple calico dresses, but because there were twenty-two in the cast, we also had to build and restore many others. Every girl in the club helped with costumes or the quilt. One became our expert ironer; others learned to gather waistbands and pin on trim. The girls ransacked their homes for shawls and aprons. Once we saw the costumes, the whole play began to seem real. We were becoming experts at the very crafts we had been reading about.

During four long Saturday rehearsals we did a combination of acting and tech work. Our set was simple—the frame of a house against the upstage wall and a number of platforms to provide levels and discrete playing areas. . . .

We decided to include several poems and the words to an old folk song about a quilting bee. I had a friend compose music for this and we used it at the end of the first act. At different points in the show, I had several girls enter and speak about the same topics: girlhood, courtship, motherhood, etc. These served as transitions or bridges. Speaking the lines about having a baby, or getting engaged, or going West, the girls noticed that perhaps their 1980s lives were not so very different from those of the young women they were acting after all—at least the feelings were the same across one hundred years. . . .

Until the dress rehearsal I had worried that although the show had taught the girls a great deal, it might be painful to watch. I was not confident that we had had enough rehearsal time, that the understudies could pull off their roles, that the other girls had the confidence to carry on no matter what happened. There were moments in the show I was still dissatisfied with, things I would have changed had the show not been created by the students. The director in me battled with the teacher in me. In short, I was not sure *Threads* would be good theatre. But magically, the opening came and the audience was spellbound.

Spring vacation came and went and we returned to school to talk about plans for next year. "How about Shakespeare?" I inquired at a Drama Club meeting. "Shakespeare," one eighth grader muttered indignantly, "you mean we're not going to write our own play?" Another member added, "What if it's not as good as *Threads?*" I laughed and reminded them about their initial misgivings about *Threads.* They looked offended; surely I had been mistaken—they always knew that *Threads* would be wonderful! I smiled back at them. We had learned a lot from one another.

The French Revolution fascinated the same students sometime later. They saw in it the dramatic possibilities for another playwriting experience when they discovered the "women's march" on Versailles and this became the focus and theme for a plot. Again, working on their research over the summer months (during which time several students actually traveled to Versailles with their families), they were ready and eager to begin. The issues were discussed, characters created, and scenes improvised from which came questions. Who were these women? Why were they motivated to march on the palace? How did they live? What was their status? What were their relationships to each other? What did they accomplish?

Further research led to the writing of a script and its subsequent production. Sticking to the facts was no impediment; the facts provided the structure for the issues, plot, and action. A coeducational high school would have handled the situation differently, but as students at a

Revolution! *A collaborative piece written and produced by students at the Chapin School, New York City. (Courtesy of Ann V. Klotz, director.)*

girls' school, the Chapin teenagers found the "women's march" a brilliant choice and an exciting adventure in learning.

Other Suggestions

The following list of topics includes a wide variety of sources that can be used for simple improvisations but can also be expanded into original plots or even well-developed plays like *Threads*. Many sources are worth time spent on research and may inspire players to work on them over a long period, eventually sharing them with an audience.

advertisements	tools
bridges	poetry
rivers	hands
cartoons	coins
photographs	the media
posters	food
sculpture	an artist
occupations	animal welfare
time	space
headlines in newspapers	sports
letters to the editor	transportation
"personal" advertisements	music
books (printing and publishing)	a disaster like the Tsunami flood

Some of the best projects come out of field trips. Field trips, because they have been planned for their content, suggest topics that can be noted by the teacher in follow-up discussions. A trip to a seaport or harbor, for instance, might arouse curiosity about old sailing ships, boats of all kinds, immigration and immigrants, marine life, and so on. Museums of natural history are obvious sources of information and should be explored for ideas on science and social studies. Art museums and special exhibitions can stimulate interest in individual artists, other periods, and foreign countries. Costume and jewelry exhibits as well as crafts and folk art appeal to young people. Trips to factories generate questions, pointing out possibilities for study that can lead into drama or documentaries. The latter, incidentally, are splendid sources for theatre-in-education (TIE) programs and can be developed by older children, often expressing a strong point of view.

A unique resource is the *Mysteries of Harris Burdick*,[3] a collection of photographs with captions and without a narrative to explain them. That part is left to the reader or, in this case, the actor. It is a work that so totally captures the imagination it results in different meanings for every individual. Unlike the use of pictures only, or captions the combination stimulates as it offers and then withdraws explanations.

---

[3]Chris Van Allsburg, *The Mysteries of Harris Burdick* (Boston: Houghton Mifflin Company, 1984).

Summary

Many beginning teachers tend to use stories exclusively as material for creative drama. Although good stories and folklore are excellent, there are hundreds of other sources available, and it is in that interest that this chapter was included. Creating plays from researched topics is difficult because the structure must be developed by the teacher and the class, but it is excellent practice in writing and can bring enormous satisfaction to the group that tries it. Yes, it is a risk, but a risk worth taking. If the first attempt is not successful, do not be discouraged; try again. The teacher and the class will learn much in the process.

Suggested Assignments

1. Take one of the topics listed in this chapter and outline a play that might be developed from it.
2. Suggest four or five other topics possible for dramatization and the grade levels for which they are appropriate.
3. Develop a lesson plan for Martin Luther King Day.

Journal Writing

1. What historical characters have you seen portrayed on the stage or screen? Did they seem true to the characters as you knew them?
2. A documentary is dramatized material on a particular subject. What documentaries do you remember from television or film? Did they hold your interest or not? Explain.
3. Has there ever been a girl or boy in your class who seemed lonely or friendless? Can you imagine why? Think of possible reasons and see if you can create a drama of his or her life.

Chapter 11

The Possibilities in Poetry

Poetry and song. And the Tide Shall Cover the Earth *by Norma Cole. (Courtesy of Amie Brockway,* The Open Eye: New Stagings. *Photograph by Adrienne Brockway.)*

Poetry teaches the enormous force of a few words.
—Ralph Waldo Emerson

Children like poetry. They are sensitive to the rhythm of it and enjoy the repetition of sounds, words, and phrases. The direct approach of the poet is not unlike their own; hence, poetry, unless it has been spoiled for them, has a special appeal. The music and language, as well as the ideas, feelings, and images of poetry, reach the younger child particularly, capturing and stimulating his or her imagination. For this reason, poetry can be used in creative drama, often with highly successful results.

Many leaders find poetry a more satisfactory springboard than prose for introducing creative playing to a group. This is probably an individual matter, depending as much on the leader as on the participants. If the teacher enjoys poetry, he or she will find that it provides a rich source of material that can be used at all levels of experience and with all ages. For children, poetry and play go together naturally. "The affinity between poetry and play is not external only; it is also apparent in the structure of creative imagination itself. In the turning of a poetic phrase, the development of a motif, the expression of a mood, there is always a play element at work."[1]

For these reasons, the possibilities in poetry as motivation are considered. What kinds of poems are usable? How can poetry and movement be combined? Has choral speaking any place in creative dramatics? For the answers to these questions, we have only to go to the children themselves as they engage in their play. Many of their games are accompanied by chants, which are a form of choral speaking. In action games, rhythm is basic, whereas some games are played to verse with the players often making up their own original stanzas. If we listen, we note the enjoyment of repetition, refrain, and the sounds of words. Only very much later does poetry become a literary form to be taken seriously, and when it does, the element of play is, unfortunately, too often lost.

Choral Speaking

Because poetry lends itself so well to group enjoyment, let us begin with a consideration of choral speaking, its purposes, and its procedures. Choral reading, or speaking, is simply reading or reciting in unison under the direction of a leader. It is not a new technique; people have engaged in it for centuries. It antedated the theatre in the presentation of ideas and became an important element of the Greek drama. Evidence of choral speaking has been found in the religious ceremonies and festivals of early peoples, and today it is still used for ritualistic purposes in church services and on patriotic occasions. In the early twentieth century, however, it was recognized as one of the most effective methods of teaching the language arts and of improving speech habits.

---

[1]Johan Huizinga, *Homo Ludens: A Study of the Play-Element in Culture* (Boston: Beacon Press, 1955), p. 14.

In the past, choral speaking was used as an important means of communication and communion; today, it is an art form as well and is employed in both ways by the theatre, the church, and the school. When working with older children or adults, the activity has two major purposes:

1. Learning (when the purpose is process and therefore participant centered)
2. Performance (when the purpose is program and therefore audience centered)

Often the former leads into the latter, but like creative drama, it does not necessarily follow that practice must result in performance. Practice has value of its own, whether or not the product is shared.

The Value of Choral Speaking

One of the values of choral speaking is that it can be used successfully regardless of space or class size. Although a group of twenty or so is more desirable than one of forty or fifty, the larger number need not be a deterrent.

Many teachers consider the greatest value of choral speaking the opportunity it provides for speech improvement. Pitch, volume, rate, and tone quality are important to the effective interpretation of material. The need for clear diction is apparent when a group is reading aloud, whereas the practicing of speech sounds alone is often a tedious and unrelated exercise. During discussion, even young children will make suggestions as to how a poem should be recited. Vocal expression and the clear enunciation of speech sounds are often acquired more easily and with greater motivation when the group works together on meaning.

A third value, and one shared with creative drama, is the opportunity it provides for social cooperation. Choral speaking is a group activity, and by its nature, it therefore directs each individual to a common goal. The child with the strident voice learns to soften his or her tone, whereas the shy child can work for more volume without feeling self-conscious. Even the child with a speech impediment can recite without embarrassment because he or she is not speaking alone and is therefore not conspicuous.

A fourth value of choral speaking is its suitability to any age level. It can be introduced in the kindergarten but is equally effective when used in high school or college classes. Not all material can be adapted to choral work, but much can be; the major criterion is that it be enjoyed by the readers themselves.

Procedures

There are many ways of beginning choral speaking, but with younger children it will probably spring from their own enjoyment of a poem and their obvious desire to say it aloud or to the accompaniment of action. With older children who have had no experience in group reading, the teacher will not only select the material with care but will give some thought in advance to its interpretation. Discussion of the meaning and of the various ways of reading the material so as to bring out the meaning give the pupils a part in planning the group reading. A second reading will reveal further meaning, as well as difficulties in phrasing and diction.

As the group becomes more experienced, students will offer suggestions about those lines that can be most effectively taken by the whole group, by part of the group, and by individual voices. Although a structured activity, choral speaking offers a real opportunity for creative thinking as each group works out its own presentation. The teacher leads, indicating when to start, and watches the phrasing, emphases, and pauses suggested by the readers. The time spent on a poem will vary, but it is more important to keep the enthusiasm alive than it is to work for perfection. With practice, the group will grow increasingly sensitive to the demands of different kinds of material, and their results will improve in proportion to their understanding and enjoyment.

Most authorities on choral speaking suggest dividing the group into "light" and "dark" voices. This is not the same as a division into high and low or soprano and alto voices but has to do with quality and resonance as well as pitch. Some leaders, however, believe that a division in which there are both light and dark in each group makes for more interesting quality. However it is done, some division is necessary for any group of more than ten participants. Some poems can be read by three groups if the class is very large. These groups may include middle voices, but again, it is the material that will suggest the groupings rather than an arbitrary division.

WAYS OF READING

Unison: The whole group reads together. Although the simplest in one sense, this is the most difficult, since using all voices limits variation. Some poems, particularly short ones, are most effective when read or spoken by the entire class.

Antiphonal: This is a division into two groups with each taking certain parts. Many poems are more effective when read in this way. The poem will dictate the way it should be read.

Cumulative: When this technique is used, it is for the purpose of building toward a climax or certain high points in the poem. As the term suggests, it involves the accumulation of voices, either individually or by groups.

Solo: Often lines or stanzas call for individual reading. This can be an effective technique, as well as a way of giving an opportunity for individual participation.

Line-around: This is solo work in which each line is taken by a different reader. Children enjoy this and are alert to the lines they have been assigned.

Ad lib: This is where the group members use their own words but all have the same emotion.

As the group progresses and attempts longer and more difficult material, children may suggest using several or all of these techniques in one poem. The results can be remarkably effective, encouraging attentiveness and self-discipline as well as imaginative planning. Occasionally, sound effects can be added. Music, bells, drums, and vocal sounds, produced by the readers themselves, provide an opportunity for further inventiveness. Teachers who have never tried choral reading with a class often ask how to divide the lines of a poem among the readers to make the best sense and to give all the students a chance to read. As an example, let's take two well-known verses: "Simple Simon" and "The Queen of Hearts."

Simple Simon

Light Voices	Simple Simon met a Pieman,
	Going to the fair;
Dark Voices	Says Simple Simon to the Pieman,
Solo	Let me taste your ware.
Light Voices	Says the Pieman to Simple Simon,
Solo	Show me first your penny;
Light Voices	Says Simple Simon to the Pieman,
Solo	Indeed, I have not any.
Dark Voices	Simple Simon went a-fishing,
	For to catch a whale;
Light Voices	All the water he had got
	Was in his mother's pail.
Dark Voices	Simple Simon went to look
	If plums grew on a thistle;
Light Voices	He pricked his finger very much,
	Which made poor Simon whistle.

(Whistle at end)

The Queen of Hearts

Light Voices	The Queen of Hearts		**Dark Voices**	The King of Hearts
	She made some tarts,			Called for the tarts,
	All on a summer's day;			And beat the Knave full sore;
Solo	The Knave of Hearts		**Light Voices**	The Knave of Hearts
	He stole the tarts,			Brought back the tarts,
	And took them clean away.			And vowed he'd steal no more.

There is really no right or wrong way of distributing the lines. Some obviously belong to a solo voice, and others require a lighter or stronger touch. Have the class try different ways before making a final decision. A major objective is to give everyone a chance to read, and the students like to be in on the decision making.

Because our primary concern is creative drama, only those poems that suggest movement or pantomime are included here. The following poems have been used successfully with groups, combining choral speaking and activities suggested by the content or sounds. The first, "Happy New Year," is an old rhyme, suggesting the simplest kind of movement as a beginning.

HAPPY NEW YEAR

Happy New Year! Happy New Year!
I've come to wish you a Happy New Year.
I've got a little pocket and it is very thin.
Please give me a penny to put some money in.
If you haven't got a penny, a halfpenny will do.
If you haven't got a halfpenny, well—
God bless you!

In England, children went caroling from house to house on New Year's Day. Their neighbors gave them money, much as we give candy and apples for trick-or-treat on Halloween. Whether or not they received a contribution, the children sang or spoke, and this old rhyme has been handed down. The group can say the verse together, with one child acting the part of the caroler, or half of the group can speak, with the other half playing the carolers. Perhaps the entire group will want to speak and move. There are various possibilities in even as short a rhyme as this. Adding pantomime can enhance it.

A very simple verse, but one that offers an unusual opportunity for imaginative movement, is "Jump or Jiggle." Not only children but adult students as well get into the spirit of it and have a good time thinking of movements that characterize the animals mentioned.

JUMP OR JIGGLE
Evelyn Beyer

Frogs jump.
Caterpillars hump.
Worms wiggle.
Bugs jiggle.
Rabbits hop.
Horses clop.
Snakes slide.
Seagulls glide.
Mice creep.
Deer leap.
Puppies bounce.
Kittens pounce.
Lions stalk—
But
I walk.

The next verse suggests the use of sound effects rather than action. Part of the group might say the first and third lines, with the others taking the second and fourth. Or, if two clocks are suggested, a solo voice might take the first and third, with the total group taking the other lines. Even so simple a poem as this provides some opportunity for inventiveness.

THE CLOCK

Slowly ticks the big clock:
    Tick-tock; tick-tock!
But cuckoo clock ticks a double quick:
    Tick-a-tock-a, tick-a-tock-a,
    Tick-a-tock-a, tick!

The next poem is fun for children of all ages because of the action, which requires some coordination. As with the others, half of the group can read it while the other half acts the merry-go-round, or, if the group is small, everyone can do the action while repeating the lines. It is probably more satisfactory handled the first way, with variety achieved by having individual voices take the lines beginning with "I." Sometimes children like to imagine the merry-go-round running down until it comes to a stop.

MERRY-GO-ROUND
Dorothy Baruch

I climbed up on the merry-go-round,
And it went round and round.
I climbed up on a big brown horse,
And it went up and down.
Around and round and up and down.
Around and round and up and down.
I sat high up on a big brown horse,
And rode around on the merry-go-round,
And rode around on the merry-go-round.
I rode around on the merry-go-round
Around
And around
And
Round.

Echoes are fascinating, and the following poem is one that may prompt a group to make up an original story about echoes. It lends itself so well to choral reading that the class should try it this way first and then discuss whether something else might be done with it. The lines in which Echo speaks are good solo lines that stimulate speculation as to who Echo is, what Echo is like, where Echo is hiding, and whether or not Echo is ever discovered. Some groups have made up delightful stories about Echo after reading the poem together first.

ECHO
Author Unknown

I sometimes wonder where he lives,
This Echo that I never see.
I heard his voice now in the hedge,
Then down behind the willow tree.
And when I call, "Oh, please come out,"
"Come out," he always quick replies.
"Hello, hello," again I say;
"Hello, hello," he softly cries.
He must be jolly, Echo must,
For when I laugh, "Ho, ho, ho, ho,"
He answers me with "Ho, ho, ho."
I think perhaps he'd like to play;
I know some splendid things to do.
He must be lonely hiding there;
I wouldn't like it. Now, would you?

A popular poet with children is Shel Silverstein. Both of the following poems simply demand movement, which classes of any age enjoy creating. Most children respond to poetry by contemporary writers, and Shel Silverstein's work lends itself particularly well to dramatic interpretation. "Danny O'Dare" could be dramatized with half the class reciting the verse while the other half plays the bears. When there is only one character like this, I strongly suggest that many children play the part at one time, thus giving everyone an opportunity rather than featuring one child.

DANNY O'DARE
Shel Silverstein

Danny O'Dare, the dancin' bear
Ran away from the County Fair,
Ran right up to my back stair
And thought he'd do some dancin' there.
He started jumpin' and skippin' and kickin',
He did a dance called the Funky Chicken,
He did the Polka, he did the Twist,
He bent himself into a pretzel like this.
He did the Dog and the Jitterbug,
He did the Jerk and the Bunny Hug.
He did the Waltz and the Boogaloo,
He did the Hokey-Pokey too.
He did the Bop and the Mashed Potata,
He did the Split and the See Ya Later.
And now he's down upon one knee,

Bowin' oh so charmingly,
And winkin' and smilin'—it's easy to see
Danny O'Dare wants to dance with me.

Everyone will want to dramatize "Yuck," so it could be played by the entire class while the teacher reads it aloud.

YUCK
Shel Silverstein

I stepped in something yucky
As I walked by the crick.
I grabbed a stick to scrape it off,
the yuck stuck to my stick.
I tried to pull it off the stick,
The yuck stuck to my hand.
I tried to wash it off—but it
Stuck to the washin' pan.
I called my dog to pull me loose,
The yuck stuck to his fur.
He rubbed himself against the cat,
The yuck got stuck to her.
My friends and neighbors came to help—
Now all of us are stuck,
Which goes to show what happens
When one person steps in yuck.

Although choral speaking is an effective way to begin pantomime, it is not the only way of using poetry. Often a poem can be introduced by the leader either before or after improvisation. The poem may serve as a springboard to action in which the whole class participates, but the improvising group does not necessarily repeat or read the verse. One short poem that has proved highly successful with many groups of all ages is "Hallowe'en."

HALLOWE'EN
Geraldine Brain Siks

Sh! Hst!
Hsst! Shssssh!
It's Hallowe'en.
Eerie creatures now are seen.
Black, bent witches fly
Like ugly shadows through the sky.
White, stiff ghosts do float
Silently, like mystery smoke.

Lighted pumpkins glow
With crooked eyes and grins to show

It's Hallowe'en
Hssst! Shssh!
Sh! Hst!

The period might start off with a discussion of what we think of when we hear the word *Halloween*. Most groups suggest pumpkins, witches, orange and black, elves, broomsticks, cats, night, ghosts, trick-or-treat, and masks. Some pantomime to music can be introduced here, with the whole class becoming witches, cats, or ghosts. After the children are thoroughly in the spirit of Halloween, the poem can be read. When the group is small, all may be eerie creatures, witches, and ghosts. When the group is large, it can be divided into several parts, with each one choosing one idea to pantomime. Pumpkins have been suggested in a variety of ways: rolling about on the floor in rounded shapes, squatting with big smiles, and moving in circles to music. Music is helpful, though not necessary. This poem never fails to arouse a response, and on one occasion it led to an informal program of Halloween poems and improvisations.

The next poem is one that has been most successful with both children and adults. The universality of its theme appeals to everyone and stimulates an imaginative response at any time of the year. It was the basis for a delightful improvisation by a group of Puerto Rican teachers, who understood and enjoyed it in English, then improvised it in Spanish with games they played in their country.

SING A SONG OF SEASONS
Alice Ellison

It's spring.
Such a hippity, happity, hoppity
First spring day.
Let's play! Let's play! Let's play!
It's summer!
Such a swingy, swazy, lazy
First hot day.
Let's play! Let's play! Let's play!
It's fall!
Such a brisky, frisky, crispy
First fall day.
Let's play! Let's play! Let's play!
It's winter!
Such a blowy, snowy joy
First winter day.
Let's play! Let's play! Let's play!

Before reading the poem, there can be pantomimes of simple sports and games. Flying kites, skating, tossing a ball, jumping rope, and playing tennis are familiar activities that serve to get the group moving and break down the barriers of self-consciousness.

After perhaps fifteen minutes of this kind of activity, the teacher is ready to read the poem. Discussion about games and sports appropriate to each season directs the thinking and often brings some unexpected suggestions. After everyone has had a chance to offer ideas, the teacher can ask how the poem might be played.

If the class is separated into four groups, each group can take a season, showing various games and sports belonging to it. Some groups create situations for each, such as going to the beach in summer, with sunbathing, swimming, picnicking, and the like. More than one group has created a scene with characters for each season, using the poem only as a springboard for an original situation. It is urged that this be done in the round, rather than on a stage or in the front of a room, to allow for as much movement as possible and easy passage into the center without breaking the mood.

IMAGININGS
J. Paget-Fredericks

Imagine!
A little red door that leads under a hill
Beneath roots and bright stones and pebbly rill.
Imagine!
A quaint little knocker and shoe scraper, too—
A curious carved key
Is waiting for you.
Imagine!
Tiptoe on doormat, you're turning the key.
The red door would open
And there you'd be.

Imagine!
Shut the door tightly, so no one could see.
And no one would know then
Where you would be.
Imagine, if you can.

A poem such as "Imaginings" lends itself to all kinds of improvisation. Every age will find an answer to the question "What lies behind the little red door?" It is a good idea for the teacher to read the poem aloud two or three times before asking what the group sees in it. If the class is not too large, every child can be given a chance to describe what he or she sees. Younger children find buried treasure, a forbidden city, thieves, a ghost town. Some may describe a place they know, with friends or neighbors inhabiting it. This particular poem is a wonderful springboard for the imagination, since it leads listeners to the threshold and then leaves them free to follow their own ideas.

Some groups have been stimulated to plan an original play involving several characters. If many good suggestions come out of the discussion, the leader may want to break the class into small groups of three or four, who will in turn dramatize their ideas. Occasionally, if a group is very small, or if the teacher wants to plan an individual lesson, each child may pantomime what he or she sees and does behind the red door.

The poem can hold a group for two or three sessions, depending on their readiness to use the material and the interest it stimulates.

SEA SHELL
Amy Lowell

Sea Shell, Sea Shell,
   Sing me a song, O please
A song of ships, and sailor men,
      And parrots, and tropical trees.
Of islands lost in the Spanish Main
Which no man may find again,
Of fishes and coral under the waves,
And sea-horses stabled in great green caves.
Sea Shell, Sea Shell,
      Sing of the things you know so well.

Although "Sea Shell" offers vivid imagery, it leaves the imagination free to roam tropical isles and savor adventure. Every child responds to the singing of a shell, and most will go on to ideas of their own. Perhaps asking the children to tell their own stories is a good beginning: What did you hear? Where did you find the shell? What is it like? What did it sing when you listened? Tell us its story.

Having a collection of shells adds to the interest as the children feel and examine them. Elaborate plays set on unknown shores have resulted, with the children responding to the thoughts of sailors, pirates, and treasures buried in the sand.

The poems of Robert Louis Stevenson have long appealed to children, and both their content and the suggestions for action make them especially appropriate for creative drama. The two poems that follow can be used with quite young children, who may already be familiar with them.

MY SHADOW
Robert Louis Stevenson

I have a little shadow that goes in and out with me.
And what can be the use of him is more than I can see.
He is very like me from the heels up to the head;
And I see him jump before me, when I jump into my bed.

The funniest thing about him is the way he likes to grow—
Not at all like proper children, which is always very slow;
For he sometimes shoots up taller like an India-rubber ball;
And he sometimes gets so little that there's none of him at all.

He hasn't got a notion of how children ought to play,
And can only make a fool of me in every sort of way.
He stays so close beside me, he's a coward, you can see;
I'd think it shame to stick to nursie as that shadow sticks to me!

One morning, very early, before the sun was up,
I rose and found the shining dew on every buttercup;
But my lazy little shadow, like an arrant sleepy-head,
Had stayed at home behind me and was fast asleep in bed.

The idea of a shadow offers all kinds of possibilities. The group might try this one all together—half being children, half shadows. This could also lead into original stories, with use of shadows as a theme. It could also stimulate the writing of original verse.

THE WIND
Robert Louis Stevenson

I saw you toss the kites on high
And blow the birds about the Sky;
And all around I heard you pass,
Like ladies' skirts across the grass—
    O wind a-blowing all day long,
    O wind, that sings so loud a song.
I saw the different things you did,
But always you yourself you hid.
I felt you push, I heard you call,
I could not see yourself at all—
    O wind a-blowing all day long,
    O wind, that sings so loud a song.
    O you that are so strong and cold,
    O blower, are you young or old?
Are you a beast of field and tree
    Or just a stranger child than me?
    O wind a-blowing all day long,
    O wind, that sings so loud a song.

Like the preceding verse, "The Wind" offers a wonderful opportunity for strong movement. The group can divide up in many ways, being everything that is mentioned: the wind, the birds, the kites, the skirts, and other things the children may suggest. Wind is a good topic for discussion, often suggesting original stories as well as the search for other stories, such as Aesop's fable "The Sun and the Wind." A whole unit could be developed on the subject of wind or on the natural elements.

The following is an amusing verse which younger children will enjoy saying and whistling. "Whistle" is so short that after two or three readings it will probably be memorized, and everyone can try it individually. Much poetry is serious and lyrical; it is fun to work on a humorous verse that deals with a familiar situation.

WHISTLE
Author Unknown

I want to learn to whistle,
I've always wanted to;

I fix my mouth to do it, but
The whistle won't come through.
I think perhaps its stuck and so . . .
I try it once again;
Can people swallow whistles?
Where is my whistle then?

Langston Hughes's poetry is rich in images and rhythms. This particular short work suggests strong movement, which older children enjoy using to create the different rivers.

THE NEGRO SPEAKS OF RIVERS
Langston Hughes

I've known rivers:
I've known rivers ancient as the world and older than the flow of human blood in
    human veins.

My soul has grown deep like the rivers.

I bathed in the Euphrates when dawns were young.
I built my hut near the Congo and it lulled me to sleep.
I looked upon the Nile and raised the pyramids above it.
I heard the singing of the Mississippi when Abe Lincoln went down to New
    Orleans, and I've seen its muddy bosom turn all golden in the sunset.

I've known rivers:
Ancient, dusky rivers.

My soul has grown deep like the rivers.

After some discussion of the places and the different kinds of rivers described in the poem, the children will be ready to use it as a springboard. Strong movement and use of the whole body are called for; perhaps large groups, moving together, can suggest the vast bodies of water better than one or two persons. What else is there to depict besides the waters? Are there any people? Does anything happen? What does the last line mean? How can this be expressed?

The next selection, "A Sioux Indian Prayer," suggests movement or mime. It can be said in unison by part of the class with the rest of the class expressing it in dance, or spoken by one with the class moving, or spoken by the entire group with one child dancing. It is a lovely piece, and students are very responsive to it. The words and the meaning behind them appeal to both younger and older children. Discussion can be expected because of the cultural context and the beauty of the form.

A SIOUX INDIAN PRAYER

O GREAT SPIRIT, Whose voice I hear in the winds, and whose breath gives life
    to all the world, hear me! I am small and weak, I need your strength and
    wisdom.

LET ME WALK IN BEAUTY, and make my eyes ever behold the red and purple
    sunset.

MAKE MY HANDS respect the things you have made and my ears sharp to hear
    your voice.

MAKE ME WISE so that I may understand the things you have taught my
    people.

LET ME LEARN the lessons you have hidden in every leaf and rock.

I SEEK STRENGTH, not to be greater than my brother, but to fight my greatest
    enemy—myself.

MAKE ME ALWAYS READY to come to you with clean hands and straight
    eyes.

SO WHEN LIFE FADES, as the fading sunset, my spirit may come to you without
    shame.

"The Blind Men and the Elephant" is a favorite on all levels and begs for pantomime. Like "A Sioux Indian Prayer," it can be handled in several ways. Not only is the humor fun, but the idea always causes discussion about how we make judgments.

THE BLIND MEN AND THE ELEPHANT
John G. Saxe

It was six men of Indostan
    To learning much inclined,
Who went to see the Elephant
    (Though all of them were blind),
That each by observation
    Might satisfy his mind.

The First approached the Elephant,
    And happening to fall
Against his broad and sturdy side,
    At once began to bawl:
"God bless me! but the Elephant
    is very like a wall!"

The Second, feeling of the tusk,
    Cried, "Ho! what have we here
So very round and smooth and sharp?
    To me 'tis mighty clear
This wonder of an Elephant
    is very like a spear!"

The Third approached the animal,
    And happening to take
The squirming trunk within his hands,
    Thus boldly up and spake:
"I see," quoth he, "the Elephant
    Is very like a snake!"

The Fourth reached out his eager hand,
    And felt about the knee.
"What most this wondrous beast is like
    Is mighty plain," quoth he;
"'Tis clear enough the Elephant
    Is very like a tree!"

The Fifth, who chanced to touch the ear,
    Said, "E'en the blindest man
Can tell what this resembles most;
    Deny the fact who can,
This marvel of an Elephant
    Is very like a fan!"

The Sixth no sooner had begun
    About the beast to grope,
Than, seizing on the swinging tail
    That fell within his scope,
"I see," quoth he, "the Elephant
    Is very like a rope."

And so these men of Indostan
    Disputed loud and long,
Each in his own opinion
    Exceeding stiff and strong.
Though each was partly in the right,
    And all were in the wrong!

Younger children enjoy acting out the story as it is being read. However it is handled, the idea provides opportunity for pantomime and food for thought.

The Creation was written by the great African American poet James Weldon Johnson. It can be read, acted, or danced. Most young people respond to its power and find in its strong, imaginative style a stimulus for expression of one or another of these dramatic forms. It should be read aloud first, then performed both in dance and in mime. Because of the numbers of creatures the poem includes, it is an ideal piece for a large group to work on.

THE CREATION
James Weldon Johnson

And God stepped out on space,
And he looked around and said:
I'm lonely—
I'll make me a world.

And as far as the eye of God could see
Darkness covered everything,

Blacker than a hundred midnights
Down in a cypress swamp.

Then God smiled,
And the light broke,
And the darkness rolled up on one side,
And the light stood shining on the other,
And God said: That's good!

Then God reached out and took the light in his hands,
And God rolled the light in his hands
Until he made the sun;
And he set that sun a-blazing in the heavens.
And the light that was left from making the sun
God gathered it up in a shining ball
And flung it against the darkness,
Spangling the night with the moon and stars.
Then down between
The darkness and the light
He hurled the world;
And God said: That's good!

Then God himself stepped down—
And the sun was on his right hand,
And the moon was on his left;
The stars were clustered about his head,
And the earth was under his feet.
And God walked, and where he trod
His footsteps hollowed the valleys out
And bulged the mountains up.

Then he stopped and saw
That the earth was hot and barren.
So God stepped over to the edge of the world
And he spat out the seven seas—
He batted his eyes, and the lightnings flashed—
He clapped his hands, and the thunders rolled—
And the waters above the earth came down,
The cooling waters came down.

Then the green grass sprouted,
And the little red flowers blossomed,
The pine tree pointed his finger to the sky,
And the oak spread out his arms,
The lakes cuddled down in the hollows of the ground,
And the rivers ran down to the sea;
And God smiled again,

And the rainbow appeared,
And curled itself around his shoulder.

Then God raised his arm and he waved his hand
Over the sea and over the land,
And he said: Bring forth! Bring forth!
And quicker than God could drop his hand,
Fishes and fowls
And beasts and birds
Swam the rivers and the seas,
Roamed the forests and the woods,
And split the air with their wings.
And God said: That's good!

Then God walked around,
And God looked around
On all that he had made.
He looked at his sun,
And he looked at his moon,
And he looked at his little stars;
He looked on his world
With all its living things,
And God said: I'm lonely still.

Then God sat down—
On the side of a hill where he could think;
By a deep, wide river he sat down;
With his head in his hands,
God thought and thought,
Till he thought: I'll make me a man!

Up from the bed of the river
God scooped the clay;
And by the bank of the river
He kneeled him down;
And there the great God Almighty
Who lit the sun and fixed it in the sky,
Who flung the stars to the most far corner of the night,
Who rounded the earth in the middle of his hand;
This great God,
Like a mammy bending over her baby,
Kneeled down in the dust
Toiling over a lump of clay
Till he shaped it in his own image;

Then into it he blew the breath of life,
And man became a living soul.
Amen. Amen.

The following work by the great Civil War poet Walt Whitman has strong imagery and power when read aloud.

I HEAR AMERICA SINGING
Walt Whitman

I hear America singing, the varied carols I hear,
Those of mechanics, each one singing his as it should be blithe and strong,
The carpenter singing his as he measures his plank or beam,
The mason singing his as he makes ready for work, or leaves off work,
The boatman singing what belongs to him in his boat, the deckhand singing on
    the steamboat deck,
The shoemaker singing as he sits on his bench, the hatter singing as he stands,
The wood-cutter's song, the ploughboy's on his way in the morning, or at noon
    intermission or at sundown,
The delicious singing of the mother, or of the young wife at work, or of the girl
    sewing or washing,
Each singing what belongs to him or her and to none else,
The day what belongs to the day—at night the party of young fellows, robust,
    friendly,
Singing with open mouths their strong melodious songs.

"I Hear America Singing" is a splendid poem for both choral speaking and dramatization. The various characters and their occupations suggest pantomime to participants of all ages. If playing in a large room, the characters can be scattered about the circle, with any number taking part. Pantomime and speaking may be done simultaneously or separately, as the group prefers. This is a poem that is particularly appealing to older students, who are often stimulated to further reading of the poet's work. The mood is powerful and usually acts as a unifying element.

Poetry and Dance

Poetry grew out of dance and song, and so they are natural companions. Bringing a dancer to the class—the dance teacher, perhaps older students who have had more dance experience than the class, or a professional dancer if one is available—adds another dimension when working with poems. For one thing, dance offers an abstract expression rather than the more literal interpretation of mime and improvisation. Dividing the class, with one half moving to the cadence and meaning of the poem and the other half speaking it, calls for imagination and cooperation. This approach is not suggested for older students only; younger children, though lacking well-developed performance skills, are often freer in interpreting poetry through movement.

Working on poetry first in mime and then in dance helps students to experience it more fully. Lyric verse lends itself best to nonverbal interpretation, whereas narrative and dramatic verse stimulate the improvisation of dialogue. Some groups respond to poetry more readily than others, but most will enjoy it if the leader's approach is positive and enthusiastic.

Working with poetry in creative drama can also be an incentive to the writing of poetry. A good way to start is to take a topic of current interest to the class and have each make up a line. The creating of a group poem is fun, and the results are often unexpected and sometimes remarkably sensitive and perceptive. Many classes will want to write poems of their own, often illustrating them. Because the poem is a short and direct form, it is particularly suitable for young writers, even those for whom English is a second language.

The poem that follows is particularly effective when interpreted in movement. It can be read aloud or written on a program to be read silently while the dancers express their reaction to the imagery. Working on the piece over a period of time brings greater depth and a more varied interpretation.

HEIGHT OF A SEASON
Anne Fessenden

The sound of leaves blowing
swaying limbs that toss
shadows on this ground
along the silver tarnished stone wall
on the mountain's south side;
dazzle of wave of wind
wandering down toward the house
by the rushing stream

Gathering of light and leaves
and limbs, sound and grass in one
round yellow day circling shatters.

The whole broad stretch of land
beyond this sun porch where I sit
is framed. Lights and shadows flicker
on the clapboard of the yellow house.

Blue intense of sky
above the maple leaves
yellow orange on branch and
carpeting the ground.
Wind bent limbs that swirl
And sweep them on.

The angled sun casts light
on this falling and rising
the whirling wind has caught.

The following poem offers many possibilities for interpretation, ranging from dance to mime. Given complete freedom students may enact it in their own ways. What does "woppa, woppa, woppa" mean? Is it action? Sound? Does it propel and describe the poet's vision? Does it suggest a story? Or is it a refrain? Experiment with different ideas.

WORKERS' SONG
Maya Angelou

Big ships shudder
down to the sea
because of me
railroads seen
on a twinners track
    'cause of my back
      woppa, woppa,
      woppa, woppa
Cars stretch to a
super length
    'cause of my strength
Planes fly high
over seas and lands
    'cause of my hands
      woppa, woppa,
      woppa, woppa
I wake
start the factory humming
I work late
Keep the whole world running
and I got something....something....
    coming....coming....
      woppa, woppa,
      woppa, woppa.

Summary

Poetry is an effective springboard for improvisation and improvisation for poetry. The directness of verse motivates the players to a response that is direct and imaginative. For this reason, poetry is a good starting point for the beginner, though it can be used at any time with even the most advanced players. Because the sounds of poetry have as great an appeal as the content and mood, poetry should be spoken as well as acted. Choral speaking is a group art and can therefore be combined with creative drama if the teacher so wishes. Some of the reasons for including choral speaking are as follows:

1. It can be done with groups of any size and age.
2. It emphasizes group rather than individual effort.
3. It provides an opportunity to introduce poetry.
4. It offers the shy child or the child with a speech impediment an opportunity to speak.
5. It promotes good habits of speech through enjoyable exercise rather than drill.

6. It is a satisfying activity in itself.
7. It can be combined successfully with rhythmic movement and pantomime.

Just as action songs are used with very young children as an approach to creative rhythms, so may poetry be used with older students to suggest mood, stimulate ideas, and begin the flow of creative energy. Chants and the repetition of words have a natural appeal. Thus poetry and nonsense verse may prove a successful method of introducing creative drama. Skill in movement, rhythms, and pantomime is increased as all children are given opportunities to participate.[2]

Suggested Assignments

1. Find several poems that you think would be effective in stimulating creative drama. Explain your selection.
2. Take a poem that you believe could be read or spoken chorally and try it out with the class.
3. Find a poem that stimulates dance or movement rather than drama.
4. Write a poem yourself and decide what else you might do with it.
5. Create a group poem. Each member of the class contributes a line on a theme suggested by the teacher: for example, "summer evening," "deserted play-ground," "the last day at camp," or "winter."

Journal Writing

1. If you enjoy poetry, try to think why you do. If you do not, can you explain why?
2. What does the word *poetic* suggest to you?
3. What are some of your favorite poems?
4. What poets come to mind with this chapter?
5. Can you remember chants or verses that you repeated as a child? What were they, and under what circumstances did you say them?

---

[2]Shel Silverstein, *Falling Up: Poems and Drawings* (New York: HarperCollins, 1996), pp. 31, 38, 51.

Chapter 12

Speech and Speech-
Related Activities

Working on speech through drama. Michele Valeri at Pilgrim Day Care, Washington, DC. (Wolf Trap Institute for Early Learning Through the Arts, photograph by Paula Jones, 1994.)

225

> Speak the speech I pray you, as I pronounce it to
> you, trippingly on the tongue ...
> —*William Shakespeare*

Most of us have difficulty with some sounds when learning a new language. For example, Asians have trouble with *l* and *r*. Some Europeans have problems with the *th* sound, Hispanics with the *j* sound; and many people in the United States, brought up in a local dialect, experience problems with certain vowel sounds. All who master these problems of pronunciation are to be applauded, but few succeed without help from the teacher.

Improved speech is a shared objective of modern educators and teachers of creative drama. Although this book is not primarily directed toward speech and the language arts but is focused instead on various aspects of dramatic techniques, the implications for improved speech habits are obvious. As the players, either children or adults, feel the desire to communicate orally with others, they will seek the words they want and will try to pronounce and articulate them clearly. This chapter suggests some activities that can be carried on in addition to improvisation and may act as an incentive for improving oral expression.

Speech depends on words. The more words we have at our command, the richer and more precise our communication. Children love words and enjoy learning new ones, given half a chance and some encouragement. Vocabulary building, moreover, is a never-ending process. Reading good literature is one of the finest ways of meeting new words, and the improvisation of dialogue offers an opportunity for putting them into practice. Different characters speak in different ways. A person's manner of speech distinguishes him or her as much as physical movements and behavior do. In assuming a role, the player learns as much as possible about the character he or she is playing: age, education, occupation, likes and dislikes, strengths, weaknesses, and other personal qualities. Knowledge of a character will help determine the words used as well as the way they are said.

The young or inexperienced player will not be able to delineate character at the outset but will slowly develop an awareness of the speech appropriate to a character and in time will be able to handle dialogue that conveys more than rudimentary information. Particularly effective in pointing out individual differences in speech and the possibilities of enriching them are the discussions held after the first and second playing. The leader may ask the player some questions about the character: would the character talk that way? use those words? use slang? suggest the occupation by the way he or she describes it? Then the leader may proceed to some general questions about characters: how would a father speak? a storekeeper? a general? a television newscaster? Would a child say the same thing in the same words and phrases? Children are quick to discern discrepancies. Moreover, they enjoy finding just the right words for a particular character and delight in using long words. Proof of this can be seen in the way very young children memorize repeated phrases and words from favorite stories: any deviation from the text on the part of a reader, in an effort at simplification, will bring an immediate correction from the listening child who knows and loves the original.

As to clarity and audibility, no activity points up the necessity of being heard and understood any better than taking part in a play. The teacher need not, indeed should not, stress such failings as indistinct or inaudible speech, but the other players will be aware of it. A far more effective way of telling a player that his or her voice is too soft is to raise questions such as these: Would an angry man sound like that? What kind of voice do you think a giant would have? How do we know that the boy is calling to someone from a distance? Too much attention to vocal projection and articulation frequently leads to an artificial manner of delivery, but attention to the reasons for a louder voice or clearer speech will accomplish the desired goals, though admittedly this approach takes longer. Observers are quick to comment when they cannot hear or understand a player. Peer criticism is far more than constant nagging by the teacher in improving a player's speech.

In recent years classroom teachers have made a conscious effort to improve the self-image of the speaker whose verbal skills are poor or for whom English is a second language. To accomplish this, voice and diction have been de-emphasized; in other words, what is said is considered of greater importance than how it is said. Other objectives—encouragement of the speaker and the building of pride in a cultural heritage—have been given priority. Although no one would quarrel with this approach as the first step in language improvement, it is to be hoped that once a degree of self-confidence has been achieved, the student will be helped to move on to better habits of speech. Clarity, audibility, and a constantly improving vocabulary are still our goals. For citizens in a democratic society, freedom of speech is of little value without the ability to express ourselves clearly and effectively. Today that ability affects almost every facet of life and most jobs. Therefore, the speech arts are more important than ever before, and it is condescending to demand anything less than the best of students in this area as well as in others. The teacher's acceptance of a patois or a sub-standard level of English does the speaker a disservice both now and later.

Most people—adults and children—enjoy nonsense verse. Probably the most familiar is Lewis Carroll's "Jabberwocky." Reading it with expression is a challenge to which most students respond readily. Who is to say what it means? The readers have carte blanche to do what they want with it. It may also prompt them to want to write non-sense verse of their own. Beyond that is the built-in necessity to articulate clearly. It is a perfect example of an exercise that is fun.

JABBERWOCKY
from *Through the Looking-Glass*

Lewis Carroll

'Twas brillig, and the slithy toves
Did gyre and gimble in the wabe:
All mimsy were the borogoves,
And the mome raths outgrabe.
"Beware the Jabberwock, my son!
The jaws that bite, the claws that catch!
Beware the Jubjub bird, and shun
The frumious Bandersnatch!"

He took the vorpal sword in hand:
Long time the manxome foe he sought—
So rested he by the Tumtum tree,
And stood awhile in thought.
And as in uffish thought he stood,
The Jabberwock, with eyes of flame,
Came whiffling through the tulgey wood,
And burbled as it came!
One, two! One, two! And through and through
The vorpal blade went snicker-snack!
He left it dead, and with its head
He went galumphing back.
"And hast thou slain the Jabberwock?
Come to my arms, my beamish boy!
O frabjous day! Callooh! Callay!"
He chortled in his joy.
'Twas brillig, and the slithy toves
Did gyre and gimble in the wabe:
All mimsy were the borogoves,
And the mome raths outgrabe.

Readers Theatre

Readers theatre, a relatively new concept in the speech arts, is particularly suitable for
older children and high school students. The simplicity of production and effectiveness of result make it singularly desirable in schools with inadequate stage facilities
and where rehearsal time is at a premium. More than that, it is a way of enjoying
good literature through guided study, a mutually agreed-upon interpretation, and
clear and expressive oral reading. *Readers theatre* can be defined as the oral presentation of drama, prose, or poetry by two or more readers, with characterization when
necessary, narration if desired, coordination of material to constitute a whole, and the
development of a special reader-audience relationship as an objective. Although traditionally a reader has handled a single role, recent performances have permitted one
person to read several parts. Readers theatre is neither lecture nor play; rather, it is a
staged program that allows the audience to create its own images through the skilled
performance of the readers.

The cast (whether large or small) usually remains onstage or in the designated
area throughout the performance, reading the various assigned portions. Generally,
readers use little movement, suggesting action instead with simple gestures and facial
expression. They must understand what the author has to say, the structure of the
piece, and the development of characters, and they must be able to interpret a variety
of roles in a matter of minutes, if called on to do so. I have seen many different types
of presentations in readers theatre, ranging from some actual movement onstage to
formal positions behind lecterns. Stools and steps are sometimes used to sit on, if an

Johnny Tremain *by Linda Blase. (Courtesy of Robin Flatt, Director of Dallas Children's Theatre.)*

effect of informality is desired or if the leader wishes to have the performers seated when they are not reading. Sometimes readers turn their backs to the audience to indicate their absence from a particular scene. The material, as well as the group's experience and preference, will determine how much or how little movement to include. In general, however, movement is minimal.

A few years ago a group of Broadway actors established a readers theatre called TACT (The Actors Theatre Company), whose mission was to find and present fine old plays that were not likely to be revived. Established as a series of five plays a season with three performances of each, TACT has been very successful in attracting large audiences with only the spoken word, eschewing scenery, costumes, and props. With a focus on speech rather than production, the TACT format is ideal for high school actors.

A good deal of readers theatre has been done by adults for adult audiences (e.g., *John Brown's Body, Don Juan in Hell, Spoon River*). The Periwinkle Players of Monticello, New York, have for years been presenting highly effective programs in the genre for elementary school children. This company uses simple costumes to suggest character or period and uses lighting effects to enrich the performance. With several programs in their repertoire, the Periwinkle Players have proved that poetry—as well as drama and prose—has a strong appeal for children. An awakening interest in words and writing was found to be an additional positive result. Although these players are adult professional actors doing a professional job, their kind of program, on a simplified scale, could be presented by children.

One particularly effective program was performed by high school students who selected and arranged a script using a group of the world's great love poems to celebrate Valentine's Day. In this instance, a narrator introduced each section of the program, giving some background material. A different but equally successful program for children was arranged by college students on the subject of the American West. Prose and poetry that told about the settlers and the frontier were combined with appropriate background music played on the guitar. When transitions were needed, folk songs were introduced. A chronological progression built interest, with the music adding a unifying colorful element. Children doing readers theatre can select material they like and then decide as a group, just as these groups did, the questions of arrangement and sequence. Choral reading is often incorporated if group speech is considered more effective than solo reading for some selections.

Other kinds of literature can be used effectively: history, biography, letters, and various documentary materials. More than one program celebrating the bicentennial of American independence featured American history and American essays. Black history has been the focus of other programs, and topics of current social and political interest can also offer powerful and dramatic content. These materials require much more arranging and editing than do drama and short stories, but they also bring a new dimension to material that is not usually read aloud. This brings up the point that selections from separate works can be combined: it is not required that only one text be used.

In 1973 the Institute for Readers Theatre was established in California. Among its services are a Readers Theatre Script Service, an international workshop held each summer in a different locale, and short workshops in the United States and Canada for various organizations such as the Foreign Language Association, the International Reading Association, the Speech Association, and theatre conferences. An impressive list of guest artists, both British and American, and an advisory board composed primarily of educators show the seriousness of the project. According to its brochure, the institute was founded to encourage academic interest in group performances of literature. Its phenomenal growth proves the interest in this approach to art and education.

The Musicians of Bremen is an example of one way readers theatre was used by older students for children. If children do it, they should act the story creatively first and then read it aloud from the script, eliminating stage movement and business. Any story can be treated in this manner. Myths and legends, which often depend on the supernatural, can be handled with ease, whereas difficulties are encountered when they are dramatized in the usual way. Appropriate music may be added, if desired, to suggest the passage of time, the movement from one scene to another, or changes of mood. Music is not necessary to this story or to readers theatre in general, but it often makes the presentation more effective, just as background music and sound effects lend color and setting to a radio play.

Costumes can be used, but they need not, and indeed probably should not, be complete or literal. The same thing is true of settings, which, if merely suggested, make demands on the audience that lead to a clearer and more accurate understanding than any attempt to duplicate a place or scene. Platforms, stools, chairs, ladders, and benches do not connote particular places; this has been one reason for their popularity. Although material may be memorized, books or manuscripts are generally used to let the audience know at once that it is going to share literature, not see a play.

The Musicians of Bremen
A Dramatization for Readers Theatre
Nellie McCaslin

CHARACTERS:
> Narrator
> Cat
> Donkey
> Cock
> Dog
> Robber

The six readers may stand throughout, reading from their scripts at lecterns or reading stands. Because the story is so simple and informal, they may prefer to sit on steps instead; they will probably be able to get more into the spirit of it if they are seated informally and close to the audience.

Narrator: There was once near the town of Bremen a farmer whose Donkey was growing old and was every day less fit for work. The farmer knew that he should soon have to buy a new donkey, and so he began to think of how he could get rid of his faithful old beast. Now the Donkey, who was not as stupid as the farmer thought, decided that he would settle the matter himself. So one day, when the farmer was in the house having his dinner, the Donkey took himself off and started down the road toward the city. "For there," he thought, "I may become a musician." He had a powerful voice which, in spite of his advancing years, could be heard for miles around when he put back his head and brayed. Yes, a musician was what he should be.

> He had not gone far when he met a Dog lying stretched out by the roadside. The Dog was panting as if he had just run a great distance. The Donkey stopped and greeted him.

Donkey: Good morning, friend Dog. What, may I ask, are you doing out here all by yourself? And why are you panting so hard?

Dog: Ah, me. I have run away, but I am an old dog and my strength has all but given out.

Donkey: Run away? Why should an old fellow like you run away? Pardon me for saying it, but I should think you'd be better off at home where you've someone to care for you than out seeking adventure.

Dog: I agree with you. But the truth of the matter is that my master no longer wants me around. I was a "fine fellow," a "good dog," as long as I was able to work. But now he grows angry when I trail behind and can no longer hunt or herd sheep.

Donkey: (*Sympathetically.*) That is too bad.

Dog: That's not the worst of it. He even threatened to knock me on the head and thus be rid of me. Then, with me out of the way, he'll get a new puppy.

Donkey: Your master is a cruel man, but I can understand how you feel, for the same thing has happened to me. My master is impatient with my slow steps and stiff joints and would like to replace me with a younger beast.

Dog: It's hard to grow old in this world. I suppose I may as well lie here till I die, for I am of no use to anyone anymore.

Donkey: Nonsense, my dear friend. Listen. I have an idea. I'm on my way to the city. There I plan to become a musician. Why don't you join me and see what you can do? We may harmonize well together, and anyhow, two are always better off than one.

Dog: I have nothing to lose by it. Yes, your words give me courage. I'll go along with you to the city.

Narrator: So the two of them set out. Before they had gone very far, they came upon a Cat sitting in the middle of the road. They stopped to speak to her.

Donkey: I beg your pardon, my lady; what is the trouble? You look as unhappy as my friend the Dog did less than an hour ago. Surely life is not all that hard.

Cat: And why shouldn't I look unhappy? You don't know what it is to grow old and no longer be welcome in your very own house.

Donkey: Indeed? Do tell us what has happened. We, too, have suffered similar misfortunes. Perhaps we can help.

Cat: Very well, I'll tell you, though there's nothing either one of you can do.

Dog: (*Sympathetically.*) Sometimes it helps just to talk.

Cat: That is true. You see, I used to be loved very much. My mistress thought me the most beautiful cat in the world. She brushed my fur—it was soft and sleek in those days—and gave me cream in a saucer each morning, and meat at night. And she praised me to all the neighbors. She said I kept the place clean of mice.

Dog: Go on.

Donkey: What happened next?

Cat: You wouldn't believe it! Because I no longer care to run about and catch mice but prefer to curl up by the fire, my mistress has said she would drown me. Is that the way to treat an old friend? I was fortunate enough to escape from her, but how I shall find enough to eat or a warm bed at night, I do not know.

Donkey: Do not despair, old friend. We share the same sorrow. Instead of sitting here in the road, why not come with us to the city? You are a good musician, I'm sure. Perhaps we can work together. A trio is much more attractive than a duet. Wouldn't you agree, Master Dog?

Dog: Yes, indeed.

Cat: I hadn't thought of being a singer. But it's worth trying, and I'm glad to have company, however it turns out.

Narrator: So the Cat got up and went with them. The three talked and exchanged stories of their youth and began to feel much better as they got acquainted. Presently they came to a farmyard, where they saw a Cock perched on the gate. He was crowing with all his might.

Cock: Cock-a-doodle-do!

Donkey: What a fine sound you make, Master Cock. Pray, what great event are you proclaiming?

Cock: Why, that it is a fair day and sunny and my mistress can safely hang out her wash.

Donkey: She must depend on you very much.

Cock: Indeed she does. She would never know when the sun had come up if it weren't for my crowing.

Dog: You don't looked pleased, somehow. What's the matter?

Cock: I've had a rude shock. Would you believe it, in spite of my years of service to her, I have just heard her say that she plans to cut off my head and roast me for Sunday dinner.

Dog: Oh, that is even worse than what has happened to us, friend Cock. Why don't you leave here at once?

Cock: Where can I go? And how do I know every other farmer's wife might not have the same idea?

Cat: Well, we have a plan . . .

Cock: What kind of plan?

Cat: Come along with us and we'll tell you.

Cock: Where are you going?

Donkey: To the city. We are going to seek our fortune as musicians. With your fine strong voice, I'm sure you will have no trouble finding work.

Cat: And if we practice together, we may work up a concert. Four voices! Do come along.

Cock: I'll join you. And I thank you with all my heart.

Dog: Anything is better than staying here, and who knows, things may turn out for the best after all.

Narrator: And so the four of them walked on together. The day was fair and their hearts were high, for they were certain that good luck was in store for them. As evening approached, they were still a distance from town, so they decided to stop at the edge of the woods for the night. The Donkey and the Dog made a comfortable bed under a tree, and the Cat climbed up on a bough where she felt safer. The Cock, however, who was used to spending the night on a perch, flew up to the very top of the tree and settled himself on a sturdy branch.

Cock: Is everyone all right down there?

Donkey: As right as my old bones can be on this hard ground.

Dog: This is better than being knocked in the head, though I shall be glad when we find proper lodging.

Cock: How about you, Mistress Cat? Are you comfortable?

Cat: Oh, I'm all right. The leaves keep out the draft, and anyhow it's not a cold night.

Cock: Well, I'll say good night then, and I'll wake you up first thing in the morning.

Narrator: Before tucking his head under his wing, however, he looked out in all directions, to be sure that nothing was amiss. As he did so, he noticed, not too great a distance away, something shining and bright. He called down to the others.

Cock: We can't be as far from the town as we thought. I see lights. There must be a house nearby.

Dog: Are you sure? It looks very dark to me.

Cat: Yes, I see it. It's a house or an inn.

Donkey: Then perhaps we should push on. I could use a softer bed.

Dog: So could I. And, who knows, the master might throw in a bone and some scraps from his table.

Cat: Yes, indeed. I would willingly exchange this bough for a spot in front of a fire.

Cock: I'm game. Let's find out what it is.

Narrator: Having agreed, the four companions got up and followed the Cat, whose eyes served best in the dark. At length they came to a house. It was a very comfortable house, in which there lived a band of robbers. The four stopped outside the door; then the Donkey, who was the tallest, cautiously peered through the window.

Cock: Well, friend Donkey, what do you see? Do they look like kindly folk?

Donkey: I see an astonishing thing. A table piled with good things to eat and a band of men sitting around it, counting their gold.

Cat: What do you take them to be?

Donkey: If I'm not mistaken, I'd say they were robbers. This is no farmer's cottage.

Cock: Do you suppose they live here?

Donkey: Either that or they've taken over the place.

Dog: Perhaps we can scare them away. I used to be good at that years ago. My master always said no robber could get within gunshot when I was around.

Cat: It looks like a fine lodging for us, if we can get in.

Donkey: Let's think of a way.

Dog: I've got it. I'll get on the Donkey. You, Mistress Cat, jump on my back, and the Cock can perch on your shoulders. Then we'll make music.

Cock: A capital idea! Let's do it.

All: (*Ad lib.*) All right—I'm for it—Good idea!

Donkey: Is everyone in place? Good. Now, all together . . . (*Each animal makes its own noise at the same time.*)

Donkey: Now, then, stand back. I'll put my front feet through the window, and we'll all go inside. (*Crash of glass.*)

Narrator: The robbers, who had been startled by the concert, were terrified when the four musicians tumbled over the sill into the room. They were out the door in a flash and scattered in all directions. The four old friends watched them go.

Donkey: Well, it looks as if we have the place to ourselves.

Dog: And the dinner.

Cat: Will you look what's on the table! This is a feast.

Cock: It would be too bad to let so much good food go to waste. What say you? Let's eat.

Narrator: So the four gobbled up every crumb. Then, their hunger satisfied, each one sought a bed to his liking. The Donkey found a pile of straw outside the back door and bade the others good night. The Dog stretched out on a rug under the table. The Cat curled up on the hearth; and the Cock, who preferred a higher spot even indoors, perched on a beam in the ceiling. Warm and tired from their travels, they were soon fast asleep.

Later on that night, however, the robbers, seeing the house dark and hearing no noise, crept stealthily back. The leader of the band was the first to venture inside. He struck a match on the fireplace, and then out of the darkness blazed two bright eyes. The Cat was on her feet in a flash and flew at him and clawed him with all her might. (*Meow!*) The robber yelled in fright more than pain. As he stumbled back, he tripped over the Dog, who bit him sharply in the leg. (*Bow-wow!*) Running out the back door, he bumped into the Donkey, who woke up with a start and kicked him with both feet. (*Hee-haw!*) All this commotion roused the Cock, who crowed at the top of his lungs. (*Cock-a-doodle-do!*)

This was too much for the robber, who ran off to his companions and told them what had befallen him.

Robber: A witch has got into the house. I saw her eyes in the dark. First she scratched me with her long nails; next she stabbed me in the leg. Then, when I tried to escape, I was struck with a club from behind, and all the while someone on the roof was yelling, "Throw the rascal out! Throw the rascal out!" I tell you, the place is bewitched.

Narrator: Well, after that, the robbers never ventured inside the house again. The four musicians were so pleased with their lodging that they stayed right there. And I shouldn't be surprised if they're living there still.

Story Theatre

Story theatre is closely related to readers theatre. According to Paul Sills, whose production entitled *Story Theatre* captivated audiences of all ages a number of seasons ago, it evolved from readers theatre. Sills had worked in readers theatre, but in his search for a new form of expression, he developed a form as an oral story rather than as a piece of literature. In dispensing with the narrator, which Sills often does, the exposition is embedded in the dialogue of the various characters. They may also speak in the third person, as in the short sketch that follows.

Like readers theatre, story theatre is hard to define because of its flexibility; no hard-and-fast rules apply. Actors are usually costumed and may speak or perform in pantomime while a narrator tells the story. There may be musical accompaniment throughout if desired, and the pantomime may approach dance, depending on the wishes and abilities of the group.

The following short play is an illustration of what is usually meant by story theatre.

Rimouski

Shirley Pugh

Music: "Gypsy Rover" melody used throughout.

Marcel: A peasant named Marcel—
Madeleine: —lived with his wife Madeleine—*(Curtsies.)*
Jeanette: —and their little daughter Jeanette—*(Madeleine cues Jeanette to curtsey.)*
Marcel: —in the tiny village of St. Fabien. But he had it in his head to travel.
Madeleine: Oh!

(A sound of deprecation.)

St. Fabien is good enough for me.

(Mimes cooking and stirring.)

I was born here, and I'll die here.

Marcel: Me, I want to see what is in the world. More than anything else, I want to see Rimouski.

Madeleine: Rimouski! How can you think of it? So far away.

Jeanette: Is Papa going to Rimouski?

Madeleine: Papa is going nowhere, Jeanette. Stop pulling at my skirt.

Marcel: Today I talked to the blacksmith. There's a good fellow—he has seen Rimouski.

Madeleine: (*Adds pepper to the pot.*) That's very fine for the blacksmith. (*She readies herself to sneeze—and the sneeze doesn't come.*)

Marcel: (*Sneezes without warning.*) Ah-choo!

Jeanette: Bless you, Papa.

Marcel: Thank you. Listen—Rimouski is a town that could swallow St. Fabien. The blacksmith says that people crowd the streets there. Have you ever seen a crowd in St. Fabien? The blacksmith says—

Madeleine: Then listen to the blacksmith and be satisfied.

Marcel: No, listen—he says there are fine shops and large houses in Rimouski. He says—

Jeanette: When is Papa going to Rimouski?

Madeleine: Play with your doll, Jeanette. Papa is going nowhere.

Marcel: No, listen. I am going, me myself, to Rimouski.

Madeleine: Marcel, you are a peasant. We are poor people. Travel is not for you. So expensive!

Marcel: I can't rest until I see for myself what is in the world.

Madeleine: You certainly can't afford to ride such a distance!

Marcel: Then I will walk.

Madeleine: What? And wear out your boots? They aren't in good repair anyway.

Marcel: Then I will walk without my boots.

Madeleine: Barefooted! Hah! A fine sight he'll be in Rimouski with no boots on his feet.

Marcel: Then I know what I'll do. I'll carry my boots in my hand. When I see the smoke from the chimneys of Rimouski, I'll put on my boots and go into the town.

Jeanette: (*Weeping.*) Why must you go to Rimouski, Papa?

Marcel: Don't worry, Jeanette. I will return.

Madeleine: (*Mimes packing a basket.*) What can be done with such a man? Marcel, do you really want to go to Rimouski?

Marcel: With all my heart.

Madeleine: Go, then. Here's a basket with sausage and bread and beer—

Marcel: Sausage and bread and beer—that will be fine. First I'll take off my boots—

(*Mime.*)

—and I'll be on my way.

(*Mimes taking the basket in one hand and his boots in the other, making ready to leave for Rimouski.*)

Madeleine: Promise me you will stop to rest, Marcel.

Marcel: Yes, well, I'll do that all right.

Madeleine: And take time to eat your sausage and bread.

Marcel: Sausage and bread. I will, I will.

Madeleine: And whatever you do, Marcel, don't leave your boots at the side of the road or they'll be stolen.

Marcel: I'm not a nincompoop. I'll keep them right here in my hand.

Jeanette: How far is it to Rimouski, Papa?

Marcel: Jeanette, it is a journey of one entire day.

Jeanette: Oh, Papa! So far!

Madeleine: And don't lose your way, Marcel. The road will be confusing.

Marcel: All right! Jeanette, mind your mama. (*Kisses her.*)

Madeleine: Oh, Marcel, it is such a distance!

Marcel: (*He kisses her.*) Don't worry, keep well, and when I return I will tell you about the wonders of Rimouski.

Madeleine: The wonders of Rimouski! Hah! (*Flounces off with Jeanette.*)

Marcel: (*Music. He walks.*) What a woman to worry, and the little one will be just like her. Do they think I can't keep my wits about me? She should see me now, on the road, a seasoned traveler.

(Music.)

The sun is high in the sky—it's getting hot. A little sausage and bread and a drink of beer will go down well. Here's a spot of shade.

(Music. Mimes eating.)

A swallow of beer—ah, that's good!—a bite of sausage—that's not so good—

(He finishes eating.)

Maybe now a small nap.

(He lies down, immediately sits up.)

But if I sleep, how will I remember which way the road goes? Ah, that's it! I'll put my boots on the ground—and I'll point the toes of them toward Rimouski.

(Mimes action.)

There. When I wake up, my boots will point the way.

(Lies down and snores gently. Threatening music.)

Thief: Now a thief happened along the road. There's a pair of boots with no one's feet in them. I could use an extra pair of boots. He's asleep, all right.
(*To audience.*) Should I, or shouldn't I? I'm going to do it anyway.

(Steals boots.)

These boots, they aren't much. Not worth the stealing. Full of holes and all run down at the heels. They are no better than my own boots.

(Puts boots down with toes pointing the wrong way.)

And he put the boots down with the toes pointing back toward St. Fabien.

(Music. Thief exits.)

Marcel: (*Wakes, yawns, scratches, stretches.*) And now it's cooler and I'm on my way. But which way does the road go? See? I'm not such a fool. There are my boots, with the toes pointing to Rimouski.

(Takes boots and basket and follows wrong direction. Music.)

There's smoke! That smoke comes from the chimneys of Rimouski! Now to put on my boots.

(Mimes action.)

Well, so this is Rimouski! Looks a lot like St. Fabien! The blacksmith said it was so miraculous here. Why, this street could be a street in St. Fabien! These shops look no finer than the shops at home. And the houses—they aren't so large. I expected a town that looked better than this. Rimouski is not so grand!

(Walks.)

I'm really in Rimouski!

(Madeleine appears, sweeping the sidewalk.)

(Jeanette appears, washing a window.)

Ah, well, this street could be my own street. As far as that goes, look. This house could be my own house. See—an ordinary wife like my own wife. A little girl like my own daughter. If I didn't know I was in Rimouski, I'd swear I was in St. Fabien!
Madeleine: Marcel! Come in the house and have your supper.
Marcel: She calls me by my name!
Jeanette: Did you bring me something, Papa?
Marcel: It is exactly like St. Fabien! I've never heard of this, but it's true. Imagine—two places so far apart, yet with streets alike, houses alike—even the people are the same! Aha! Now I see! There is someone just like me who lives in this house, here in Rimouski. Maybe at this moment, he is visiting my house at St. Fabien.
Madeleine: Marcel, stop talking to yourself. Go in and eat your supper.
Marcel: Yes, I know. I know all about it. Tomorrow he'll come back here. Well, I'll stay in Rimouski and wait until he comes.

(Goes into house, sits, and eats.)

Jeanette: (*Puzzled.*) And he's still waiting.
Madeleine: And he still thinks he's in Rimouski.

(A single minor chord from the musicians.)

(BLACKOUT)

Public Speaking

A good way of improving speech is speaking before an audience, even if that audience is just the class. Beginning with "Show and Tell" in the early grades, assignments become more demanding by middle school and can range from introducing a class play to a book report or discussion of a current event in high school. Whatever the assignment, speech should be a pleasurable experience for both speaker and listeners. While this book makes no pretense of being a text on public speaking, it does point up the fact that to be effective, speech must be loud enough to be heard and clear enough to be understood. Performing and discussing ideas with the class will also help to prevent stage fright later on.

Summary

The number of activities that can be incorporated into a curriculum to improve speech and teach the language arts is almost limitless. Show and tell, storytelling, sound and motion stories (discussed in Chapter 13), group discussion, monologues, improvisation, readers theatre, and story theatre are activities most young people enjoy. We are living in a period of experimentation and change, however, and new forms are being created every day. Hard-and-fast rules no longer apply. The combining of forms and the use of nondramatic material for oral presentation suggest possibilities to the imaginative teacher and student. Whereas the produced play was once considered the logical outcome of a semester's work or a unit of drama, it is now only one of numerous possibilities. What is more, the loosening of the rules that previously governed form makes possible the invention of interesting and often exciting new structures. Not all of these inventions will be successful, but school is a place in which experimentation should be encouraged.

Speech is our most important means of communication, although the written language receives the greater emphasis in schools. It is through oral language, however, that our earliest learnings take place; through it we are able to express our thoughts and feelings, our needs and desires. The actor and public speaker are not necessarily more gifted in its use than the average man or woman; they have simply developed their skill through diligent and daily practice. Good speech is within the reach of everyone, except, perhaps, persons with certain disabling conditions that speech therapy cannot overcome.

The creative drama class offers a rich opportunity for practice in oral communication. Class discussion, planning sessions, and participation in plays all demand the ability to use the language and to use it well. Students are motivated to work on voice and diction when they participate in these and other activities. Because drama deals with ideas and literature, vocabularies are enlarged and the ability to express thoughts clearly is strengthened. Interpretation of characters brings color to the voice and melody to the speech as players take a variety of roles.

The student who achieves a good standard of speech does more than present himself or herself well; he or she shows consideration for the listener. Communication, be it oral, written, or sign language, is a two-way affair; the giver and the receiver have a relationship that is strong or weak, depending on their ability to express and comprehend meanings.

Suggested Assignments

1. Arrange a short piece of prose, poetry, or drama for readers theatre.
2. Rehearse and perform it for the class.
3. Put a short children's story into story theatre form.
4. Rehearse and present it to the class.
5. Using a tape recorder, record everyone in the class. Listen and discuss what you hear.

Journal Writing

1. If you have ever attended a readers theatre performance, how did it affect you? In what ways was your involvement different from your involvement in theatre or film?
2. What values do you find in readers theatre, both practical and aesthetic?
3. Whether or not you have seen it, what is your reaction to story theatre?
4. Do you experience stage fright when speaking before an audience? Why? Think about it and answer the question.
5. Seize every opportunity to make an announcement or a speech. Then analyze your reaction and that of your audience.

Chapter 13

Storytelling

Storyteller Rives Collins weaves his magic on young listeners. (Photograph by Jim Ziv.)

And therein lies a tale.

—William Shakespeare

Storytelling is an ancient art that is experiencing a resurgence of interest in spite of, or perhaps because of, our technical advances in communication. Storytelling can be an end in itself, a means to an end, or the first step in the creation of drama. It appeals to people of all ages, and its flexibility makes it adaptable to a variety of uses and occasions. Though we tend to think of storytelling in relation to young children, its use has not always been so restricted. Indeed, in many societies storytelling has been an important means of disseminating information and handing down the culture, reaching the oldest as well as the youngest members of the society. Before going further, perhaps we should define this art that we so easily take for granted and examine some of its uses and techniques.

Why Tell Stories?

Very simply, storytelling is the act of communication between the one who knows the story and the ones with whom it is shared. Storytelling implies a special skill, however, that lifts the communication above the level of mere reporting. Good storytelling enhances and gives life to a story. It captures and holds the attention of the listeners, inviting involvement in the narrative and identification with the protagonist. It stirs the imagination, recalling the familiar to mind with colorful images as well as constructing a bridge to the unfamiliar. It brings its listeners a heightened awareness that involves a sense of wonder, mystery, and creativity. Television brings a vast array of entertainment into our homes, but it can no more replace the living storyteller than film can take the place of the living theatre.

Storytelling predates theatre, and theatre in one form or another has existed for more than two thousand years. Historically, storytelling has been used for the following purposes:

to entertain
to educate
to transmit the culture
to instill values
to nourish the spirit

Most of us think of entertainment as storytelling's primary purpose, and indeed, it must engage the listeners or it will fail in its purpose, no matter what that purpose may be. In many instances, entertainment *is* the raison d'être. Good stories, interestingly presented, constitute a performing art, with literature as the material to be interpreted and shared.

A second reason for telling stories has always been, and still is, to educate. Through a story, an idea can be explored and a lesson learned. Whereas direct teaching is often construed as preaching, the same points can be made effectively through the reading or telling of a story. Listeners identifying with the protagonist share his or her experience vicariously and so can comprehend the meaning of the problem or conflict. "Storytelling can bring much of the classroom curriculum to life. A lesson in electricity will be much more meaningful, for example, if students first listen to a story about the life of Edison and his successes, failures, and especially persistence."[1]

At the same time, the listeners are learning something about another place, time, and social or family group. Through heroic tales and narratives of ancient times, history, religious beliefs, and social customs are handed down. Great deeds are described, and values are instilled. Occupations of people, geography, foods, homes and furnishings, articles of clothing, arts and crafts, beliefs and values—a wealth of information can be absorbed within the context of a story. Attentive listening to a good piece of literature is an excellent way of finding out about people who are different from ourselves. The current interest in our cultural diversity can be well served through the sharing of our literature and legends.

The student of folklore is interested to see how material has been shaped and modified through repetition. For example, before the days of newspapers, a raconteur, passing the night at an inn, was often described as telling tales of his travels and spinning yarns of foreign lands for the pleasure of those gathered around him on the hearth. Tall tales and legends were carried from one end of a country to the other, sometimes from one land to the next. Details were added and incidents embellished by the individual storytellers, thus adding fresh layers to the original anecdote. Often the same story turns up in the folklore of several different countries; it may differ in setting but retain the identical theme and structure. Many stories with universal and timeless appeal are still told and handed down to each succeeding generation. "Beauty and the Beast" and "Cinderella" are examples of favorite tales that appear in the folklore of more than one country. *The Three Cinderellas: The World's Favorite Fairy Tale,* dramatized by Lowell Swortzell, is a fascinating collection of plays based on the same theme but told through the perspective of three different cultures.[2] During the Middle Ages in Europe, wandering minstrels offered entertainment to the common people through song and story just as the commedia dell'arte troupes brought improvised drama to the village square in Italy, France, Spain, and England. With the invention of the printing press in the fifteenth century, however, profound changes took place, affecting both storytelling and improvisational theatre. Literature was frozen for the first time; hence, there was less need for the oral transmission of tales. In essence, the book replaced the storyteller; material previously passed along by word of mouth was now cast into a permanent form and could no longer be cut, lengthened, or changed in response to audience reaction.

In Japan, however, the storyteller is still used to impart information, much as theatre was used in the Soviet Union to teach a way of life. Historically the storyteller

---

[1]Liz Rothlein and Anita Meyer Meinbach, *Legacies: Using Children's Literature in the Classroom* (New York: HarperCollins, 1996), p. 217.

[2]Lowell Swortzell, *The Three Cinderellas: The World's Favorite Fairy Tale* (Charlottesville, VA: New Plays, 1992).

Don Doyle, master storyteller, in Tempe, Arizona.

has always played a significant role in the education and entertainment of the Japanese people. Through him the folklore was handed down and dramatic material adapted for use in the *kyogen* or folk plays. When I visited Iceland a few years ago, I was told that storytelling in that country is the favorite form of entertainment for children, surpassing both film and television in popularity.

Both in the United States and the United Kingdom, there has been a strong revival of interest in storytelling, resulting in the founding of numerous centers and the emergence of individual artists. Among the better-known centers here is Weston Woods in Weston, Connecticut, established by Morton Schindel in 1953. Aware of his own children's enjoyment of literature presented in this way, the young filmmaker was inspired to reach many listeners by combining storytelling with the media. He began by adapting picture books on film, working in a quiet rural area. Consulting authors of children's books, publishers, illustrators, and teachers, he selected material of good literary quality appropriate to the medium. The slogan "Fidelity to the original" was a guiding principle from the beginning and has been a major factor in the success of the project.

In 1988, *The New Yorker* carried an article on Ray Hicks, a champion storyteller in North Carolina.[3] In his late sixties at the time the article was published, Hicks was holding audiences spellbound. He specialized in the "Jack Tales" of the Blue Ridge Mountains, often telling them without charge to tourists who sought him out, to neighbors, and locally to students in schools and colleges. Once a year he was persuaded to travel to the town of Jonesboro, Tennessee, for an annual storytelling festival. First in the country, the Jonesboro Festival now has many imitators and many participants,

---

[3]Gwen Kinkead, "An Overgrown Jack," *The New Yorker,* July 18, 1988, pp. 33–41.

but Hicks is considered the patriarch. Although other storytellers have become professional, doing research and making tapes of their performances, Hicks from the beginning worked in the simple oral tradition: no agent, no press kit, no fees of any sizable amount.

Two theatre professors who have attracted a large following as master storytellers are Don Doyle, formerly of Arizona State University, and Rives Collins of Northwestern University. For many years, colleges, particularly teachers' colleges, have offered courses in storytelling; today, however, we are finding a new emphasis with training given in both theatre and education departments. Although we cannot all hope to become great storytellers, most of us can become good ones. Sincerity, imagination, good judgment, a pleasing voice, and vocal expression are basic equipment.

Through storytelling we can foster a love of literature, for a good story gives vent to the emotions, permits the imagination to soar, and gives the listener a chance to experience the adventures of other persons both in the past and in the present.

Finally, one of the best storytellers I have ever heard was Reverend Edee Chase Fenimore, a pastor in a large urban church. A good delivery, an appreciation of the story, and the ability to relate a story to the theme of the sermon are invaluable assets both for the leaders of sophisticated adult congregations and for actors in the theatre.

Guidelines for the Selection of Stories

The first ground rule is that the teller must like the stories he or she is going to tell. No amount of preparation will help if the teller does not respond positively to the story in the first place. Next are the questions that the teller must ask:

1. What are the age and background of the listeners?
2. Will the material hold the listeners' interest?
3. Am I able to handle the material? to do it justice?

Of course, the audience is not always known in advance, but it is important that an effort be made to find out something of the listeners' interests and background. In this respect the classroom teacher has an advantage over the librarian or the assembly performer. In time, however, the neighborhood children's librarian will learn who is likely to appear for story hours and will become aware of these children's particular interests. In an effort to expand the children's knowledge of the world through literature, the librarian will sometimes deliberately pick stories of life in other ethnic or social settings. A regular story hour in the library or on the playground is a wonderful way of introducing children to different cultures as well as to prose and poetry that they might not discover on their own. Camp counselors and volunteers in hospitals, working in more isolated settings, can also make a special contribution, for literature fills a need in the lives of listeners who are temporarily removed from the attractions and distractions of contemporary life.

When telling stories to very young children, there are often pictures to be shared. While this presents another technique to be mastered, it is well worth the effort, for the illustrator of a children's book frequently contributes as much as the author. Children should see as well as hear the work. Who among us can conceive of *Alice in Wonderland* without the Tenniel illustrations? or *Peter Rabbit* without Beatrix Potter's drawings? or *Where the Wild Things Are* without Maurice Sendak's art? Material selected for any group should be worth sharing, and illustrations add another dimension to the experience. A word of warning, however: pictures should be shown only when the group is small and close enough to see them. Attempting to show pictures to a large group is frustrating and a distraction. A better solution in that case is to tell the story, then put the book on display so that the pictures can be seen at close range by everyone.

I do not suggest that material must always be serious; but I believe that there should be values in theme, character, narrative, or language. Most children love humor, and there are many stories with amusing situations and comic characters. Repetition and funny sounds are especially amusing to the very young, and truths can be found in the folk and fairy tales. We tend to think only in terms of fiction when planning a program, but in fact, nearly every form of literature can be shared orally. In the category of fiction are both old and modern stories, but poetry and nonfiction, like biography and essays, can be enjoyed by older children. There is such a wealth of literature from which to choose that the problem soon becomes not one of finding good material but rather one of selection.

A trap into which many storytellers fall is thinking only in terms of arbitrary age levels. Groups respond differently according to their readiness for the ideas, and readiness is not necessarily dependent on age. In tribal cultures the storyteller is the wise one, who does not distinguish between child and adult. We do, primarily because today's storyteller usually has a group of listeners of approximately the same age. Some selections obviously require more help from the teacher than others. In a folk tale like "The Fisherman and His Wife," there is a clear message for all ages, and all understand it. Rachel Carson's *The Sea Around Us,* in contrast, is a long and philosophic work that should be read aloud for its literary value. Because the point is to elicit appreciation and understanding, some works need orientation. Older groups, particularly if there has been a study of environmental issues, will find Carson's work moving and relevant.

Poetry like John Masefield's "Sea Fever" and "Ariel's Song" from *The Tempest* sing their messages. But it is the enjoyment of the reader that is the greatest factor in stimulating a similar response in the listeners. This brings up the question of whether to tell or read selections aloud. When the language is so beautiful, so integral to the work, or so necessary to the meaning that it would be lost in a telling, then it should be read. Where content and theme are more important than the language in which they are couched, the material will probably be more effective told.

Storytelling is probably the easiest way of acquainting students of all ages with the customs and values of people of different groups. In fact, through storytelling we are even better able to appreciate our own cultures; describing family and community traditions deepens appreciation as we share stories. We are blessed today with a burgeoning library of children's literature, both fiction and nonfiction, in which the lives of young people throughout the world are described accurately and sympathetically. It is a commonplace that with knowledge, prejudice can be overcome; yet how often we fail to achieve this. Through a judicious selection of literature, however, the teacher can do much to create an understanding of members of minority groups in the class and an appreciation of their traditions and values. Sensitive issues can often be handled most effectively through stories, much as Aesop used animals to depict human frailties as a way of teaching. Storytelling enables the teacher or librarian to impart information indirectly without obvious teaching or preaching. The more we learn about a person or group, the less likely we are to believe the damaging stereotype.

The neighborhood library is a rich resource and the children's librarian a valuable resource person. In addition to books, there are illustrations—photographs and drawings—which help to stimulate interest and imagery. Exhibits in the classroom can augment the story with pictures of the people, their homes, crops, foods, clothing, arts and crafts. It is safe to say that everyone loves a good story, and when it can be enriched with related experiences it becomes a lasting memory. The renaissance that story-telling is having today may be more than coincidental; there is so much we all have to tell, so much we have to share with each other.

Preparation of the Material

The storyteller's most important possession is an annotated card file, listing titles and authors of stories, poems, and nonfiction, giving sources and other information. The second most important possession is a well-chosen personal library. After deciding on the selection or group of selections, the storyteller should become thoroughly familiar with every detail. Pronunciations and definitions of unfamiliar words and references should be checked, for once in front of a group, the storyteller is the "authority" and may be asked about meanings. There is a difference of opinion regarding memorization. Some experts believe that to retain the beauty of the language or the style of the author, the performer should memorize the words and deliver them exactly as written. Other storytellers disagree, contending that extemporaneous presentation is the only way to give the story life. My own preference is for a thorough knowledge of the material but an informal, nonmemorized presentation. In some cases certain phrases and words should be incorporated in the telling to give the original flavor. When telling favorite stories to young children, the storyteller may be expected to repeat some words and phrases a number of times, and any change in the wording is sure to bring a protest. The listeners in all probability already know the original, and paraphrasing it will prompt immediate corrections.

Part of the preparation is keeping the structure in mind. All stories have a beginning, a middle, and an end. To be planned, then, are the exposition, the rising action, the climax, and the dénouement. A word of warning: children love the excitement of a conflict or an adventure, but when the problem is solved, the storyteller should not belabor the point. Older children have a longer attention span and can become involved in a more complicated narrative, and the conflict may be one that they will want to discuss later.

Mention has been made of wording and word choice. Here we have not only an opportunity to enhance the tale but a means of enlarging vocabulary. Obviously the age of the group will determine the choice of words used, but children love sounds and enjoy learning new words that are presented in a pleasurable way. Embellishing the facts is, after all, what distinguishes a story from a report.

Some Techniques Used by Storytellers

The techniques of storytelling have changed radically in the past few years. It was once emphasized that the storyteller was not an actor and must resist the temptation to become one; today, however, some of our most successful storytellers use mime and movement freely. The recent revival of interest in the oral tradition has resulted in imaginative ways of telling stories. Instead of rejecting the actor's techniques, many of our younger storytellers make full use of them, including vocal effects, strong facial expressions, and physical activities that can border on the acrobatic—for a frankly theatrical result. Many of them memorize their material and wear costumes, or at least garments that are different from ordinary street clothes. Some add musical accompaniment or work with a musician. Who, after all, is to say that something is *not* storytelling because it breaks traditional rules? Librarians and teachers favor the traditional approach—first, because they are not giving a performance, and second, because they are in a quiet place and are concerned about noise. The professional who comes in for an assembly program or special occasion *is* a performer, educated in theatre techniques, and he or she serves a different purpose. It is not suggested that the teacher and librarian should discard the older conventions to keep up with the times. The point is simply this: we can no longer lay down ironclad rules regarding any art form and refuse to recognize the changes that artists may make.

Whatever the style of the presentation, however, the voice of the reader is paramount. A pleasing tone and flexible vocal range will hold the attention far better than a monotone or strident quality. Vocal expression includes inflection, intonation, emphasis, change of pitch, and the use of pauses. All are necessary for effective oral interpretation. Pause and hesitation, incidentally, are not synonymous. The former is an intended period of silence and can be highly effective; hesitation, on the other hand, implies a lapse of memory or poor preparation. Diction should be clear and words articulated clearly but without affectation. The type of material told or read will suggest whether the delivery should be rapid or slow. Under any circumstance, vocal expression comes from the literature and is not imposed on it. Dialogue generally calls for more vocal variation than simple exposition. Dialect is sometimes appropriate, but unless the storyteller can use it easily, he or she should not attempt it. Good use of accent adds color to the dialogue, but when speech patterns are not true to the region, they are not convincing and merely call attention to the effort.

Rehearsals are necessary. No matter how well prepared the storyteller may be, an audience poses problems. Rehearsing a piece is like rehearsing a play: the important details are set in rehearsal, thus establishing a structure that aids the memory and instills self-confidence. Rehearsal is also the time to get acquainted with your room or audience, to experiment with pantomime and gesture. By the time different ways have been tried, perhaps cast aside, modified, or changed completely, the sentence structure is improved and vocabulary selected for meaning and sound. Rehearsals help the storyteller to approach the audience with confidence, not wondering "How am I doing?" but rather "Do the listeners understand and enjoy the story?" The beginner who is worried about forgetting should carry a few note cards. They are inconspicuous, and if they put the speaker at ease, there is no reason not to use them; sometimes just having them available is all that is necessary.

Some common pitfalls lie in the path of the storyteller:

1. Selection of inappropriate or dull material.
2. Excessive explanation. Too many details will confuse or bore the listeners, causing them to lose the point of the story rather than understand it better.
3. A tendency to go off on tangents.
4. Changing the theme or intent of the author. If the storyteller is unsympathetic to the theme, the story is probably not a good choice.
5. "Watering down" or lowering the level of the material in an effort to appeal to what the storyteller considers to be the underdeveloped appreciation of the listeners. This practice is condescending, and children recognize it as such. Slang and poor grammar should be used only when they are integral to the story.
6. Obvious teaching, disguised as entertainment. Although it has been stated that some of the best learning takes place while listening to stories, children resent what they feel to be manipulation.

Two variations of storytelling are tandem and participatory storytelling. In tandem, a pair of storytellers take turns telling different parts of the story. In participatory, the listeners are asked to join in by repeating a refrain or chant or, where the teller asks for collaboration, by adding details that are then woven into the narrative. These variations are recommended when working with young children for whom English is a second language.

Further Values of Storytelling

Storytelling elicits questions and stimulates class discussion. It improves listening ability, and it encourages students' interest in reading. Values apart from those, however, include the human need for security and to belong, to achieve, to have exciting adventures, and to enjoy aesthetic pleasure. Specifically, the need for security involves material, emotional, intellectual, and spiritual satisfaction. There is much controversy these days as to the meaning that the old folk and fairy tales have for modern children; how can they relate to princes and princesses or visualize castles and the lives of royalty? Those who object believe that contemporary material should be stressed: stories of the here and now, current social issues, exploration of values for children growing up in a confusing world, colloquial speech. Although I agree that storytelling should include contemporary material, I am unwilling to make it an either/or situation. I believe that the old tales still have something to say to us. They have survived the honing of the centuries and should not be summarily dismissed in favor of the new.

Children pay rapt attention to a story told by Don Doyle.

In fact, where there is conflict between old and new values, group discussion can be particularly rewarding. Content seems to me like the language; remember to start where the group is, but do not remain there. The hope is that the listeners will learn to relate to more than one period, place, or social group.

The desire for material security—shelter, food, and clothing—may be satisfied in part by the old tales, in which there is wealth with food and raiment in abundance. True, most American children have never seen a king or a castle, but in their imagination they can create images that bring certain satisfactions in the symbols of material goods. This satisfaction should not be interpreted as an opiate but rather as a temporary respite from life's harsh realities. Presented by a good storyteller, the images are believable for the length of the tale, leaving unforgettable memories for the rest of life. Bruno Bettelheim, in his *Uses of Enchantment,* says that he finds the fairy tale more satisfying than any other genre to all kinds of children at every level of intelligence: "And to attain to the full its consoling propensities, all its symbolic meanings, and, most of all, its interpersonal meanings, it should be told rather than read."[4]

Descriptions of home life and family relationships in books help to satisfy certain emotional needs of children. Some professionals today question whether books should present a picture of middle-class family life that is fast disappearing. They contend that in view of the changing times and problems that many children face, more realistic fiction should be presented. Life in poverty, the single parent, the painful breakup

---

[4]Bruno Bettelheim, *The Uses of Enchantment* (New York: Knopf, 1976), p. 150.

of a family, death: these are the experiences that many children know. The point is well taken, and these experiences should not be ignored or glossed over; yet living for even a short time with beloved literary friends provides vicarious warmth.

As to a child's intellectual needs, information about persons, places, and things is to be found in fiction as well as in textbooks. The desire to learn can be gratified in the story hour as well as in the class. No matter how entertaining or amusing the piece, there is always something to learn in a book read for the first time. In a good book there are several levels of meaning, each to be discovered when the listener or reader is ready.

The need to belong, to love and be loved, to have friends grows out of our basic human need for emotional security. Whether it be in the description of life in another culture, the story of an outsider who is taken in, or an animal tale, the child finds identification. All of us have felt "outside" at one time or another; therefore, the experiences of a protagonist who yearns to belong has reality.

Heroic tales, old and new; science fiction; biography; history—all tell of human achievement. Today an effort is being made to present the contributions of heretofore neglected groups: racial and ethnic minorities and women. The storyteller has an ideal opportunity to build positive social attitudes and break down old stereotypes through literature and group discussion. In stories, as in creative drama, children can go wherever they want and can be whomever they choose, for books offer a chance to do the impossible.

Finally, through exposure to good literature, children are given aesthetic pleasure that may be the beginning of a lifelong appreciation.

Sound and Motion Stories

Joanna Kraus has coined the term *sound and motion stories*. These consciously use the young child's natural impulse to participate in a story being read or told. Her collections of tales, suggesting places in the text where sounds and actions can be incorporated, are excellent examples of what the teacher can do to involve the group more actively in the experience. Using sound and motion is also a way of beginning a creative drama session or encouraging participation when time and space are limited. With a little practice, the teacher can find places in a text where sounds and motions add a dimension and are fun to do. Needless to say, sound and motion stories demand close attention and concentration.

Because words grow out of sounds, sound and motion is a valid approach to the teaching of speech. Children love the sounds of words, and their enjoyment of sound for its own sake should be encouraged. Difficult sounds can be practiced in this way without the dullness of drill.

Sound and motion stories provide a technique that can be used when space is limited or when desks are fastened to the floor. At the same time, the imagination is stimulated, providing freedom within the boundaries of space, time, or the ability of the students to handle more demanding material. This technique is especially popular with children in the primary grades. If a class enjoys the participation, the teacher can find other stories that lend themselves to the technique, marking the participation points accordingly.

The following is a delightful story from Joanna Kraus's collection of tales; children with whom I have worked love it. It is modern, a contrast to the folk and fairy tales, and children enjoy a situation that they can easily imagine and visualize. In the story, (S) calls for a sound, (A) for an action.

The Night the Elephants Marched on New York

Joanna Kraus

There they were, stranded in a railway yard in New Jersey, two hundred animals from Gambelli Brothers Circus.

Thirteen miles away in President Gambelli's New York City office, the phone rang. (S)

"What! What! I can barely hear you," President Gambelli yelled into the telephone.

From the other end of the wire came the sound of nineteen hungry elephants. (S)

The chief animal trainer was trying to explain, but President Gambelli could only hear half of what he said.

" . . . railway strike . . . in the yard at South Kearney, New Jersey . . . can't get the animals through to New York City . . . two o'clock opening tomorrow . . . ."

President Gambelli heard the roars of nine lions and fifteen tigers in the background. (S)

"I'll do what I can," called President Gambelli and hung up the receiver. (A)

He paced his office. On the wall was a large poster of a circus elephant, which he knew thousands of schoolchildren had seen. He knew thousands of mothers, fathers, aunts, and uncles had bought tickets for the two o'clock performance of the Gambelli Brothers Circus.

Violetta, his assistant, rushed in with the morning papers and put them on his desk. He picked up the first newspaper. (A) "Rail Strike," announced the headlines. He picked up the second newspaper. (A) Large black letters spelled out the disaster. "Nationwide Rail Strike. Country Comes to a Halt."

"If the animals don't arrive on time, there won't be a circus," he said to Violetta. "Do you know there are over two hundred animals in the unit stranded in South Kearney, New Jersey!" Luigi Gambelli put his head in his hands. (A) How was he going to move two hundred animals by two o'clock tomorrow?

"We could put the smaller animals in vans, if we can find some," Violetta suggested, "but eight thousand pound elephants . . . I don't know. There won't be a van big enough anywhere."

"It sounded like the jungle when the chief trainer telephoned me. We've got to do something fast," answered President Gambelli.

"JUNGLE! That's it. That's where they're from—any kid knows that," said Violetta excitedly. "Well, it's only about thirteen miles from South Kearney to midtown Manhattan. In India the elephants walk farther than that."

"But they don't have rush hour traffic in the jungle," he reminded Violetta. Then Luigi Gambelli threw back his shoulders and looked sternly at the pile of newspapers on his desk. (A) "Gambelli Brothers Circus has never missed a performance, and it's not going to now! Get the governor on the phone, and then the mayor! I will *not* disappoint all those children."

The governor found vans to carry the smaller animals. He authorized a yellow permit slip for the larger animals to march to Lincoln Tunnel. (A) The mayor authorized a blue permit slip for the animals to finish their march to Madison Square Garden on the public streets of New York City.

Late that night the gorillas, lions, panthers, and tigers were sent in huge vans across the Hudson River over the George Washington Bridge.

President Gambelli, the chief animal trainer, and his assistants lined up the elephants, trunk to tail, and chained them together. As they worked they fastened each chain carefully. (A) When the elephants moved, you could hear the clinking of the heavy metal chains. (S) At the end of the line was a baby elephant. Tied to her tail were a zebra, a llama, and a Shetland pony.

The chief animal trainer carefully guided the lead elephant by the ear with his bull hook. (A)

A few miles from Lincoln Tunnel, a grocer rushed out to the street. "Luigi Gambelli," he said, "I heard about the animal march on the radio. You and the elephants are invited to have supper in my store." Nineteen elephants flapped their ears happily, as the grocer and his two children fed them thirty-nine cents a pound peanuts and fed carrots to the other animals.

A little later Miss Page, the Lincoln Tunnel toll booth attendant, waved hello to the motorists she recognized who drove through the tunnel every night at that hour. (A)

It was nearly eleven o'clock. Soon she could go home too. At her feet her pet dog, Bouncer, was dozing and dreaming of a bone. (S) For a few minutes there were no cars and she glanced at the new report forms she had to fill out. After "Accidents" she wrote "None." After "Unusual Events" she sighed and wrote "None."

Suddenly Bouncer pricked up his ears and let out a low growl. (S) Miss Page looked up startled. (A) She listened carefully, then looked uncomfortably about. (A) She could not see a car or a person. But way down at the end of the tunnel there was a noise that sounded like a movie she had just seen on television. The movie had been all about the jungle. The sound grew louder . . . and louder, as it got nearer and nearer. (S)

A minute later President Gambelli, the chief animal trainer, and his assistants arrived at the toll booth. Miss Page could only stare at them. President Gambelli took off his hat. (A) "Gambelli Brothers Circus," he explained. "They're part of a mixed animal act," the chief animal trainer added.

Miss Page looked quickly through the pages of *Traffic Rules, Regulations and Toll Rates.* There were twelve categories of vehicles in the little green book. "But there's nothing here about elephants," she told them. Then she turned back to the page on Class 2 Vehicles: "Animals, ridden, led or herded, and motorcycles." "Fifty cents an elephant," she said.

President Gambelli counted out nine crisp new dollar bills. (A) The chief animal trainer counted out five dimes. (A) "What about the zebra, llama, and the Shetland pony?" the animal trainer asked.

Miss Page and Bouncer leaned out of the booth. (A) Neither had ever seen a zebra, a llama, or a Shetland pony before. Timidly, Miss Page put out her hand and patted the pony. (A) "Aw, let them have a free ride," she said. "I know there's nothing in the regulations about zebras, llamas, and Shetland ponies."

After they had thanked her, they marched away. Miss Page could hear the elephants trumpeting at the end of the tunnel. (S) She picked up her report. Next to "Unusual Events," she scratched out the word "None." (A) Miss Page wrote rapidly. (A) She could still hear the sounds of nineteen elephants, one zebra, one llama, and one Shetland pony marching away. (S) "They'll never believe it," she said to Bouncer.

The next day at two o'clock exactly, Gambelli Brothers Circus opened. There were loud trumpets as the house lights dimmed. (S) The news photographers snapped pictures of Luigi Gambelli standing with the mayor and the governor. (A) President Gambelli told the press, "Gambelli Brothers Circus has never missed a performance."

"The Night the Elephants Marched on New York" could tie in with a circus theme. Or it could be a stimulus to finding stories and local anecdotes in the news to write or tell, as well as discovering good places for sounds and actions. I like to use sound and motion stories for starters, going on to improvisation and a total involvement after the limited participation required by this technique.

Creative Writing

Finally, there is a clear link between storytelling and creative writing, making it possible to move from one to the other in either direction. Although both are treated at length in other chapters, creative writing is discussed here because it is an excellent way of explaining and sharing cultures. Two examples illustrate the possibilities.

One class of fifth graders went on a field trip to Ellis Island. They were fascinated and moved by the experience and wanted to do a project about it for a school assembly. The teacher followed their lead with the result *Children of Ellis Island—A Rainbow Called America,* a play/pageant exploring the various experiences of immigrant children who had come through Ellis Island to their new home in the United States. From the information they gathered and the empathy they felt, the children created a script that neither they nor the rest of the school would forget.

Another example is a project sponsored annually by the Police Athletic League of New York City in which students of all five boroughs are invited to take part in a creative writing contest. The topic, "Stories My Grandparents Told Me," is described in Chapter 10.

Summary

Students enjoy telling stories themselves. Through daily show and tell, children in the primary grades improve their oral communication and gain self-confidence. Older children find storytelling an enjoyable assignment through which they strengthen their power of visualization, expand their vocabularies, and develop poise speaking before a group. The teacher who is a good storyteller provides his or her students with a good model.

An excellent practice for high school and college students is telling stories to audiences in community and senior centers. I have seen how much older adults enjoy hearing familiar tales and contemporary literature shared in the intimacy of a small room or parlor. Incidentally, this often leads to a lively discussion of the material and an invitation to come again!

Regardless of the stories we tell and the way we choose to tell them, there is another component that transcends all techniques and methods. Author Barry Lopez says, "The stories people tell have a way of taking care of them. If stories come to you, care for them. And learn to give them away where they are needed. Sometimes a person needs a story more than food to stay alive. That is why we put these stories in each other's memory. This is how people care for themselves."[5]

Suggested Assignments

1. Assemble a small card file of stories suitable for children on three different grade levels.
2. Tell an anecdote or joke to the class. Brevity and carefully selected details sustain interest and lead to the point.
3. Tell a story of your own choice, not exceeding five minutes in length.
4. Experiment with different ways of telling a story, and find the one most comfortable for you.
5. Read aloud a piece of literature that you consider better read than told.
6. Make up an original story with a particular group of children in mind.
7. Tell or read a story to a group of very young children, showing the illustrations as you go along.
8. Tell or read selections for adults in a retirement or nursing home. In what ways does preparation for this session differ from that for the classroom?
9. Find a short piece you can mark for sound and motion. Try it out in class.
10. Prepare an annotated bibliography of use to the storyteller.

Journal Writing

1. Did you have the pleasure of listening to a good storyteller in your childhood? What do you remember about him or her? What made the most lasting impressions?
2. If you have an opportunity to hear a good professional storyteller or a children's librarian who reads or tells stories, notice the techniques used and the listeners' reactions. What holds their interest? Does the interest ever flag?
3. What were your favorite stories when you were a child? Why do you think they made such a strong impression, so that you wanted to hear them again and again?

---

[5]Frederic A. Brussat, "Twenty-seven Ways to Live a Spiritual Life Every Day," *Utne Reader,* July–August 1994, p. 94.

Chapter 14

Drama as a
Teaching Tool

Metro Theater Company actor Christopher Gurr planning with sixth-grade students at Lincoln Acceler School, St. Louis, MO. (Photograph by Kitty Daly.)

> The school of the future will, perhaps, not be a
> school as we understand it—with benches,
> blackboards, and a teacher's platform—it may be a
> theatre, a library, a museum, or a conversation.
>
> —*Leo Tolstoy*

Tolstoy's prediction of a century ago has taken place; today, we find both receptivity and active involvement of community resources in the education of children and young people. One of the most effective resources is theatre. The use of drama as a tool for teaching is not new: historically, both drama and theatre have long been recognized as potent means of education and indoctrination. The ways they are used today, however, are new, and they differ in a number of respects from the ways they have been used in the past.

Most familiar to us in the Western world is the theatre of ancient Greece, which developed from celebration and dance into a golden age of theatre. Athenian education in the fifth century B.C. was based on music, literature, and dance. Physical activities were emphasized, whereas music included the study of rhythms and harmony as well as the instruments of the time. Because dance was basic to religious festivals, it was stressed, and the chorus of young people received a rigorous training subsidized by wealthy citizens. Dramatists were highly respected, and drama was a major educational force. Plato, in *The Republic*, advocated play as a way of learning. Aristotle urged education in the arts, distinguishing between activities that were means and those that were ends.

The medieval church taught through the medium of mystery plays and, in so doing, helped to restore theatre to its proper place as a great art form. By the last half of the sixteenth century, drama was an important part of the curriculum of the English boys' schools; not only the reading but the staging of classic plays flourished. We could go on through the centuries, nation by nation and culture by culture, finding examples of the various ways drama and theatre have been used to inform, inspire, entertain, and indoctrinate.

The United States has only recently discovered the relationship between theatre and school. Indeed, the twentieth century was well advanced before the arts began to have any real impact on public education in this country. Private schools often offered opportunities in the arts, but usually as extracurricular activities or as minor subjects, rarely placed on a par with the so-called solids. On the secondary school level, they were given even less emphasis. All the arts tended to be what the teacher made them; thus they reflected the teacher's background, interests, and attitude. In the minds of many, theatre and dance were even questionable as part of a young person's education. Drama, in fact, followed music, athletics, and the visual arts into the curriculum. The publication of the *National Standards for Arts Education* in 1994 has had an impact, but the states are still uneven in acceptance and implementation of these standards and are therefore far from the subtitle: "What Every Young American

Should Know and Be Able to Do in the Arts."[1] Nevertheless, a milestone was reached with a document that offers guidance to sequential learning across the four disciplines: music, dance, visual arts, and theatre.

Despite progress, however, the dispute regarding the importance and function of drama in education continues. Is it to be included in the curriculum as a means or as an end? Are we primarily concerned with its use as a teaching tool, or do we regard it as a discipline in its own right, to be taught for its own sake? Augusto Boal, in his introduction to *Theatre of the Oppressed,* states the question clearly: "Should art educate, inform, organize, influence, incite to action, or should it simply be an object of pleasure?"[2] From Aristophanes to the practitioners of today, these objectives have been discussed and argued. Indeed, today the arts are practiced in every category mentioned, for needs vary and interests differ. Adherence to one use does not, and should not, exclude the others. We need the arts for every reason given. Since the 1920s, many of the foremost practitioners in the field of drama education have warned against the exploitation of drama/theatre to achieve other ends, that is, making it a handmaiden to other subject areas. This exploitation, incidentally, has been of concern to teachers of the other arts as well. Are the visual arts, for instance, to be respected as art, or are they to be used for the preparation of school decorations, posters, party invitations, stage sets, and so on? This concern is not to be confused with inclusion of the arts in integrated projects, in which the same activities might be performed, but in which they are related, often brilliantly, to a unit of study. The influence of the British theatre-in-education (TIE) companies and drama-in-education (DIE) on American schools and producers of children's theatre began a new era in the seventies, as many of their concepts and methods have been adopted here. Leaders insist that every subject in the curriculum can be taught through drama. It is the aim of this chapter to discuss some of the ways in which that can be done.

Integrated Projects

Projects integrating drama, music, dance, creative writing, and the visual arts with social studies and literature have been popular since the early days of the progressive education movement in America. Even the most traditional schools have found integrated projects an effective way of teaching and learning. Arts educators have generally endorsed integrated projects because they place the arts at the core of the curriculum rather than on the periphery. Such projects continue to find popularity in schools whose staff members are able and willing to work closely together. Such cooperation is often more easily accomplished in small private schools, where the schedule allows for flexibility and where there is concern for student interest.

The integrated project usually starts in the social studies or English class. With the topic as a base, various aspects of it are explored. Take, for instance, the topic of a

---

[1]Consortium of National Arts Education Associations, *National Standards for Arts Education* (Reston, VA: Music Educators National Conference, 1994).
[2]Augusto Boal, *Theatre of the Oppressed* (New York, NY: The Theatre Communications Group, 1985), p. xlll.

foreign country such as Egypt. In the exploration of the topic, Egyptian history, geography, climate, religions, homes, clothing, food, occupations, myths and legends, and arts and crafts are all included, and from this study a project evolves. One fifth-grade class became so fascinated with Egypt that the students made shadow puppets and presented them in a program of short plays based on their favorite Egyptian legends. The project lasted for several weeks and involved teachers of art, music, and social studies; the results showed both interest and understanding on the part of the students.

Such integrated projects are part of schoolwork, done during school time, and if shown they are seen by an audience of schoolchildren. Occasionally, a project reaches into the community or is of such magnitude that a wider audience is invited to see the work. One memorable program given in New York City early in 1979 celebrated the International Year of the Child. This was an extremely effective project in which performers from Asia, Africa, and Latin America, children from the Third World Institute of Theatre Arts Studies, and children from the United Nations International School worked together on a multiethnic pageant. Titled *A Third World Litany*, it brought dance, chanting, music, and religious rites together, concluding with a pledge to observe the rights of children everywhere.

Whether drama should be taught as a subject in its own right or employed as a medium for the teaching of other subjects is at the heart of a continuing controversy, and each side of the argument has its proponents. It is not that the two points of view are incompatible. Many teachers holding both points of view achieve successful results. When the teacher subscribes strongly to one point of view, however, that separate point of view is given a priority; it is for this reason that drama/theatre as an art and drama/theatre as a learning medium are examined separately.

Drama as an Art in Its Own Right

When drama is taught as an art form, the goals are both aesthetic and intrinsic: aesthetic, because product is emphasized; intrinsic, because the child as artist is a major concern. Overall objectives in such teaching include range of perception, sincerity, and the deepening of feeling and thought, for arts education is "education of the senses, of the intuition, not necessarily a cognitive or explicit didactic education."[3]

Drama classes include work on movement and rhythms, pantomime, improvisation, character study, and speech, often following a progression similar to the one I use in this book. The teacher helps students to develop greater awareness as they create dramatic situations. The problems of structure, organization, unity, and plot are studied through guided improvisation and group discussion. Characters and their relationships to other characters are analyzed for insights into motivation for their actions. Students are encouraged to express their own ideas and interpretations and to offer suggestions to the group. Indeed, the teacher's first job is to create an atmosphere in which the players feel comfortable and at ease with one another while working together.

---

[3]Robert J. Landy, *A Handbook of Educational Drama and Theatre* (Westport, CT: Greenwood Press, 1982), p. 260.

The teacher of creative drama on any level usually begins drama instruction with simple group activities and theatre games. As the players develop and grow, they are given longer and more demanding assignments. Folklore and literature that lends itself to dramatization make excellent material for creative playing. The teacher enriches the experience by bringing in appropriate materials: music, pictures, and other visual aids. Properties and bits of colorful costumes help to stimulate the imagination, and if it is available, stage lighting helps to enhance the mood. A stage, however, is not necessary and is, in fact, undesirable until much later, when or if students reach the performance level. Even then, performing in an all-purpose room or in a large classroom, arena style, is preferable.

When players are stimulated and freed to make full use of their creative powers, they produce work that not only is satisfying to them but communicates to others. As Susanne Langer put it, "art creates perceptible forms expressive of human feeling."[4]

The aesthetic growth of a student has little, if anything, to do with his or her chronological growth, for the aesthetic sense is individual and so differs from one person to another. In a sound program of arts education, students are encouraged to interpret in their own way the world as they see it. Far from being an escape from life, art is a deep involvement in life, one that enriches the participant now and afterward. In the lower grades, children enjoy the act of creating or pretending. Few little children ask on their own to give plays for an audience. The process of playing itself brings fulfillment. In the middle and upper grades, however, product assumes a greater importance. Performing for an audience carries the experience one step further. It must be emphasized that this is not an essential or automatic outcome of every lesson in creative drama, but older children generally do reach the point where they want a performance. When this happens, the teacher should support the request and help them plan the details, adding the necessary showmanship so that the program or play will be a success. The teacher makes sure, however, that the children's work remains theirs and is not transformed into a show with an adult-imposed structure and style that turns guidance into exploitation.

If the program or play is developed through an improvisational method, process is stressed before product. Even though a script will be used for performance, working for meaning before casting or memorization of dialogue puts the emphasis on the play rather than on pleasing an audience. Thus process leads into product, which is the normal result of studying a performing art. Performance, to be satisfying to both players and spectators, calls for education of the adults in the audience as well as the children in the cast. Parents, teachers, and administrators need to understand what they are looking for and why: to appreciate the work that has gone into the performance; to perceive the growth and share the excitement of the players; to commend the result but not overpraise individuals, laugh at mistakes, or expect skills that are not yet developed. Performing can be a wonderfully rewarding experience if approached and received in the right spirit.

---

[4]Susanne Langer, *Problems of Art* (New York: Scribner, 1957), p. 80.

It is to be hoped that performances by children are confined to school assemblies, where a sympathetic invited audience will view the product with knowledge of the process through which the product was developed. Honesty and understanding are important, not technical skills that children do not have and cannot be expected to acquire until their bodies and voices have matured.

The other important component of aesthetic education is the experience of seeing good theatre. Providing this experience is often easier said than done because of the wide variation in both availability and quality of plays for the child audience. Availability depends on the community and its geographic location; quality, on the standards of the producing groups. There is no single pattern throughout the country. Professional, university, and community theatres all contribute, but not all meet the same standard of production. In some areas college theatres offer excellent plays and tour them to nearby towns. In other areas civic or community theatres provide regular and ongoing seasons of plays, including one or more for children and youth. In still other communities schools sponsor performances by professional touring companies whose work also varies in quality. Few plays designed for the adult audience are appropriate for elementary school children, though many adult plays hold interest and are recommended for high school students.

Good dramatic literature, well performed and artistically costumed and staged, is welcomed by every drama and classroom teacher as the other aspect of aesthetic education. A fine production nourishes as well as gives pleasure and, moreover, holds up a standard of excellence. Although the involvement of the spectator is rarely as deep as that of the participant, it can bring a child excitement and make a lasting impression. In addition, theatre helps build an appreciation of an art form that is different from the response one has to film and television. The live performance, in which the audience plays an integral part, touches us on a deeper level.

Drama as a Learning Medium

The 1970s, which brought new concepts of drama and theatre education to this country, caused some far-reaching changes in our practices and a reexamination of our methods and goals. Classroom teachers, more at home with the use of drama as a technique for teaching other subjects than with the production of plays (for which they had little or no background and insufficient time to rehearse), discovered creative drama to be an exciting and useful addition to the curriculum. Proponents of the new techniques offered the suggestion that administrators might find drama and theatre more acceptable as educational media than as aesthetic education. This argument would be further strengthened, they said, if research could prove that children's learning was enhanced when drama and theatre had been used as teaching tools.

The difference between drama employed as a specific teaching technique and drama taught as an art form, an end in itself, is primarily one of intent. Many of the same procedures may be followed, but in the case of drama as a learning medium, the teacher is using these procedures to reach certain extrinsic goals: to convey knowledge, arouse interest, solve problems, and change attitudes. Through the process of studying

Julia Morris teaching young children using a puppet as a tool. (Courtesy of Julia Morris.)

a conflict and the persons involved in it, material is illuminated and interpreted, just as it is in the preparation of a play.

British educator Dorothy Heathcote's approach to drama is particularly appealing to classroom teachers, who find in it techniques that they can use in their own teaching. She works, as she says, from the inside out, and her concern is that children use drama to expand their understanding of life experiences, to reflect on a particular circumstance, and to make sense of their world in a deeper way. There is no area of the curriculum in which she has not used drama. She begins with process and in time moves to a product that may take an audience into account, though this is not her major concern. She consciously employs the elements of drama to educate, according to Betty Jane Wagner, and aims to bring out what children already know but don't yet know they know.[5]

In lieu of putting on plays and dramatizing literature, Heathcote prefers to help children find the dramatic moment in an event or unit of study. She believes in helping the teacher use drama to teach more effectively, but not by exploiting it to sugarcoat nondramatic material. She encourages the teacher to work with children as a guide and resource person. When there is a drama specialist in the school, Heathcote advocates having the classroom teacher follow up the lesson with the drama specialist's

---

[5]Betty Jane Wagner, *Dorothy Heathcote* (Washington, DC: National Education Association Press, 1976).

suggestions. When there is no specialist, the classroom teacher must learn how to discover the tension, conflict, or point of greatest interest in a topic; how to collect relevant source materials; and how to guide the class through an original piece of work. This process may last for a few periods or for an entire semester, depending on the scope of the study and the interest of the children.

Dramatizing an event, Heathcote believes, makes it possible to isolate and study it. She starts with discussion, using the children's ideas and encouraging their making decisions. Once the direction is clear, she suggests a choice of procedures: analogy, simulation, and role. Of the three, Heathcote prefers the last because she believes it fixes an emotional response. She therefore assumes a role, taking part as a character in the drama. When clarification is needed, she steps out of role, stopping the drama for discussion; she then resumes the improvisation. It is this technique that most differentiates her work from that of American creative drama teachers, who rarely take an active part or stop a scene that is going well to discuss it.

Teachers following this method collect the best reference materials, literature, and artifacts they can find. The children are encouraged to spend much time studying them in order to build an original drama. Social studies, current events, and moral and ethical problems become grist for the mill because we are concerned with both cognitive and affective learning. Possible topics for drama might be the study of a particular community, an industry, energy, pollution, transportation, immigration, a disaster with social implications, or a great or well-known person. The possibilities are endless and may come from any area of the curriculum; the point is that by employing drama in this way, the teacher helps students to see below the surface of an event or topic and thereby gain a better understanding of it.

As an example, consider a disaster. Go beyond the immediate situation: What is the impact on the community? on the families of the victims? What are the ramifications of a major disaster, and what steps are taken by the government to prevent future catastrophes like it? The objective is to gain understanding, challenge thinking, and develop compassion.

The collapse of the World Trade Towers was a catastrophe that many teachers had to handle without preparation or any previous experience. Drama therapists were called in some cases. This was a disaster that will be recalled vividly for years to come, with drama still an effective way of coping with it.

Gavin Bolton of Durham University in England has worked with Dorothy Heathcote in the United States on numerous occasions and has also offered workshops of his own. Although they share the same educational philosophy, Bolton's techniques differ in certain respects. He stated his aims in drama education as follows:[6]

1. To help students understand themselves and the world they live in
2. To help students know how and when (and when not) to adapt to the world they live in
3. To help students gain understanding of and satisfaction from the medium of drama

---

[6]From notes prepared for London Teachers of Drama by Gavin Bolton, 1973.

Bolton admits to being primarily concerned with the cognitive aspect of the drama experience. Although he does not recommend neglecting the aesthetic element, he says that he teaches through it rather than for it.

Another of the current and respected voices in drama-in-education is Cecily O'Neill. As she says, she shares the philosophy of Dorothy Heathcote and Gavin Bolton, but realizing that many American teachers and students have difficulty applying it to their own work, she is trying to clarify the method by working with them over a longer period. The following excerpt from a paper written by Cecily O'Neill for me may help both teachers and students understand this practical use of drama-in-education.

Drama as a Significant Experience

For me, the most important task in drama-in-education is the creation of a shared dramatic context, a fictional world, in which it is possible to explore and examine ideas, issues, relationships, and content areas. Like theatre, drama is a paradoxical activity. It is both real and not real at the same time. Both drama and theatre require an active engagement with the make-believe, a willingness to be caught up in and accept the rules of the imaginary world which is created on stage or in the classroom. . . . I want my students to experience the pleasure, insight, and satisfaction of balancing these opposites. There will be a growing sense of mastery and delight in cooperatively manipulating the make-believe and sharing perceptions and cognitions with others.

A central concept in my work is role-play. In both theatre and drama the participants adopt roles. They pretend to become what they are not. By taking on roles they transcend their everyday selves and get a glimpse of their own potential. Roles can be assumed, modified, elaborated, refined, and relinquished. But the result is not merely that the participants' role repertoire is expanded. By exploring the different perspectives offered by fictional roles, students may come to recognize, and, if necessary, modify their habitual orientation to the world.

. . . In drama we are not seeking solutions or finding answers, as is often the case when role-playing is used as an instrument in the curriculum. We are trying to release students into finding their own questions. The power of the teacher-in-role comes not from theatrical skills or a desire to perform but from a capacity for courageous, imaginative, and authentic engagement with students in the co-creation of an imagined world. In my work with teachers I have tried to share this sense of structure. I want them to gain confidence in manipulating elements of the drama experience so that it is satisfying for both leader and participants.[7]

Again, as in every area, similar work is being carried on successfully in the United States, without publicity, by classroom teachers who have created their own methods of teaching. One of them is the Echo Project, designed by two young teachers in Middle College High School of La Guardia Community College, Long Island City, New York.

---

[7]Nellie McCaslin, *Children and Drama,* 3rd ed. (Studio City, CA: Players Press, 1999).

The Bongo Workbook, a manual for teachers of science and social studies, was made possible by grants from the National Endowment for the Arts and administered by the Research Foundation of the City University of New York. The teachers, Paul Jablon and Terry Born, realized the special needs of this city's at-risk urban high school population and to that end designed an interdisciplinary team-teaching program in the late 1970s. By the late 1980s its success was recognized, and a workbook explaining their methodology was completed. Published in 1987, it became available for use by other teachers in the field. A popular technique described throughout is creative drama.[8]

Drama can be used to illuminate the study of science in middle school. With a grant from the Appalachian College Association, Professors R. Rex Stephenson and Mike Trochin collaborated on the play script *Galileo, Man of Science.* With a guide to extend the experience in the classroom following the performance, teachers are offered a wealth of ideas for further work in science, math, creative writing, playwriting, character study, history and ethics.

Ferrum College students perform Galileo, *a play commissioned by the Appalachian College Association for middle school students. (Courtesy of R. Rex Stephenson, director. Later published by New Plays, Inc.)*

---

[8]Terry Born and Paul Jablon, *The Bongo Workbook* (Long Island City, NY: Middle College High School at La Guardia Community College, 1987).

An interesting project was instigated by a teacher of first and second grades in a New York inner-city school. Discovering that the children had never experienced sharing a traditional Thanksgiving dinner with a family or community group, the teacher used the holiday as a way of learning about the first Thanksgiving and how some of our customs and practices have evolved. He included songs, arts and crafts, and the enactment of appropriate legends and stories in his plans. The children made Native American headdresses and strings of paper beads to wear for the occasion and paper mats to be used on the tables. With the cooperation of a parent-teacher committee, a complete Thanksgiving dinner was prepared. The children counted and peeled potatoes, apples, and squash, measured brown sugar, and made butter and stirred gravy, thus meeting the curriculum goals of science and math as well as social studies. Local merchants supplied food, including a large turkey, and a florist friend of the teacher contributed flowers for the tables. I was invited to the festivities held at noon on the day before Thanksgiving, and I was both charmed and touched by the enjoyment and pride of the children as they presented their simple program and then looked for their places at the tables. It was evident throughout that much learning had taken place through the use of the arts.

Two Sample Lesson Plans

The following lesson plans can be adapted to any grade level, depending on the curriculum and unit of study. This is the reason I have suggested procedures rather than specific books or stories. For "Animal Partners" there is a wealth of literature available in most libraries, from which the teacher can select the most suitable material. The Humane Society of the United States, the ASPCA, and most animal shelters have publications and films that are easily available. Reading about animals leads to discussion and the enactment of stories.

Animal Partners

Objectives

1. To teach a unit on humane education, using drama as a medium for learning.
2. To promote understanding and compassion for animals by studying their habits and needs and our relationship to them.

Preparation

Put pictures and photographs of different kinds of animals on the bulletin board. These may be pictures of domestic animals, wild animals, or both, depending on the focus.

Procedure

1. Begin with a discussion of the animals we know best. Talking about pets usually elicits anecdotes, for the children will have had experiences and stories they are eager to share. Lead the discussion into the care and feeding of dogs, cats, gerbils, guinea pigs, birds, and horses and our responsibility toward these domestic animals.

2. Most cities and many small towns have an animal shelter. Arrange for a class visit. Staff members are usually glad to welcome school groups and can answer questions such as "Why are the animals here?" "Who brought them in?" and "What happens to them if they are not adopted?" Staff members will explain some of the problems such as finding homes for old animals or animals with health problems and raising funds to support animal shelters.

3. The visit will lead to discussion in the classroom and afterward, and environmental and ethical issues may come up as a result.

4. If wild animals are included in the study and there is a local zoo, try to visit it. There the class will see wild animals as opposed to the domestic animals they saw in the shelter. A docent is usually available to lead the tour and answer questions.

5. Back in the classroom continue the discussion and read some of Aesop's *fables*, explaining how Aesop used animals to show human faults and foibles. Have the children enact the fables, which are short but offer opportunities to play animal roles. This is also a good time to think of ways in which animals are used today to help people: as guide dogs, for horseback riding, and in pet-assisted therapy, for example. In what other ways do animals and people care for each other? (Try to avoid discussion of animals in entertainment, research, hunting, etc., where there may be abuse. With older children these issues can and should be explored, but they involve ethical and legal problems that require mature consideration.)

6. Creative writing, stimulated by stories and class discussion, may include original stories, poems, or plays. Children in the intermediate grades and older may want to write a play about animals for an assembly program. Adaptations of favorite animal stories or original plots are equally good as experience for young playwrights.

7. When children are playing animals, it is usually better not to have them attempt walking on all fours. Standing upright not only is much easier but makes the player work on interpretation of the animal character rather than attempt to imitate stance and movement. Some movements can be suggested; helping the players find which ones is the challenge.

The Westward Movement

Objectives

1. To understand the reasons why people leave their homes and friends to make long, difficult journeys to new lands.

2. To experience the journey to the West through the medium of drama.

Preparation

1. The teacher leads a discussion on moving from one's home to a new neighborhood, perhaps in another city or country. Ask the children questions:
   a. How many in the class have had this experience?
   b. How did you feel about it?
   c. How long did it take to make new friends?
   d. What were the best things you remember about the move? the worst?
2. Select books, appropriate to the grade level, that explain the westward movement.
3. Select photographs and pictures of the country, the wagon trails, the housing, vegetation, and animals.

Activities

1. Study the route one family took, and make a map showing it. If there is time and the students are interested, each child can make a map.
2. Plan the important scenes and improvise the action that might take place before starting out, along the way West, and after arriving at the destination.
3. Write a play based on the scenes.
4. Share the work by performing the play for a school assembly or for an invited audience of parents or another class.

The Situation

This is the story of a family that makes the trip to the West. The characters have the difficult task of deciding what they must take with them and what to leave behind. They have strong and mixed feelings about the prospect of leaving friends and familiar surroundings for the strange and unknown. The father believes that he can provide a better living for his family. The mother is willing to go but apprehensive. The son is eager for the adventure, but the daughter does not want to leave her friends and her school. The family lives in the Northeast; if they go out West, they will be able to homestead and settle new territory, to be part of a new country.

The Scenes

Scene 1: Broaching the subject. The father gathers the family members together to tell them about the proposed move. Each one reacts to it in his or her own way.

Scene 2: Telling friends and neighbors. Some reactions are positive, some negative.

Scene 3: Preparing for the journey. The family must make the hard decisions as to what to take and what to leave behind.

Scene 4: Stopping to rest along the way a month later. Everyone is tired but eager to push on.

Scene 5: Stopping three months later. Exhausted, the family almost gives up, but after they have traveled so far and for so long, it would be hard to turn back.

Scene 6: Getting settled in their new home a few months later. They have found some good things, and there have been some disappointments.

As the students improvise the scenes, they will create the action and the reactions of their characters, who will become richer with each playing. Only a skeletal structure is given so as to offer the students maximum opportunity of developing the story in a credible and sympathetic way.

Questions

Where is the family going? What is the country like? What are the individuals' reactions when they finally reach their destination? What are the possibilities of farming the land, meeting neighbors, making friends? What about school? church? social life?

The students may want to add an additional scene or two as they work on this play telling the story of one family's experience of going West. Although I have included this as an appropriate topic for elementary classes, it is also one that high school students can relate to and handle on a more sophisticated level.

A delightful example of teacher-in-role was described to me by a young assistant teacher of preschool children. Asked to introduce a unit on animals, she donned overalls, boots, and a straw hat, entering as Farmer Jess. The children, after a few moments of silence, asked where Ms. Morris was. The teacher explained that *she* was Ms. Morris, but with the help of a costume and her imagination, she had become Farmer Jess. Their curiosity satisfied, the children spent the next thirty minutes eagerly immersed in a new level of teaching and learning. They discussed the different animals that could be found on a farm, their habits, their food, where they slept, and the care they required. At the end of the period, when Ms. Morris left the room, she suggested, that the children draw pictures of Farmer Jess's farm. Not only did they respond to the suggestion, but for several weeks afterward they talked about animals, described them in pantomime, and begged for more stories about them. This is an example of a lesson by an imaginative young teacher who at that point had never heard the term *teacher-in-role* yet used the technique with success.

Artists in the Schools

Another approach to drama/theatre education is the artists in the schools program, which brings performers into the classroom for a morning, a day, a week, or sometimes a much longer period. Here actors perform, demonstrate, or work directly with the children. This provides an opportunity for the teacher to learn new techniques that help him or her to continue alone after the actors have gone. It also exposes children to the creative artist, whom they would otherwise probably never meet. Throughout the United States, actors, dancers, musicians, painters, puppeteers, and poets have been brought into schools through funded programs. Information on available artists (both groups and individuals) is available through state arts councils and state departments of education. Today many theatre companies offer workshops or residencies following performances.

Playwriting with Young People

Since the sixth edition of this book was published, there has been a developing interest in playwriting with and by children and young people. It is too soon to tell whether or not this is a trend, but some unusual opportunities have been made available to both elementary and secondary school students and their teachers to learn more about this form of writing. The participation play, by involving the audience in the process as well as in the performance, introduces children to dramatic structure in a way that the formal proscenium production does not. Whether the idea of bringing a playwright into the classroom is in any way related to participatory theatre is hard to say, but it is obvious to anyone who has ever been in a child audience that children are extremely perceptive regarding character, plot, and motivation. Though children do not necessarily observe a linear pattern in their writing any more than they do in their improvisations, there is a logic in their dramatic writing which, if given encouragement and basic technical help, can lead to some impressive results.

One program that has attracted attention is the Young Playwrights' Project, initiated in 1980 by the Dramatists' Guild. To direct it the guild engaged Gerald Chapman, a young Englishman whose work in playwriting with young people at the Royal Court Theatre in London brought him to their attention. Chapman launched the project by offering workshops for students and teachers in the New York metropolitan area and later in other cities. By 1982 the Young Playwrights' Project had become highly successful, with seven hundred plays submitted that season, ten of which were produced with professional casts. The brochure for the following season announced workshops for young people from fourth through twelfth grades and a festival in the spring offering professional production of the award-winning scripts. Critics, educators, and directors have acclaimed the project as "an innovative design for learning," "a bracing theatrical occasion," "an opportunity for children to acquire not only a sensitivity to the art of playwriting and drama but a contribution to their cognitive, social and emotional development." The project has continued with winning plays given production every spring in one of New York's most prestigious off-Broadway theatres. Collections of the plays are also available in paperback.

A quite different approach was used by the late Aurand Harris, a well-known American children's playwright, who was playwright-in-residence in a number of communities throughout the country in the 70s and 80s. He spent a month at a time in elementary school classrooms, working directly with children, stimulating them to writing but without awards or eventual production. His educational objectives were to foster an ongoing interest in the dramatic form and to stimulate improvement in written communication.

Guided experience in writing plays performs a number of services for the student. Its contribution to the language arts, however, can be summed up in the following simple statement concerning plays as literature: "The important feature is that they [plays] are primarily linguistic, narrative constructs; they are all part of the unique relationship between language and form we call literature."[9]

---

[9]*Plays Considered as Literature as Well as Theatre for Young People from 8 to 18 to Read and Perform*, compiled and discussed by Aidan Chambers (South Woodchester, Stroud, England: Thimble Press, 1982), p. 6.

It is heartening to see that children's plays have finally been recognized as literature and accorded a place in some elementary school textbooks and anthologies of children's literature. Stories, poems, and essays have traditionally made up the content of these books; today, however, with a growing number of excellent plays by gifted children's playwrights, a new genre of literature has become available, one to which most children respond. It is also interesting to note that the range of subject matter has broadened. Plays with characters from different ethnic and racial backgrounds are being written, and some leaders in the field are also taking an active part in making fine religious dramas available to young people. For the junior and senior high school student there is practical help in Carol Korty's handbook *Writing Your Own Plays*.[10] Clear organization and practical suggestions make this a valuable resource for both teachers and students.

A recent book, *Bringing the Word Alive—Children's Writings: Process to Performance* by Pat Hale and Trish Lindberg, makes the point that writing does not necessarily mean playwriting, although an original play may be the objective.[11] Let me explain. The authors accept all kinds of writing that children offer: stories, personal anecdotes, poems, journals, even songs. What children write is typically brief, often fragmented, and rarely linear. Their work may, however, become the raw material for performance in time. It is the teacher who stimulates and collaborates with the children in bringing a script out of a patchwork of forms.

Creative writing, handled in this way, provides a link to the curriculum, engaging children in a variety of learning styles and challenging them to think dramatically. Story starters, or phrases that can trigger the imagination, are effective ways of beginning:

It was a cold and stormy night.
I lost my boot in a snowdrift.
That haunted house on Pineapple Street ...
The last day of vacation ...
The present I didn't want ...
When we moved to a new neighborhood ...

Props stimulate imaginative responses in writing just as they do in creative drama. Show the children an unusual item. Ask what it is or where they think it came from, what it might be used for, whether they think it is valuable, or to whom might it have belonged.

The authors suggest brainstorming for issues related to a particular subject, especially if it is controversial or the objective is a socially conscious presentation. They describe an original play called *Just Between Friends*. The issues related to it were peer pressure, loneliness, families, fears, self-esteem, and hopes and dreams. After reading what the children submitted, the authors sorted the writings for their dramatic possibilities. The questions that always arise at this point are, "Do you try to

---

[10]Carol Korty, *Writing Your Own Plays* (Studio City, CA: Players Press, 1996).
[11]Pat Hale and Trish Lindberg, *Bringing the Word Alive—Children's Writings: Process to Performance* (Charlottesville, VA: New Plays, 1996), pp. 8–9.

include everything, and do you change what the children have written?" The authors say that they do not make changes, except occasionally for grammar, but they may shorten a piece that is too long. They may also ask the writer to rewrite a piece for the sake of greater clarity. What can develop from this process may be either a play or a collage of the various writings that are submitted. In the latter case, everything can be included.

Playwriting, therefore, is not the only genre that drama can generate. Stories, poems, journals, letters, children's personal reactions to experiences are all possible, as described in *Children's Writings: Process to Performance.* The authors list the educational values of drama as a stimulus to creative writing:[12]

1. Providing a new way to motivate writing
2. Engaging children with a variety of learning styles in a collaborative process drawing on kinesthetic, spatial, musical, and interpersonal intelligences as well as language and logic
3. Linking writing to curriculum
4. Enhancing academic performance in children who may previously have lacked the confidence that comes from achievement
5. Challenging children to think and write dramatically
6. Empowering children and teachers to think of themselves as creative individuals

Group Poems

Group poems are adaptable to every grade level. The procedure for writing a group poem is as follows:

ESTABLISH GOALS

To involve everyone in the process of composing a poem.
To stimulate strong imagery.

PLAN ACTIVITIES

1. Brainstorm for ideas or, if the group is not ready for that, suggest a topic that will lead to a creative response.
2. After allowing two or three minutes to think about the topic, have each student contribute a line, a phrase, or even a word stimulated by the topic.
3. Write down the suggestions as they are spoken.
4. Read the resulting poem to the class, and discuss the strengths of the work, the structure of a poem, and the writers' feelings as they composed their lines.

Some of the topics I have used with success have been the last day of school, birthdays, the band concert, fire engines, in-line skates, skyscrapers, the school bus, and winter mornings.

---

[12]Ibid.

After having written a group poem, the children may want to try writing poems of their own. It is important that they not be concerned with rhyming; original work phrased in their own words or in free verse is a fresh approach, and the results will have far more authenticity than a struggle with a form that is neither childlike nor poetic. Although I include this as an appropriate activity for elementary classes, it is also one that high school students can relate to and handle on a more sophisticated level.

Other kinds of writing can be started in the same way, that is, with a group effort. This is particularly true of playwriting. Dividing the class into small groups of three, four, or five gives an opportunity for discussion of characters, plot, motivation, and dramatic action. The teacher must keep in mind the fact that children's logic is quite different from that of adults; by eschewing the linear form, they often come up with something delightful in its originality. Have a scribe in each group write down the dialogue, unless the recording is done by student teachers or aides. Reading the parts aloud when scenes are finished enables the playwrights to see where the weaknesses are and what filling out is needed. Drama is the best way to begin a playwriting unit.

A number of years ago when I was teaching in the intermediate grades, I often went to the teachers of language arts and social studies to see how we could work together. In every instance a unit in one or the other would be an exciting starting point for my creative drama class. For example, James Whitcomb Riley was celebrated annually in Indiana schools but I went beyond the poet and his work. We also studied the period in which he lived and wrote, the people and the customs as reflected in his verse. Choral reading, tableaux, and improvisation preceded writing. When the students were ready to begin, I divided the class into groups of three, each group taking one area. We worked out the scene that evolved, discussing and rehearsing for several weeks, finally presenting them in an assembly program for the school.

Other topics that the class found fascinating were "France in the Middle Ages" and "Taxation," both of which had tremendous ramifications. As the drama teacher, I consulted with the classroom teachers; the classroom teachers, wanting to use drama to illuminate the material, had the advantage of preparing in advance, calling visual materials, and stimulating interest through questions.

Special Arts Projects

Supplementing curricular offerings are the many special arts projects that have been funded by the U.S. Office of Education to promote intercultural and interracial communication for students, teachers, and community members. Although all the programs are subject to budget cuts, they have contributed to various areas:

1. The artist-in-residence program. Before each residency, the artist holds a workshop with teachers about his or her craft. Artists may include a poet, a dancer, a media specialist, a visual artist, a dramatist, and a musician.
2. Special series programs. In this area there are performances by actors, orchestras, ballet companies, mimes, and puppet theatres.

3. Speakers and field trips.
4. Arts camps.
5. Publications.
6. School-community relations. The aim is to involve more parents and community organizations in the purpose and implementation of the special arts projects program.
7. Teacher training. Workshops help teachers in ongoing arts programs.
8. Project replication. This may involve visits to other school systems and preparation of helpful materials.

An organization that has been a help and source of inspiration to many communities is Young Audiences. Founded in 1952 as a national nonprofit organization, it has as its stated purpose to enhance the education and, in doing so, the quality of life of young people by introducing them to the performing arts. To achieve this purpose, Young Audiences sponsors professional musicians, dancers, and actors who present programs in public and private schools. Students learn about the creative process directly from the performers. These are some of the offerings:

Programs for students. Performances and demonstrations are given in primary and secondary schools. Workshop and residency programs are also offered to teach students about the arts in a series of presentations conducted over a longer period of time.

Programs for the education community. Arts education is sponsored at the local, regional, state, and national levels. The programs encourage integration of the arts into teacher training.

Third graders make costumes and props. (Courtesy of Susan Sleeper, Dallas Children's Theatre.)

Programs for artists. Programs and training for artists are designed to meet the educational and cultural needs of the individual communities served. The organization provides—and sustains—career opportunities for performing artists.

Programs for growth. To expand its representation throughout the United States, Young Audiences is committed to strengthening affiliations among the thirty-eight chapters in its national network. Young Audiences researches techniques for developing arts education programs and distributes the published results to professionals in the field of arts education.

One of the benefits of a high-quality performance is the stimulating effect it has on students' own creative work. When the teacher makes use of the excitement engendered by an artist, the results are often imaginative and strong. When performers come into the classroom, another point is made: that art can be created and enjoyed anywhere; it is not confined to the concert hall. Young children have no problem with this; it is only the adult who thinks in terms of auditoriums, lights, curtains, and so on.

This brings up the point made earlier that drama is the least expensive of all arts to implement. It requires no elaborate equipment and no special materials. A room, a leader, and a group of children are the only requirements. A piano and tape recorder are useful but not necessary. Nor is stage lighting needed, although it adds atmosphere if it is available. Costumes and props can be supplied by teacher and students, but they act as stimuli rather than as dressing for players or stage. Education of the leader is important, but the many classes and workshops that are available today in most communities make it relatively easy for the interested teacher to find the help he or she needs. Pointing out the fact that creative drama is not the production of plays and therefore does not require a theatre rules out the first objection of an administration that believes drama is too expensive.

The Circus Arts in Education

Some startling facts emerge in a study of circus arts in modern education. Although it is generally known that some schools and colleges offer them on an after-school or extracurricular basis, the extent to which they are being offered is surprising. Today, according to Jean Paul Jenack, more than 150 colleges and universities have well-developed programs in circus skills, with many of the courses offered for credit.[13] Some programs approach the work from a cultural or performing arts point of view, some from a physical education base, still others as entertainment.

The first circus arts programs appeared in U.S. schools in the mid-1920s, but there was no further record of activity until the 1930s. This took the form of magic shows, popular as entertainment both in and outside the classroom. Again, this did not lead to any well-developed programs in the circus arts. After World War II, circus skills were introduced into physical education departments as new body-building techniques. By the 1980s, a combination of many of these techniques reappeared, followed by a pattern

---

[13]Conversation with Jean Paul Jenack, 1995.

Educational Television. Using a puppet to teach basic English. (Courtesy of Kannie Chung, Hong Kong.)

of real growth. In England, circus arts were equestrian based, whereas in Eastern European countries, troupes worked for excellence in professional performance. The trend in the United States, in contrast, has been for circus performers to join in partnership with educators and community leaders. In recent years psychologists and the clergy have also found therapeutic values in the circus arts. Some companies emphasize production, preparing and sending out teachers' study guides in advance of a performance and giving a follow-up session afterward in the classroom.

Some schools and studios enroll children as well as adults in a carefully structured curriculum. Other circus professionals work closely in or with the schools, using the circus arts as tools for reaching boys and girls who show little motivation in academic areas. One thing the new circus professionals have in common is a strong academic background, often including a graduate degree.

It would be a mistake to think that all circus performers of the past were roustabouts or runaways lured by a romantic notion of life under the big tent. Circus people were not formally educated, for a variety of reasons, but they were not ignorant or illiterate. To the contrary, they were highly educated in discrete areas, generally taught by their families, with daily practice for perfection. The tradition was for families to hand down their expertise if the child showed promise. Education began at an early age, much like the training of the ballet dancer. Whether the young performer followed in his or her parents' footsteps as aerialist, equestrian, clown, or animal trainer, early acquaintance with the field was necessary to ensure success in a demanding and often dangerous profession. Formal education was out of the question because of the heavy touring schedule, which made regular school attendance impossible. As to mathematics and science, some basic elements were mastered through the rigging of tents and wires, and practical information was gained where errors of judgment could be fatal.

Technology and Drama Education

A direction that I suspect we shall be seeing more of in the future is the use of technology in the study of the arts, particularly drama. Whereas interactive theatre has been with us for a long time in one form or another, the combining of video conferencing, the Internet, and creative drama represents a new strategy. Creatively and judiciously handled by a skilled leader, technology can reach a generation that may have had little direct experience in the arts. It is not by accepting the new technology carte blanche but rather by discovering the possibilities for its use and linking those possibilities to the study of drama that we can chart a new course. For example, at New York University in 1998, an intensive summer workshop for young people eight to fourteen, college students, and teachers, in connection with a group of children in Eastern Canada, did precisely that. Directed by Professor Alistair Martin-Smith, technology and the arts were brought together under the rubric Dram Tech.

Summary

Increasingly evident forces are attempting to change the direction of education from a purely intellectual emphasis to one that recognizes latent potential and therefore includes the arts as a basic component. Many teachers use arts as a tool for teaching as well as disciplines in their own right—not to sugarcoat other subject areas but to illuminate and interpret them. This is less a change, however, than it is an expansion of goals. The many and varied approaches to these concepts represent a new vitality in arts education.

Circumstances rather than specific methodology, however, should be our guide. Leaders share certain common objectives, but they assign priorities according to their situations, strengths, and needs. In other words, although there have been significant changes in the philosophy and the methods employed by teachers of creative drama, there is perhaps less actual than apparent difference from the approach of the past. All methodologies subscribe to a primary concern for the student; most place process above product; all hold certain educational goals in common.

A word of warning: a method is only as good as the person who uses it. A popular method may not be for you, whereas you may have devised a strategy that works well in your situation.

The controversy regarding drama as means or end is not settled and perhaps never will be. Compelling arguments on both sides press for a curriculum in which there is a place for each. Leading educators have declared drama and speech to be central to a language curriculum. They believe that drama can motivate writing and improve oral skills; they believe that it stimulates reading. Some insist that it can be used to teach any subject effectively.

Many educators agree that study of the arts gives form and expression to human feeling and that attending the theatre as a spectator is a rich experience not found in film and television viewing. In the foreword to a publication released by the State University of New York in 1978, a strong stand is taken regarding the place of the arts in education: "The arts are a means of expressing and interpreting human experience. Quality education of individuals is complete only if the arts are an integral part of the daily teaching and learning process. The integration of the arts in the elementary, secondary and continuing education curriculum is a key to the humanistic development of students."[14]

Statements of purpose distinguish the attitude toward arts education today from that held in the past. Hundreds of agencies and foundations—federal, state, and private—contribute to the arts as a further expression of support. Although we have far to go before we can point with pride to schools in which the arts and the academic areas have equal emphasis, progress has been made.

The National Standards for Arts Education lists note what students should know and be able to do in the arts by the time they have completed secondary school:

1. Communicate proficiently in at least one art form.
2. Develop and present basic analyses of works of arts from structural, historical, and cultural perspectives.
3. Have an acquaintance with major works of art from different periods and cultures.
4. Relate their knowledge and skills throughout arts disciplines.

Suggested Assignments

1. Investigate the work of Dorothy Heathcote, Brian Way, Gavin Bolton, or Cecily O'Neill. Books are readily available in most college libraries. Discuss in class the philosophies and methods of these leaders.
2. Design a lesson that you consider to be drama-in-education rather than creative drama. Consider goals, methodology, and expected results.
3. Design a lesson that you consider to be drama-in-education for a specific grade and area of study. What is the subject matter, and what are your goals, methodology, and hoped-for results?
4. If you are doing student teaching, ask if you may do some creative writing with the group. Bring the results to share with your college classmates.
5. Plan and then teach a lesson to your classmates.

---

[14]*The Arts as Perception (A Way of Learning),* Project Search, The University of the State of New York (Albany, NY: State Department, Division of Humanities and Arts Education, 1978), p.iii.

Journal Writing

1. What is the relationship between means and ends?
2. Compare creative drama and drama-in-education in regard to goals and values.
3. Must there be controversy regarding the values of either approach? What do you see as the principal arguments on each side?
4. If your teacher were to evaluate you, what do you think he or she might write?

Chapter 15

Creative Drama for the Special Student

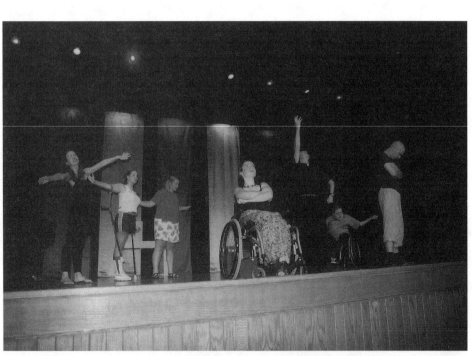

A cabaret performance of the National Theatre Workshop of the Handicapped. (Courtesy of Br. Rick Curry, S.J. and John Spalla.)

> Let each become all that he was created capable of
> being: expand, if possible, to his full growth; and
> show himself at length in his own shape and
> stature.
>
> *—Thomas Carlyle*

This chapter considers creative drama in one of the newer areas of education: special education, or the education of the exceptional student. *Special education* can be defined as any program of teaching techniques designed to meet the needs of children whose abilities deviate markedly from those of the majority of boys and girls of their age. Included in this group are children who are intellectually gifted, cognitively disabled, physically disabled, emotionally disturbed, or economically disadvantaged; children for whom English is a second language; and underachievers whose problems have not been identified.

The purpose of this chapter is to:

1. Raise the consciousness of the leader to make him or her more aware of the needs of the person in the group who has a disability or is special.
2. Offer encouragement to try creative drama and puppetry with persons who are disabled.
3. Introduce some of the materials in the field.

Until recently very little has been done to help these students, whose basic needs are the same as those of others but whose individual needs require special educational services. A difference of opinion still exists about whether, or when, these children should be integrated into regular classrooms, but their special needs must be met. All children should be helped to take their places with their peers in as many areas as possible and as soon as they are able to do so. One of the greatest obstacles to this goal has been the widespread notion that children with special needs are different from other children. Modern educators and psychologists have pointed out the value of getting these boys and girls into regular classrooms while they are receiving remedial help, therapy, or, in the case of the gifted, additional enrichments. Remediation should be an aid to their instruction rather than a separate program of instruction.

Mainstreaming

Mainstreaming is the term used to define the integration of exceptional students into regular classrooms. The major objective is social: to assist all children in working and living together. To this end, various practices can be followed. Drama, because of its total involvement—physical, mental, emotional, and social—offers a wealth of activities that have therapeutic value if properly handled.

Speech therapy, remedial reading, language classes for non-English-speaking children, psychological counseling, and special classes for students who are partially sighted, blind, or deaf can be included in the school day without removing a child from the group for more than a class period or two at a time. Most schools do not have an extensive program of special services, but many do meet the more urgent needs. Special activities are often added as enrichment for the economically disadvantaged as well as for the gifted. In all these programs there is an opportunity to use creative drama.

One community that has been applauded for mainstreaming children with special needs is Woodstock, Vermont. According to a front-page article in the *New York Times* in 1997, "Woodstock is singular in its commitment to keeping 9 out of 10 of the severely disabled in regular classrooms."[1] Some students are also assisted by one-on-one tutoring or a laptop computer, but all are given a chance to participate in the arts and the social life of the school.

The Student Who Is Gifted

One group of students which has received very little attention, perhaps because they are able to move ahead on their own, is the intellectually gifted. Some educators and parents have taken constructive steps to enrich the curriculum so that these boys and girls can receive the stimulation they need by participating in extra classes and following individual interests. One of the areas that has been used most successfully for enrichment is the arts. This is not to imply that *all* children should not have wide and continued exposure to the arts, but because this is an area with endless possibilities, it has often been selected for use with the gifted. Arts programs have been designed both as after-school activities and as additional classes during school time. Some programs include field trips to museums, theatres, and concerts, although funds given for this purpose are generally allocated for the use of all children rather than for one specially selected group.

Some courses are designed for students of above-average ability; the curriculum is characterized by intellectual rigor and a challenge to students to make full use of their abilities. Children who are gifted have the ability to think of many things at the same time; therefore, drama, with its wide range of responsibilities, is an ideal choice. When dealing with these children, the leader must always present a challenge. Classes in drama, dance, music, and the visual arts offer children who are gifted a chance to use their abilities in putting on plays—often written by the children themselves—and in designing and making costumes and scenery.

Profiles of gifted children suggest they tend to fall into four categories:

High-achieving students. Such students work hard in drama, as in other subjects, though their work is frequently conventional rather than original. Improvisations are structured and detailed and are likely to be rehearsed and well performed. Their objectives, which they usually achieve, are a good product, a serious involvement, and better-than-average performance skills.

---

[1]Tamar Levine, "Where All Doors Are Open for Disabled Students," *New York Times*, December 28, 1997, p. 1.

Social leaders. They produce superior work in groups. They also work hard but have the additional ability to lead their classmates to desired ends.

Creative intellectuals. Many of these students have originality. They like the freedom to choose situations, and they produce work that is original, often humorous.

Rebels. These are the mavericks in a group, as likely to be disruptive as to be supportive. With guidance, these students can produce excellent results, but they are not always easy for their peers to work with.[2]

Despite being stereotypes, these categories correctly imply that students who are gifted are a challenge and that the results, when gifted children are well taught, are often brilliant and original.

The Student Who Has Mental Retardation

Mental retardation describes a condition, not a disease. Although it can refer to any degree of retarded mental development, the classifications most commonly used refer to the types of supports an individual needs: intermittent, limited, extensive, and pervasive. This discussion of creative drama in the education of the child who has mental retardation centers on the first category. It is with this group that play can be most rewarding both as a teaching tool and a pleasure. Play constitutes an important role in the all-around human development of the child.

The nature of drama makes it a versatile tool for working with these youngsters. Rhythms, dramatic play, and pantomime are activities widely used by many teachers of children needing intermittent support. Adaptations of the techniques used with other children and developed over a longer period can bring both immediate satisfaction and lasting benefit. According to one teacher who has used creative drama successfully, some of the best material comes from the very social situations that cause the child to be stared at and shunned: entering a restaurant; ordering food and eating it; going on a bus, train, or plane trip; and dressing. These are mostly simple daily activities.

Like all children, the child who has mental retardation wants to be a member of a group, to contribute to it, and to have the contribution accepted. Drama offers this opportunity. One characteristic of these children is difficulty in using imagination or dealing with abstract ideas. Some teachers believe that children who have mental retardation become more imaginative when placed in a regular classroom.[3] Whether they are in a regular classroom or a special class, however, their pace is slow. Recognizing this, the teacher can guide their dramatic play and stimulate their response. Frequently, the leader errs in expecting too much too soon. These children need more help and encouragement than other children; they need to repeat experiences more

---

[2]Richard Courtney, *Re-Play: Studies of Human Drama in Education* (Toronto: Ontario Institute for Studies in Education, 1982), p. 106.
[3]Sue Jennings, *Remedial Drama* (New York: Theatre Arts Books, 1974), p. 4.

often; and, finally, they must learn self-confidence and feel the satisfaction of having their contribution accepted. The game of pretending can help them learn to use imagination, to prepare for new experiences, and to lay a firmer foundation for oral communication. Experienced teachers state that dramatic activities help to develop the skills of listening and looking. In this way, attention is engaged.

Rhythms and movement games are excellent beginning exercises. They aid the development of large muscles while they motivate use of imagination. The acting out of simple stories comes much later. At first, children with mental retardation will be more comfortable participating in a group than working individually. They probably have experienced frustration and the sense of being different; their need for praise and encouragement, therefore, will be great. Children who show interest in moving out of the group to become specific characters—someone other than themselves—are ready for the next step. Now, instead of general group activities, individual roles may be undertaken. At this stage the teacher will not only need to provide stimulation but also must give clear and simple direction: Who is the character? How does the character walk? What is the character doing? How does he or she do it? What does the character say?

If social ease and a sense of security are our first consideration, oral expression is the second. Guided dramatic play is a way of introducing oral vocabulary and developing concepts that prepare the child for reading. A variety of experiences will help to provide the child with a better understanding of his or her world, and acting out words will give them meaning. Acting out descriptions of actions such as *jump, run, skip, skate,* and *throw a ball* helps children learn by doing. Nouns such as *letter carrier, mother,* and *grocer* can become the basis for dramatic play and pantomime. Children who have been guided carefully and slowly through dramatic play will eventually be ready to dramatize simple stories. By this time they will have achieved some personal freedom and mastered a functional vocabulary. The procedure of planning, playing, and evaluating is the same as that followed in the regular classroom, except that with these children, the task and the process must be simpler and will take longer.

One particularly important point to remember is that adjustments in all activities for the child who has mental retardation should be made on the basis of the child's interests and needs. Stories selected for dramatization should, in addition to being clear and simple, reflect the interests that give meaning to the child's life. As his or her interests widen, a greater variety of stories can be introduced, with new words to express and describe them.

Not only literature but other subjects as well can be taught through the medium of improvisation. For example, one teacher had the children in her arithmetic class be plus and minus signs and pieces of fruit; through acting out simple problems of subtraction and addition, the children were able to see the correct answers. So-called creative walks, on which children became trees, flowers, stones, birds, and animals, helped them to observe and recall what they had seen after they returned to the classroom. With these children, communication and social development are the primary goals; art is secondary. The potential in drama for motivating and reaching these primary goals validates its use. In time, other objectives can be established, but they are not possible until the child has developed a sense of security, has acquired some freedom of expression, and has mastered a working vocabulary that will enable him or her to take on the role of another.

A continuing program of creative drama offers an opportunity for social growth, emotional release, and a way of learning. These students often astonish us with what they have learned.

The Student Who Is Emotionally Disturbed

It is with the child who is emotionally disturbed that the classroom teacher must exercise the greatest caution. We know so little about these children and the causes of their problems that the possibility of doing harm is greater than it is with any other group. Indeed, it is often a challenge to distinguish between the child who is emotionally disturbed and the child who has mental retardation because of their frequently similar behavior. Often, repeated testing must be done to determine the nature of the condition. What might be a rewarding activity for the child who has mental retardation might not be appropriate for the child who is disturbed. Psychodrama and play therapy are accepted techniques in the treatment of these children, but they can be damaging in the hands of the layperson, regardless of his or her background and skill as a teacher of creative drama. The teacher who is not a therapist must carefully consider whether creative drama techniques are appropriate with some children. Seriously disturbed children are often enrolled in a special class or school and provided with special services, which may or may not include psychiatric help and play therapy. Often children in special schools are referred to outside clinics or therapists, and drama may be part of their treatment.

Some readers have suggested that violence be addressed in this chapter. The request is understandable in view of the many reports of serious, even tragic, consequences of violent behavior in schools and on playgrounds. These cases require professional attention, which the drama teacher is not qualified to give; therefore my advice is an immediate psychiatric referral, if and when warning signs appear. Inability to get along with others, lack of trust, and out-of-control anger should alert teachers to potential trouble.

Remedial Drama

Remedial drama is an umbrella term used in Britain and to a lesser degree in the United States. As was stated earlier, drama/theatre has been a part of society through-out human history. In preventive and therapeutic work we are primarily concerned with communication and therefore in helping individuals and groups build better relationships. According to Sue Jennings, author of *Remedial Drama,* "[it] does not differ in content or technique from other types of drama, although great care must be taken in selecting and applying drama techniques to remedial work."[4] Her emphasis is

---

[4]Jennings, *Remedial Drama,* p. 4.

on experience, and the goals of drama, used in this way, are socialization, creativity, and insight.

Eleanor Irwin, a well-known drama therapist, drew a distinction between a therapeutic experience and therapy as a treatment. She said that "any experience which helps an individual to feel a greater sense of competence and well-being may be thought of as therapeutic."[5] All drama is therapeutic in one sense, but it is important to understand that not all drama is therapy.

Drama therapy, role playing, psychodrama, and *sociodrama* are terms frequently heard with reference to remedial drama. They differ both as to technique and thrust. The National Association for Drama Therapy defines drama therapy as "the intentional use of creative drama toward the psychotherapeutic goals of symptom relief, emotional and physical integration, and personal growth."[6] Drama therapy, like the other arts therapies, applies a creative medium and establishes an understanding or contract between the client and the therapist. Thus it is differentiated from creative drama in the school.

Psychodrama Dr. Robert Landy describes this form of drama therapy as follows: "Psychodrama is one of several action-oriented therapies that lie at the roots of drama therapy. Developed in the early 1900's by the Austrian psychiatrist J. L. Moreno, psychodrama is a form of group therapy where clients act out events of significance in their lives. Through role playing and role reversal clients are led to experiencing and then understanding the dimensions of a conflict."[7]

Sociodrama, as the name implies, deals with the group and with group problems or conflicts. A class in creative drama may become a sociodramatic experience when a real-life situation is employed, leading to discussion with benefits to all participants. Classroom teachers and recreation leaders sometimes use sociodrama in a limited way to help solve problems that arise and persist in having a damaging effect on the group. In sociodrama the group and group relationships are the primary concerns.

Another use of sociodrama is described in an article by Robert Landy and Deborah Borisoff: "'Reach for Speech' is a program to help young people in New York City develop speech skills. Departing from conventional methods of skills teaching and debates, it focuses upon sociodrama. It centers on an examination of significant social problems within New York City communities and empowers secondary school students to address these problems in the roles of a wide variety of characters."[8]

The "Reach for Speech" method proceeds in several discrete steps:

1. Students and teacher choose a relevant social issue.
2. The group identifies appropriate roles that relate to the issue.
3. Group members select roles.

---

[5]Eleanor Irwin, "Drama Therapy with the Handicapped," in *Drama/Theatre and the Handicapped,* ed. Ann Shaw and C. J. Stevens (Washington, DC: American Theatre Association, 1979), p. 23.
[6]National Assoc. for Drama Therapy brochure.
[7]Robert J. Landy, *Handbook of Educational Drama and Theatre* (Westport, CT: Greenwood Press, 1982), p. 139.
[8]Robert J. Landy and Deborah Borisoff, "Reach for Speech: Communication Skills Through Sociodrama," *English Journal* 76, no. 5 (1987): 68–71.

4. Students do research through readings and interviews of role models in the community.
5. Students enact roles in class; they act "as if" they were particular characters, presenting their characters' point of view through speech and movement. The role playing is deepened through a process that includes role reversal and a critique of the role playing.
6. Students shape their role playing, preparing for a final presentation.
7. The students, in role, present the dimensions of the social issue to a particular audience.

There is a difference of opinion as to the desirability of drama therapy of any kind, however, for the child who is seriously disturbed. Some therapists believe that role playing is beneficial; others, that the child's problems present difficulties that may make this form of expression less desirable than participation in the other arts. Children who are seriously disturbed need to make sense out of their own environment before they can enter another; moreover, until they know who *they* are, they will have difficulty being someone else. Their greatest needs frequently include the ability to interact and to develop language. Until they can express themselves, they will find it difficult, if not impossible, to enter into the simplest form of dramatic play. Dr. Haim Ginott writes, "The playroom behavior of immature and neurotic children is characterized by an excess of inhibition or aggression."[9] Inasmuch as play therapy requires special training techniques, we shall confine ourselves to the consideration of appropriate activities for the child with less serious emotional problems who is taught in the regular classroom.

According to some therapists, dramatic play, when first introduced to the child with emotional problems, should include reality-based situations rather than fantasy. Highly imaginative situations may cause young children who are not in touch with reality to meld with the idea or to identify too closely with the characters played. All children tend to become deeply involved in dramatic play. Most children can suspend disbelief for the duration of the period and then return to reality. However, the child who is disturbed may not be able to shake off the role so easily; hence, "de-roling," or helping the player withdraw from the drama and return to everyday life, may be necessary.

Dance, rhythms, and ritual movement are excellent for children who are disturbed. Physical activity gives them a sense of the body; the large movements, such as skipping, galloping, stretching, and moving the arms, are wonderful exercises for those who are poorly coordinated. Reaching for the sky or pushing away the clouds, feeling big, growing tall—all are movements that contain an element of drama.

Many teachers have reported that the nonverbal child can develop the ability to express feelings and knowledge through the use of movement and pantomime. In this the child finds a means of communication, and motivation for speech may follow. The teacher may also discover capabilities and awareness that remain hidden in the usual classroom situation. The other arts therapies—dance, the visual arts, and music—are particularly successful with the nonverbal child.

---

[9]Haim G. Ginott, *Group Psychotherapy with Children* (New York: McGraw-Hill, 1961), p. 40.

A good exercise for any group, but particularly good for those who are emotionally disturbed, is the following:

1. One child begins a pantomime. This might be a man shoveling snow. Another child, who knows what the first child is doing, steps up and joins in. The second child may also shovel snow or do something that relates to it. The pantomime is kept up until all the children have entered into the activity, one at a time. This is an excellent means of focusing attention and assisting each to "join" the group in a natural and logical way. If the class is large, two smaller groups can be formed, each taking a turn at the same exercise.

2. Another suggestion is a variation on the old game of "statues." One person comes into the center of the room and strikes a pose. The child freezes as another joins in. All stay in their poses until the entire group has come together, forming a large sculpture. This exercise is not drama therapy but is pantomime with possible therapeutic benefits, inasmuch as it encourages both observation of others and movement that relates to them.

3. The mirror game (described in Chapter 5) is often suggested for children with emotional problems. It focuses the attention and encourages concentration. Although it is only an exercise, repeating it from time to time makes for greater precision, and most people of all ages enjoy it.

4. Role playing and role reversal, which offer an opportunity to experience both sides of a problem or situation, are particularly helpful and appropriate for children and teenagers with emotional problems.

5. Storytelling, followed by story acting, offers work on speech, language, concentration, and a sense of sharing. Stories should be short and, if acted, good for dramatization. (For a group of immigrant children, stories with ethnic backgrounds are particularly appropriate.) Children benefit from sharing their backgrounds with one another, and they enjoy learning stories, dances, and music of other lands. Sue Jennings suggests improvising "shopping" in ethnic neighborhoods. Players lead others into stores and describe the items they see and what they are used for. She made a point of stories' being short, clear, and clearly told, with satisfying endings. For children who are disturbed, "calming down" endings are important.

6. Choral speaking (described in Chapter 11) has values beyond the activity stage. One value is that members of the group work together, rather than as individuals, for reading or performance. Large spaces such as gymnasiums should be avoided. Smaller rooms have boundaries, important for children with emotional problems. The exception to this is the player in the wheelchair, who needs more space.

Attention deficit disorder (ADD) is a term for behavior that most teachers have witnessed at one time or another. It identifies the abnormally short attention span of some children, which interferes with their concentration and frustrates the efforts of their classmates. For these children, only very short activities are indicated. Group work is difficult, yet music, movement, and creative drama, because they involve the whole person, can be successful. Patience, understanding, and discipline are essential ingredients in working with ADD pupils.

Although all groups benefit from starting a session with movement, it is essential for children with emotional problems. Through ritual, they find security; through warm-ups, comfortable use of the body; through moving as a group, a lessening of self-consciousness. Dance involving physical touch is often helpful, and patterned dance with its structure is a better starting place for some children than freer dance forms. Under any circumstances, rhythms that involve the whole body, clapping the hands, and making sounds to a beat are all good ways of getting and holding attention.

Both finger puppets and hand puppets have been found to work successfully with children too inhibited to assume roles themselves. Such children usually have a poor self-image; thus, it takes longer to build their interest and ego strength to the point that they are able to move out of the group to assume roles and sustain them through improvised situations. Again, we are speaking of children with knowledge of themselves and their reality. When they can enter into dramatic situations with relative ease, these disturbed children will begin to derive some of the same benefits found by other children. In terms of objectives, first on the list are interaction with the group, ability to concentrate, ability to express themselves orally, and ability to take the part of another. After these objectives have been met, children with emotional problems should be able to work with joy, accomplishing as much as, and sometimes more than, the others in the group. Their sensitivity, if properly guided, can be an asset to their understanding of a character and creation of a characterization.

A professional organization with stringent requirements, the National Association for Drama Therapy, was formed in 1978 to set standards and goals. Both specialists and generalists benefit from this formalization of principles and practices. Conventions and regional conferences offer programs featuring speakers, demonstrations, and discussion groups, as well as an opportunity to view new films and publications. The Association for Theatre and Disability and the American Alliance for Theatre and Education often meet together, recognizing their similarity of goals. Special education, once a discipline apart, is today a close colleague of both the classroom teacher and the specialist in drama.

The Student Who Is Physically Disabled

In many ways students who are physically disabled present fewer difficulties to the classroom teacher than children who are emotionally disturbed or those who have mental retardation. Physical disabilities often are visible and the children's limitations obvious. Their problems are easier to identify, and depending on the seriousness of the disability, decisions have already been made as to whether they can function in a regular classroom. As with all exceptional children, the physically disabled are thought to be better off in a regular classroom rather than segregated; if their disability is so severe that they require special services, however, they may have to be enrolled, at least for a time, in a special school or in a hospital.

For our purposes we shall consider children who are physically disabled to include those who are hearing impaired, partially sighted, or blind, as well as children whose functions are limited because of some other physical disability. Frequently, children with physical problems have emotional problems as well; for both reasons, they need all the support and encouragement the teacher can give as they struggle to reach their goals. Because of the conspicuousness of their disability, however, they are generally treated with more compassion and understanding than a classmate with emotional problems, whose behavior may at times be inappropriate or immature. People whose psychological problems cause them to behave in a socially unacceptable manner are often criticized or ridiculed, prompting the question "Why must they act that way?" The person on crutches, on the other hand, rarely prompts this response, for we know that person is walking as well as possible.

The child who cannot hear, see, or speak clearly, like the child who lacks physical coordination or cannot walk, needs an opportunity to escape the body on the wings of his or her imagination. Creative drama offers this opportunity, though admittedly the activities must be modified. Every drama therapist to whom I have spoken has agreed that the same techniques and principles that work with the able-bodied can be applied with persons who have physical and emotional disabilities, either in a school or a clinical situation. In the latter, the clients tend to exhibit more acute symptoms, and therefore, the therapist will focus on psychological issues. According to Dr. Robert Landy, the focus on cognitive learning for children who have serious emotional problems should be carefully balanced with affective, sensory, and social learning.[10] For children who have mental retardation, greater attention should be given to motor coordination, speech, and social and communication skills rather than to abstraction through dramatic action. There should be no pressure for memorization of lines; however, storytelling and improvisation are excellent activities for older students. For administrators, a performance or demonstration of class work, well executed, helps to justify the time and money spent on dramatic activities; performance on any age level is questionable, however, unless it is the wish of the class.

Most drama teachers and drama therapists begin a session with warm-ups; the length and content depend on the age and abilities of the group. Singing, which requires the participation of everyone, is a popular way of beginning; this is usually followed by movement and rhythms to work off tensions and establish concentration. One teacher of preschool children combines voice and body work by first asking the children to say their names. Next she tells them that they must wake up their bodies and asks for suggestions. If a child says "Toes," she will say, "Wake up, toes!" and all the children wiggle their toes at the same time. After two or three minutes she will say, "Goodbye, toes!" and all stop. The next suggestion may be hands and the same procedure is followed, with "Hello, hand!" and "Goodbye, hand!" While they are doing this activity, the children are warming up and developing concentration. When the

---

[10]Robert J. Landy, *Drama Therapy: Concepts, Theories, and Practices* 2nd ed. (Springfield, IL: Thomas, 1994).

Intergenerational Theatre. Roots and Branches. (Courtesy of Lauren Scott, photograph by Elena Olivo.)

teacher is ready to begin the lesson for the day, she explains that body and voice are some of the tools the class will be using.

The Little Theatre of the Deaf

The Little Theatre of the Deaf, which achieved national prominence at the end of the 1960s, was a shining example of what can be done by actors for children who cannot hear. Because oral communication is emphasized in early education, deaf children are at a disadvantage when attending theatrical performances, just as they are in ordinary classroom situations. Pantomime is the obvious means of reaching those who are hard of hearing, and it is in this form that the Little Theatre of the Deaf has succeeded so brilliantly. A cue can be taken from the success of this company: pantomime is an area of drama that allows the child with hearing loss to participate as well as enjoy theatre as a spectator. In another medium, television, we have become accustomed to seeing interpreters using sign language to bring important programs to nonhearing viewers.

Again, movement is an ideal way to begin activities. Large physical movements come first, then rhythms and dance. Small muscle movements follow. Sensitive to the keen visual perception of many deaf children, the leader can move from dance to pantomime. There will be motivation for speech in drama, but the easiest communication will be through pantomime, in which the child who is deaf can achieve success. Stories can be told in this medium, giving pleasure both to player and observer. Observing creative drama classes in a school for the deaf, I saw remarkable possibilities for learning and emotional release.

Children who are visually impaired or partially sighted face different problems. They are at home with speech, so storytelling is an excellent beginning activity. Choral speaking, like music, is also an art in which they can excel and at the same time find pleasure. Original poetry composed by the group offers the children a chance to express feelings and personal responses. Free movement is more of a challenge for them than for sighted children, but it is not impossible. Carefully guided improvisation may be attempted, although the formal play, in which movement is predetermined and not changed in rehearsal, is by its nature easier for these children. For the player who is visually impaired or partially sighted, formal or scripted drama offers greater security than improvisation. One director who has had great success with a drama group of actors who are blind stressed the fact that she never moves scenery or props after their placement has been established. A knowledge of where things are enables the players to move freely and easily about the stage.

Children with physical problems that prevent them from running, walking, or easily using their arms or legs have also found drama to be within the range of their capabilities. Group participation while the children are seated is an excellent way of involving everyone in pantomime, choral speech, and puppetry. In preparing a dramatization, the roles of narrator and storyteller are highly regarded and can be handled by a child who is not able to engage in more physical participation. The imaginative teacher can find a place for disabled children where they are able to add to the group endeavor, thus enhancing their self-image and giving them a sense of achievement.

Puppetry

Persons who are physically disabled can do and enjoy a much wider range of dramatic activities than was formerly thought possible. Most obvious but little used in the past is puppetry. The puppeteer in a wheelchair is able to run, jump, dance, fly—in short, to perform every physical activity through the puppet. In most cases, the child is at no disadvantage. The Kids' Project, a puppet troupe created in 1977 in response to the problems of mainstreaming, has become an effective and growing medium for reaching schoolchildren who have physical disabilities.[11] The puppets represent a variety of disabling conditions: blindness, deafness, cerebral palsy, and cognitive and learning disabilities. Two nondisabled puppets are also included in skits in which they learn to accept the others. One segment of the performance is devoted to each of the puppets with disabilities, followed by a question and answer period. The originator of the Kids' Project, Barbara Aiello, was a special education teacher who realized that putting children with disabilities into regular classrooms, in compliance with the Education

---

[11]"Puppets Depict Life of Disabled," *New York Times,* July 10, 1983, sec. 1, p. 39.

for All Handicapped Children Act of 1975, demanded attitudinal changes if true integration were to take place. After years of separation, both those with disabilities and the nondisabled needed to understand each other.

Theatres with Special Programs for Persons Who Have Physical Disabilities

There are now a number of theatre groups across the nation for persons with physical disabilities. Robert J. Landy's *Handbook of Educational Drama and Theatre* lists Theatre Unlimited in San Francisco; Process Theatre with the Handicapped of the Alan Short Center in Stockton, California; the San Diego Theatre for the Disabled; and the National Theatre Workshop of the Handicapped in New York City.[12] One group that must be given special mention is the Rainbow Company in Las Vegas, Nevada. There, classes in creative drama, mime, technical theatre, makeup, costuming, and playwriting have been held since 1976 for children from preschool age through high school. The Rainbow Company has received national acclaim for the quality of its work with performers who have physical disabilities; in 1982 it was selected as a model site for the fourth consecutive year by the National Committee, Arts for the Handicapped.[13]

The National Theatre Workshop of the Handicapped in New York City is an integrated group of physically disabled and able-bodied persons founded by Brother Rick Curry, S.J., in 1977. The workshop's stated objectives are the same as those of any other drama school. Through training in mime, improvisation, and acting, students develop an appreciation of the theatre arts, learn theatre techniques, and improve their own performance skills. Most important, they gain confidence and a better understanding of themselves. Originally established for adults, it now has classes for children.

Recently I visited a creative drama class at the National Theatre Workshop of the Handicapped in New York City. The children, age five, six, and seven years old, came by bus from a public school during the school day. The instructor, who also teaches adult classes at the workshop, was assisted by three parents who acted as aides. All the children were visually impaired, some more than others; one child was in a wheelchair, and one five-year-old used a walker. The teacher had arranged a circle of chairs, but the only other piece of furniture in the room was a piano. This circle made a safe playing area for those whose ability to see was limited. The teacher began the session by asking each child to say his or her name and age. She then asked the children to shake their arms, next their hands, and then to roll their heads from side to side, back and forth, up and down. Finally she had them beat a rhythm on the floor with their feet. The two who could not stand did the same exercise by beating the rhythm with their hands on their knees. No one was exempt, and no one was made to feel different.

She next divided the group into pairs for the mirror game, which required greater concentration. The children exchanged roles after a few minutes and enjoyed the

---

[12]Landy, *Handbook of Educational Drama and Theatre*.
[13]A 1982 brochure from the Rainbow Company reported that "this designation has been made to only ten sites in the country"; it indicates "exemplary programming in the arts by, with, and for the handicapped."

challenge as they became more efficient in repeating the movement. Following the mirror game came playground activities. The children were asked to think of something to do on a playground but not to tell what it was. They thought of swinging, going down a slide, jumping rope, playing ball, hopscotch, and so on. Those who could move easily improvised the action; others worked out their ideas with help from the teacher. The little girl with the walker, for instance, pushed it forward, then moved it back slowly, repeating the action several times until the other children guessed the right answer—going down a slide, then climbing back up and sliding down again. As I watched, I realized that each exercise had built on the preceding one.

The last activity of the morning combined voice and body in the song "Winnie the Pooh." The children sang it first with the help of the teacher and piano accompaniment; then they added appropriate pantomime, much of it original and delightful; finally they had memorized the words and music without realizing it.

The class lasted for an hour and a half without a break, an extremely long period of time for children of that age. It came to closure not because the children were restless but because it was twelve o'clock and time for lunch before getting back on the bus. Their enjoyment was obvious, but it was reinforced by the pictures they drew of their last class, which their teacher brought to show the National Theatre Workshop. The point I want to make is that everything they did that day can be and is being done in classes on every age level; the lessons were simply adjusted to meet the special needs, age range, and abilities of the group.

Very Special Arts

There have been some major developments in the arts, education, and disability fields in this country since the first edition of this book was published in 1968. One was the founding of Very Special Arts (VSA) in 1974 by Jean Kennedy Smith. This international nonprofit organization, which now has affiliate organizations across the United States and worldwide, was founded as an affiliate of the John F. Kennedy Center for the Performing Arts to provide an array of performing, visual, and literary arts programming for children, youth, and adults with disabilities. VSA believes that the arts play a vital role in the lives of all people by providing a universal language through which we can enhance education, communicate experiences, and explore diverse cultures. VSA serves to communicate the power of the arts as a means to achieve personal growth, increase inclusion, and positively shape the lives of people with disabilities. In 1991, VSA developed an early childhood program that engages children in a variety of artistic activities designed to support academic learning experiences. Start with the Arts provides young children with valuable, lifelong academic and social advantages by using the creative and communicative power of the arts to enhance learning and social skills. This educational program for four- to six-year-olds with and without disabilities is designed to provide educators and parents with objective-based, thematic learning experiences in the arts. The program supports the development of basic literacy skills and offers engaging activities in visual art, creative movement, music, and creative drama. By offering an opportunity for children to communicate their ideas and feelings creatively through the arts, Start with the Arts utilizes the benefits of the artistic experience to strengthen learning environments and support inclusion.

The Rehabilitation Act

The other and much more comprehensive development affecting arts programs, as well as other educational programs, is the Rehabilitation Act of 1973 regarding persons with disabilities. Section 504 of this act states: "No otherwise qualified handicapped individual in the United States . . . shall, solely by reason of his handicap, be excluded from the participation in, be denied the benefits of, or be subjected to discrimination under any program or activity receiving Federal financial assistance." This regulation applies to all recipients of federal funds, including elementary and secondary schools, colleges, social service agencies, and hospitals. The effects of this legislation have been felt in numerous ways, and they are bound to increase in the future. The arts, as part of the educational system, will be affected, and so will public attitudes. In 1990 Congress passed the Americans with Disabilities Act, a far-reaching federal statute that prohibits discrimination in employment as well as other areas of life. With each piece of legislation, consciousness is raised to a higher level, as reflected in our treatment of both children and adults.

A related topic is creative drama with the aged. Some creative drama teachers and group leaders have successfully applied the same classroom techniques with senior citizens and nursing home patients. This practice opens up a new area. Funds are becoming available for programs for the senior adult, and teachers of the arts, particularly those experienced in working with children and the arts therapies, will have much to offer. Books and articles dealing with the arts and this population are beginning to appear; meanwhile, the basic principles and practices of creative drama are finding a new use.

Intergenerational Theatre

Intergenerational Theatre has proliferated within the last thirty years. Some community theatres and university drama departments offer an occasional or even annual play of this genre, while other theatre companies operate year-round with an intergenerational focus. An example of the former is the Blue Ridge Dinner Theatre in Virginia, which ends its summer season with several performances of a play for family audiences, often with as many as four generations in the cast. Roots and Branches, on the other hand, is a professional New York ensemble that hires actors from age eighteen to eighty. Actors tell their life stories, dramatizing them as well as working on plays with themes of conflicts and problems of youth and elders. Discussions with the audience follow performances and are an important component.

Courses and Workshops

A number of courses and workshops offer training in drama therapy. Robert J. Landy, in his *Handbook of Educational Drama and Theatre,* published in 1982, listed California State University in Los Angeles, Avila College in Kansas City, Antioch University in San Francisco, and Loyola University in New Orleans. He described New York University as having one of the most comprehensive programs in educational theatre. By 1988 it had the only program in the United States to offer both a master's degree in drama therapy and a doctorate in educational theatre with a concentration in drama therapy. Students are required to take work in the related fields of drama/theatre and psychology and to do supervised field work in one of New York's hospitals, in special schools, or in community institutions that serve persons with disabilities. Certification under the title of registered drama therapist is now offered by the National Association for Drama Therapy.

On the undergraduate level a unique example is the curriculum of Gallaudet College, located in Washington, D.C. This well-known institution specializes in the education of students who are deaf or hearing impaired. The theatre arts department at this school recently reviewed its goals and objectives, initiating a new program designed to prepare students to work with children in educational, recreational, and social settings in which the arts can be integrated to facilitate learning. The Gallaudet major in developmental drama, as it is called, represents a collaboration between the theatre arts department and the departments of psychology, education, and sociology. The program comprises theories of dramatic play, creative drama techniques, the use of a visual and gestural approach in working with children who are hearing impaired, classes in the theatre arts, and leadership training.

Extensive outreach services for teachers of deaf children are offered by the Gallaudet staff. The college also works closely with the Wolf Trap Foundation in early childhood education. Improvisation, role playing, movement, puppetry, storytelling, and mime are taught through visual and gestural communication.

An outreach program, Sunshine Too, was founded in 1980 at the National Technical Institute for the Deaf at the Rochester Institute of Technology. Deaf and hearing actors comprise a company of six, which tours shows for children and youth. More than 650 performances a year are given, and the company appears on television, does residencies at schools and colleges, and participates in national and regional conferences. Sunshine Too states that it is the only college program in the world that offers a full curriculum of theatre, dance, and music for students who are hearing impaired.

Recently the Seattle Children's Theatre established a Deaf Youth Drama Program funded by the U.S. Department of Education. The program trains deaf student actors; the first play by these young people was presented in the summer of 1994.

Another community resource, Enact, is a New York not-for-profit corporation organized in 1987 for the purpose of using drama to assist students in their efforts to acknowledge and transform personal and social obstacles to self-awareness and communication. Since then, Enact has been working with students of all ages, serving more than fifteen hundred during 1992–93. This program is an example of a close and effective school-community relationship. Classes involving teachers and therapists are held at the center, and occasional performances are given in an intimate space for small selected audiences and teachers. Students improvise and sometimes write their own plays, with diagnostic and therapeutic results.

In 1986 the Big Apple Circus added a new dimension to its program of community service. With the Clown Care Unit at Columbia Presbyterian Medical Center, it moved into the ranks of health professionals. Today thirty-five specially trained clowns serve six New York hospitals, going into children's hospital rooms where they work their magic to help seriously ill children and teenagers overcome their fears. Supervised by the medical staff of each hospital, clowns in the garb of doctors work side by side with staff members, making the rounds two or three times a week, fifty-two weeks a year. In addition to circus skills such as juggling, mime, and magic tricks, the clowns use special hospital techniques that stimulate participation and laughter among patients and parents: white coats, outsize stethoscopes, red nose "transplants," chocolate milk "transfusions," and parking tickets for children who stay too long. Doctors and nurses welcome the Clown Care Unit, which provides a unique service, easing anxiety and bringing laughter through drama into the wards.

A necessary ingredient of successful work with the ill and disabled of any age is a sensitivity to their situation; this is a quality that members of the Clown Care Unit have, in spite of their grotesque appearance and exaggerated reactions. Beyond the positive impact on the individual is the validation of the clown's place in education and drama therapy. In many cities, clowns are involved in Meals on Wheels; their antics amuse elderly and housebound men and women.

The Student Who Is Economically Disadvantaged

Since the advent of the Head Start program, we have been hearing much about the child who is economically disadvantaged. This is not a new problem in our society but one that, for a variety of reasons, is now attracting wide attention, with government and private foundation funds allocated for the establishment of educational and recreational programs. The arts, including dramatic play and creative drama, are emphasized in many of these programs. The values cited in Chapter 1 have tremendous implications for those who have been born into an environment lacking books, playing space, supervision, the arts, and, in many cases, the English language. According to one group of leaders at a conference on the subject of creative drama in special education, the problems of these children are manifold. For example, poverty may preclude treatment of a physical disability; the disability causes feelings of inadequacy, and this results in emotional disturbance. Hence we have a combination of problems requiring understanding and skill beyond the qualifications of the average well-prepared teacher.

Nevertheless, the classroom teacher can do much for inner-city children. Actually, the first work in children's drama in this country was initiated in the settlement houses of our large cities at the turn of the century. It is significant that the first theatre for children in America was established at the Educational Alliance in New York City in 1903 for the children of immigrant families of the Lower East Side. This enterprise attracted wide attention, and in the following twenty-five years many settlement houses and playgrounds introduced storytelling and drama to the children of the poor. Most of the classes were conducted by social workers and Junior League members, some of whom had theatre training. All the leaders realized the potential of drama in teaching English, brightening the lives of the boys and girls, and bringing strangers together socially in a new land.

Since that time the schools have taken up the challenge, although community centers have by no means abdicated their responsibilities. During the 1960s and 1970s the phenomenon of street theatre began to appear in our cities: these are free performances of drama, music, and dance, often in poor neighborhoods, where strength is drawn even as it is given. Some of these productions have been subsidized by state

A class in creative drama at the National Theatre Workshop of the Handicapped, New York. (Courtesy of Br. Rick Curry, S. J.; photo, Jorge Boetto.)

arts councils, some by municipalities, others by churches and colleges. Some have been part of a two-pronged program involving both participation and spectator enjoyment.

The schools have been concerned in recent years with bilingual education and the teaching of English as a second language. Particularly in many large urban areas, there is a need for teachers with a knowledge of Spanish and the ability to teach English in the early grades to children who enter school speaking another language. One technique used and discussed today involves movement and pantomime. Dance is recommended as a beginning because it forces more concentration on the use of the entire body and mind than does pure verbal exercise. Folk dances involve a physical response to oral commands. Pantomime makes the spectator guess what the performer is doing and thereby ties the word to the act.

Creative drama with bilingual children does not differ from creative drama with other groups except in the matter of vocabulary. The most common error in dealing with these children is underestimating their ability and overestimating their verbal skill. By giving them very short but interesting activities, the teacher ensures that these children can be successful and thus at the same time gain confidence.

Programs that support professional and community theatre groups benefit the economically deprived by making performances and workshops available. Drama experiences are available to the inner-city child if school administrators take advantage of artists-in-the-schools programs, theatre-in-education teams, and professional and highly competent nonprofessional performers in the community.

Summary

This chapter has introduced the subject of arts education for the special or exceptional student in the most cursory way. Leaders of any group or class in which there is a child with a disability should avail themselves of the growing literature in the field.

A practical starting place for the beginning teacher is with self-assessment and assessment of existing programs and of the facilities that are available.

Regardless of the condition that sets him or her apart, the exceptional child suffers isolation. Life is dependent on one's social network, but in the case of the exceptional child satisfying relationships are all too often lacking. Drama is an ideal environment for meeting and working with others and for establishing interpersonal relationships through a shared interest.

The exceptional child merits individual attention, and each teacher knows the capabilities as well as the disabilities of the various children in the group. Although they cannot do everything that other children do, they can do some things well and, from this experience, can move forward, thus gaining pleasure and a sense of accomplishment. One successful teacher stressed *listening* as the first and most important element of the teaching process. What are the children trying to tell about themselves, their desires, their frustrations? What is unspoken and why? Important cues are there to be picked up by a sensitive ear.

In working with students with special needs, it is important for the leader to

Create a comfortable, nonjudgmental atmosphere.
Set up the physical space with clear boundaries.
Determine the theme and structure for the day.
Establish ground rules.
Bring the class to closure.

The final activity in each class session not only should reinforce the theme but should allow the children to leave with a sense of accomplishment and anticipation of the next meeting. In evaluating the class, the teacher should ask herself or himself each day whether it went well as a group activity and whether the needs of each individual in the class were addressed.

The classroom teacher does not presume to be a therapist, but with knowledge of the exceptional child in the class—his or her problems and needs—the teacher can apply the techniques of drama to effect growth, strengthen abilities, and build a more positive self-concept in the child. Moreover, the teacher can work with therapists to their mutual benefit.

Suggested Assignments

1. Find a workshop or class in drama for children with special problems, and ask to visit one. What did you learn from your observation?
2. Study a particular disability (a hearing or vision problem, a physical or other disability) and think of dramatic activities that would be possible for participants who have this disability.
3. Prepare simulations of disabling conditions and bring them to class. Provide your classmates with earplugs, bandages for eyes, slings for arms, and so forth. Have each student take one and experience what it feels like to be blind or deaf or to lack an arm or leg. This activity will lead to a lively class discussion.
4. Find information on violence in schools and report your findings to the class.

Journal Writing

1. If you have ever had a disability, even temporarily (laryngitis, a broken arm, conjunctivitis, an accident, etc.), think back to what it felt like. Note the compensations we all make when we are unable to perform ordinary everyday tasks.
2. What help does our society and your town in particular provide persons with disabilities?
3. Have you ever had a disabled friend? If so, what accommodations did you make in your social life together?
4. Would you welcome a disabled roommate? Think about it.

Part II

Programs Beyond the Classroom

Although creative drama is not yet as widespread in the classrooms of America as we hope it will become, it has spread dramatically in areas beyond the classroom. Many leaders of creative drama programs have been educated in college or university theatre departments, and the work they do frequently supplements school programs. Some of the more innovative uses of creative drama beyond the classroom could be replicated anywhere.

Some of the alternative spaces include libraries, museums, parks, camps, community centers, churches, and the streets of the city. Not all these venues are new; the community center, or settlement house as it was once called, was home to children's dramatic activities at the turn of the century, predating drama and theatre in the classroom. The early leaders, however, were volunteers, usually amateurs, who combined their love of the theatre with their desire to work with children. The new community center, on the other hand, is often part of an arts center and is staffed by trained leaders who offer classes in creative drama, acting, puppetry, movement, music, dance, and film. The leaders supplement the curriculum by providing after-school programs and conducting workshops that follow plays attended by school groups. Frequently the actors are adjunct teachers in universities and private schools.

The circus, not an educational resource in the past, is today providing social and educational services in numerous communities. An outstanding example is the Big Apple Circus, which offers four outreach programs: Circus Arts in Education; the Clown Care Unit for hospital patients; the Ticket Fund, which provides complimentary circus tickets to disadvantaged children and senior citizens; and Circus of the Senses, an annual performance for boys and girls with visual and hearing disabilities.

Among my own graduate students have been professional storytellers, actors, clowns, mimes, and puppeteers. It is therefore no longer possible or even desirable to separate creative drama as taught in the classroom from that provided outside; we are connected and interrelated, with benefits for all.

Included also in Part Two is work shared with an audience. After preparing a play in the classroom, children often want to share their work with an audience, which usually means moving into the school auditorium or all-purpose room.

There are many excellent drama and theatre programs throughout the country, each with its own unique features and strengths. One of the first to develop several discrete areas is the program in Educational Theatre at New York University, which offers the B.S., M.A., Ph.D, and Ed.D degrees; a summer study abroad program; a storytelling series in the fall; and staged readings of new scripts of plays for young audiences in June. Internships are available for students at institutions such as the New Victory Theatre, at community centers, and in hospital settings. Obviously, offerings are in part dependent on the location and size of the university. Departments in small towns and rural locations have the opportunity of touring children's plays to neighboring schools, while communities with theatres designed especially for children's theatre have an advantage over the touring companies. In urban areas schools bus students to performances during the school day with performances for children and family audiences over the weekend.

Chapter 16

Sharing Work with an Audience

Audience for a puppetry workshop. Shiny Shoes Children's Theatre, Taiwan. (Courtesy of Spica Cheng-Wobbe.)

> What children do is more significant to them than
> what they see and hear. They would rather act in
> a dramatization instead of sitting in the audience.
> —*Winifred Ward*

Sooner or later most groups want to "put on a play" or at least invite their parents to see their work. This is the point at which creative drama becomes theatre. The formal play, in contrast to creative drama, is primarily audience centered and has, from the beginning, performance as its goal. A script is either written or selected in advance and memorized by the players. It does not matter whether the lines were written by a playwright or by the children themselves. The use of a script distinguishes the formal play from creative drama, and the script supplies the structure—plot, theme, characters, and dialogue.

It would be unwise to attempt to cover both informal and formal dramatic techniques in one book, whatever its length. It is hoped that teachers of young children will confine their efforts to creative drama. But for teachers of older children and junior high school students who may wish to share their work with others, a few suggestions are offered as to the smoothest way of moving the play to the stage.

A momentary digression: as I stated in the preface to the sixth edition of this book, my attitude toward children's performing has undergone change since the first edition of this book nearly forty years ago. There are a number of reasons for this. First, theatre is a performing art, and to refuse the performance, when actors are eager and ready to share their work, is to frustrate a natural desire. Second, after fifty years of drama education in America, plays by very young players, often taught gestures by imitation and lines by rote, are disappearing, if they have not almost vanished from the scene. Third, and less a philosophic conviction than a reality, is the effect that television has had on young people. Spectators from birth, children see skilled performers and technical scenic effects daily and so take for granted the idea of performance as the natural goal of rehearsal. Whereas before the advent of television children were taken to an occasional film or play, statistics show that many children spend more hours before the screen each week than they spend in the classroom. For better or worse, television has conditioned them to want to communicate their work or to move from drama to theatre at a much earlier age than their forebears. Although this may appear to be a pragmatic and therefore questionable reason for change, it is a fact of modern life, which, added to my basic belief, is part of a rationale for supporting performance. Performance does not, however, justify exploitation of child actors; it does, I hope, urge understanding of children's needs and capabilities on the part of the responsible adult, whether teacher, administrator, recreation leader, or parent.

The transition from classroom to stage should come easily and naturally to the group that has spent many hours in improvisation; for boys and girls who have played together informally for some time, the result is more likely to be one of "sharing" than "showing," and to this end the teacher should be able to help the players achieve their goal: successful communication with an audience. Public performances, regardless of their popularity, should be infrequent, however, and then planned only for other classes or parents.

Unless the teacher has had some theatre training, directing a play can be a difficult experience. That is the reason for emphasizing simplicity: a long script, requiring elaborate scenery and costumes, poses problems for the most seasoned director. The average teacher does not have the background, time, or facilities to cope with such problems, but he or she can support and help enthusiastic young players as they prepare and demonstrate their work. In guiding beginners of any age, the most important single element is the approach of the leader. Enthusiasm and guidance help young players to cross the bridge between self-expression and successful communication.

Creativity is less dependent on training and past experience than it is on a special way of feeling, thinking, and responding. It is therefore possible for the teacher to be a highly creative person without having specialized in the theatre arts. Nevertheless, the formal play does make technical demands that the teacher must realize; an audience is involved, and, therefore, a product. The teacher must be prepared to take an additional step by supplying showmanship and maintaining discipline.

Choosing the Script

Ideally, a play presented by children in the lower and middle grades is one they have written themselves. When the script comes as the result of enthusiasm over a good story or as the culmination of the study of a subject, it is much more likely to have meaning for the class. If, for example, a class has been studying another culture (Native Americans, China, the Middle Ages) and the children dramatize material relating to it, the play emerges from this background as a natural result. The children may decide to dramatize one of the stories or legends they have read. After playing it creatively a number of times, children will be ready to write the dialogue or to have the teacher write it as they suggest it. The results will be childlike and crude, but the story itself has stood the test of time and therefore serves as a good scenario.

Sometimes a group wants to try an original plot. This is infinitely more difficult. Again, if it comes as the result of great interest in a subject the class has been studying, the children will know something of the background (time, place, occupations of the people, beliefs, superstitions, education, food, housing, folk or tribal customs). Their very enthusiasm is the primary requisite. Beyond that, they will need the guidance of the teacher in planning a story and developing characters who motivate the action. Inexperienced playwrights of any age cannot be expected to turn out well-made plays. What they *can* do is demonstrate their understanding of the subject matter about which they are writing and show believable characters involved in the story. The play that comes as the result of integrating drama with social studies, music, literature, dance, or art will have its greatest value to the players. Another class will enjoy seeing the work and perhaps will be stimulated to try a play of its own. These are sufficient reasons for deciding to share the project, but unless the children are older and the teacher has had considerable experience in drama, it should not go beyond the school assembly audience.

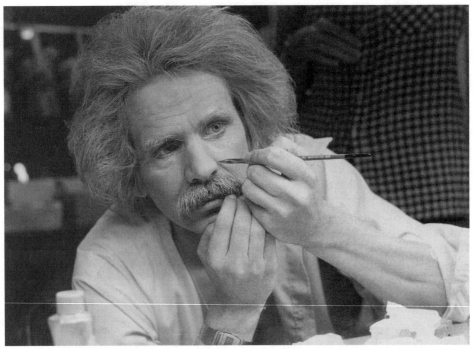

Making up as Mark Twain. (Courtesy of Rex Stevenson, Blue Ridge Dinner Theatre and Ferrum College, VA.)

Occasionally, however, a class of older students will want to do a play that is not related to class work. When this request comes, the problem is somewhat different. There is the question of finding a good script that will offer as many roles as possible, without featuring three or four talented players. There is a scarcity of such material, though there are some good short plays available that have been written with the class or drama group specifically in mind. The values cited in Chapter 1 should be considered when choosing the script: Is it worthwhile material? Are the characters believable? Does the dialogue offer enrichment? Is the play interesting to the players? Has it substance? Beyond that, we must ask whether it has enough parts and opportunities for participation to involve the whole group.

The text, no matter who writes it, should be literate. Language should help to create character, provoke action, further plot, and offer color and credibility. The construction of the play is of equal importance, for content and form should work together. A good play will offer opportunity for young people to interpret not only its literary content but its production requirements: scenery, costumes, lighting effects. Finally, a good play generates interest beyond itself—beyond its subject matter, ideas, or characters. It should stimulate thought in both performers and audience. This is a big order, and not all plays meet these demands equally, but material that is worth working on must meet some of them.

Within the past few years a number of good collections of plays for children have appeared on the market. Consult the catalogues of publishers who specialize in this area of dramatic literature. Visit bookstores that carry their material. If you have no resources of this kind in your community, write for scripts; most publishers are helpful in supplying information and books for examination.

Many short plays by major dramatists are suitable and challenging for junior and senior high school students. These plays are seldom considered, but they offer excellent material. Moreover, one of these plays will hold the attention of an audience of peers if the cast enjoys the play and can project its meaning and dramatic value. The choice of play is important because it is the foundation of the production. A play of good quality is worth all the time, effort, and study that will be required in the weeks that follow.

Occasionally, a junior high school group will want to do a Shakespearean play. This is a challenge to the teacher as well as to the class, but it can be done intelligently and effectively if approached in the right way. First, the play will be far too long as it stands. If the teacher familiarizes the class with the story, has the children improvise scenes from the play, and then cuts the play to a manageable length, the project will be possible. Rather than cutting within the play, it is better to select key scenes to work on. In this way there is no dilution of the literature; what is done has been carefully selected to be performed as written.

And the Tide Shall Cover the Earth *by Norma Cole. (Courtesy of Scot Copeland, Nashville Academy Theatre.)*

Shakespeare requires more time to prepare than a modern play because of the language and the necessary orientation. Yet children who can experience Shakespeare as *theatre* rather than a textbook assignment are amazingly quick to grasp meanings and see the humor. *A Midsummer Night's Dream, Twelfth Night, As You Like It, Julius Caesar,* and *The Merchant of Venice* are among the plays I have seen or done with seventh and eighth graders, and they have all been successful.

Not only Shakespeare but Molière, Goldoni, and Rostand as well have appeal for older children. Again, only scenes should be performed rather than the full-length play, although the actors must have knowledge of the entire work. An advantage of working on classics is the fact that scenery is rarely important. Two or three chairs, a bench, a table, perhaps some sturdy boxes, a screen—these are all pieces of furniture and props that schools and community centers have on hand. The classics are certainly not for beginners or for the very young. Still, for children who have had previous work in creative drama, they provide a real challenge and can establish a lifelong love for some of the world's greatest dramatic literature.

Many plays for the adult theatre are suitable for high school students but with the limited amount of time available for rehearsals, I would urge preparing individual scenes rather than the entire play. A half hour or forty-five minutes of good quality work is preferable to a mediocre two-hour program.

The Director

The teacher moves from being guide to being director during the rehearsal periods. Some directors are permissive and allow much opportunity for individual interpretation. Others plan action carefully in advance and supervise every detail. The director of inexperienced casts often finds the greatest success in an approach that is somewhere between the two extremes: giving enough direction to make the cast feel secure but providing enough leeway for individual interpretation and inventiveness. Regardless of method, however, the use of a script and the anticipation of an audience automatically place the emphasis on product rather than process.

Production also implies scenery and costumes; hence, time and effort must be given to their design and construction. These need not be elaborate—indeed, they seldom are in school or club situations—but the mounting is an important aspect of the formal play. When children can assume some responsibility for scenery, costumes, and properties, additional learning experiences are provided, as well as the opportunity for integrating arts and crafts with drama. Cooperation between the players and the backstage crew is essential to success and is certainly one of the greatest satisfactions a group can experience. For the seventh or eighth grader, there are values to be found in the sustained work of production.

It is suggested that before any work on a play is begun, the director have the group play the story creatively. Improvisation helps the players become familiar with the plot, get acquainted with the characters, and remain free in their movement. When the cast is thoroughly acquainted with the story, it is a relatively easy matter to rehearse more formally.

Childhood *by Thornton Wilder, Palace of the Pioneers Youth Theatre in Moscow, Russia. (Courtesy of Xan Johnson, Theatre School for Youth, University of Utah.)*

Floor Plans

The director should make a floor plan or diagram of the playing space in advance. On this he or she will sketch in the essential pieces of scenery or furniture and indicate the entrances. This is not a picture of the set but rather a careful diagram of the floor area that indicates where each piece of scenery will be placed, its relative size, and the space left on the stage for easy movement. The director will be careful to put entrances where the actors can use them most comfortably and effectively. Although the scenery will probably not be available much before final rehearsals, the director will try to find pieces of comparable size so that the cast becomes used to the plan and will have as little trouble as possible adjusting to the setting when it appears. For example, three or four folding chairs will suggest a sofa; coatracks, trees; and so on.

The beginner will find that the simpler the setting, the fewer the problems and, incidentally, the more effective the stage will probably be. Children can be involved in all the details of the production; they will enjoy and learn from the experience.

Arena Stage

The term *arena stage* is used to describe a center playing space. Some smaller theatres are built with the playing space in the center and the audience seated on all four sides; others, often called thrust stages, have seats on only three sides. In either case a different style of acting is demanded from that required by the proscenium stage, but it is one that is often easier for the less experienced player than for the professional adult actor accustomed to the techniques of the proscenium stage (see 310). In schools with an all-purpose room, plays are frequently given in the round. Although such areas lack proper lighting and good acoustics, they have the advantage of being familiar territory to the students, and they require little in the way of scenery. What

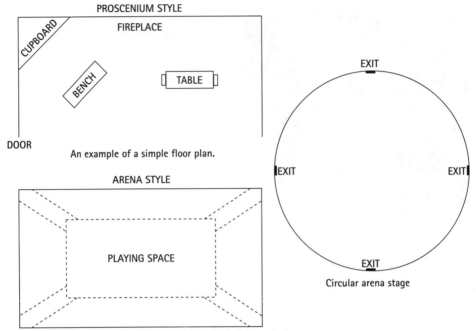

An example of a simple floor plan.

The audience is seated on three or four sides of the indicated playing space.

scenery there is should be simple and low so as not to block the view and so light-weight that it can be carried on and off the stage in front of the audience. Entrances can be indicated by putting masking tape on the floor. The audience when seated must be told that the taped-off areas will be used by the actors and must therefore be kept open. Audience participation is much easier to handle in the round than on an elevated proscenium platform.

Whatever the space, it should be small, with the best acoustics possible to put the actors at ease and help to prevent the constant reminders "Speak up" or "Louder, please!" These admonitions all too often lead to a stilted, unnatural performance, with children talking to the audience rather than to the other characters in the play. Large high school auditoriums are probably the worst possible places in which to perform. A small room, on the other hand, de-emphasizes the lack of performance skills and puts the attention where it should be, on the play.

The Auditorium

One aspect of producing a play that is frequently overlooked is the auditorium seating area. Ushers may be members of the class who have worked on play committees and so are free when the dress rehearsals are over. Ushering is an excellent way for these students to perform a necessary function. If there are programs, the ushers may hand them out, although in an informal situation a narrator is preferred to impart necessary information to the audience.

Attendance should be by invitation only rather than by ticket. When tickets are sold, there is an added emphasis on perfection and a felt obligation to make elaborate settings and costumes. Young players feel the strain, and the "sharing with" too often turns into "showing off."

The Stage Manager

The job of stage manager is important and one that responsible students can do and enjoy. A stage manager should be appointed at the same time as the cast is selected and given a script. A stage manager attends all rehearsals and keeps a record of all cuts, action, and business. It is a good idea for the stage manager to sit at one side of the stage where he or she can not only see and hear but also call the actors for their entrances.

Under most circumstances, the stage manager will be able to pull the curtains and handle or give cues for the lights. The stage manager works closely with the director and assumes as much authority as the director feels he or she can when the play is presented. The stage manager has a chance to grow in the job, for this person is important to every aspect of the production and learns, by doing, the meaning of the word *responsibility*.

Casting the Play

This preliminary work done, the director is now ready to give attention to casting the play. In creative drama the cast changes with every playing. In the formal production, however, there is one cast that rehearses each scene a number of times in preparation for the performance. The matter of casting is therefore important. The director tries to get the best possible cast together and usually does this by means of tryouts.

The director is obligated to do a certain amount of typecasting. For example, a giant must be played by a very large child; a dwarf or elf, by a child who is small; other characters who may have certain specified physical characteristics, by children with similar characteristics. To cast for any reason other than theatrical effectiveness is a questionable practice. The audience must believe in the reality of the characters, and if they are too obviously different from the description or implications in the script, an audience cannot find them acceptable. Likewise, older players feel uncomfortable if they realize that they are not believable, and so the good that the experience may do them is negated by their own feelings of inadequacy. This is one of the strong arguments against public performance by children.

Planning the Production

Stage Movement

Stage movement is the movement of actors about the stage. The director who plots it in advance will find that valuable time is saved in rehearsal. Writing notations in the script, or even making diagrams, will help the director see at a glance where the various characters are. Although most published scripts have action included, it seldom works, because no two stages are alike. For example, an important entrance, which the script indicates should be from the right, may have to be reversed if the wing space in the school auditorium cannot accommodate it.

It is an advantage to have the cast memorize the movement along with the lines. Once the general movement is set, the cast is free to develop appropriate business and work on characterization. Early memorization of lines also helps the group move ahead, giving attention to the rhythm of the play, the building of climaxes, projection of voice, and general polishing. Perfection is never the aim when working with children, but their satisfaction will certainly be greater if they can feel well prepared and able to enter into the performance with a sense of security. Encouragement, plus necessary constructive criticism, will help to make the rehearsal period one of pleasure and learning.

Business

Business is the small movements the actors make to suggest character, occupation, and emotional state and necessary mime or use of required props. Knitting, setting a table, reading, sweeping, putting on gloves, cleaning glasses, playing with jewelry, arranging flowers, and eating are common bits of business that help to establish character and move the play forward.

Music

Many children's plays require music. It may be taped or live. Instrumental music is often suggested by the playwright (guitar, flute, recorder, drum). Live music is best if musicians are available; otherwise, taped music works well.

Lighting

Lighting is the area in which children are usually least involved. Lighting equipment is dangerous, expensive, and too sophisticated for a young and inexperienced crew. An all-purpose room is rarely equipped with stage lights, so the problem does not exist there. Occasionally, a school auditorium will have a few simple spotlights that can be added to the general lighting; in this case children in the intermediate grades and up can learn how to operate them, and they enjoy the magic of transforming a scene with colored lights and dimmers.

Scenery

Scenery means the large pieces that suggest the locale of the play. There is always controversy as to the difference between scenery and properties, or "props." Scenery is background, whereas properties are those items used by the actors.

Platforms and steps are helpful in creating different levels, thus adding variety in appearance and making for interesting movement. A bright tablecloth, a few large flowers, and two or three benches or stools often provide all that is needed. Children have wonderfully imaginative ideas for suggesting scenery; what they need is practical help in constructing it. If the director works closely with the art department of the school, most backstage problems can easily be solved. Best of all, the stage crew or scenery committee will have an ideal opportunity to learn techniques of painting and handling materials.

Scenery is usually not needed until the final rehearsals. If it can be ready a week in advance of the first dress rehearsal, the players will have a chance to get used to it and will not have to add that adjustment to costumes and other last-minute details. A few *dos* and *don'ts* about scenery may be helpful: it should

1. Enhance, not distract.
2. Be firm, not flimsy.
3. Unify the production.
4. Be in keeping with the mood of the play.
5. Suggest the time and place of the story and the circumstances of the characters.
6. Be planned together with costumes.

Properties

Very little needs to be said about *properties*—all the objects (usually small) used by the players. If the school has a property closet, many commonly used items can be kept and brought out when needed. A creative drama teacher should have these items anyhow, for they are often used in class. Baskets, canes, wooden bowls, china (better yet, plastic dishes), swords, and the like are basic equipment. Some things must be borrowed, some made. It is a challenge to the ingenuity of the property committee when, for example, items such as a golden goose, a snowman, a roast chicken, or a birthday cake are called for. Papier-mâché and Styrofoam are excellent materials for the unusual item, but, again, the young or inexperienced committee needs help in construction.

One other word regarding props: the property committee learns through its assignment what responsibility is all about, for objects are often needed at particular moments in the play, and their absence can ruin an otherwise excellent scene. Properties should be checked before and after every rehearsal and performance and, if damaged or missing, replaced. It is a good idea to begin gathering the properties as soon as the play goes into rehearsal so that the actors will have ample time to get used to handling them.

Costumes

Costumes, like scenery, can be a source of worry and frustration to the teacher whose group is too young or inexperienced to assume responsibility for them. Sometimes parents take a hand with the costumes, and sometimes the art department offers assistance. The former may be a satisfactory arrangement, but all too often it builds what should have been a simple performance into a major production. Too much emphasis is put on the mounting and the public performance when adult contributions take precedence over the learning. The second arrangement—assistance from the art department—is decidedly preferable, since it keeps the play within the framework of the school and may give the class an opportunity to help design or even make some part of the costumes.

If neither type of cooperation is available, the teacher should try to solve the matter of clothing by merely suggesting it or adapting easily obtainable garments to the play. For example, aprons, hats, vests, capes, boots, and shawls are easily acquired and go a long way toward suggesting various kinds of characters. Children accept simple suggestions readily and do not demand complete or authentic outfits. Blue jeans, tights, and colored T-shirts are in the wardrobes of most children and young people today, regardless of economic circumstances. If these things can be chosen with a color scheme in mind, they can be used as costumes for many folk tales or for plays with historical backgrounds. One way of handling costumes is to have a coat tree on stage. Garments such as hats, shawls, and coats can be hung on it and picked up by the players when needed. This is particularly effective when presenting folk tales.

Here are a few suggestions as to the function of costumes: they should

1. Suggest the personality, age, occupation, and financial circumstances of the characters.
2. Belong to the period and setting of the play.
3. Be appropriate to the season of the year, as suggested by the story.
4. Help to unify the production.

Try to make sure that the players are comfortable and that the clothes or costumes add to the individual and overall effect. Attention to cleanliness, color, design, and fit need not take up much time, but it is worth every minute spent and will avoid the amateur look of the old-fashioned school play.

Rehearsals

The director is now ready to set up a rehearsal schedule. It is hoped that, for the teacher or director, this will be an informal procedure. Even though a performance date has been set and the work planned, the director must try to avoid the anxiety and boredom that mar rehearsals of so many nonprofessional productions. For this reason, rehearsals should be frequent but short. Scenes, rather than the entire play, should be rehearsed first; complete run-throughs come later.

Early memorization of lines is advocated, since it frees the player to move and to develop pertinent business. Most important is interpretation. Discussions along the way help the actors to learn who the characters are and why they behave as they do. First, there should be an oral reading of the whole play. Then questions such as these should be answered:

1. How would you describe the character you are playing?
2. What does the character have to say about himself or herself?
3. What do others have to say about him or her?
4. What are his or her relationships to other persons in the play?
5. What are his or her aims? motivations?
6. What are his or her individual qualities? Name details that help in understanding him or her (personality, temperament, age, occupation, background, likes, dislikes, education, beliefs).

Improvising scenes from the play should precede memorization of lines and movement. Any misunderstanding or lack of understanding will be cleared up if players create their own dialogue, characters, and motivations.

One word of caution: the dramatist's intention must be respected in interpreting the play. Altering the meaning is dangerous and disrespectful. If the group does not like the play as written, it would be better to give up the project and select something else rather than alter the script. Changing mood or meaning will throw the play out of focus. Leave the spoofs for older and more experienced players, if they wish to tamper; it is a questionable practice at best and not for young players.

Composition, or stage picture, is something else for the director to bear in mind. Even an experienced actor cannot see the grouping on the stage when he or she is part of it; hence, the director, who is watching closely from the front, must be aware of the composition. Are the players hiding each other? Can important business be seen? Are entrances blocked? If there are several players together, do they make a pleasing picture?

If dances or songs are included, they should be rehearsed and integrated as early as possible. It is always a temptation to let them go, but the director will find that this neglect makes for a weak spot or a slow transition. Such business should appear to spring from the play and belong to it; it should not be imposed for the purpose of adding more people or relieving monotony.

As the rehearsal period proceeds, the play should grow in feeling, understanding, technical competence, and unity. Smoothness will come as lines are learned, the business is perfected, and the actors develop rapport with each other. Rough spots should be ironed out in the beginning rather than left to the end for polishing. Finally, if the director can maintain a spirit of fun, the rehearsal period will be a source of pleasure as the cast shares the satisfaction of building something together.

As in creative drama, the director occasionally finds a show-off or clown in the cast. The director does not want to inhibit inventiveness, but he or she cannot afford byplay, which disrupts the rehearsal and takes the attention away from the script. Clowning must be stopped at once, for it can jeopardize the entire performance. Most

High school students share their work with audiences at Friends Seminary, New York City. (Courtesy of Jennifer Fell Hayes, Director.)

children and young people, if approached constructively, will see that practical and private joking are out of order, and for the good of the production their energy must be used to build, not break up, a scene.

The Dress Rehearsal

The dress rehearsal can be either a day of confusion or a satisfying culmination of weeks of group effort. When details have been well planned and the scenery and costumes are ready, there is no reason why the dress rehearsal should not be the high point of the rehearsal period. The old adage "A poor dress rehearsal makes a good show" is fallacious.

Two or even three dress rehearsals are desirable and should be planned from the beginning. At the first one, the scenery should be finished and in place. At the second and third, costumes should be worn so that by the time the play goes on, the cast and backstage crew will have mastered all the problems. After each dress rehearsal and performance, costumes should be hung up carefully and properties checked. This practice not only helps to keep things in good order but also instills a sense of responsibility in the players. Even in the most informal of plays, the actors should remain backstage and not mingle with the audience. Food and other refreshments have no place in a dressing room. They are a risk to the costumes and distract the players from their responsibilities.

Makeup is rarely necessary in a children's play. Teenagers, however, like working with makeup; for them it is another learning experience. Again, makeup extends or enhances a character; it does not create one.

If there is to be a curtain call, it should be rehearsed so that the players are ready to come out and bow to the audience. One curtain call is sufficient for the audience to show its appreciation. Although there is some difference of opinion about this, the curtain call is a convention of the formal theatre, and an audience should be given a chance to observe it.

The Performance

Once again, a performance by beginners or children should be simple and informal. The director has the greatest responsibility here, for an attitude of calm encouragement will be contagious. If the director regards the play as a good piece of work that the cast and crew take pleasure in sharing, they will view it much the same way. They will look forward to the performance with anticipation rather than with anxiety. Both excessive criticism and excessive praise are as harmful at this stage as at any other. The most satisfying response a group can be accorded is the appreciation of the audience. The players will know that they have succeeded in achieving their goal: successful communication.

One performance of a play is recommended for younger children, for they plan and anticipate it as a special event. Repeating the experience rarely recaptures the fun; the play lacks the original spontaneity, and the players become bored with what was once a lively involvement. Junior and senior high school students, however, can gain a great deal from the experience of giving a play two or three times. As the product assumes more importance, there is the challenge of trying to improve it and discovering in the process the responses of different audiences.

In a children's production, the director supplies the necessary showmanship. This does not mean dictating the way lines should be read or imposing a style that is unnatural to young players. It means being sensitive to their ideas and helping them express those ideas most effectively. It means checking costumes and props to make sure everything is ready before a performance. Attention must be given to composition and blocking only to insure visibility and projection of voices.

Teamwork is both a necessity to a good performance and a source of deep satisfaction to the players. There is probably no experience comparable to the camaraderie that develops during rehearsals. For players of junior and senior high school age, this experience may be the highlight of the year and leave a lasting impression. A special feeling binds a group together when it shares the hard work, the creative effort, the interdependence, and the fun of rehearsing and presenting a play.

Now, having discussed the production of a school play in some detail, I must say that there are times when a very young group is not ready to perform, yet the students would be bitterly disappointed if they had to forgo the experience. I have faced that dilemma with children in the primary grades and finally hit upon a solution that satisfied all of us: Send an informal invitation to the parents and principal to observe a demonstration lesson or rehearsal of a work in progress. This eliminates the need for costumes, scenery, props, and programs. And, of course, the rehearsal should take place in the classroom, not the auditorium. The children are freer because they are not burdened with a script, and it gives an understanding audience a chance to see how we work and learn.

The following lesson plan is included in this chapter for a specific reason. There are times when you may wish to invite parents to observe their children's work, and for very young children a demonstration is much better than attempting a performance. The children will enjoy it without the anxiety of putting on a play. I suggest that when parents come they sit informally around the room rather than in straight rows. Applause should be limited and discouraged. Expressing their enjoyment without excessive praise does no harm and makes for a pleasant occasion all around.

The Imagination Station

A lesson by Julia M. Morris—"Curriculum for Younger Children," originally developed for preschool children, but easily adapted for older groups

Story: "The Selfish Giant," by Oscar Wilde

1. Imagination Transformation Activities

Forest of Trees. Tell the children that you have noticed a forest of trees growing up around them, that in fact they each have their own tree in front of them with baskets at their feet. Explain that these trees grow all sorts of different things. Model for the group what grows on your tree and then ask them to share their own ideas. "On my tree, there are oranges . . . Alex, what grows on your tree?" Together, the children begin to reach up and pull down the goodies on the trees. Rhythmically recite: "Reach, reach—reach, reach, reach." After each reaching sequence, ask the children how we might reach for things that are higher up in the trees or that are in the tree next to us. Try any suggestions that are given (such as up on tiptoes, reaching to the side, jumping, using a ladder). This activity works especially well when accompanied by music.

Introducing Pantomime. Have the children sit down and begin to eat the various items that they picked from the imaginary trees. They are exploring the skill of pantomime. Have the children mime (use gestures without voice) how they would eat or use the items in their trees. If it is a tree of puppies (remember, these trees are magic so anything grows on them), ask students to show you how you might hold the puppy, pet him, even feed him. The group guesses each child's pantomime. Then you, as the teacher-facilitator, begin to pick an orange out of your basket and peel it. Give the children clues about this fruit, describing its texture and showing, through pantomime, the peeling process. See if they can name the fruit. Take out a seed from the orange and ask for responses as to what this tiny, stone-like object might be. Ask for ideas about what can be done with a seed and what happens when you plant it in the ground.

Planting Finger Play. Introduce the "planting song." The song can be sung to the melody, "I Had a Little Tea Pot" but works equally well as a chant.

> Hold a seed between your finger and thumb
> Kiss it, reach, show it to the sun
> Crouch way down
> Dig a hole in the ground
> Place it, pat it, make a growing sound

Introduce finger and hand gestures simultaneously with the song. Repeat it twice.

2. Dance Drama

Growing Dance. Talk again about what happens when seeds are planted in the ground. Next, initiate the children's movement: "We are all seeds in the ground now. Show me how you would grow." Put on growing music. Describe the growing movements that you see. "I see different stems that seem to be slowly stretching towards the sun." Have everyone sit down and ask what their seeds grew.

3. Introduce Story

"Wow! What a beautiful garden we have just made with our bodies and imaginations! It was filled with (name some of the plants and flowers which the children created). I am now going to tell you about another beautiful garden. It is a magical garden and it belongs to my friend, the giant." Ask the children for their background knowledge of a giant. "What does a giant look like? Have you ever seen one? How do you think a giant walks?" Allow for giant walking demonstrations.

"Well, my friends, in the giant's garden it is spring all year around! Here and there over the soft green grass stand beautiful flowers which bloom like stars. The birds sit on the trees and sing sweetly. Unfortunately, my friend is having trouble with his garden. He needs our help, but in order to help him we must go visit him in his garden." Explain that they will go there today on their bikes. Introduce your special "biking bag" and explain that inside this bag there is a bicycle for each one of us. Open the bag. Let the bikes ride out. Each student has a bike roll.

4. Drama Journey into the Story Setting

Bike Ride. Everyone gets on an imaginary bike. Start to ride by lying on your back and pedaling with legs up in the air. Together, you are traveling up and down hills of different terrain. You pedal up and down a steep hill covered with pointy brambles, a muddy, sticky slope, and then, finally, a hill of soft, billowy clouds. You finally arrive at the entrance of the giant's garden.

5. Exploring the Setting (The Giant's Garden)

Everyone takes off their bike helmet and follows you to the "entrance gate" of the garden. Tell the children that there are great high walls around the garden but they can take a peek through the gate. Peer in through the gate or over one of the walls by standing on tiptoe. Tell the children that the giant does not seem to be home because his house is boarded up. Begin to point out things that you notice in the garden and give the children the freedom to do the same. "I see flowers that look like rainbows . . . I can hear some sparrows singing a strange melody . . . what do you see/hear?" The children will join in with their own observations.

Slowly, with the children's help, open up the squeaky gate. Urge everyone to walk around and observe the surroundings. Remind the children that if they touch the giant's plants or flowers, they must do so gently. Try to initiate responses as to what the flowers smell like and what it feels like to touch the soil and the various greenery in the garden. While the children are walking around, you find a mysterious sign (with big letters printed on it) and a small note attached to the other side. This sign seems to have fallen behind some rose bushes. Gather the children closer and read the sign and note to them.

The sign reads:

DO NOT ENTER

The note says:

It always snows and nothing grows!

–G

Discuss the sign. "Who do you think wrote these words? (Who is G?) If the giant wrote this sign, why do you think he does not want people to enter his garden? What do you think he means when he says that nothing grows?" Tell the children that if we wait, we can talk to the giant and ask him any questions we have. Make sure they are willing. "Have you ever talked to a giant before? What if he is mean and perhaps steps on us?" Remind them that this giant is your friend and today he needs our help.

6. Meet the Story Character

Storytelling Through Teacher in Role (The Selfish Giant). Ask children to clench their fists, close their eyes, and count to ten with you or another teacher. "The giant is sometimes shy, so let's count to ten softly and see if he comes over to us." Open your eyes. The teacher-in-role[1] is wearing a hat or an article of clothing that represents the giant. The giant (teacher-in-role) is talking quietly to himself and pacing. He makes it clear, through his body movements and his muttering, that it is no longer spring in his magic

---

[1]"Teacher-in role" refers to a classroom teacher taking on the role of one of the main characters. In the original curriculum project, which served to demonstrate and model this type of work for preschool teachers, either my project assistant or I brought these characters to life through the teacher-in-role strategy.

garden and that a very cold winter has set in. "Nothing grows . . . it always snows, nothing grows . . . oh, what am I to do? This is supposed to be a magic spring garden!" The giant suddenly notices the children a few feet away and is happily surprised. He introduces himself and explains that he used to have a glorious garden. Everyday it was spring in his garden and the children of the town used to play there.

"But you see I got very angry that the children were using my beautiful garden. Everyday, they dug under my fence and began playing in here! I wanted it all to myself and I wanted to make sure that all my flowers, plants, and trees were safe. So I built a big wall to keep people out. I even put up a sign that said . . . now what did it say exactly?" The children will remind him that it said DO NOT ENTER. "That's right. I wanted everyone to know that they were not allowed to play here. But (becoming very sad) now my magic garden has changed. It is always winter here and all the flowers are gone. There are no more fruits or vegetables and the trees are sleeping so they don't have any leaves. It is cold and snowy all the time. I don't know what to do. I have this garden all to myself now, but it isn't as beautiful and I feel lonely. I am so glad you are here. I need your help to bring my garden back."

The giant (teacher-in-role) fosters a discussion with the children by asking them: "Have you ever had something that you didn't want anyone else to play with? What was it? What did you say when you were asked to share? I really want my garden to come to life again and I want children to play here again. Does anyone have any ideas of what I might do?"

7. *Brainstorming Solutions for the Character's Conflict*

Take suggestions from the children as to what the giant might do or how the children might help him. Some possible ideas and suggestions:

- Take down the wall
- Teach the giant the "planting song"
- Plant new flowers, vegetables, trees, etc., for him using the seeds they brought
- Play in the garden with him. (He might not know how to play so the children and the teachers will have to teach him.)
- Teach the giant new words to use when people want to play in his garden. ("You may use my garden, but be careful with the plants," "Maybe we can share the garden together," etc.)

Follow through on whatever suggestions the group offers.

The garden is restored. The giant gives each child an imaginary camera. They can now go around the garden and take pictures of what they see. Ask children to tuck the cameras and their pictures into their pocket when they are finished taking photographs. The giant says good-bye and thanks the children for their help. He says he won't be lonely anymore and will be happy to have other children playing in his garden again. "I can't wait to share this beautiful place we have created together."

Return Journey: With the giant's help, children close their eyes to return to the classroom instantly. "I know you went to a lot of trouble to get here. My gift to you is to sprinkle magic dust on you as you close your eyes. You will be back with your teacher in the classroom by the time you count to five. One magic dust . . . two magic dust . . ."

8. Closure

Open your eyes. The teacher is out of the role of the giant. Children show and describe photographs (imaginary) of the giant's garden. They talk about the giant, the garden, and sharing. If there is time, sing a final good-bye song.

9. Present the Story Book

Show the class the story book of *The Selfish Giant*. Remind the children that the story they created using their bodies, voices, and imaginations might be a little different from the way the author wrote the story. Explore together how in some places the book is the same as the story drama and in some places it is different.

Writing Extension: Ask the children to draw illustrations of the plants in the garden. Leave room below for words to describe the story setting. You can transcribe what they say or, depending on their ages and abilities, they can write themselves.

This plan can be split into two lessons on even these. If so, each session must be properly introduced (warm-up) and closed (discussion/closure activities).

Summary

The presentation of a scripted play for an audience should be done only when older children are involved, and then infrequently. For both younger or older children, informality and simplicity should be stressed if the basic values of communication and sharing are to be realized. There is a difference of opinion about whether children should ever appear before an audience, for fear of destroying their spontaneity and naturalness. This is a valid argument, but my contention is that performance does no harm if it is done without pressure, thus avoiding drudgery.

The teacher must become director, supplying showmanship and making certain decisions. As teacher, however, he or she tries to involve every member of the group so that the procedure is as democratic as possible. Most important, children should not be exploited to show the value of the content—*or* the instruction. In our zeal to present an excellent product we must avoid exhausting or alienating performers.

In the school, club, or camp play, educational and social values come first. The product will hold interest for the viewers if they are properly oriented and their appreciation is the natural consequence of a successful attempt at communication. There is probably nothing that binds a group together more closely than the production of a play and no joy more lasting than the memory of a play in which all the contributions of all participants have dovetailed so well that each member of the group has had a share in its success.

A scene from Tin Pan Ali, *produced by the Palo Alto Children's Theatre, one of the oldest community theatres for children in the United States. (Courtesy of Patricia Briggs, director; photograph by Steve Bonnel.)*

Finally, let us not forget that theatre is a performing art. The suspicions that have surrounded the theatre in our country from the beginning are still here, if masked. When we cut the arts from the budget in times of depression and de-emphasize *acting* in favor of *learning,* we are giving tacit acceptance to an old prejudice. Some funding agencies request a product as proof of the effectiveness of the programs to which they have given financial support. A product need not be interpreted as a full-fledged production, however; in fact, a good demonstration can meet the requirement just as well, often better. You may find a production desirable, but if you do not, consider demonstrating creative drama or an open class by showing what it is, what it does, and how it works. If there is one thing that recent experimentation in the arts has shown us, it is that there are few, if any, rules that must be obeyed.

Suggested Assignments

1. Try to find a play or program that children are presenting for an audience. Attend a performance and answer these questions:
   a. Was the material worthwhile and worthy of the players' time and attention?
   b. What educational values did you find in it?
   c. Describe the audience and its response to the children's efforts.

2. Read several plays written for children to perform, and select one that you like particularly. Explain your choice.

Journal Writing

1. If you have ever been in a play, what values did the experience have for you?
2. Do you believe that performing for an audience is important? Which has greater value, the product or the process? Explain the reason for your answer.
3. Why do you think some educators disapprove of all performing for children under age twelve?
4. Discuss the social value of theatre.

Chapter 17

Applied Theatre

Playing Lear, an intergenerational play. Roots and Branches Theatre. (Courtesy of Lauren Scott, photograph by Elena Olivo.)

325

> I believe that all the truly revolutionary theatrical
> groups should transfer to the people the means of
> production in the theatre so that the people
> themselves may utilize them. The theatre is a
> weapon, and it is the people who should wield it.
>
> —*Augusto Boal*

Applied theatre[1] is a term used by Philip Taylor and is the best term I know for describing the ways in which theatre techniques are used to effect social changes. It is an umbrella term covering TIE (theatre-in-education), conflict resolution, playback theatre, and intergenerational theatre. Although drama therapy also belongs in this rubric, it has become a discrete discipline separate from theatre education with a special curriculum. Specific degree requirements prepare candidates for the drama therapy field and so drama therapy will not be discussed here. The classroom or drama teacher is not a therapist, although we have all seen the beneficial results of creative drama on the students in our classes.

Theatre in education was defined in Chapter 1. What place does further discussion of the subject have in this textbook on creative drama? Simply that theatre-in-education has created so much interest in this country in the past twenty years, and is so closely linked with creative drama, that it merits more space than the few paragraphs it was accorded in earlier editions of this book. Originating in England in the 1960s, the TIE concept spread to other English-speaking countries and, soon afterward, to many other countries around the world. TIE often uses creative drama in activities preceding and following a performance; teachers cannot only work with teams in this way but can also use creative drama as a natural method of solving problems and exploring curricular material and social issues.

Australian educator John O'Toole described TIE as based on an extension of children's play and a combination of theatricality and classroom techniques to provide an experience in its own right; the glamour of strangers in dramatic roles and costumes provides both a stimulus and a context not normally available to the teacher.[2] Whenever players put themselves in the place of others, they become better able to comprehend other people's concerns and problems in both affective and cognitive ways.

The potential of drama for reaching young people is now generally accepted in the United States, although the approach and techniques used by various companies are far from uniform. Some groups pattern their work on the British model, whereas others adapt the concept to meet American needs and interests. Many children's theatre touring companies in the United States advertise an educational component, but not all of them interpret the term *educational* in the same way, nor do they necessarily offer TIE pieces exclusively. Some children's theatre companies perform plays that qualify purely as entertainment; others describe their work as educational. Few, however,

---

[1]Philip Taylor. *Applied Theatre* (Portsmouth: Heinemann, 2003).
[2]John O'Toole, *Theatre in Education* (London: Hodder and Stoughton, 1976), p. vi.

attempt the more difficult task of offering controversial subject matter in a theatrically aesthetic form.

The basic difference between traditional children's theatre and TIE is *intent*. The traditional group comes into the school to entertain, whereas the mission of TIE is to effect change or to illuminate subject matter through the medium of the theatre. The desired result of TIE is

1. To change an attitude, thereby leading to a change in behavior
2. To stimulate intellectual curiosity
3. To motivate the pursuit of a particular topic or issue

Although a play may produce any or all of these results, that is not the playwright's or producer's intent. Children may, and often do, reenact what they have just seen on the stage, but the motivation comes from their enjoyment of the story or the impression made on them by the actors. Although TIE has often been criticized as being didactic, at its best it is excellent theatre in both content and form. But let us see how it evolved.

In *Applied Theatre* Philip Taylor describes the terms *drama-in-education* and *theatre-in-education*, clarifying the uses and values of each. He gives examples of communities in need of change and the way theatre can be bought in to help. A poignant example was the case of a group of fifth graders who had witnessed the collapse of the World Trade Towers. The drama therapist who worked with the children had them tell what they had seen and felt. Through their stories, told and retold, and their role-play, they created a drama that was later shared with their families and the school community. This is an example of the healing power of theatre for a deep psychological wound.

Theatre can also be applied to social crises, an example of which was a community devastated by poverty, unemployment, domestic violence, crime, and teenage suicide. A theatre company was commissioned to help the people talk together, define the problems, and seek a solution that would ultimately transform a desperate community. In this situation participatory theatre was used to bring the adults and young people together to work on the conflicts that were destroying their lives. Applied theatre in every case is a collaborative endeavor. It is called "applied" because—"it is taken out of the conventional mainstream theatre house into various settings in communities where many members have no real experience in theatre form. The theatre becomes a medium for action, for reflection, but most important, for transformation. . . ."[3]

Background of Theatre-in-Education

TIE as a concept originated in England in 1965. The first company was established at the Belgrade Theatre in Coventry, primarily as a way of drawing the young people of the community into the theatre. The first program was a piece called *Out of the Ashes*.

---

[3]Philip Taylor, *Applied Theatre*, p. xxx.

Freedom Is My Middle Name *by Lee Hunkins,*
performed at the Open Eye, New Stagings, New
York City. (Courtesy of Amie Brockway, director;
photograph by Scott Humbert.)

It dealt with life in Coventry during the blitz and its aftermath and was developed through improvisation and subsequently put into script form with the assistance of a local playwright. Gordon Vallins, who designed the first programs at the Belgrade, was concerned not only with building an audience for the future but also with the way in which theatre was being presented to young people. Vallins noted:

> The local authority bought out two matinee performances a year for particular productions which were felt to be suitable. These tended to include the annual Shakespearean play, an event treated by many schools as a jolly afternoon out. This event was loathed by the actors. Most of the young people came ill-prepared and demonstrated little respect for the play or the actors. Consequently, the actors tended to rush the performance and garble their lines. For most actors it was a negative experience. Although some attempt had been made by the theatre to provide preparatory talks before the theatre visit, it was administratively impossible to visit every school. The situation was embarrassing and obviously needed reassessing. For most of the young audience it was as if the play had been spoken in a foreign tongue, the action remote, played on a platform behind the proscenium arch, with the actors talking to each other and never to their audience.[4]

Vallins attacked the situation with a pilot project in which he sought a new way to capture the attention of young audiences and hold their interest. The material, he believed, must be direct, challenging, and relevant to their lives. It need not be current or even familiar, but it must contain an issue or a problem to solve. He was

---

[4]Gordon Vallins, "The Beginnings of T.I.E.," in *Learning Through Theatre,* ed. Tony Jackson (Manchester, England: Manchester University Press, 1960), p. 6.

acquainted with Brian Way's work at the Theatre Centre in London and knew the value of audience participation. The Theatre Centre at that time produced specially scripted plays, written and produced to include audience participation. The participation might be vocal, physical, or verbal and was sometimes necessary to the outcome of the plot, but Way's primary purpose was to entertain rather than to educate the audience. Theatre-in-education, in contrast, was created with an awareness of the limitations of the school curriculum and the lack of impact that the theatre was having on young people. If audiences could be moved to participate, Vallins reasoned, children's restlessness might be dispelled and replaced by a genuine involvement in the content.

"In essence," wrote Tony Jackson, "TIE needs to be seen as a new genre, a form of theatre that has arisen in direct response to the needs of both theatre and schools and which has sought to harness the techniques and imaginative potency of theatre in the service of education."[5] In time TIE companies developed a variety of plays for different age levels. "Infant," junior, and secondary school programs were devised, sometimes even on the same theme but handled in different ways, with increasing complexity on the upper levels.

By serving a large population, teams were able to qualify for funding from the British Arts Council and local authorities, though not necessarily from local education authorities. Many TIE teams were attached to regional theatres and some, as mentioned, to academic institutions. Standards and goals varied, reflecting each individual team's perspective and point of view. Some teams were highly political; others were not. All, however, researched and prepared their own material and created programs that they considered relevant to the lives of young people.[6]

At the core of the concept was the conviction that the best learning takes place through personal or hands-on experience. Actor-teachers would engage the students' interest in the subject and then give them the details necessary to bring the material to life. From there on it was a cooperative effort, with the team guiding the class through an exploration of the problem.

The classroom teacher was to be a key person in helping students derive maximum benefit from a visit; therefore, cooperation from the schools was enlisted. Many teachers were enthusiastic about this new and different approach, and it was not long before it had captured the imagination of the English-speaking world and of drama teachers on the European continent. Although there have been changes in TIE since its founding, the basic tenets have remained.

By 1973 the TIE concept had proliferated to the extent that a two-week festival was organized and held in London. Two venues were selected to accommodate the thirty-eight companies that responded to the invitation to participate. These sites were the Young Vic and the Cockpit, both theatres with active companies of their own and good performance spaces. A wide variety of programs, ranging from simple pieces for preschoolers to sophisticated programs for teenagers, was offered to delegates from the United Kingdom and abroad. TIE in England is no longer as widespread as it was a

---

[5]Tony Jackson, ed., *Learning Through Theatre* (Manchester, England: Manchester University Press, 1960), p. viii.
[6]Many of the scripts were later published and so made available to other groups.

generation ago, but it has contributed a lasting service in raising consciousness of theatre that challenges, stimulates participation, and transforms.

Strategies for Theatre-in-Education

In TIE, children are expected to enter into a situation and are asked to make decisions or solve problems. This participation is believed to help them become much more deeply involved than they do when merely seeing a production that is entertaining or having a lesson taught traditionally in a classroom. Also, with young children, having a teacher participate in-role (assuming a part) also heightens the experience, although it is not necessarily a part of the program. Some programs are humorous, some are serious, but all are thought-provoking.

Although audience participation is commonly used in TIE, the two concepts are different. Indeed, audience participation is frequently used in children's theatre. In TIE, however, participation makes a greater demand on the audience: it means decision making, thoughtful discussion, and cooperative effort that may affect the outcome of the program. Both the *intent* and the *extent* of participation differentiate TIE from participation used in other types of plays.

Creative drama is often employed following a performance, but it, too, is only one of many methods suggested by the team to make the most productive use of the

The Lonely Loch Ness Monster. *(Courtesy of Penny Jones, Early Childhood Puppet Theatre.)*

visit. In other words, there is no exact formula for a program or for the varieties of participation and combinations of techniques employed.

One effective method that is sometimes employed is simulation. A scene or situation is simulated with an entire group of students taking part. *Factory,* which took place in the Curtain Theatre in London in the 1970's, is an example of simulation. The secondary school students for whom it was planned were divided into groups, with the factory workers on the shop floor and the white-collar employees on an upper floor. Each group was introduced to its responsibilities and then led through the schedule of an entire working day. By experiencing the job, the hierarchy, and the rewards and problems faced by factory personnel, the students developed a much better understanding of both the work and labor relations than they had had before. Simulation requires much careful planning and supervision; it is time-consuming, and it also involves fewer students than a program that takes place in an auditorium. Nevertheless, it is an effective and unique way of learning. As opposed to traditional learning, simulation aims to help students develop critical judgment and a sense of personal responsibility rather than a passive, unquestioning acceptance of society as it is. By living through a simulated situation, the participant is better able to assess it. Imaginative thinking is encouraged, and a deeper level of feeling is aroused.

Another effective technique is anthology, used primarily in the teaching of history. According to John Hodgson, formerly of Bretton Hall College, anthology is a collection of authentic material from a particular period. It can be music, poetry, prose, plays, or any form of actable, livable, presentable, communicable idea or sound or facility. In other words, explains Hodgson, "It's all about people in history. It's about people living in an age, what they did, what they said to each other, what they thought about each other, what they wrote to each other and about each other."[7]

Tony Jackson, in his introduction to *Learning Through Theatre,* described the theatrical event, whatever it may be, as the central stimulus of the TIE program, but it is only one of several elements. The team provides teachers' workshops in advance to explain the aim and describe the manner in which the program will be presented. If teachers are to take part in-role, they are taught how to proceed and are given a packet containing research materials and suggestions for further activities. The performance elements come next; last of all is an opportunity for the team and the classroom teacher to assess the effectiveness of the program. The following criteria were suggested as guidelines for engaging a company and reviewing its work:[8]

1. Is the content worth presenting, and how far does it go in arresting, informing, and challenging the audience?
2. Is the material well performed, and does the team have good audience contact?
3. Is it performed for the right age level and the most appropriate size of audience?
4. To what extent are the teachers involved, and does the program relate to the school curriculum?

---

[7]Robert J. Landy, *Handbook of Educational Drama and Theatre* (Westport, CT: Greenwood Press, 1982), p. 53.
[8]Jackson, *Learning Through Theatre,* p. 33.

Periwinkle National Theatre production of Halfway There, *a drug prevention play. (Courtesy of Sunna Rash, Director, Monticello, NY.)*

5. How committed are the actors to the objectives of their work? Are they open to discussion and criticism? Do they attempt to evaluate their work?
6. What unique contribution will this company make to the children's education?

Although this is by no means a definitive list of questions, it directs the attention of the sponsor or teacher and the team to the most salient points.

Bretton Hall College in Yorkshire was one of the colleges in the forefront of the TIE movement from its inception, and it was the campus selected by New York University's program in educational theatre for several years for its overseas summer school. John Hodgson of Bretton Hall and Nancy Swortzell of New York University designed a curriculum for U.S. graduate students in educational theatre, who could elect twelve credits toward a master's or doctoral degree. This curriculum gives students a thorough grounding in TIE techniques, and a highly successful project was formed in New York: the Creative Arts Team (CAT).

CAT defines itself as "a new kind of provocative and challenging theatre which questions, probes, involves, and finally motivates personal response and action . . . a catalyst for thought on social and curricular issues, enriching the lives of both young people and adults by the vitality, immediacy, and pertinence to the concerns of today's society."[9]

Projects change according to sponsors' needs, but there is usually a new one each season. These are six of CAT's projects:

Conflict Resolution Through Drama: performance, workshops, and videotapes that address issues such as AIDS prevention, prejudice and racism, and independent living skills

---

[9]Touring productions have included such issues as child abuse, substance abuse, racial prejudice, and the violence it engenders, and teen suicide.

Project Communication: original theatre performances on timely issues and interactive drama workshops, aimed at strengthening communication skills

Drama Unlimited: interactive drama workshop residencies that address specific educational priorities and promote multicultural understanding

Special Express: workshops that meet the needs of students who are learning disabled, emotionally disabled, or hearing impaired or have other special needs, as well as the professionals who serve them

Early Learning Through the Arts: interactive drama workshops that heighten preacademic and socialization skills for students in Head Start and city board of education pre-kindergarten classes

Special Projects: specially designed drama workshops and performances for a wide range of populations and organizations

Through workshops, seminars, and summer institutes, the Paul A. Kaplan Center at the City University of New York trains classroom teachers, drama specialists, and actors in the use of drama and theatre to address critical social issues facing young people for twenty-five years.

One student, stimulated by the Bretton Hall experience, developed an unusual project in the Boston area. His use of TIE was aimed at creating a bridge between local historical events and the persons involved in or affected by them. Through research into the lives of actual people who had lived in Concord at the time of the Revolutionary War and were known to have taken part in the events that happened on the night of April 19, 1775, a living history piece was developed. It was titled *Cannon Fields* and played for several weeks during the summer of 1982 at the visitor's center in Minute Man National Historical Park in Concord, Massachusetts. This was an example of family theatre for both community and tourists in the area, but the procedures followed in creating the piece and the values derived from it are the same as those designed for schools. Many teachers made use of this documentary, but the performance dates and location precluded the kind of follow-up that is part of a regular TIE program.

Theatre-in-Education in Developing Countries

Today in many parts of the world, theatre is used to teach, to entertain, and to stimulate discussion about important social issues. For example, in Africa, where tribal societies have long used narrative and other forms of theatre to pass on tribal history, religious beliefs, and moral values, today it is being used to educate for the future. From Nigeria to Swaziland, theatre companies similar in structure to TIE are presenting programs on topics such as health care, family planning, conservation, sanitation, and alcoholism. Theatre is a particularly effective way of reaching country people in areas where there is no electricity to run movie projectors or television sets. The audiences respond to live performance, often joining in singing and dancing but also engaging in serious discussion afterward.

Some of the plays call for audience participation; some are purposely left open-ended. Most are used for instruction rather than for entertainment. The director of the National Theatre of Zaire described theatre as a particularly useful way of informing illiterate people of local issues and different ways of solving local problems. Often story lines are selected after polling the people for their suggestions. The government of Mozambique has used theatre to show villagers the serious responsibilities that come with independence. Used with adults as well as with young people, drama and theatre are potent techniques for consciousness raising and teaching in developing countries.[10] They are also effective in developed countries. When the South African musical *Sarafina!* came to Broadway in the spring of 1988, American audiences responded to it so enthusiastically that the limited engagement was extended indefinitely to accommodate the crowds who stormed the box office. Many high school teachers in the area made use of *Sarafina!* as a field trip for their students. Printed materials explaining the content and process of creating the musical were in the best TIE tradition.

Conflict Resolution

Instructors wanting to use this technique begin with a familiar conflict, which has the potential for serious results if left unresolved. An excellent textbook for high school and college students is Patricia Sternberg's *Theatre for Conflict Resolution*. The author makes the point that simple conflicts over minor issues often escalate into violence if not resolved amicably. Why? Because young people tend to act first when aroused and think later. By that time the damage has often been done.

This is not a situation confined to youth, however; cultural prejudices, national issues, domestic conflicts, and adult disagreements all challenge us to improve our communication, to listen to each other, to think, and to make an effort to diffuse emotions rather than to allow conflict to escalate. One-liners are excellent exercises for starters. For example:

1. "You never do anything right!"
2. "All you people—"
3. "It's all your fault!"

More complicated situations can be dealt with later but the idea is to use dialogue, not violence, to confront the issues. This is theatre.

Intergenerational Theatre

Intergenerational theatre may or may not deal with social problems but it is a way for two or more generations to work together. The hoped-for result is better understanding and respect for what others have to offer. It can also be theatre at its best, though this is accomplished only when the group works together cooperatively and creates an ensemble. Used therapeutically, intergenerational theatre can be an effective way of

---

[10]"Drama in Africa Is Used to Educate Audiences," *New York Times*, April 4, 1983, sec. 3, p. 12.

developing better human relationships. Both improvisation and scripted plays are appropriate, depending on the age readiness and desire of the groups.

Summary

A key link between applied theatre, TIE, and traditional youth theatre is the word *play*. As already implied, both educational drama and simulation games have their roots in the way children's play ritualizes forms of exploration. In both, the process is enjoyable if it is challenging, clear, and progressing toward some kind of satisfying conclusion.

The manner in which theatre-in-education is employed varies as greatly as the content and orientation of the company. The age and needs of the groups to be served determine the objectives; the financial aspect offsets the time that can be spent in a school as fees are usually based on the length of time that a company spends with students and teachers. Nevertheless, three components are always included in TIE:

1. Preparatory material, sent in advance of the team's visit to the school or community center in which the program is to appear
2. The presentation by the team
3. Follow-up activities for use in a workshop after the performance or for discussion later with the classroom teacher

Suggested Assignments

1. If there is a TIE company or a company that occasionally uses TIE techniques in your community, attend a presentation and analyze the content and the response of the audience.
2. In groups of five or six, take an issue that particularly interests you and explain how it might be presented. Explain your plan to the rest of the class, and lead a discussion on it.
3. List several topics that you think will challenge an audience. Consider the age of the audience, the cultural background, and the location. Where will you get material to support a theme?

Journal Writing

1. Is there a difference between a TIE program and a play based on the same theme? What is the difference?
2. Do you find any problems with TIE? any dangers?
3. If you have ever seen a TIE program or an issue-oriented play, what were your reactions? Try to analyze your response.

Chapter 18

Playgoing for Appreciation and Learning

The New Victory Theatre. Programs for youth family and audiences in New York City. (Photograph by Eliott Kaufmann.)

Theatre is one of the most enriching experiences a
person can have. Not only does it widen one's
experience with life but it helps develop skills for
coping more effectively with life's real problems.
I am certain that human dignity has its roots in
the quality of young people's experience.

–Dr. Lee Salk

To generate excitement among children, just announce a play for assembly or a class
field trip to the theatre. This can be merely an entertaining hour or a much richer experience, leading to a desire for more information, a deeper understanding, or some
creative expression. The last is what is meant by aesthetic education: an integration of
the arts into our lives, resulting in a lifelong appreciation.

Since the publication of the first edition of this book, there has been a phenomenal
growth in cooperation between educators and artists, who are no longer suspicious of
each other. The majority of children's theatre producers now write study guides, lead
workshops following performances, offer residencies, and seek help from teachers in order to make their work more relevant. Theatre-in-education companies create programs
on curricular topics and social issues most troubling to school and community. Moses
Goldberg, former director of Stage One, the Louisville children's theatre, says, "In selecting the season, I look at the goals of the schools. Some of them are interpreting other
cultures, or learning a second language. Others are working in groups and figuring out
career choices. . . . We make a covenant with the teachers. If they come and see a play
on Monday, we'll help them use the experience in the classroom on Tuesday."[1]

Because today schoolchildren are likely to see plays in assemblies and community
theatres, a chapter on theatregoing is important to include. The distinction between
creative drama and children's theatre, once clear, has become blurred or is at least
recognized as more flexible than we once regarded it.

Although an ancient art form, the theatre reflects society's most current ideas and
problems. A good play offers the audience not only entertainment but substance; to
engage our attention, a play must first entertain, but to hold our interest, it must have
content as well. A play that merely entertains palls in time; a play that attempts to educate without entertaining bores. A children's play, even more than a play for adults,
must have an interesting story, content worth spending time on, and a performance
by a skilled and talented company. Beyond that, it may have scenery, costumes, special
lighting effects, and perhaps music and dance. These visual elements enhance a performance, but they are not found in every production, nor are they always necessary.
They explain, however, why the theatre is often described as encompassing all the arts
and why it has such a universal appeal.

---

[1]Andrew Adler, "KERA Is the Key to Stage One's 1994–95 Season," Louisville *Courier Journal,* April 17,
1994, pp. 1–5.

In early societies, all members of the community took part in dramatic celebrations. As time went on, some persons emerged as superior dancers and musicians. This eventually led to a separation between those who performed and those who watched—between actors and audience. Today, except for children's participatory plays, when we attend a performance, we go as spectators. But to get the most out of the experience, we need to know something about the play that we are going to see—not every detail or the outcome but the theme, some idea of the plot, and the style and kind of production. As adult theatregoers, we read what the critics have to say, or we talk to friends who have already seen a performance.

Children's plays are not, as a rule, professionally reviewed. This may account, in part, for the popularity of the traditional folk and fairy tales both with children and with the adults who select their entertainment. The appeal of the familiar is strong, and the announcement of a well-loved story brought to life on the stage has tremendous drawing power. The adult who selects a child's entertainment is also inclined to respond to the known over the unknown title. A growing number of playwrights are bringing new stories and modern themes to the theatre, however, including some of the problems that young people face. To help children better understand and enjoy these plays, it is more important than it has been in the past for the teacher to take on the role of reviewer. The orientation that he or she can provide will stimulate interest and prepare a class for a valuable and exciting experience.

Adults responsible for setting up field trips should be aware of a number of criteria for evaluating plays for the child audience:[2]

1. Is the story suitable for the children who are going to see it?
2. Is the story worth telling? Does it have content and meaning?
3. Is it entertaining?
4. Is there an opportunity for identification? Usually, a play is stronger if the audience can identify with the character to whom the story belongs.
5. If it is an adaptation, are the essential elements of the source material retained so that the audience will not be offended by the change?

Values of Attending the Theatre

Much has been said about the values of theatre for youth, and basic to this subject is the script. The children's playwright, who cannot anticipate the age level of the audience, has a special and difficult task. Chances are that those who will be attending the play will range in age from five to twelve, perhaps a span even greater. Efforts have been made in some communities to try to control the age of the audience, either by adding a statement in the publicity or by presenting two series of plays. Age-level programming is controversial and a problem facing the playwright.

---

[2]Adapted from "CTAA Guidelines for Writing Children's Plays."

Children's interests change. Although fairy and animal tales are popular with younger children, the eleven- or twelve-year-old prefers adventure, history, biography, and stories of real life. The attention span of the older child is longer; hence, the older child can be absorbed for as long as two hours, whereas the younger child probably cannot give full attention for more than an hour.

High school students, if given adult entertainment, can easily be absorbed for the length of the play and are eager to discuss the material afterward. Raising standards applies in the theatre as well as in the classroom; for too long we have underestimated young audiences, watering down material instead of challenging students with demanding themes and scripts.

To younger children, a character is all good or all bad. As they grow older, children begin to comprehend motives and can see a combination of faults and virtues, or weakness and strength, in a single person. Children identify with characters of high motives and brave deeds. Through this experience they grow, gaining appreciation for the ideals and standards by which people live. Values, therefore, are important to both young and old. Material that confirms values such as honesty, integrity, and social concern holds the interest of all and can be presented without condescension.

In our preoccupation with ideals and values, we sometimes forget the appeal that comedy holds. There is a time for serious study, but there is also a time for fun. A good comedy has many values, not the least of them laughter. Children of all ages love humor, though what is funny to the younger child—riddles, jokes, repetition, slapstick, the chase—does not appeal to an older brother or sister. Comical characters, ridiculous situations, and amusing lines are the materials of comedy and may teach even more effectively than the serious play. Some of our social critics have used comedy to point up the defects and flaws of society.

In children's theatre, the values may be categorized simply as aesthetic, educational, and social, to which the following elements contribute.

1. A Good Story

A good story holds the interest of the audience from beginning to end. Something happens as the result of a conflict or problem that must be solved. Beyond that, a good story has literary value, vocabulary that enriches, ideas that challenge, and dialogue that strikes our ears as true.

2. Credible Characters

Credible characters are those in whom the audience can believe, whether or not they are real. In other words, the characters may be witches, giants, ghosts, or elves, but the audience must accept them as real. Children are quick to detect the false or inconsistent, but they will accept the most fantastic characters when they are well developed and consistent. Children will identify with credible characters and empathize with them. (*Empathy* is the emotional relationship that exists between the character in the play and the spectator.)

"Dance Cuba." The New Victory Theatre, NY. (Courtesy of Lauren Danilov, photograph by Eduardo Patino.)

3. Well-Developed Performance Skills

Well-developed performance skills include speech that is clear and audible; music well played or sung; dances choreographed and performed by disciplined dancers; and other skills that may be called for, such as juggling, fencing, and acrobatics. These must not detract from the story but should be so well integrated that unity, as well as a high standard of performance, is maintained throughout. Sometimes a director will add songs and dances to enliven a show, but unless they are an integral part of it, they will take away from the production, actually weakening it.

4. Beautiful Visual Effects

Although not every play requires elaborate mounting and costumes or special lighting effects, some plays do, and children respond with delight to them. The word *beautiful* encompasses color, a sense of proportion, and good composition; therefore, even a slum setting or a simple screen can achieve an aesthetic quality. Likewise, a costumer can use color and design to bring beauty to the poorest garments without sacrificing the authenticity of the wardrobe. I shall always remember the inner-city children who attended plays at a college where I once taught. Their response to a beautiful scenic effect was as thrilling to the cast and backstage crew as the set was to the audience. The gasp of appreciation that was heard when the curtains opened was clear proof of the joy that color brought into their lives, contrasting with the drab neighborhoods from which they came.

Many producers today dress their actors in a uniform costume, such as jumpsuits or leotards. There are reasons for this choice, and in many cases, the uniform is appropriate and effective. The Paper Bag Players of New York City, for example, aim to stimulate the imagination of the audience and so are always dressed alike, except for color. To save time in their succession of short skits, the actors simply add bits of clothing to suggest different characters. In general, however, the elimination of costumes deprives the audience of one of the theatre's most colorful components, spectacle, and one of its aesthetic values.

5. Challenging Ideas

Challenging ideas stimulate thinking about attitudes, solutions to problems posed in the play, or social values. Consciousness often can be raised more effectively through theatre than in any other way. Even the folk and fairy tales that have been handed down to us convey valuable lessons, which is one of the reasons for their survival. Modern plays and theatre-in-education programs present issues more directly, but unless the plays are too didactic, children are affected by them and are concerned with the message. Children want to see justice done, an almost universal response reflecting their strong sense of fair play.

6. Experience as a Member of an Audience

Going to a play, unlike reading a book or even watching television, is a social experience. It involves being part of a large group that is sharing a common experience. It also provides material for discussion later, either at home or at school.

An elaborately mounted production of A Tale of Cinderella. *(Courtesy of the New York State Theatre Institute, photograph by Timothy Raah/Northern Photo.)*

7. Involvement with the Players

This element relates to being part of the audience. The living theatre differs from television and film in that the response of the audience affects the performance. Theatre is communication; hence, the rapport between actor and audience is an essential component. Actors are quick to state that no two performances of the same play are ever alike because of the differences in audience response.

8. The Opportunity to Learn About Other People and Different Cultures

In the theatre, we are able to view other cultures and learn about people different from ourselves. Characters living in foreign lands or at different times come alive on the stage, often making an indelible impression. This, incidentally, leads to another reason to ask for truthful and accurate portrayals onstage. Far too many stereotypes have been imposed on children, both in the theatre and on television, for us to ignore misrepresentations. Aware of this, responsible producers are making a conscious effort to show characters as they really are, by treating them with respect as individuals and as members of a social group. This principle, incidentally, should always hold, even in comedy. To be genuinely funny, characters should not be consistently presented in a derogatory light, for it is the exception that amuses us and the unusual situation that makes us laugh.

A stereotype, in which all members of a particular group are presented as identical, reinforces an impression that not only is untrue but is difficult to erase. The villain

A Midsummer Night's Dream, *Nan Smithner, Director, Program in Educational Theatre. (Courtesy of New York University, photograph by Chianan Yen.)*

should not always be presented as foreign and dark; the hero as tall, handsome, clever, and strong; the heroine as blond and beautiful. Onstage, as in life, human beings come in a wide assortment of colors, ages, and backgrounds, each one possessing individual strengths and weaknesses. An honest portrayal helps children to distinguish between them and, in doing so, to develop the values and insights that are characteristics of an educated adult.

9. A Strong Emotional Response

Aristotle wrote of the catharsis of theatre. Anyone who has ever been in a children's audience can readily understand what he meant, for their emotional responses are strong and spontaneous. Children are caught up in the excitement of the drama. They cheer the hero or heroine and may even "boo" the villain, and they often participate vocally by calling out advice to the actors. Unless it gets out of hand (and an experienced cast will see that it does not), this expression is a natural outlet for emotion. The children have a vicarious experience, one that they probably would never have in real life. They participate in a great adventure; they identify with the protagonist; and in the end, they win through just and honorable actions. In some modern plays, the spectator is left with an ethical or a moral question to think about after the final curtain has closed. The emotional response has come first, however, and now comes the time to consider alternative solutions and their consequences.

10. The Foundation for an Appreciation of the Theatre

Good theatre experienced when one is young often leads to lifelong pleasure. Few persons pursue the theatre as a profession, but all of us can enjoy it as members of the audience. A child's opportunity to see even a few fine plays, well produced, under optimum conditions, is the best possible preparation for appreciation later in life.

The values of theatre can scarcely be overestimated. Granted that not all children's entertainment is of the quality we would like to see offered, much of it is, and it is improving constantly, thanks to better-educated producers and the numerous funding sources now available. By orienting children to the best at an early age and helping them to extend the experience, we are able to increase these values immeasurably. Let us see how we can best go about it.

Preparing Children for the Occasion

By the time children are in the fourth or fifth grade, they may have attended several plays and will be looking forward to seeing others. It is possible, however, that some children have attended only informal performances in an all-purpose room or gymnasium and so have never been to a community or university theatre or seen a play produced formally in an auditorium. In that case, the subject of theatre etiquette and conventions should be part of the orientation. This information should not be presented as a disciplinary measure; rather, it should be explained as courteous and expected behavior.

Orientation

By the time children have reached the middle grades, they are ready for substantial background material that will spark interest and enrich the performance. Many producers send packets of teaching material to the school in advance; these materials are well worth using, since they provide additional information for the class before seeing the play. Producers often list books they have found useful in doing their own research on the subject. These books may even be in the school library. Sometimes, when a company tours a region on a regular basis, it will develop a program for a particular grade-level curriculum. In this case, it is easy to relate the play to the unit of study. The class may already be familiar with the major character, and the children will be eager to see him or her brought to life on the stage.

In contrast, the protagonist may be a well-known figure in real life. I am reminded of a production I saw based on the career of Jackie Robinson. He was a hero to the audience, so the story of his boyhood and struggle as he rose to fame had a strong attraction.

Assuming that the class does not know what the play is about and that the title is also unfamiliar, the teacher will want first to introduce the theme and then, if it is important to their understanding, to give the class an idea of the plot. Preliminary study has the same effect as knowing a story and then seeing it dramatized. It is the time to bring in relevant background material—historical, biographical, cultural—so that the class will gain a better idea of where and how the characters lived or live. If the play takes place at a former time or in another place, not only will the clothing be different from ours, but so will the furnishings of the homes, the occupations, the props, and the lives of the people. Social attitudes may differ also; therefore, the class will get more from the play if the children understand why the characters behave as they do. Speech patterns may be strange, so some knowledge of the dialect used makes for appreciation rather than confusion. The extent of the orientation that teachers give varies, depending on the play and the amount of time they have at their disposal. I believe that some information about the prospective assembly program or excursion is always desirable in order for the audience to derive maximum pleasure and benefit.

By the middle and upper grades, students should have some knowledge of dramatic form. They know the difference between comedy and tragedy and are familiar with a few of the more common theatrical terms. Opportunities for attending plays as well as creating and writing them help young people gain a deeper understanding of an art form that involves the work of many artists, yet does not live until it is shared with an audience.

The following evaluation form was designed specifically for teachers, administrators and parents responsible for booking or purchasing tickets to plays for young audiences. Because committee members often differ in their views and communities vary, an instrument of this kind is helpful in establishing the guidelines for choosing entertainment.

EVALUATION FORM FOR CHILDREN'S THEATRE PREVIEWERS

Production Title _____

Date Previewed _____ Estimated Number in Audience _____

Name of Auditorium _____ Seating Capacity _____

Producer _____

           (Name)   (Address)   (Tel. No.)

Note to Previewers: The prime criteria we use in children's theatre is a respect of the production for the audience—of the audience for the production. Does the production present an idea worthy of children's consideration? Does it do so in a manner which honors their intelligence and integrity? Does it evoke honest reponses to quality in the theatre?

Report on this form by applying this rating code:

Excellent	Good	Adequate	Fair	Poor	TOTAL:	
5	4	3	2	1		

Using the question as a guide, rate each category by the NUMBERS SHOWN ABOVE. Feel free to comment in answer to any specific question and enlarge on it.

1. DOES THE PRESENTATION RESPECT THE AUDIENCE IN THE PLAYSCRIPT?

  ☐ *Content:*
  Is it worth doing?
  Did you feel the children were involved enough to care about the people in the story and what happened to them?

  ☐ *Dramatic Development:*
  Is the story line clear and forward moving?
  Is the piece well paced, or does it drag? (Or, is it too hectic?)

  ☐ *Dialogue:*
  Does the vocabulary, which is essential to the comprehension of the plot, come within the range of the audience?
  Beyond that, does it offer enrichment?
  Is the dialogue suitable to the style and mood of the piece?

  COMMENT:

2. DOES THE PRESENTATION RESPECT THE AUDIENCE IN THE PRODUCTION?

  ☐ *Direction:*
  Is stage business pertinent to the situation and style? (Or, inserted for its own sake?)
  Does the director have a point of view which unifies the elements of the play?
  Is the physical movement in keeping with character and style?
  Does the director achieve an ensemble performance?

  ☐ *Mounting:* (Costumes—Scenery—Lighting—Music)
  Are settings and costumes expressive of the style, the characters, the locale, and the period?
  If there is available equipment, is the lighting also consistent?
  Are settings and costumes fresh looking and attractively executed?

  ☐ *Acting:*
  Do you believe the actor in character? In relation to the style of the piece? (Or, does the actor ever step out of character?)
  Is there a sense of joy in the performance? (Or, is it flat?)
  Is dialogue well spoken (Voice? Diction? Interpretation?)
  Are songs and dances well performed?

  COMMENT:

  Question: Did you enjoy it? _____

Audience Participation

Some theatre companies, both commercial and educational, perform what is called *participatory drama*. This means that instead of acting on a stage, they perform in the round in an all-purpose room or a gymnasium, with the audience seated on three or four sides where spectators can become actively involved in the performance. The actors request help from the children from time to time, asking questions or persuading some to come into the playing space as fellow actors. Occasionally, a company will invite suggestions about what course of action to take, and the responses may alter the outcome of the story. An experienced cast is able to handle audience participation skillfully, thus giving children a dual experience: as spectator and as participant.

Before a participatory play is given, actors usually go into the classrooms of the children who are going to attend. They discuss the play and may rehearse the scenes in which the class will be taking part. The performance can be a rewarding experience when it is carefully planned and rehearsed. Participatory theatre is most effective with younger children; beyond the fifth or sixth grades, there is an inherent risk involved in asking the audience to take part, unless the techniques are sophisticated and the children are used to participation. The majority of companies that offer plays for middle and upper grades perform on a proscenium stage in a traditional manner.

Theatre Etiquette

One aspect of theatregoing that must be treated is etiquette. Accustomed to television, with its frequent breaks for commercials, younger children must be told that the theatre makes certain demands on the audience so that all spectators can see and hear well. Although older children do not have to be oriented in the same way, they may have to be reminded that a good audience observes the following rules:

1. *Does not talk aloud or annoy others.* Once seated, the members of the audience should refrain from whispering, standing up, or leaving the auditorium without permission.
2. *Does not bring food into the auditorium.* Candy, gum, potato chips, and other easily accessible foods interfere with attention in addition to causing clutter on the floor. The practice of eating while watching television has cultivated a habit that must be discouraged in the theatre. Eating may take place before or after the performance but never during the play.
3. *Does not run around the auditorium during the intermission.* An intermission need not be a trying period for teachers and ushers if its purpose is explained. It is a time to move and stretch, to get a drink of water, or to use the rest rooms while scenery is being changed. Some producers are afraid of intermissions, but I have never seen one misused when the play held the interest of the audience.
4. *Does not destroy printed programs.* Some companies provide printed programs, a theatre convention that children should understand. Programs are not to be made into airplanes or balls and thrown around the auditorium. They are to be read. In addition to information about the play, they often include activities for children to try at home or in class afterward.

A young viewer reads the program. New Victory Theatre, New York City. (Photograph by V. Amessé.)

5. *Waits for applause and curtain calls.* Applause and curtain calls are theatre conventions. Applause is our way of thanking the actors for the good time they have given us, and curtain calls let us see the actors as people instead of as characters in the play.
6. *Leaves the auditorium in an orderly manner.* Putting on coats, getting up before the curtain is closed, slamming seats, and running noisily up the aisles are bad manners. If children realize this, the majority of them will wait till the lights in the auditorium are turned on and it is time for the audience to go.
7. *Meets the cast afterward, if invited.* Some casts make a practice of meeting the children in the lobby on their way out, and many youngsters enjoy it. I have mixed feelings about this practice, for it removes the mystique that the cast has taken pains to establish. But some older boys and girls have questions about the play or technical effects that they want to ask, and this is an ideal way to have them answered.

The Performance

The day of the play has finally come. Ideally, the students have been well prepared and are in their seats five to ten minutes before the curtain opens. If the play is presented in the school auditorium, the teacher can easily gauge the time it will take to go from the classroom to the reserved section of seats. If it takes place in a community theatre or the auditorium of another school or a college, more planning is involved to be sure that the group arrives on time, neither late nor too early. When school buses

The Cat's Meow *by the Paper Bag Players.*
(Courtesy of Judith Martin, photograph by
Jean-Marie Guyaux.)

are employed, it is important to arrange the arrival in plenty of time to allow the children to hang up coats, or at least to remove them, and to be comfortably seated before the performance begins. I have often seen classes come into a darkened auditorium fifteen to twenty minutes late, which is unfortunate because they can never catch up on what happened before they arrived; in addition, of course, they disturb others who are absorbed in the story.

If the audience is restless under ideal conditions, something is wrong. It may be that the script is geared to a younger age level than is present or is over the heads of the audience. Most children are willing to reach up to the latter, but they are bored by anything they consider "babyish." It also may be a poor production. This is another matter altogether, which should have been discovered before the arrangements were made. So many excellent college theatre departments are sending out student groups and so many good professional touring companies are available that there is little excuse for engaging a mediocre company. This can happen, however, and when it does, it is a problem for the faculty and administration. Good companies are expensive, but one good show is worth far more than half a dozen poor ones. When college or university troupes are available, they are an ideal resource. Not only are their performances less expensive to attend, but their standards tend to be consistently high, their choice of material usually is excellent, and the student actors are sensitive to the interests and needs of children.

Theatre of Mime and Dance, Montanaro-Hurli, Portland, ME. (Courtesy of Tony Montanaro.)

Although carrying on conversations during the performance is inconsiderate, this does not mean that an audience should observe total silence. Indeed, it is a pity when children are made to think they cannot utter a sound. There is nothing wrong with laughter, cheers, even calling out spontaneously to the actors when the comments are appropriate; an experienced cast can handle such responses, and most actors enjoy having this rapport with the audience.

Although a good performance of a fine play will certainly stand by itself, the experience can be enriched by a follow-up period afterward. As adults, we like to discuss a play or film we have seen, and children respond in much the same way. They will discuss the play on their own, but with proper guidance the discussion can be made richer and more lasting. There are many ways of starting. Least likely to lead to discussion is the question "Did you like it?" But questions relating to the underlying theme or the characters and their solutions to problems will usually generate a lively discussion. Depending on when and where the action took place and the way of life or the social attitudes of the characters, questions will be raised, offering an ideal opportunity for further exploration. Although children find many programs diverting, they are capable of remarkable insights when guided toward a more discriminating point of view.

As in all teaching, we are most successful when we begin where the children's interests lie, following their lead before making suggestions. The following discussion covers some of the successful ways in which teachers have followed up a performance.

A traditional but still worthwhile activity is writing letters to the cast. This activity should not be imposed on children as a tedious assignment; when it represents an honest expression of appreciation, however, it is an outlet for feelings, a courteous act, and a valid exercise in writing. Actors, incidentally, love the letters children write and often keep them in their scrapbooks.

Painting or drawing pictures of the play is another favorite activity. The Paper Bag Players of New York City, aware of the effect that their performances have on young children, sometimes put up yards of brown wrapping paper on the walls of the lobby, where space permits, so that audiences can draw pictures before and after the production.

The Jack Tale Players of Ferrum College in Virginia play to audiences of all ages year-round, indoors and out. When performing in theatres they supply drawing paper and chalk in an adjacent room for children who arrive early. In the weeks following the performance teachers often send the director pictures of the show that the children have painted; the director, in turn, posts the pictures on a bulletin board in the lobby for actors and audiences to see. This establishes a friendly rapport with schools in the area. Sometimes children will draw scenery or a character who was not on the stage but who exists in their imagination.

Some teachers' packets include folk songs and dances that children can learn. Many folk tales, particularly those of Native Americans and Eskimos, suggest tools and artifacts that children can make. Masks, jewelry, woven fabrics, pictures of the clothes people wear, and photographs of the land are always fascinating, especially to children in urban areas. I have seen many excellent exhibits of artwork stimulated by a performance of Joanna Kraus's *Ice Wolf,* a serious drama that invariably arouses discussion.

Many children are eager to enact scenes from a play they have seen. Besides being a sure sign of interest, this enthusiasm encourages further improvisation. New scenes, action that might have taken place, different endings—these things can begin with questions such as "How else?" or "What if?" Creative drama and the scripted play are different, but the one often leads to the other. Seeing a play may stimulate creative drama, just as creative drama may result in an original play.

Some teachers find that other forms of writing come more easily as well after children have seen a play. The release of emotion into verse is not unusual. Older children are often led to further study of a culture and will share their findings in oral or written reports. The theatre reaches us on many levels, and because it embodies all the arts, it elicits various verbal, visual, and physical responses. Whatever form the expression takes, the ramifications of theatre go far beyond the enjoyment of the performance, when time and opportunity are offered.

A word of caution: although there is no doubt that preparation and follow-up activities enhance the experience, the teacher must never give the impression that he or she is testing for right or wrong answers. Children who think that they are expected to reply in a certain way are robbed of the opportunity to give spontaneous, honest responses. Reaction to a work of art is an individual matter. Adults do not always agree about what they have seen, and we should not expect agreement among children. Appreciation of any art form is difficult to assess. Sometimes it takes days, weeks, or years to integrate what one has thought and felt. This does not mean that everything a child sees should embody a lesson or aim to teach.

The Broadway Theatre Museum

Plans for a theatre museum are currently being developed by the Broadway Theatre Institute in New York. Located in the heart of the theatre district, the Institute arranges trips to Broadway and Off-Broadway plays and offers workshops conducted by professional actors for area schoolchildren. According to Helen Guditis, director and president, the museum is another way of introducing young people to the art of the living theatre as well as extending performances they have seen.

Operating currently as a museum at large, with a provisional charter from the Board of Regents of the University of the State of New York, the museum's focus is twofold: cultural preservation and theatre arts in education.

Meanwhile, the Broadway Theatre Institute continues its educational programs and is expanding its workshops for teachers and administrators. Through interactive programs educators learn to incorporate theatre arts education into their curriculum with the goal of improving students' literacy, language arts, and math skills. Seminars and exhibitions further augment current offerings.

New Kinds of Plays and Programs for Young Audiences

The folk and fairy tales have been a staple of children's theatre in America from the beginning, and they should not be discarded. Their endurance is based on solid values and familiar plots, and most children respond to them. Today, however, we are hearing tales told by new immigrants who describe life in their native lands as well as their experiences in America. This material is different in content and style from that of the earlier storytellers, for the demographics have shifted from the European migrations of the nineteenth and early twentieth centuries to the recent waves of immigrants from Asia, the Middle East, the Caribbean, and South America.

Besides the wealth of new material brought by recent immigrants, foreign artists and theatre companies bring their perspectives. Seen first only in our large cities, many of these companies of actors, dancers, musicians, and puppeteers are now being sponsored for tours across the country. These are expensive enterprises, to be sure, requiring substantial funding and local sponsorship. But when theatre is made available through generous foundation and community support, tickets can be priced so that children attending public schools are able to see a performance.

Located in New York is the Chinese Theatre Workshop (CTW), founded by Kuang-Yu Fong in 1990. Its mission is to preserve and promote traditional Chinese opera and literature by performing and teaching students and general audiences of both Chinese and non-Chinese ethnic backgrounds. The other aspect of its activities is the creation of new works that combine Eastern and Western theatre techniques to address contemporary social issues and cultural concerns. CTW also tours.

The scale of productions varies from tabletop "object theatre" shows such as *Kasper as a Banana,* which told the story of illegal Chinese immigrants, to the large-scale music, dance, mask, and puppet production of *Instinct,* a collaboration with the Ninth Street Theatre, which focused on issues of pollution and the environment. Two recent productions, *Zhang Boils the Ocean* and *Climbing Gold Mountain,* co-produced with the Henry Street Settlement, combined Peking opera, puppetry, masks, dance, and original music; it explored issues of cultural identity, stereotypes, and economic hardships affecting the Chinese community in America.

Hawaii, a center of Asian and Pacific Rim culture, also takes pride in offering plays with ethnic themes, along with puppet shows for young audiences. For some time the Honolulu Theatre for Youth has exploited the wealth of material available from Asia and the Pacific islands, earning an enviable reputation.

The Puerto Rico Traveling Theatre and the Don Quixote Children's Theatre tour bilingual productions along the East Coast, and other children's theatre companies along the Mexican border, offer plays performed in English and Spanish. Canada shares its bounty of Eskimo tales and legends, many of which are dramatized and performed in the United States by professional children's theatre companies and puppet troupes. Our Northwest takes pride in its Native American arts and crafts, myths, and dances. In the Southeast we find the folk tales and folk arts of the mountain people; the Blue Ridge, for instance, is a gold mine for scholars and folklorists. For nearly thirty years, students at Ferrum College in Ferrum, Virginia, have taken the "Jack Tales," authentic material dramatized for the stage, and toured them to schools, community centers, nursing homes, and hospitals. Audiences of all ages are enchanted with the humor, folk wisdom, and fresh appeal of America's tall tales and legendary characters.

The New Victory Theatre, which opened in New York City as 1995 drew to a close, is far more than professional theatre for young audiences; it is an institution with a multicultural mission. As many as fifteen attractions a year from around the world are available to school audiences, family audiences, and general audiences at low prices. Previewers travel throughout Europe, Asia, and South America as well as the United States in search of the best theatre, music, puppetry, and dance companies they can find for fees they can afford. All performances are preceded and/or followed by workshops for school and family audiences. For example, *Romeo and Juliet* was given an interpretation to appeal to young audiences, and discussions afterward helped the audience to see the tragedy and futility of feuds in which hate divides and kills. *Salvador,* on the other hand, was a new play about a Peruvian boy from the mountains who wanted an education to become a writer. In order to understand his struggle, it was necessary for the audience to learn about his country; his culture; the legendary ancestors, the Incas; and the poverty and poetry in which the boy grew up. A poignant and fascinating narrative, *Salvador* painted a positive portrait of the young South American protagonist, whose ambition and family support led to success. These are but two examples of the variety of productions that are designed to attract young audiences and engage them in discussion or workshop activities after the performance.

In the Midwest a familiar entertainer is African American folklorist and singer Ella Jenkins, who has been performing for forty years. Growing up during the Depression on Chicago's South Side, she was fascinated with the music she heard on the streets on summer evenings. Although it would be years before she began to sing professionally, the encouragement she received and the enthusiasm with which she was greeted eventually led to performances, recordings, and television appearances. Native Americans and Asians have also joined the ethnic voices throughout the United States, performing in schools and community centers. Indeed, every brochure and professional journal I read today announces performing artists and programs that differ fundamentally from those of twenty years ago.

Our country's diverse population and its ethnic, indigenous, and historic communities are finding their voices and parallel histories and sharing them through many different art forms. It is through the arts that we cross borders among individuals, cultures, themes and new forms. The following words of Ben Brantley, while not written with theatre for young audiences in mind, could not be more appropriate as we survey the scene.

"Theatre rides along the edge of social change, reinventing itself with each generation. Its survival depends on theatre artists who find new pathways, new symbols, new languages to engage the audience of the future." Ben Brantley, The New York Times.

Summary

Theatregoing can be one of the richest experiences of a child's life. With its aesthetic, educational, and social potential, a good play, well produced, can lead to appreciation of a great art form and add to knowledge and deeper understanding of humankind. Orientation to the event prepares children by familiarizing them with the theme, the style of the production, and any other information that will enhance their enjoyment. Less preparation is needed for a traditional story, but for the majority of children, who have grown up watching television, some orientation to live performance is necessary. For many, the school assembly program may be their first exposure to theatre.

Theatre etiquette, simple as it sounds, is also necessary if we are going to teach consideration for the right of others to enjoy the play and to show respect for the actors. The theatre makes demands not only on our hearts and minds but also on our social awareness, for the living theatre is shared enjoyment.

Follow-up activities in the classroom offer a further opportunity for enrichment. Most children enjoy reliving a performance; hence, giving them the time and place in which to do it is a welcome extension of the experience. Theatre can be limited to a single hour of entertainment, but, as teachers and producers have discovered, it can be much more than that.

Suggested Assignments

1. Attend a children's play with a child audience. Were the children around you absorbed all of the time? part of the time? How could you tell?
2. Can you interpret the attention the children gave during the performance? the lack of attention at any points?
3. Discuss production details: scenery, costumes, sound effects, music if it was used.
4. For what age level would you consider the play most appropriate? Explain why.
5. Check a newspaper for cultural activities or special events. Make a list of them, giving information as to location, sponsorship, dates, and type of event.
6. Attend an event, either alone or in a group. Report on your trip in class.

Journal Writing

1. What are the similarities and differences between theatre for young audiences and theatre for adults?
2. Consider television programs for children. What good ones do you remember from your own childhood, and why do you cite them?
3. What values does the living theatre have that film and television lack?
4. Do you remember any cultural events—festivals, celebrations, exhibitions—in your community when you were a child? What impression did they make on you?
5. Are there any traditions in your background that your family preserves or celebrates? What are they? Did you and do you take pride in them?
6. As a child, did you have a friend whose cultural background differed from yours? Did he or she share it with you? Describe it.
7. Have you ever felt any prejudice that was changed through the arts? Can you describe what happened?
8. What ethnic arts do you respond to most? Why?

Chapter 19

Creative Drama in Alternative Spaces

African Tales of Earth and Sky *by the Dallas Children's Theatre. (Courtesy of Robin Flatt, photograph by Linda Blase.)*

All the world's a stage.

—William Shakespeare

This chapter is concerned with the special environments and features that outside locations possess and some of the ways in which they can be used effectively. They include museums, churches, libraries, community and recreation centers, civic theatres, parks, and historical venues.

Drama in Museums

Museums play a central role in preserving the cultural, artistic, and historical heritage of each generation. Through their education departments, they have become more than repositories of treasures; lectures, films, special exhibits, and programs are offered to attract a larger public. Some art museums, in expanding their community services, not only are providing more educational programs than they have offered in the past but also are providing space where outside groups can perform. Some museums offer classes in the performing as well as the visual arts; for example, the Brooklyn Museum inaugurated an innovative drama program a number of years ago. Paintings and sculpture provide stimulation and inspiration, and galleries are used for playing space. Students also view as well as create plays in a special gallery that seats no more than one hundred persons. At the museum, the use of theatre techniques parallels Piaget's contention that children are motivated to gain a greater understanding of their world and to restructure their knowledge when they encounter experiences that are dissonant with their previous assumptions.

In the museum, children find objects removed from their original context. Helped to understand that these objects once belonged to a particular society and were expressive of that society, children re-create a cultural context for dramatization. In this context they explore the environment and the relationship between the objects of art and the people who created them. An appreciation for aesthetic standards that differ from their own, as well as cognitive learning, results when children visit the museum in this way.

Many museums sponsor educational and theatre-related programs. Museum-school collaboration creates an educational experience that meets the needs of both institutions. Holiday programs provide family audiences with programs to stimulate interest in particular collections. Informal theatre events for special exhibitions create quick theatrical "happenings" to point up or highlight an exhibit, with vignettes written and performed by staff members and student actors. Staff involvement in theatre encourages participation on the part of both children and adults. Furthermore, the museum has found that audiences who participate are motivated to return.

One Brooklyn museum-school collaboration was the Chinese mythology theatre "collage" titled *Can You Hear the River Calling the Moon?* This piece was created and performed by elementary school children for the general public over the Christmas holidays. A class of schoolchildren visited the Brooklyn Museum for ten weekly sessions,

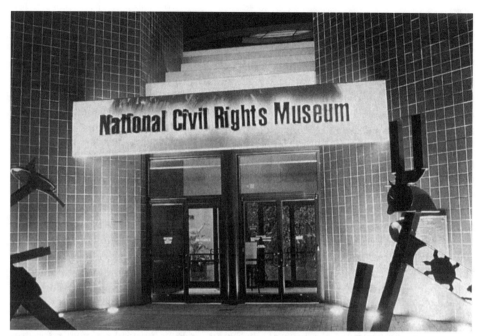

Facade of the National Civil Rights Museum. (Courtesy of the National Civil Rights Museum, Memphis, Tennessee.)

during which time Chinese art and culture were the subject of study. The children acted Chinese myths improvisationally and made their own costumes and props in the museum workshops. The script that evolved was based on the myths and put into written form by the museum instructor. As described in a museum newsletter, the protagonist of the collage was a river that flowed from a landscape painting and introduced the various components of the production: a shadow puppet play, showing the creation of the land; large puppets in a morality legend; and a group of children performing a dragon myth.

The play told of the relationship of the people to the land and explained the conventions of Chinese landscape painting. A Chinese musician accompanied the performance on traditional instruments. Following each performance the audience was invited to tour the galleries, where they viewed the original paintings of the characters, dragons, waterfalls, and landscapes that they had just seen portrayed. After the weekend performances at the museum, the play was given in the school auditorium for the rest of the children. This project illustrates one way in which schools, museums, and communities can work together on a project involving all the arts, emphasizing educational and aesthetic values equally.

The Children's Museum in Boston is another museum with an extensive program of activities, including classes in drama and weekly children's theatre performances. Both a Sunday series and a Friday night series of entertainments are open to the public and are held in a small area called the Sit Around Space. Because the space is small, puppet shows, storytelling, magic shows, and singers are featured, though plays are offered on occasion.

An excellent book on the use of drama in the museum cites a number of other innovative programs, some in detail. *Pioneer Journeys: Drama in Museum Education* by Jennifer Fell Hayes and Dorothy Napp Schindel provides an overview, a rationale for drama/theatre in the museum, lesson plans, teacher preparation, and material on docent training.[1] The authors describe a variety of settings that affect the ways drama and the other arts can be most effectively utilized. Included among the most successful examples are the Queens Museum of Art located on the old New York World's Fairgrounds, which is visited by thousands of schoolchildren every year. Its performance-oriented and process-based drama are popular offerings. At the University of Texas at Austin, the Huntington Gallery uses creative drama to make the museum more accessible to teachers and students. In Massachusetts, Old Sturbridge Village enlists students to play the parts of villagers who might have lived there in 1830. At Plymouth Plantation, actor-teachers live a day in a specific year and answer questions in role. At the Old South Meeting House in Boston, children are prepared in advance to be particular characters at the Boston Tea Party. At the Philadelphia Art Museum, monthly performances attract the public to the museum. At the Fraunces Tavern in New York City, docents are trained in creative drama techniques. This small historic museum offers an extensive program for grade-school children to "become" characters who might have visited the tavern at the time of the American Revolution. Participating in this way gives depth to the experience as the children create men and women of different social classes interacting and solving problems relevant to the period. This program could be replicated in any historical building or location.

Hayes and Schindel were involved in the founding of a new museum in New York City, the Lower East Side Tenement Museum. Visitors, including school groups, tour one of the oldest tenements in the city. Home to nineteenth-century immigrant families, it has been restored. After a tour of each floor, visitors attend an audience-participation play in a space on the ground level. The opening production in June 1994, *Whippersnappers,* was an appropriate choice, as it told the story of teenage tenement life at the turn of the century, giving a vivid picture of the problems and the camaraderie of ghetto youth. Following the performance the four professional actors held a discussion and answered questions the children had about the tour and the play. In small historical museums such as the Edison House in Louisville, Kentucky, limited space precludes drama on the premises. An educational program, however, may include a film, a lecture, and a hands-on tour; the Edison House provides a wealth of material on the life and work of Thomas Edison for dramatization afterward in the classroom.

The Abigail Adams Smith Museum in New York City has been the seat of interactive performances about life at the Mt. Vernon Hotel circa 1830. School groups come to first tour the grounds and premises, then see the play, and afterward ask questions of the actors. Teachers find the learning that students gain from this kind of experience

---

[1]Jennifer Fell Hayes and Dorothy Napp Schindel, *Pioneer Journeys: Drama in Museum Education* (Charlottesville, VA: New Plays, 1994).

*Facade of the Lower East Side
Tenement Museum. (Courtesy of
the Lower East Side Tenement
Museum in New York City,
photograph by Dorothy Napp
Schindel.)*

of enormous value in their study of history and the social and political life of a period: "In a true partnership between school and museum, there is a mutual valuing of time, expertise and experience. Teachers who have examined the potential find it exciting. Parents who have enjoyed these resources in their own lives would look at them with fresh perspective; those who had not, would learn along with their children. These are real experiences as opposed to TV in terms of shared family experiences."[2]

As the authors of *Pioneer Journeys* point out, there are unlimited possibilities for drama in every kind of museum, including science museums, a choice that only now is catching on. Cleveland's Museum of Natural History was the principal venue chosen for a children's theatre festival held in that city in the spring of 1982. The imaginative architectural design of the building afforded a variety of spaces for performances of plays, dance, and music. Large museums have traditionally offered educational programs for both adults and children, but these informal grassroots programs in which children are active participants define the museum in new terms. The museum, once a hushed and awesome sanctuary, is today proving to be a lively and suitable location for classes in drama, movement, and mime.

---

[2]Nina Gibans, "School-Museum Partnerships," *Cleveland Plain Dealer,* October 21, 1992, p. 3.

Scene from Whippersnappers *by Jennifer Fell Hayes, directed by Dorothy Napp Schindel. (Courtesy of the Lower East Side Tenement Museum.)*

Bruno Bettelheim, commenting on the value of the museum to the child, said that irrespective of what a museum's content might be, it serves "to stimulate his imagination, to arouse his curiosity so that he wishes to penetrate ever more deeply the meaning of what he is expected to admire in the museum, to give him a chance to admire in his own good time things that are beyond his ken, and, most important of all, to give him a feeling of awe for the wonders of the world. Because a world that is not full of wonders is one hardly worth the effort of growing up in."[3] Bettelheim was not writing of drama when he made that statement, but the role of children's drama in the museum serves two of his purposes: first, to offer an aesthetic experience in a welcoming cultural institution; and second, to bring the child into the museum, which he or she might otherwise not have entered.

The growth of this venue for drama was indicated when the *AATE Newsletter* announced the formation of the Theatre in the Museum Network in 1997. This network encompasses a large number of approaches and strategies, including TIE, audio-guide script writing, interactive theatre production, museum-to-classroom outreach programs, vignettes in the galleries, storytelling, living history museums, and enactments. A few

[3]Bruno Bettelheim, "Children and Museums," *Children Today* 9, no. 1 (Jan.-Feb. 1980): 23.

The Edison House, Louisville, KY. (Courtesy of Ruth Warner.)

large museums have a full-time staff person to handle these activities, but most do not. People interested in any aspect of museum drama or theatre programming are invited to get in touch with the AATE members listed in the newsletter.

Drama in Parks

Since the early part of this century, parks and playgrounds have included drama among their activities for children. In many cases this has meant an informal program of storytelling, improvisation, puppetry, and traveling theatre companies who perform free of charge. In recent years, however, more structured programs have been designed, with well-qualified leaders and better facilities for both classes and performances. An example of the latter is Wolf Trap Farm Park for the Performing Arts in Virginia, where programs for adults and children take place all summer. Children's productions are presented in both indoor and outdoor settings. Drama lends itself to this type of structure, which combines recreational opportunities and picnic and sport areas with performances of drama, mime, dance, and music. Today, Wolf Trap's program includes classes in creative drama, with a textbook designed especially for use there. This beautiful facility, with its fine staff and superb location, is an example of what can be done when a community sets out to do the best possible job, making maximum use of its resources. Not all parks or community centers are blessed with so much, but every place, like every individual, has a unique character. The trick is to find and build on its distinction and advantages. Again, this is not an isolated example, but it is probably one of the better-known parks providing excellence in teaching and entertainment.

Drama in Churches

The church has historically had a close relationship with the theatre. The medieval theatre was born in the church, and despite the repudiation that theatre has suffered from the church periodically, an unquestionable connection and acceptance of certain common values and goals exist between them. It is therefore no surprise to discover that a growing number of drama and theatre groups are housed in church buildings of various faiths. Some of these groups are companies that produce plays on religious themes. Others are groups to whom space is given for classes in acting, creative drama, and dance. Many churches support extensive programs in the performing arts, including professional resident companies. Like museums and libraries, churches offer space to outside groups for whom commercial studios are unavailable or beyond their ability to pay. Indeed, one has only to look at a history of the community theatre movement in this country to see how many successful ventures were begun in churches. Many church facilities provide large meeting rooms; a stage, if or when one is needed; after-school and Saturday morning hours for classes; and low rent (or no rent). In large cities where rents are prohibitive, the church is often a haven for the performing arts.

In addition, there is now an awakened interest in drama written on religious themes and in plays posing moral and ethical questions relevant to modern life. Both educators and church people are involved in writing, directing, and promoting this new kind of religious drama. Also available is a body of information on choral reading, monologues, and clowning, and there are a number of textbooks on creative drama and improvisation. Successful Broadway plays like *Joseph and the Amazing Technicolor Dreamcoat, Godspell, St. Mark's Gospel* with Alec McCowen, and recent productions with religious themes may have been the precursors of this new wave of interest; they may also account for the strengthened relationship between theatre and church.

A feature article in the *New York Times* described the proliferation of vacation Bible schools in which drama is used to make the Bible stories more accessible to the students.[4] The focus today, however, in contrast to the past, is to learn about cultures outside the country and to offer opportunities to practice rather than just study religious ideals. Although drama is not a component of every curriculum, it is significant in many church programs as a way of helping children explore social issues and ethical and moral questions.

A related interest is biblical storytelling. An international organization, the Network of Biblical Storytellers, was formed in the early 1980s to assist a diverse membership in sharing its love of biblical stories. Today the network covers a wide variety of geographic regions, cultural backgrounds, and faith traditions. Styles of presentation range from the simple telling of the stories to improvisation and acting in costume. This ancient body of literature is once again found to have fascinating characters and exciting plots with problems not unlike those we face today.

---

[4]Jennifer Steinhauer, "Bible School for a Changing World," *New York Times,* August 14, 1994, metro report, pp. 5, 40.

A library is host to the program in drama education offered by the Honolulu Theatre for Youth. Daniel A. Kelin, 11, leader. (Photograph by Sergio Loes.)

Drama in Libraries

Not all libraries offer classes in creative drama, but many include storytelling, puppetry, and children's films among their special services. Story dramatization grows naturally from storytelling, and librarians who have worked with it report its popularity. Older children are eager to enact favorite stories, whereas little children are drawn to tales they have just heard told, and they want to try on the various roles. Surrounded by walls of books, children meeting in libraries have literary resources at their fingertips—an advantage over groups meeting in other venues. Whether the creative drama class is conducted by the children's librarian or by an expert who comes in each week, the environment is conducive to the pursuit of creative drama, particularly story acting, and to the building of the language arts.

According to Nancy Pereira, author of *Creative Dramatics in the Library*,[5] drama has benefits to the library as well as to its young patrons. First, drama brings children into the library and encourages their return. Children discover the library's resources and in the process get acquainted with the staff. They find people who will answer their questions, show them filmstrips and other materials, and help them locate periodicals and books. A strong connection with the local public library is an advantage for any child.

One problem that often comes up is noise. If there is an activity room (and many libraries have one), noise is not a problem. Some libraries have more than one room available for storytelling, lectures, and classes. Large urban libraries often have auditoriums

---

[5]Nancy Pereira, *Creative Dramatics in the Library* (Charlottesville, VA: New Plays, 1974).

with stages where films are shown and plays can be given. Because of the noise level when a group of children get together, the most soundproof quarters available should be chosen for classes in creative drama. If, on the other hand, the library is small or consists of a single room, the hours for creative drama have to be set when the fewest patrons tend to use the library. This will affect the program, but a way can usually be found to include drama if it is really wanted. Storytelling and puppets, which require very little space, make a good beginning. It may be that a simple rearrangement of furniture is all that is necessary to create a larger space for human actors. The cooperation of the staff, however, is essential under any circumstances.

Drama in Other Locations

Classes in creative drama are to be found in a variety of other places as well, both indoors and out. Among them are department stores, shopping centers, hospitals, housing complexes, grange halls, and beaches. In some cases they are established, ongoing programs; in other cases they are little more than informal play groups to which children come while parents are shopping. One cannot expect a high level of accomplishment when attendance is irregular or when weather conditions affect the meeting of the class. Nevertheless, these informal drama groups are not to be written off as lacking direction or continuity, for a number of highly successful ventures were begun in playgrounds and parks under skillful leadership. The key to success is the leader: a dedicated, well-prepared person who is able to work in prevailing conditions while seeking funding and more permanent quarters.

One project that has found a generous sharing of space in several institutions is Creative Theatre Unlimited of Princeton, New Jersey. The McCarter Theatre, the 150-year-old Trinity Church, and selected historic sites in the area have all contributed to its continuing growth. In 1983–84, public creative drama workshops were funded by the Mercer County Cultural and Heritage Commission. Sites for these workshops were selected on the basis of their relationship to labor and industry because many plays and programs are based on industrial themes and problems. Working in the actual place is an effective practice. Summer and winter programs make for a year-round community service and clearly illustrate how local facilities can enable a fledgling group to gain a foothold. The availability of a lawn is an attractive feature of the summer program, which culminates in a work in progress on the stage of the McCarter.

A different kind of program was offered to retired seniors by a recently retired professor of theatre. Living in the neighborhood of the university in which he had taught for many years, he knew that some of his former colleagues were interested in reading and discussing dramatic literature but not in performing. He proposed a play reading group which became very popular. This is the kind of activity that could be replicated anywhere with no cost to the class except the purchase of scripts.

"Patchwork" is a multilingual medley of music, dance, storytelling, and games for all ages in a variety of venues. Performers in the East River Theatre Company of New York represent different ethnic and racial backgrounds, who share a wealth of material

Rehearsing a play in an outdoor space. (Courtesy of Professor Hsiao-Hua Chang, National Taiwan University of Arts.)

from their own cultures with American audiences. For example, a Valentine program in 2004 included love songs and dances from Russia, Korea, Turkey, China, Ireland, and the United States, much of it presented in native languages. Whenever possible, time and space permitting, plays invite members of the audience to join the fun and learn about countries whose cultures are different from their own. Although "Patchwork" can be given on a proscenium stage, it is most effective done in the round.[6]

Intergenerational Drama

Intergenerational drama has been around for a long time, and some community centers and retirement homes have sponsored it successfully. Today, however, with many families broken and scattered, it has particular importance for the participants. Young people are often amazed at the willingness of seniors to participate, and the adults welcome an opportunity to work with the young. When different generations can work together, a sense of community is established. Activities have to be geared to the group—its interests, backgrounds, and experiences. Although even a single

[6]Ann McCormack, director.

meeting has value, an ongoing program gives participants an opportunity to explore interests and problems in depth and to better understand and appreciate each other.

One of the largest and best documented intergenerational programs, "Youth and Elders Inter-Act," is located in Newark, New Jersey. Sponsored by the Newark board of education, the program takes place in the schools, where elders join students from fourth through seventh grades. The program began as a pilot project in 1990; five years later, 250 students and nearly 100 adults participated in a pageant at the Newark Public Library, in which players slipped into the roles of each others' lives, showing what they had learned about the interests and concerns of each other's generation. A book by program director Rosilyn Wilder describes the project in detail.[7] While other leaders have experimented with this mixing of ages with degrees of success, it was not until Wilder's documented report on a program carried out over a period of years was made public that both process and product were available for study.

Autumn Stages is a good example of a group that performs regularly in nursing homes, retirement communities, hospitals, and colleges in New Jersey. Described as an "interactive Lifestory Theatre of Elders" under the direction of Rosilyn Wilder, the troupe has received awards and grants for its work over the years for its intergenerational drama programs, workshops, and performances.[8] Besides giving pleasure to participants and audiences, Autumn Stages helps to diffuse the negative stereotypes so often associated with seniors. Patients in nursing homes enjoy singing, dancing, and seeing familiar stories acted by children. Although many have hearing and vision impairments, the presence of young performers is a highlight in what are long, quiet days.

Today a number of groups report experimenting with intergenerational theatre. "Roots and Branches" in New York and the "Blue Ridge Dinner Theatre" in Virginia have impressive records of achievement in bringing from two to four generations together on the stage. They have found that persons of all ages attend plays for what is truly family theatre.

Environmental Theatre

An alternative space of a different sort is what in avant-garde adult theatre is called environmental theatre. This is the deliberate staging of a play in a venue in which the action could logically take place or in an environment as nearly like it as possible. Sometimes, where there is enough space to accommodate several settings simultaneously, scenery is arranged around the area, with the audience moving from one location to another. The backstage crew does not shift sets but rather moves chairs during intermissions so that when the audience returns, it is facing in a different direction and, therefore, another setting. For example, a play based on a court trial could be given in a local courthouse where trials once took place, or a historical play could be given in a park that was the site of the original event. Environmental theatre can be extremely effective, especially if the location provides the appropriate scenery and atmosphere.

---

[7]Rosilyn Wilder, *Come, Step into My Life: Youth and Elders Inter-Act* (Charlottesville, VA: New Plays, 1995).
[8]*Encomium Arts, Inc.,* vol. 5, issue 1, Spring 1995.

A play about the environment done out-of-doors. (Courtesy of R. Rex Stephenson, Ferrum College, Virginia.)

One group in Vermont, the Monteverdi Players, offered a summer production of *The Tempest* in an outdoor woodland setting. A film describing the production shows the company planning the action, rehearsing the dances and the music, and building a ship for the opening and later scenes. It also shows the members of the audience streaming in across the meadow and seating themselves on the grass. Actors appear through the trees, hiding behind bushes and disappearing into the forest beyond. The play could have been staged in a theatre, but the Monteverdi Players chose the outdoor setting for its environmental value.[9]

A play I directed for a college group was laid in a dormitory. We gave the play first on a stage; then, as an experiment, we gave it again in a dormitory drawing room. We were fortunate in having a small raised platform at one end of the room, with a step down into the main section. This was an ideal location for the small invited audience. The room could accommodate no more than fifty persons, and lighting was simply what was already there with the addition of two spotlights. The result was realistic and appealing. The obvious drawbacks were the space limitation for regular performances and the fact that we were taking over a popular room in a college building. There was no objection to a one-night stand, but it could not have been done on a regular basis.

---

[9]John Carroll, director of the Monteverdi Players, currently artist-in-residence in the Gallatin School, New York University; personal communication.

Another idea, reported by a young teacher in a junior high school, was the creation of a setting for a Halloween show that the children in her class wrote. They wanted to put on a spooky play, but instead of staging it conventionally, they chose an old building on the edge of the schoolyard that was used as a potting shed and for storing lawn mowers, wheelbarrows, and so on. Granted permission to convert the building into a haunted house for one night, the class designed the setting so that the audience would walk through a dark corridor to find seats on the floor close to the actors. Audience participation was required from the moment guests walked in the door and throughout the performance. Although the evening could hardly be described as anything other than entertaining and social, it demanded imagination and hard work to execute it; as the students discovered, the production was far from easy, but it was satisfying and fun for everyone.

One drama class of teenagers I visited in Vienna always performs in alternative spaces. Originally, they made this choice because they have no auditorium. This lack of a facility, however, led to ingenious solutions, including use of the spacious garden of a park, a café, and various outdoor settings. Obviously the location must be appropriate to the play, but that is only one benefit, for environmental theatre teaches the players to be flexible and creative and to handle the unpredictable without the protection of an auditorium. What the performances may lack in finesse is outweighed by the experience of rehearsing and performing in an unorthodox venue.

A docudrama written from newspaper accounts describing a disruptive labor/management dispute in the early 1900s was performed in the building where the union had had its offices. The university students who took part felt that the impact of the play would be greater if it were performed in the original location, despite poor acoustics and inadequate lighting, rather than on a conventional proscenium stage. They were proved right, an encouraging example for other groups with scripts that might be far more effective staged in an authentic venue. Many theatre-in-education programs are handled in this way because of the opportunities that are offered for simulation and credibility.

Dramatizing history or taking the roles of real or imagined persons who lived at that time or in that place makes an indelible impression on young participants. Follow-up activities in the classroom afterward (if the workshop is a school event) may include further improvisation, creative writing, or arts and crafts. Teachers find these experiences an opportunity for greater enrichment and another dimension in learning. During the bicentennial year, both historic sites and significant dates led to imaginative workshops throughout the country. I have heard college students recall with pleasure their experiences in both seeing and creating plays arranged by their teachers with local children's theatre companies. Their memories of the learnings that took place during that period are still amazingly vivid.

In a bank in Switzerland, I once saw storytelling for very young children while their parents were standing in line or engaged in bank transactions. It seemed to me a wonderful way of keeping preschoolers occupied and quiet in a public place.

Every community has a multitude of possibilities that an enterprising teacher or theatre company can exploit, often at little or no extra cost. Workshops may be one-time events or presented throughout the semester; either way, they are examples of the unique value that a special space has to offer.

Creative Drama in the Camp

Except in the arts camps, of which there are a growing number, drama/theatre is rarely one of the more important activities of the camp program. Camps exist primarily to give city children an experience in group living in an outdoor setting. An opportunity to engage in a variety of sports is provided, with nature study, music, arts and crafts, and drama, as well as other activities from which to choose. Because of this broad emphasis, children should not be expected to spend long hours indoors in rehearsals but rather to enjoy drama and share the results of their work in occasional informal programs. Creative drama is an ideal activity for campers of all ages and backgrounds. Pantomime, improvisation, and simple out-of-doors pageantry can contribute both to the participants and to those occasions when the group comes together for programs.

Community Arts Agencies

In 1974 there were approximately two hundred community arts agencies in the United States. By 1984 there were two thousand. By 1998 there were four thousand. Most of these agencies were established through local initiative because citizens wanted arts programs in their own communities. The purpose, regardless of structure, is mainstreaming the arts into all areas of the community—working with seniors and in the schools, among many other areas. Community arts agencies can be catalysts for new approaches to problems in urban and rural areas. Rural communities, which heretofore were isolated from the arts, are now bringing in professional artists and nationally known arts companies. Government-supported public television programs, arts periodicals, artist-in-residence programs, and improved transportation have made the arts accessible to rural citizens. Most encouraging has been the support of local artists and the increased opportunities for participation in the arts that the community programs provide. Although there is great variation in type and quality of programs, this seems to be a grassroots movement supporting the stated belief in the arts as essential to an enlightened and humane society.

Arts Centers

One of the most exciting developments of the past twenty-five years is the growth of large cultural centers. Some of them are arts complexes that have incorporated services for children and youth; others were designed specifically for children and have since extended their services to include workshops and training programs for teachers. Best known among the former is the Kennedy Center for the Performing Arts in Washington, D.C. There an extensive series is offered to children free of charge under the aegis of its education department.

In New York City, Lincoln Center developed a somewhat different program. The Lincoln Center Institute is responsible for bringing children to performances and for taking artists into the schools. In addition, numerous teacher and student workshops in all the performing arts supplement and enrich the program.

The following organizations, each different in inception and program, carry on extensive programs for school audiences and the general public: the Children's Theatre Company of Minneapolis; the Nashville Academy Theatre; the Dallas Theatre Center; the Alliance Theatre Company in Atlanta, Georgia; the Mark Taper Forum in Los Angeles; the Louisville Children's Theatre; the Seattle Children's Theatre; and the New York State Theatre Institute in Albany.

An unusual center also deserving of mention is the O'Neill Memorial Theatre Center in Waterford, Connecticut. Best known for its theatre of the deaf and its playwrights' conferences, the O'Neill Center is involved in numerous other programs. These are its major areas of activity:

1. Playwriting
2. Developing new forms and uses of theatre
3. Raising standards of performance
4. Reaching young audiences
5. Sponsoring a center for theatre research

Summary

The leader of a group that meets in a nontraditional setting is wise to take stock of its assets—to consider what the facility has, not what it lacks. For instance:

The *library* has rich resources in literature, visual aids, and research materials. In addition to favorite stories, the library has new literature and authors to introduce to children.

The *museum* has collections and special exhibitions, and its education department can provide a wealth of resources. Leaders can work with the staff to add another dimension to the creative drama experience.

The *church* has meeting rooms, often a stage, and access to a piano. Its staff is accustomed to having groups of young people around, and the schedule will probably have more time available there to work or rehearse.

The grange halls and community centers also have spaces. While these are in greater demand, they are usually available if requested well in advance. A careful clean-up after use is the best assurance of acquiescence to future requests.

Other spaces vary so widely that one has to discover their unique advantages. Most will have some positive features. If you do not find the first setting suitable, look for another place in which to hold your class. A room, a leader, a group, imagination, and a regular meeting time: these are the prerequisites. One warning: remember that alternative spaces were not designed for classes in creative drama and will therefore lack some of the features that teachers expect. Respect them, use them, but do not abuse the hospitality of the institution. Your successful use of its resources is a measure of your *own* creativity—and perhaps a new program will grow tomorrow from the roots you put down today.

The large arts centers have spacious quarters, but advance planning and scheduling is necessary. More than a fringe benefit is the opportunity of knowing about other programs that take place in the center. Children who live in a city that boasts such facilities are fortunate, but the fun of discovering unexpected venues for classes or performance is possible everywhere.

Suggested Assignments

1. If there is a children's museum in your city, visit it. If you are student teaching, try to arrange to take the class there on a field trip. Plan ahead for an orientation to what the children will be seeing. List the possibilities that you find there for a drama lesson; if possible, work on one of them with the class.
2. Most cities or towns have a community center that offers classes in creative drama or acting for young people. Visit it and write a report on what you find.
3. Investigate other drama programs in the community: church, library, community theatre. Investigate them and write a report or present the information to your class.
4. From your investigation, where do you find the greatest emphasis: primary level, intermediate grade level, junior high level, or senior high level? How do the programs compare in terms of the strength of their offerings and their popularity in the community?
5. If you can find nothing in your community, design a program that you think would be an asset. List content, meeting hours, goals, age levels, staff, and physical requirements such as space, equipment, and so forth.

Journal Writing

1. What was your earliest exposure to a museum? Was it a positive experience or not? Describe your reaction and explain why you reacted as you did.
2. What kinds of exhibitions do you enjoy most today?
3. Do you enjoy any of the programs offered by a museum—lectures, music, drama, or film?
4. Think about follow-up activities for children after a field trip to a museum or a play. What could be negative about the experience? How would it affect your activities?
5. How would you use drama in the library?

Chapter 20

The After-School Drama Program

Just Before Sleep, *by James Still, directed by Jennifer Fell Hayes for City Lights Youth Theatre, New York City. (Photograph by Susan Lerner.)*

372

Choose to have fun.
Fun creates enjoyment.
Enjoyment invites participation.
Participation focuses attention.
Attention expands awareness.
Awareness promotes insight.
Insight generates knowledge.
Knowledge facilitates action.
Action yields results.

—Oswald B. Shallow

There are both similarities and differences between after-school and weekend drama programs and the classroom. First of all, the after-school program should be fun and a period of relaxation for both children and leader, for it is a voluntary activity. To be successful, however, it must be more than that. It should be recreation in the true sense of the word: to "re-create," leaving the participants refreshed at the close of the session so that they leave with satisfaction in their creative efforts and with substance to nourish mind and spirit. The leader should be as well educated as the specialist in the elementary and secondary schools but should also be prepared to handle the production of plays, as this is often part of the job. While there is wide variation among after-school programs, many sponsoring organizations expect public performances or demonstrations of some kind in addition to classes in creative drama, acting, movement, and mime. It is true that the classroom teacher may also be expected to present programs for school assemblies during the course of the year, but these are meant for school audiences rather than for outsiders.

Both classroom teachers and specialists in after-school programs are primarily educators; however, the drama teacher in a community center (or after-school program located in a public school) is also very much concerned with social goals in order to form and keep a group together and thereby be able to achieve long-range artistic goals. He or she should have as broad a background as possible, including drama/theatre and the liberal arts, a knowledge of child development, and psychology.

Leaders involved in weekend programs are in a somewhat different situation in that there is usually more class time available on a Saturday or Sunday than in the late afternoon of a weekday. The boys and girls are fresh, coming from home rather than from school. Also, the excitement that is generated in the morning in an arts center, large or small, is contagious; visitors as well as students feel it when they come through the door, and they are stimulated by it. Here a production, exhibition, or final program of some kind is almost mandatory and is anticipated by parents and community. In large centers, professional actors and artists are often on staff, adding another dimension to the experience. This connection, incidentally, frequently leads to tickets to plays and programs in local theatres, a fringe benefit for young people who cannot afford tickets and those who may be unaware of the offerings–plays, concerts, recitals, exhibitions–that are available.

Many leaders in community centers have some background in social work and experience working with different populations and a variety of age levels. Indeed, the earliest drama leaders in this country came from the ranks of social workers, as there were no programs in educational theatre to prepare them. The goals of both teacher and after-school leader were, and are, basically the same, although the ranking order may differ. The classroom teacher, for example, will rank educational, aesthetic, and social goals in that order, whereas the leader of the after-school program will list, unconsciously if not consciously social goals first with artistic and educational goals following. Neither purports to prepare actors for the professional stage, although many actors claim to have had their start in a community arts center or civic theatre.

Differences Between After-School and In-School Programs

Typical after-school and weekend programs in the large arts centers resemble the university curriculum in a number of ways. They include classes in movement, modern dance, and ballet; creative drama, acting, and musical theatre; music, visual arts, and film. What they do not include are a list of prerequisites, class credits, and degree requirements. Classes and workshops give appropriate age levels but do not require auditions for acceptance. Arts centers and community centers offer entertainment for both adult and young audiences at a fraction of the cost of the professional and even nonprofessional theatre. Often programs are so good and faculty of such high quality that they attract students from a wide area and in some instances are accepted for college credit. Because the center's primary goal is social rather than academic, financial support comes from different agencies and benefactors.

To begin with, because the after-school program comes at the end of the school day, children are tired but eager to move after sitting down for many hours indoors. Released physically and mentally, they must make the transition from school to the drama class. The children are coming from different schools and/or different grades in the same school, so they arrive at different times. This is a challenge for the leader who has to handle the fifteen or twenty minutes until all have assembled, a challenge not shared by the classroom teacher, whose students come in the door as a group. Therefore some activity must be planned to keep order and to turn a collection of restless boys and girls into a cohesive unit.

Some leaders use the time with an active game that latecomers can easily join. "Simon Says" is a favorite with younger children, who know and enjoy it. Singing is an effective technique, especially if the teacher plays a guitar or has a musical background. Movement is particularly good, not only because it can involve all the children but because it gives them a chance to exercise vigorously before settling down to serious work. In some cases storytelling is preferred; drawbacks are that it requires children to sit quietly again and listen and it can be difficult for latecomers to follow the story. Each leader, however, draws from his or her own bag of tricks to fill the preliminary period, a period that is extremely important because it is this time that cements the group. It also acts as a warm-up, thus making any further warm-ups unnecessary. Too much time spent on theatre games and physical and vocal warm-ups is wasteful of class time that should be spent on more challenging material, and players who are anticipating drama soon tire of the games. What is to be avoided under all circumstances is rowdy behavior, using the drama room as a place to let off steam with movement unrelated to the purpose of the class and counter to the tone the leader wishes to set. For this reason structured movement such as the activities suggested in Chapter 4 and 5 may be the best way to handle the first part of the class and at the same time satisfy the children's need for physical activity. Students of all ages need to move, and this is an ideal time to do it. If the material that the teacher plans to work on (play, story, study of a period or a place) calls for folk dancing, tumbling, fencing, mime, or any special type of movement that can be done by the entire group, this is an opportunity to practice it, incidentally saving rehearsal time later on.

Another difference between the after-school programs and the in-school class is the length of the period. Drama as a part of the curriculum is often limited to twenty to forty minutes, whereas the after-school class is longer and the length more flexible. Ten or fifteen minutes more usually makes little difference, unless the space is being used immediately afterward by another group. This is a decided advantage when the children's interest is high and they are working on a special project.

Problems That Arise

The after-school class is not immune to problems, however, despite the fact that it is elected by the participants, some of whom return year after year. Irregular attendance is the problem most often reported, although I suspect that it is rarely a serious problem for an effective, well-prepared leader. It is important to remember that the players, whether children or young adults, have chosen this activity from among many others and therefore have certain expectations. If the leader does not meet these expectations and succeed in capturing their interest from the beginning, the players are free to leave. They are not captives and can drop out or join another class or activity, a move that is destructive to group morale. The classroom teacher does not have this problem because attendance is required. It is true that most children enjoy drama, but the leader must prepare carefully, be sensitive to the dynamics of the group and to individual needs and interests, and maintain discipline; and perhaps most of all, the leader must share his or her personal enthusiasm for the work. Only with this approach is it possible to spark the interest and hold the attention of players over a period of weeks or months.

A second problem is interruption in the schedule. This may be frequent or only occasional. Whereas the classroom teacher has few interruptions during class time, the after-school leader can expect such interferences as the scheduling of special events that conflict with the class or use of rehearsal space; doctors' and dentists' appointments; family plans; and even severe weather conditions, causing children to go home immediately after school. If the interest is strong, however, and the group has a real sense of commitment, the children themselves can do a great deal to maintain regular attendance and keep interruptions to a minimum.

Finally, a perennial problem is budget. Arts centers depend on outside funding, for the tuition is low, and expenses must be met for maintenance of the building, basic equipment, supplies, staff salaries, and special events. Receiving a grant one year does not automatically mean that it will be given the following year; indeed, most agencies support different institutions and organizations and vary the amounts annually on principle. Fund-raising therefore has become an important part of running today's arts centers.

Advantages of the After-School Program

Now, having said that, I may have given the impression that the leader of an after-school or weekend program is in for a grim time of it, trying to spark the participants' interest, maintaining their interest to keep up attendance, suffering interruptions in the schedule, and feeling anxiety over budgets. As most leaders will tell you, however, there are advantages to the extra-curricular program that often outweigh the disadvantages.

A scene from Ragged Child, *produced by the Palo Alto Children's Theatre, one of the oldest community theatres for children in the United States. (Courtesy of Patricia Briggs, director; photograph by Tim Berger.)*

Among them are freedom from a set curriculum, no requirement for grades at the end of term, and a free choice in the matter of content, which is based on the interests and abilities of the children. Depending on the resources of the institution (community center, civic theatre, large arts center, church, temple, or school), there may be other assets such as large costume closets, scenery, a special budget for plays, and the presence of staff members or other adults who are interested in young people and are willing to cooperate with the production of a play. Having other adults involved is a great help if the leader is responsible for direction, mounting, publicity, and business.

Finally, strong involvement in the culture of an ethnic neighborhood or in social issues of concern to the players can result in original work that is particularly meaningful both to the cast and the people of the community. When the center is located in an ethnic neighborhood, children come with stories, traditions, and special holidays that they are eager to celebrate; drama leaders are wise to take advantage of these riches and make an effort to learn more about the people and the local resources. Plays based on this kind of material not only will attract local audiences but will help to educate children of other cultural backgrounds, who may be in the group or live in the neighborhood.

An interesting play was created in New York recently by a group of teenagers who, with experienced guidance, studied the records of two immigrant families who had lived in the neighborhood at the turn of the century. The group collaborated on the writing of a script titled *Hope*. Students tried out for parts as the characters whose lives they had researched. The result, a documentary, was presented in the Lower East Side Tenement Museum, a restored building in which the families might have lived. The work was of great interest to both the neighborhood and general audiences; it was a rare opportunity for the children to learn about a chapter of local history by studying it and putting their findings into dramatic form. The small playing space in the tenement, far from being a handicap, was an asset because of the sense of authenticity it provided.

The opportunity to stage plays with exciting possibilities for production in the time and the space the after-school center provides can also be a plus for older groups. Public performance is certainly a way of holding the interest of the players; and it is also, because of its visibility, a way of showing the community what young people can do, thereby helping to build a strong ongoing program.

The choice of program or play for an after-school group depends on many things, as it does with every drama group or club: the number of players, their age and previous experience, the amount of time available for rehearsals, the budget, and the stage or playing area. Young people are ambitious. They are eager to give plays with spectacular technical effects or to perform sophisticated scripts they have seen on television. Here the director or teacher must be prepared to guide the choice by bringing in appropriate scripts or brainstorming for ideas. What every leader wants above all is a positive experience for the players and a product in which all can take pride. Success breeds success, and the word soon gets around that the class is wonderful and the productions are great.

One teacher, feeling strongly that her children in an inner-city program have missed the folk and fairy tales, produces a traditional story like "The Sleeping Beauty" once a year with music and colorful mounting. Her rationale, shared by few these days, is that these children are well acquainted with the problems of the street and for that reason need the beauty of an imaginative production. She also finds that the fairy tales have universal and timeless themes for discussion.

As for another type of program, two young women in one of my graduate classes taught after school in religious institutions. Their challenge is to find, or create with the children, suitable programs on religious themes for special holidays. One Jewish, one Christian, they shared their search and findings with the other students in my class. Appropriate plays and stories have to qualify as good theatre and are often difficult to find. Their choices are obviously limited; on the other hand, the children they teach are deeply religious and are enrolled in the classes by choice.

And, finally, there is the example of a young Chinese woman who founded a Chinese theatre workshop some years ago in a large arts center. Her mission is obvious, but I cite it because it illustrates the kind of freedom some after-school programs offer leaders. Her goals are clear: (1) to teach the traditions of the Chinese theatre and (2) to create artistic productions for family audiences. Folk tales, performance style, costuming, face painting, and other elements of the Chinese theatre have made this one of the most fascinating after-school projects I have been privileged to see.

Some large arts centers have enviable facilities, but all have unique features, and it is incumbent upon the drama teacher to discover them. A disadvantage in a small center may be lack of a stage or space large enough to accommodate a production. One solution is an appropriate outside venue such as a museum, library, park, church, grange hall, or clubhouse, as described in Chapter 19. A play I saw a few years ago in Europe was even staged in a restaurant! The teenage students had studied the French Revolution in school; they saw its dramatic possibilities and wanted to write a play dealing with some aspect of it. Their after-school teacher, who was also an actress and dancer, supported their request and worked with them on a script; she made arrangements for the cast to perform it in a café called La Guillotine. The manager and waiters knew when the troupe would be coming in and helped, even to minor participation. The performance was a rare experience for the young players, as it certainly was for the diners, who had had no foreknowledge of the evening's entertainment. This was a unique solution to the problem of performance space, but an imaginative director can find many other venues. These examples illustrate only a few of the wide variety of after-school and weekend programs that can be found in a large city, and often in a singe neighborhood.

I have not suggested specific activities in this chapter because the range of possibilities is so great and the circumstances are so varied. The individual teacher is best qualified to create his or her own methods and to find the most suitable material for the group. Earlier chapters include exercises, stories, and ideas that are just as appropriate for after-school classes as they are for the classroom. The chapters on imagination, movement, pantomime, and improvisation all contain suggestions that can be used in after-school programs.

Sometimes a community is so torn apart by social and political issues that the implementation of a conventional program is doomed from the start. Within the past forty years, however, the tool that has proved most effective in dealing with these issues and establishing an ongoing leadership is theatre. The drama teacher or theatre director is rarely prepared to deal with serious problem areas by using what Philip Taylor calls applied theatre techniques.[1] "Applied" because the drama is taken out of the theatre facility and put in the hands of the community, where it becomes a medium for social action, reflection, and transformation. It is here that a special person is needed, a leader trained to resolve conflicts.

In order to become an agent for change experienced leadership is required; the leader must be able to discern and address the issues and help the community attack and resolve them. Augusto Boal, the South American leader, is the one most frequently cited in describing the use of applied theatre in the community. When the problem areas are serious, theatre directors need help from experienced leaders.

I cannot conclude this section without mentioning a unique use of theatre techniques called "aqua drama," described by Milton Polsky in his book on acting in waist-high water. Obviously this activity belongs to the camp program or at least a venue that provides a shallow swimming pool where people can stand in water to the waist. It would also be an appropriate technique for some special education classes that promote creative movement and group cooperation.[2]

Summary

The after-school program has become a significant adjunct to arts education today. With school budget cuts, many communities depend on after-school arts programs to supplement or even replace work that had previously been part of the school curriculum. Such programs give children and teenagers an opportunity for creativity, learning, and the experience of working cooperatively.

The content varies with the leader, who is aware of the children's interests, the philosophy of the center, and his or her own expertise. Today's after-school leaders have backgrounds comparable to those of teachers in public and private schools, and, as mentioned earlier, often professional actors, dancers, and artists are on the staff. Many arts programs are excellent and are enthusiastically supported by schools and members of the community.

In any case, it is important for the leader to become acquainted with the students from the beginning. Unlike the schoolroom, the center will be new to many of the children, and they should be made to feel welcome and comfortable at once so that a spirit of ensemble can be established. It is equally important for the leader to become acquainted with the community because the center has been founded to serve it, and the better informed the leader, the better the relationship between staff and neighborhood. Knowing what has been done in the past and what the expectations are for the future will enable a new teacher to start out with ideas that are compatible with the philosophy and practices of the center. Understanding its history and goals prevents

---

[1]Philip Taylor, *Applied Theatre* (Portsmouth: Heinemann, 2003).
[2]Milton Polsky, *Aquadrama* (Winona: Drama Editions, 2002).

disappointment on both sides. The good teacher can then adapt his or her methodology to the needs of both the children and the institution, with gratifying results for all. A successful start is a good omen.

Many cities have special features that they share with the schools and community centers. Because these offerings are nontraditional they must take place in specific locations. For example, there is the Big Apple Circus in New York, which has a group of highly skilled performers/teachers. The Clown Care unit goes to children's hospitals, where members entertain patients while working closely with doctors and nurses. The physical education unit, with an emphasis on acrobatics, attracts inner-city children with whom they work in large spaces off-site. Programs like these supplement traditional educations and health care and are reportedly popular with both children and staffs.

The Jack Tale Players, previously mentioned, are college students who earn academic credit for performing in community centers, retirement homes, farmers' markets, and other off-campus locations. Funding these special offerings may require a search, but the results enrich the educational experience of young people and provide unique recreational opportunities.

Finally, stated or implied throughout this chapter, is the aesthetic contribution that a good, well-funded weekend program makes to the families of a community. Many touring theatre companies today visit these centers, presenting appropriate plays of good quality at affordable prices. Like the settlement houses a century ago, the weekend programs offered by the community centers provide a popular and valuable service.

Suggested Assignments

1. Visit an after-school drama program in your community to find out what is being taught and how the material is adapted to the children's or teenagers' interests.
2. Ask the leader what problems he or she encounters and how they are handled.
3. Plan a lesson for an after-school program in a center with which you are acquainted. State the kind of institution, the size and age range of the group, the days and hours of classes.
4. Plan a course outline for a particular population. This can be a lengthy paper or simply your ideas to be discussed with the class.
5. Why do you think the after-school and weekend programs have proliferated in the past few years?

Journal Writing

1. If you were a member of an after-school group of your own age, what would most interest you: ethnic material, modern plays for young audiences or for adult audiences, religious material, or something else?

2. What would most draw you to a group? What would you find unappealing? If you were dissatisfied with a program, would you simply leave, or would you discuss your dissatisfaction with the leader?

3. Would you like to teach in an after-school program? Why? Analyze your reasons for your reaction to the question.

4. Have you ever been involved in an after-school or extracurricular activity of any kind? What do you remember most about it—the most positive and the most negative aspects?

5. What is your reaction to the term *applied theatre*?

Chapter 21

A Final Word

The Paper Bag Players' Rubbish! She Cried, *written and designed by Judith Martin.*

Teachers live in human lives, not in books.

—May Sartan

With so much concern regarding the future of the theatre arts for children, is it not appropriate to raise some questions regarding the teacher? What special qualifications should he or she have? What kind of education best prepares a person to teach drama and/or theatre at this time?

Is a purely theatrical background a disadvantage? Are workshop experiences sufficient preparation? Dare the teacher or leader embark on a program without some specialized training? Is certification necessary?

Without discrediting academic preparation, what seems most important are those personal attributes that make a good teacher. If a person already possesses the qualities of sympathetic leadership, imagination, and respect for the ideas of others, he or she has the basic requirements. Sensitivity to the individuals in a class is necessary to an activity that is participant centered, with the growth of each person an objective. In other words, although one is teaching an art and should therefore have some knowledge and appreciation of it as a form, a genuine concern for the players is of equal importance.

Successful creative drama teachers guide rather than direct. They are able to work with others, offering and accepting ideas. To them, sharing is more important than showing; thus, their satisfaction will come through the process as well as from the product. When they do show the work of their group, they will be clear as to what is demonstration and what is performance.

Teachers of creative drama find their own way. No methods courses can prepare them perfectly, for no two groups are alike. What works well with one class may not work with another. Materials and methods that arouse a response in one group may be totally inadequate in a second whose cultural background, age, and experiences are different. Knowledge of the neighborhood in which one is working is just as important as a knowledge of literature and drama. Teachers must find out for themselves what stimulates and what fails to elicit a response. Familiarity with techniques is an invaluable asset, but imaginative leaders will, in the end, create their own methods.

A sense of humor helps teachers over those periods when nothing goes right. The ability to laugh with the group, as well as at themselves, enables them to carry on in spite of failures and frustrations. Because they are interested in all kinds of things, they will have an expanding background of information from which to draw. They learn constantly from their pupils. They must also learn not to expect good results each time the class meets. Many efforts will be pedestrian and disappointing, but, as Hughes Mearns points out, "those who work with children creatively are compelled to discard or ignore a hundred attempts while they are getting a mere half-dozen good ones."[1] It is these "good ones" that inspire others and encourage the leader to keep on trying.

---

[1] Hughes Mearns, *Creative Power: The Education of Youth in Creative Arts,* 2nd ed. (New York: Dover, 1958), p. 33.

Teachers maintain high standards, knowing that what they accept in the beginning is what the group is capable of at the time but that they can expect more from it later. By establishing an atmosphere in which all feel important, teachers will challenge their classes to give only their best; a teacher will wait for this, without demanding or pushing. For this reason, it is more difficult to teach creative drama than formal theatre. The absence of a basic structure, or script, demands flexibility, judgment, a willingness to accept the efforts of the shy and inarticulate, patience, and the confidence that something of value is forthcoming.

A background that includes both education and theatre is ideal, but interested leaders, whatever their preparation, can acquire, through course work and reading, additional information and techniques. Some knowledge of music and dance is invaluable and should be part of the teacher's preparation. Classroom teachers, professional actors, and social workers have all achieved notable results. Because of their belief that creative drama has a contribution to make, they have adapted their own individual skills to its use, with intelligence and imagination.

A successful creative drama leader keeps abreast of the times. The world is changing rapidly. With constant exposure to television, children and adults have access to the same information. Children are no longer excluded from discussion of subjects once considered inappropriate or taboo. In his book *The Disappearance of Childhood,* Neil Postman documented the ways modern technology has destroyed the boundaries separating the world of the child from the world of the adult.[2] This melding of worlds has important implications for the teacher, both generalist and specialist. For us to assume, however, that children today "know more" than children of previous generations is facile. They no longer inhabit a protected environment, but this does not mean they have a mature understanding of complex social, psychological, and political issues. What it does suggest is that the teacher must be prepared for a variety of new subjects and problems to come up and must be ready and able to handle them. Children today are bombarded with images of sex and violence and news of crime in high places; many of them experience divorce, drugs, alcoholism, and death in their own homes or neighborhoods. Often they suggest situations dealing with these topics for improvisation. The teacher must be able to accept what is offered and help the group deal with it.

The first step is to create an atmosphere in which every student feels at ease. Here are some basic suggestions:

Build on students' strengths rather than focusing on their weaknesses.

Be sure that all students are involved in the activities and exercises of the class.

Show your own appreciation of the cultures represented in the group.

Try to pair minority students with nonminority students when children work as partners.

Have frequent, even running, exhibitions of books, maps, photographs and pictures, costumes of different cultures, and so on.

---

[2]Neil Postman, *The Disappearance of Childhood* (New York: Delacorte, 1994).

Invite parents to visit classes and attend programs featuring speakers who present interesting material on cultures being studied.

Recognize ethnic and religious holidays.

Take field trips to places of interest: cultural centers, ethnic neighborhoods, and museums.

Finally, remember that a method is only as good as the teacher who uses it. What is right for one is not necessarily right for all. Learn, listen, then trust your instincts. Like first impressions, instincts tend to be right. If not, learn from the experience and try again. We learn as much, if not more, from our mistakes, creating another and clearer path to success.

Summary

Creative drama can be viewed as an art form, a way of learning, a means of self-expression, a leisure-time activity, or a therapeutic tool. In each instance, learnings include self-knowledge, knowledge of others, information acquired through the process of drama, and aesthetic appreciation.

Creative drama can also lead to performance, for, as the years have passed and areas have been defined, the lines of demarcation blur. Creative drama and children's theatre often merge as styles change and values shift. Yet, the three original objectives—aesthetic, educational and social—remain and guide us.

In his message to the International Theatre Institute on World Theatre Day, 1994, Czech president and playwright Václav Havel said, "It seems that the more tightly this variegated community is crowded together by contemporary civilizations and compelled to accept common values and codes of behavior, the more powerfully will various groups feel the need to define their national, racial, cultural autonomy and identity."[3] In our modern world, a multicultural approach to the study of drama is mandatory. The arts are universal, flourishing best in an open and accepting society.

Conclusion

The greatest challenges we face in the new millennium may be to find the monies to finance arts programs and to overcome the discouragement that prevails regarding employment. The programs that the pioneers envisioned, the practitioners have created, and the researchers are finding viable and of value are in jeopardy; it is up to us to discover new ways to support and preserve them. I believe that a third challenge has grown out of our own zeal to make drama/theatre meaningful: to preserve the *fun* of theatre (a word chosen consciously and with care). In our effort to enrich education through drama, to sponsor children's theatre with greater substance than it has had in

---

[3]Václav Havel, Letter to Members of the International Theatre Institute, New York, Spring Newsletter March 27, 1994.

the past, and to focus on scientific research, we sometimes lose sight of the *fun* that theatre brings to our lives. We who have worked zealously to improve the quality of dramatic literature and performance skills risk losing the spirit that infuses the best theatre. Fun in this sense is not to be confused with the trivial and banal or with "camp"; rather, fun is the joy that comes from creating drama or from watching superb performers in vehicles that may or may not be concerned with serious subject matter.

Finally, a basic requirement of any activity is that it be a satisfying experience for both leader and group. Educational and social goals are closely related in drama; therefore, a climate in which the players feel relaxed and good about themselves and others is conducive to learning. The basic principles of creative drama apply to all ages, and the concept of a warm and supportive environment as a positive influence is applicable everywhere. It is this kind of environment that we should try to create, an environment in which all persons can grow.

To repeat, do not overestimate students' information nor underestimate their intelligence. Every student has something to offer, and it may not be what you had in mind. Respect for the contribution, constructive criticism, and encouragement are basic to successful teaching at every level.

Suggested Assignments

1. Find out whether there are any intergenerational arts programs in your community. If so, visit one and report your findings to the class.
2. Visit a state arts council, if possible; otherwise write for information. These groups are usually generous with programs, printed materials, and newsletters. Share with your classmates.
3. Discuss the differences and similarities between aesthetic education and the arts as a medium of learning.
4. After reading this book, what interests you most of the various areas covered? Why? Write a paper or give a report on your research on this topic.

Journal Writing

1. As you reflect on this course, what have been the most significant learnings for you?
2. Has your appreciation of the dramatic arts changed? If so, in what way?
3. If you plan to continue your study of drama with children, what aspect, age level, or situation most interests you (e.g., classroom, after-school programs, aesthetic education)?
4. How are drama and theatre the same and how do they differ?

National Standards for Theatre Education

The National Standards for Arts Education are a statement of what every young American should know and be able to do in four arts disciplines—dance, music, theatre, and the visual arts. Their scope is grades K–12, and they speak to both content and achievement.

The Reform Context

The standards are one outcome of the education reform effort generated in the 1980s, which emerged in several states and attained nationwide visibility with the publication of *A Nation at Risk* in 1983. This national wake-up call was powerfully effective. Six national education goals were announced in 1990. Now there is a broad effort to describe, specifically, the knowledge and skills students must have in all subjects to fulfill their personal potential, to become productive and competitive workers in a global economy, and to take their places as adult citizens. With the passage of the Goals 2000: Educate America Act, 1992 the national goals are written into law, naming the arts as a core academic subject—as important to education as English, mathematics, history, civics and government, geography, science, and foreign language.

At the same time, the act calls for education standards in these subject areas, both to encourage high achievement by our young people and to provide benchmarks to determine how well they are learning and performing. In 1992, anticipating that education standards would emerge as a focal point of the reform legislation, the Consortium of National Arts Education Associations successfully approached the U.S. Department of Education, the National Endowment for the Arts, and the National Endowment for the Humanities for a grant to determine what the nation's schoolchildren should know and be able to do in the arts. This document is the result of an extended process of consensus building that drew on the broadest possible range of expertise and participation. The process involved the review of state-level arts education frameworks, standards from other nations, and consideration at a series of national forums.

The Importance of Standards

Agreement on what students should know and be able to do is essential if education is to be consistent, efficient, and effective. In this context, standards for arts education are important for two basic reasons. First, they help define what a good education in the arts should provide: a thorough grounding in a basic body of knowledge and the skills required both to make sense and make use of the arts disciplines. Second, when states and school districts adopt standards, they are taking a stand for rigor in a part of education that has too often, and wrongly, been treated as optional. This document says, in effect, "an education in the arts means that students should know what is spelled out here, and they should reach clear levels of attainment at these grade levels."

These standards provide a vision of competence and educational effectiveness, but without creating a mold into which all arts programs must fit. The standards are concerned with the *results* (in the form of student learning) that come from a basic education in the arts, *not with how those results ought to be delivered.* Those matters are for states, localities, and classroom teachers to decide. In other words, while the standards provide educational goals and not a curriculum, they can help improve all types of arts instruction.

The Importance of Arts Education

Knowing and practicing the arts disciplines is fundamental to the healthy development of children's minds and spirits. That is why, in any civilization—ours included— the arts are inseparable from the very meaning of the term *education.* We know from long experience that no one can claim to be truly educated who lacks basic knowledge and skills in the arts. There are many reasons for this assertion:

> The arts are worth studying simply because of what they are. Their impact cannot be denied. Throughout history, all the arts have served to connect our imaginations with the deepest questions of human existence: Who am I? What must I do? Where am I going? Studying responses to those questions through time and across cultures—as well as acquiring the tools and knowledge to create one's own responses—is essential not only to understanding life but to living it fully.

The arts are used to achieve a multitude of human purposes: to present issues and ideas, to teach or persuade, to entertain, to decorate or please. Becoming literate in the arts helps students understand and do these things better.

The arts are integral to every person's daily life. Our personal, social, economic, and cultural environments are shaped by the arts at every turn—from the design of the child's breakfast placemat, to the songs on the commuter's car radio, to the family's nighttime TV drama, to the teenager's Saturday dance, to the enduring influences of the classics.

The arts offer unique sources of enjoyment and refreshment for the imagination. They explore relationships between ideas and objects and serve as links between thought and action. Their continuing gift is to help us see and grasp life in new ways.

There is ample evidence that the arts help students develop the attitudes, characteristics, and intellectual skills required to participate effectively in today's society and economy. The arts teach self-discipline, reinforce self-esteem, and foster the thinking skills and creativity so valued in the workplace. They teach the importance of teamwork and cooperation. They demonstrate the direct connection between study, hard work, and high levels of achievement.

The Benefits of Arts Education

Arts education benefits the *student* because it cultivates the whole child, gradually building many kinds of literacy while developing intuition, reasoning, imagination, and dexterity into forms of expression and communication. This process requires not merely an active mind but a trained one. An education in the arts benefits *society* because students of the arts gain powerful tools for understanding human experiences, both past and present. They learn to respect the often very different ways others have of thinking, working, and expressing themselves. They learn to make decisions in situations in which there are no standard answers. By studying the arts, students stimulate their natural creativity and learn to develop it to meet the needs of a complex and competitive society. And, as study and competence in the arts reinforce one another, the joy of learning becomes real, tangible, and powerful.

The Arts and Other Core Subjects

The standards address competence in the arts disciplines first of all. But that competence provides a firm foundation for connecting arts-related concepts and facts across the art forms, and from them to the sciences and humanities. For example, the intellectual methods of the arts are precisely those used to transform scientific disciplines and discoveries into everyday technology.

What Must We Do?

The educational success of our children depends on creating a society that is both literate and imaginative, both competent and creative. That goal depends, in turn, on providing children with tools not only for understanding that world but for contributing to it and making their own way. Without the arts to help shape students' perceptions and imaginations, our children stand every chance of growing into adulthood culturally disabled. We must not allow that to happen.

Without question, the standards presented here will need supporters and allies to improve how arts education is organized and delivered. They have the potential to change education policy at all levels and to make a transforming impact across the entire spectrum of education.

But only if they are implemented.

Teachers, of course, will be the leaders in this process. In many places, more teachers with credentials in the arts, as well as better-trained teachers in general, will be needed. Site-based management teams, school boards, state education agencies, state and local arts agencies, and teacher education institutions will all have a part to play, as will local mentors, artists, local arts organizations, and members of the community. Their support is crucial if the standards are to succeed. But the primary issue is the ability to bring together and deliver a broad range of competent instruction. All else is secondary.

In the end, truly successful implementation can come about only when students and their learning are at the center, which means motivating and enabling them to meet the standards. With a steady gaze on that target, we can use these standards to empower America's schools to make changes consistent with the best any of us can envision, for our children and for our society.

Additional material is available from the Office of the American Alliance for Theatre and Education, 7475 Wisconsin Ave., Suite 300A, Bethesda, MD 20814. *The Stage of Art*, vol. 16, Issue 2, Spring 2004, Bethesda: AATE publication. This issue is devoted to the subject of standards and can be obtained from the national office.

Appendix B

Student Evaluation

We come now to the most difficult task of all: evaluating and assessing student work. In formal theatre this evaluation is easier because the product is obvious, but in creative drama we are assessing more nebulous qualities (creative efforts rather than performance skills). How do we measure these efforts and still maintain students' courage to try, to experiment, and to trust the one who is evaluating the results?

To evaluate student work in any area, a leader must know the *characteristics, abilities, needs,* and *interests* of the particular age level. These are not present to the same degree in all children; guidelines, however, can help the leader set expectations. Human beings grow at different rates, so there can be no arbitrary rules governing growth and development. Experienced teachers know what children of different ages are like, but for the inexperienced teacher, or the teacher working with drama for the first time, the following explanations will be helpful.

Characteristics of the First-Grade Child

Physical. Energetic, alert, active; responds with the entire body; enjoys frequent change of activity and position; needs quiet time after active periods; follows rules of the game.

Mental. Capable of reproductive images and concrete operations as well as movement for its own sake; has ability to think independently; short attention span; is curious and investigative; enjoys symbolic play.

Social. Begins decentering in cognitive and social areas; likes to be with other children of the same age; has strong feelings and is expressive; must learn to take turns.

Interests. Family, home, local activities, and occupations; toys, animals, machinery; holidays and field trips.

Activities. Fifteen- to twenty-minute drama periods recommended. Enjoys rhythms, imitative movements, and simple pantomimes; likes to enact short verses and nursery rhymes; favorite stories often played many times; should work in large groups rather than individually; enjoys having the teacher participate with class.

Characteristics of the Second-Grade Child

Physical. Enjoys using the entire body; active, eager to participate; has improved coordination and better control of small muscle movements than the first-grader.

Mental. Is moving from concrete thinking to more conceptual mode of thought; vocabulary is expanding; developing critical ability; enjoys short discussion periods; creates anticipatory images as well as reproductive images.

Social. Greater enjoyment of other children; more socialized and more independent.

Interests. The community; holidays, guessing games, and riddles; animals; stories, both familiar and new.

Activities. Thirty-minute drama periods recommended. Enjoys dramatizing stories and poems; likes fairy tales and fantasy; "show and tell" is a favorite activity; is easily stimulated and can work in groups of two, three, or four as well as in large groups; enjoys pantomime.

Characteristics of the Third-Grade Child

Physical. Developing well-coordinated movements; likes to run, jump, skip, gallop, and dance; has noticeably finer development of small movements.

Mental. Capable of critical and evaluative observation; able to organize ideas more quickly and clearly; plans scenes and sequences with ease; enjoys humor.

Social. Strong sense of justice and fair play; often cites the moral of a story or fable; follows directions and works well with peers.

Interests. Interests broadening to include other peoples and other lands; interested in fantasy, royalty, folk and fairy tales, but moving toward stories of the here and now.

Activities. Thirty- to forty-five-minute drama periods recommended. Enjoys challenging work on literature, projects, and exercises; will bring in relevant materials such as pictures, games, stories, and songs; likes to work on integrated projects involving social studies, literature, and the arts.

Characteristics of the Fourth-Grade Child

Physical. Constantly gaining better control of the body as he or she grows older, taller, and stronger; works and plays hard; is active, spontaneous, eager to try new things and to learn.

Mental. Becoming more self-motivated; enjoys discussion and group planning periods; likes to solve problems.

Social. Independent but likes working with others; can share ideas and work cooperatively on scenes and class projects.

Interests. Adventure, sports, strong heroes and heroines; enjoys new stories and more demanding exercises.

Activities. Forty- to sixty-minute drama periods recommended. Classes may include exercises, stories, poems, suggestions for creating scenes; interest in play structure; can handle more complicated plots and create original plays; able to work for longer periods and study subjects in greater depth.

Characteristics of the Fifth-Grade Child

Physical. Continued improvement of physical skills, including tumbling, acrobatics, circus acts, and clowning.

Mental. Growing ability to solve problems and create well-rounded characters; motivation for characters' behavior becomes important; likes words and can create dialogue appropriate to characters and situations or periods in which the story is laid; accepts constructive suggestions from the teacher or leader.

Social. Able to analyze feelings; continues to work well in a team; fair play important; still needs help in commenting on the work of others so as not to hurt feelings.

Interests. Similar to those of the fourth grader but with a constantly widening spread; fantasy and fairy tales become less interesting as interest in the lives of real persons and tales of heroic acts grows.

Activities. Forty minutes to an hour or more can be spent on a variety of activities. Can handle longer and more complicated stories; still childlike in spontaneity but more perceptive and thoughtful; able to sustain interest in one activity for a longer period.

Characteristics of the Sixth-Grade Child

Physical. The preadolescent is undergoing change; physical growth is reflected in the finer muscle coordination; often self-conscious because of body change but capable of refined movements, well-developed pantomime, and circus skills.

Mental. Interested in detail and motivation of characters; talkative and investigative; enjoys discussion; shows more mature reasoning ability; has keener critical judgment; is often surprisingly perceptive.

Social. Interested in the opposite sex; sensitive and aware; has had more experiences on which to draw; vocabulary much larger; can be expected to offer well-thought-out ideas and well-expressed criticism.

Interests. Many and varied interests; romantic interests as well as love of adventure and mystery; adolescent problems may begin.

Activities. Can work for an hour to an hour and a half. Likes writing and may enjoy playwriting as well as performing; can integrate learnings and engage in long-range projects involving social studies, literature, and the arts; may want to put on a play for an audience.

Characteristics of the Seventh-Grade Child

Physical. Growing rapidly at this age; some preadolescents are more mature than others; energetic and strong; capable of fine physical coordination, including the mastery of some circus skills.

Mental. Curious; enjoys the challenge of more difficult material; continued eagerness to discuss ideas with classmates; developing good reasoning power and critical judgment.

Social. Uneven development as some children now show considerable social growth, whereas others are self-conscious and sensitive to criticism; experience in dramatic activities an effective way of facilitating social growth and poise.

Interests. Interests broaden, including those noted in the sixth grader.

Activities. Can sustain interest over a longer period. Has a definite desire to perform for an audience outside the class.

Characteristics of the Eighth-Grade Child

Physical. As teenagers, children show greater physical maturity, with girls often appearing two or three years older than their chronological age; awkwardness in some cases because of this rapid growth. Dance and physical activities should be included in drama sessions.

Mental. Capable of solving more complex problems; eager for the challenge of new ideas to pursue and discuss with peers.

Social. Uneven social development and skills; many are now comfortable, however, working with peer groups, including opposite sex; expanding vocabulary contributes to improved communication.

Interests. Wide range of interests, especially among children who read. Most young people of this age concerned with adolescent problems and ways of solving them. Theatre-in-education companies coming into the school are of particular interest and a source of stimulation.

Activities. Ability to work for two hours on projects of interest. Often exhibits ability in writing and knowledge of theatre production; most children of this age are ready and eager to perform plays for outside audiences.

Characteristics of Ninth- and Tenth-Grade Students

Physical, mental, and social growth continues but now at a slower pace. In some school systems ninth graders are in high school, where they are pursuing a more advanced curriculum. Interest may shift sharply toward performance and the production of full-length plays, although pantomime and improvisation are still popular. Young people of this age are capable of difficult and often remarkably artistic work.

Characteristics of Eleventh- and Twelfth-Grade Students

As for eleventh- and twelfth-grade students, we find a maturing and growing interest in adult theatre. Because they watch adult programs on television and read the same books their parents read, they are ready for more work on performance skills. They still enjoy mime and improvisation; and some opportunity should be given to work on these areas. I have found little difference between the high school senior and the college freshman; both can handle classical and contemporary material, although variation in abilities and interests are to be expected. On all age levels multiple sources of information and observation over a period of time yield the best results.

Using an Evaluation Chart

Although grading in the arts is to be avoided, a simple checklist may be helpful in evaluating growth and development. The evaluation chart on page 398 was designed to show the major areas of concern and should serve as (1) a guide to the emphases in teaching creative drama and (2) an aid to the identification of children's individual needs and progress. It is suggested that children be evaluated three or four times a semester to note change and improvement.

We do not look for performance skills in elementary school children, nor do we expect the level of achievement possible among all high school students. Involvement, sincerity, imagination, freedom of movement, and cooperation with the group are the basic goals in teaching creative drama. Beyond that, vocal expression, vocabulary, and the ability to plan and to organize material are important, but they come with experience. The criteria applied to adult actors are inappropriate for children and should not be used. These criteria are audience centered and therefore do not belong to creative drama, in which the participant is central. Even when children's work is shared with others, the goals remain the same, with the audience prepared for the occasion rather than the players drilled for a performance.

It is suggested that instead of giving letter grades to children in the primary school, teachers assign the following three numbers to indicate quality of response in the specific category:

1. Shows good response
2. Is adequate
3. Needs special attention

The Areas of Concentration

Students are developing a variety of skills as they participate in creative drama.

1. *Listening.* Listening is an important skill for hearing instructions, discussing topics in class, responding to questions, and helping to create a climate in which all children are able to express themselves freely.
2. *Concentration.* The ability to hold an idea long enough to respond thoughtfully or creatively is essential in any discipline. It is particularly important in drama, for a breakdown in concentration on the part of one participant invariably affects the concentration of all. Group work requires the concentrated attention of every member.
3. *Response.* Responses can be varied; the important thing to note is whether or not the student is able to respond physically, verbally, or emotionally to the challenge.
4. *Imagination.* Imagination is the element that distinguishes a response as original, creative, or interesting.
5. *Movement.* Young children tend to be free in the use of their bodies as a primary means of expression. As they grow older, children become more inhibited in their physical responses. Tight, constricted movement suggests self-consciousness or fear. Unlocking the muscles therefore helps the performer to express ideas and feelings more openly.
6. *Verbal ability.* The older the student, the greater the verbal ability to be expected. Increased vocabulary and added experience in speaking should improve oral communication.

7. *Cooperation.* Cooperation includes the ability to offer and accept the ideas of others easily and graciously. It is an important part of successful living in a democracy.
8. *Organization.* Planning, seeing relationships between parts, making choices, and arranging the components of a project require thought, maturity, and patience. As children work together, they develop the ability to organize materials in such a way as to communicate with others.
9. *Attitude.* Attitude is the feeling or disposition toward the work and the other members of the class. A positive attitude not only enhances the quality of the individual student's work but also contributes to the combined efforts of the group. A negative attitude, on the contrary, detracts and may even be a destructive force.
10. *Understanding.* Understanding means more than comprehension of meaning. It includes the ability to use the material: knowing what it is and how to handle it.

Although there are other important goals in teaching creative drama, those listed above are the most important in assessing the progress of children in the elementary and intermediate grades or, indeed, of beginners at any age. Teachers may want to keep brief anecdotal records as well as a checklist. The space at the right, marked "Comments," provides for such entries. Specific instances of change, "breakthroughs," or problems of individual students can be written here.

"Class progress" is the overall picture of the group at work. In the adult theatre, this overall ambience is referred to as *ensemble.* Ensemble means the quality of work done as a group rather than by individual actors. It is not developed in a day or a week; after a month or so, a tentative evaluation can be made. Individuals develop at different rates, and some have problems that must be resolved before it is possible for them to become absorbed in a group project. An accurate statement of group progress therefore cannot often be made until near the end of a semester.

Other Yardsticks

The best method of evaluating student progress is personal observation made on a daily basis. These observations lead to the information needed for a checklist. Because the teacher's attention is on the lesson and the group, however, and because he or she must move on to other lessons, daily rating is impractical and actually undesirable. If there are student teachers in the room, ask them to be responsible for watching response and variations in behavior from day to day. Should there be more than one student teacher assigned to the class, each can be given a group to observe over a period of time. This practice has two advantages: (1) it is a help to the classroom teacher, freeing him or her for teaching the group; and (2) it sharpens the student teacher's ability to discern growth and development. Again, it must be stressed that teaching comes first and that at no time should evaluation become important to students or take on the appearance of assigning letter grades. When children try to *please* adults, they lose the most important value of the experience.

Date:_____

Students' names	Listening	Concentration	Response	Imagination	Movement	Verbal ability	Cooperation	Organization	Attitude	Comments
Doe, John	1	2	2	1	3	1	3	1	2	

Teacher's evalution of class progress:

Another yardstick, possible in some schools but not in most, is videotaping of the class. This is an ideal way to compare work done at different periods in the semester and to take a second look at a performance that one does not clearly remember. The obvious disadvantage of taping is that when children know they are being filmed, they tend to become self-conscious, thus negating two of our principal goals: sincerity and involvement. Therefore, where videotaping is possible, it should not be done until halfway through the semester, by which time the students are comfortable and working easily together. Taping should seem a natural way of recording group work and not like filming a show.

Books on Child Development

Bruner, Jerome. *The Process of Education*. Cambridge: Harvard University Press, 1960.

Coles, Michael, and Sheila Coles. *The Development of Children*. New York: Scientific American Press, 1993.

Day, B. D. *Early Childhood Education: Creative Learning Activities*. New York: Macmillan, 1983.

Dittman, L. L., and M. E. Ramsey, eds. *Today Is for Children*. Washington, DC: Association for Childhood Education International, 1982.

Flavell, J. H. *The Development Psychology of Jean Piaget*. Princeton, NJ: Van Nostrand, 1963.

Gesell, Arnold, and Frances Ilg. *The Child from Five to Ten.* New York: Harper & Row, 1946.

Hendrick, J. *Total Learning for the Whole Child.* St. Louis: Mosby, 1980.

Mallory, Bruce L., and Rebecca S. New, eds. *Diversity and Developmentally Appropriate Challenges for Early Childhood Education.* New York: Teachers College Press, 1994.

Maxim, G. *The Very Young Child: Guiding Children from Infancy Through the Early Years.* 2nd ed. Belmont, CA: Wadsworth, 1985.

Maynard, Olga. *Children and Dance and Music.* New York: Scribner, 1968.

Piaget, Jean, and Barbel Inhelder. *The Child's Conception of Movement and Speed.* New York: Basic Books, 1969.

——. *The Psychology of the Child.* New York: Basic Books, 1969.

Santrock, John W. *Children,* 5th ed. Madison, WI: Brown and Benchmark, 1997.

Spodek, Bernard, ed. *Handbook of Research in Early Childhood Education.* New York: Free Press, 1982.

Books on Assessment

Gangi, Jane. *Encountering Children's Literature—An Arts Approach.* Boston: Pearson, 2004.

Hart, Diane. *Authentic Assessment: A Handbook for Educators.* Menlo Park, CA: Addison Wesley, 1994. The subtitle cites the readers to whom the book is directed. It is clear, practical, modern in philosophy, and valuable to educators searching for an alternative to standardized tests and conventional evaluation.

Heller, Mary F. *Reading-Writing Connections: From Theory to Practice,* 2nd ed. White Plains, NY: Longman, 1995. Although this book is directed toward the classroom teacher seeking new methods of teaching the language arts, it is well worth reading by the teacher of creative drama. The author discusses journal writing, a technique that is of great value in any area of study. The subject of assessment is covered in view of the great diversity we now find in our classrooms.

Kieff, Judith E., and Irene M. Casbergue. *Playful Learning and Teaching.* Boston: Allyn and Bacon, 2000.

Levy, Jonathan. *Practical Education for the Unimaginable: Essays on Theatre and the Liberal Arts.* Charlottesville: New Plays, 2001.

Ravitch, Diane. *National Standards in American Education: A Citizen's Guide.* Washington, DC: Brookings, 1995. This book is both timely and readable. It is short but comprehensive in its handling of the many complex problems that plague American education in the 1990s.

A Sample Drama Workshop

The following study guide is included because of its excellence. Although it has been cut because of the length, I believe that the major points are clearly made: how to use the material in a dramatic context, how the material can be adjusted for different grade levels, and what metaphoric images the material may have for the students. In addition, the guide can help to lead students into an exploration of the meanings of animal and human traits in myths. The following study guide focuses on the Anansi story.

A Multicultural Drama Study Guide

By Professor Nancy Swortzell

Although this study guide has been designed for upper elementary, middle, and junior high school students, with simple modification of the ideas and experiences it also can be adapted for younger children. The aims are fourfold:

1. To stimulate students to become active participants with their teachers or leaders in exploring the multicultural themes inherent in the myths dramatized in *The Mischief Makers*[1] and in other trickster fables or myths.

---

[1]Lowell Swortzell, *The Mischief Makers* (Charlottesville, VA: New Plays, 1994).

2. To lead both students and teachers to reflect upon the *similarities* found in *diverse* cultural heroes through acting out roles and narratives.
3. To stimulate students in creating original contemporary multicultural myths and narratives through process drama.
4. To encourage and assist teachers in employing drama as a mode of learning.

The workshops are designed to take place following a theatrical performance or reading of *The Mischief Makers* or a fable of Anansi, Reynard, or Raven. Workshops may be conducted in a classroom, theatre, or recreational center. Teachers (leaders) and students (group members) are invited to examine cultural similarities as they enact issues and backgrounds inherent in the stories of the *Spider* (representing parts of Africa and the Caribbean worlds), the *Raven* (of the Northwest Pacific coast of the United States and Canada), and the *Fox* (from the cultures of Northern Europe).

Students can become aware of the ideas, traditions, art works, and social institutions of both their own culture and that of others. By being placed in the roles of both spectator and participant, students experience the center of the action. They empathize with the characters and issues, think about them, and subsequently make decisions that can alter their opinions and attitudes.

The Mischief Makers is a play that tells the stories of the three protagonists: the Raven, Anansi the Spider, and Reynard the Fox. In turn the stories they tell are acted out. Because the dramatic structure consists of three plays (or stories) within a play, the accompanying drama workshops stress conventions of narrative, story theatre, and dramatic action as they appear in the script. So, the following sessions offer participants the opportunity to become involved in all three forms.

The first sessions are devoted to *narrative* in which the storyteller supplies plot descriptions while the players mime the action. These activities are designed to encourage students to develop their own original narratives. Later workshops are devoted to the convention of *story theatre*, in which performers both speak directly to the audience in their own words as they describe their actions and feelings, and also deliver (sometimes even in the same speech) improvised dialogue in-role as the character they are playing. To facilitate this style, teachers can step into the role of a *narrator* who focuses the story as it moves from situation to situation. This method of performance freely combines sections shown in dramatic action with those that are purely descriptive. The conventions of *story theatre* are ideal for classroom and workshop use.

These two forms (*narrative* and *story theatre*) may be developed in brief scenes by the entire group or in smaller units.

First Drama Guide
Designed for Newcomers to Process Drama

These workshops are conducive to establishing a unified working group. Members introduce themselves and learn something about each other and about the nature of drama itself. Such sessions also initiate a different classroom atmosphere, one inviting a freedom to experiment and to play that is seldom possible during the normal school day. It is particularly important to note that when working with multicultural goals, youngsters must trust one another and develop attitudes that permit understanding of people who are different from themselves. Process drama allows opportunities for students to step into diverse roles and to subsequently reflect upon how they individually differ yet remain the same. They come to respect that we all possess equal but different talents and contributions. Diverse ideas, therefore, are considered, then put into action and reflected upon without respect to race, creed, or gender. An understanding of similarities and differences becomes immediate as stories are shared, improvised, and evaluated. Frequently, conclusions are deliberately left open-ended, to help make participants aware of the validity of diverse cultures in our society.

These first sessions include more theatre games than those to be found in later classes. Such workshops are intended to be ice-breakers. They give children opportunities to experience commitment to each other and to the content of the drama.

Goals:

1. To establish an atmosphere that provides the freedom to play while working as a group, in which individual students introduce themselves and learn about one another.
2. To initiate theatre games, improvisation, and subsequent reflection on the three stories dramatized in *The Mischief Makers.*
3. To introduce the Spider, Raven, and Fox as "tricksters."
4. To introduce the practice of *Narration.*

Materials:

1. An open space large enough for individual and group movement.
2. Colored markers for each student.
3. Three separate large-line drawings, about three feet square, of the Spider, the Raven, and the Fox.

Warm-up:

1. Form a circle seated either on the floor or chairs. Proceed counterclockwise with students calling out their first names.
2. Ask children to introduce themselves to the person both on their left and right sides. Make certain that they are secure with their immediate neighbors.
3. Explain that you are going to a Northwest Pacific Native American "potlatch." Briefly describe this kind of celebration. Demonstrate this theatre game by enacting the first sequence with the group:
   a. Clap hands, turning to the student to your left and saying, "Hello, Jane."
   b. Jane replies: "Hello, X."
   c. You reply, "I hear you are having a marvelous potlatch. May I bring my friend John? (student to your right)"

    d. Jane replies, "Yes, X, you may bring John to our celebration. Come in."

    e. Jane turns to her left. Claps hands and repeats: "I hear you are having a marvelous potlatch. May I bring my friends, X and John?"

4. This dialogue is repeated until all participants have been invited. If the group is exceptionally large, form two circles and play the game simultaneously. If memory fails a participant, the leader should encourage group coaching.

NOTE: The Potlatch game may be too challenging for very young children. If so, establish names and proceed to the first drama activity.

Beginning the Drama Activity

1. Ask students to review first names again, but this time by calling out their first names and the name of their favorite animal from *The Mischief Makers* or from another fable.

2. Put the three large-line drawings on the wall. Distribute colored flow pens to each participant and instruct students to write descriptive or characteristic adjectives about each animal. (This drama technique is called *Role on the Wall.*) Encourage children to contribute to the drawings. The pictures should be covered with descriptors. Review the portraits created for each animal, questioning the group along the following lines:

   • Why do you like this animal?

   • How do his actions influence other characters?

   • What does the animal do?

   • How is he clever?

   • In what ways is he different? In what ways the same?

   • What kind of trickster is he?

3. Establish groups of three and have each student choose one of the animals and discuss its characteristics (*animal imagery*). Instruct them to make a still picture (*tableaux*) of the scene in the play in which Reynard plays dead and traps both Anansi and the Raven. Each group will share its picture; after preparation, call "Freeze," and select a cluster to present its tableaux. You may wish to use an empty camera and call out "Freeze" as you pretend to take a picture of each presentation.

4. After seeing the pictures, question participants as follows:

   • Why did you recognize each animal?

   • How did each picture make you feel?

   • How do you think that the Spider and Raven might escape?

Explain that the Fox role appears in the writings of many cultures, not just in the numerous tales of Reynard, which are French in origin. This animal character also is found in Asian stories and fables. Read aloud or tell Lawrence Yep's adaptation of the classic Chinese tale, *The Ghost Fox.* (If the drama group would more readily experience multicultural similarities and differences through Korean culture, choose any of the animal stories found in Suzanne Crowder Han's collection, *Korean Folk and Fairy Tales.* In either case the drama process is the same.) Ask students how the characters in this story feel about the Fox as well as why this Fox is both the same and different from Reynard. Outline with the group three major scenes from the story and have three volunteers serve as *narrators* who link the episodes. *Improvise* the adaptation (either in mime or with dialogue) accompanied by a student's narration. As enrichment, question the class about the conclusion. Ask students to create other possible endings and enact their ideas for alternate endings. Discuss how roles and ideas were changed.

Extended Activities:

1. Ask students to research animals considered to be endangered species today. Improvise scenes that communicate ways to preserve these animals.
2. Briefly explain that the famous Russian director-actor Konstantin Stanislavsky developed a theory based upon the observation of animals in order to help actors create characters. He watched his cat for months until he could imitate its every movement and then continued to observe until he understood the motivations behind the animal's behavior. Ask children to observe their pets or visit a local pet store, or plan a field trip to a zoo where they can observe and draw their animal of choice. Ask group members to write stories reflecting the attitude of the animal. Encourage them to write in-role as the animal.

Second Drama Guide
For Participants with Some Drama Experience

Goals:

1. To examine the nature of tricks and tricksters through enacting animal images.
2. To **transform** animals into human beings.

Materials:

1. An open space with classroom chairs for participants.
2. Sheets of paper and markers.
3. Sheets of paper indicating animal roles

Warm-up:

1. Seat children in circle to establish the group.
2. If students do not know one another, choose a name game, perhaps from the First Drama Guide, and play until they are familiar with each other.
3. Walk behind students, tapping each on the shoulder and assigning each an animal: Spider, Raven, or Fox. If the group numbers fifteen, there will be five of each animal. Select a student to be "It." Place "It" in the center of the circle. Call out "Raven," whereupon all Ravens stand and run to exchange places, as

in playing Musical Chairs. When you call out "Animals of the forest, "everybody changes places. After the "It" calls an animal, he/she will try to sit in one of the vacated seats, leaving another player standing, who then becomes "It." The new "It" rapidly calls another animal and the game continues. Explain that the "It" tries to trick the group and the group to trick the "It."

4. Divide the group into pairs who stand apart holding hands at arm's length. Ask for volunteers or appoint a Fox and a Rabbit. Explain that the Fox will try to catch the Rabbit, who runs around the room trying to escape. To be safe, the Rabbit will run in between the outstretched arms (the rabbit hole). The student will face one player who forms the "hole" and takes hands. The person behind the Rabbit immediately becomes the new Rabbit and runs from the Fox. If the Fox tags the Rabbit before it reaches the safety of the hole, the Rabbit becomes the Fox.

Drama Activity:

1. After players are reseated, explain that there are different kinds of tricksters in the play *The Mischief Makers*, performed by three very different characters. In discussion, ask students to describe the differences in mischief making. Ask them to define what they mean by mischief, pranks, tricks, and magic. Make lists of examples on the chalkboard or on large sheets of paper with flow pens.

2. Explain that we can learn a great deal about human behavior, both physical and emotional, by observing animals. Write the following pairs of animals on paper and distribute. Duplicate pairs as necessary.
   cow and mosquito
   lion and mouse
   frog and dog
   fly and bear
   spider and pig
   turtle and rabbit
   spider and pig
   turtle and rabbit

3. Students decide which animal each will play, and then discuss the animal's qualities. As students work in pairs throughout the space, visit each group, asking them specific questions that relate to size, color, weight, activities, likes/dislikes, movement patterns, diet, intelligence, rhythm, and attitudes. Urge players to enact the *essence* of the animal, standing upright. Explain that plays frequently contain animal roles (*The Wizard of Oz, Peter Rabbit, Androcles and the Lion,* etc.). Actors in such plays are costumed to suggest animals but are usually played standing like human beings.

4. Ask participants to devise a story in which one animal in the pair tries to trick the other. Then put the story into action without speaking. Share these brief pantomimes. Bring the group together for questions and reflection.
   • What was the nature of the mischief?
   • How did the actors show this?

- Were the intentions or attitudes of the roles clear?
- How did you feel about the mischief?
- How did the animals remind you of human behavior?
- What activities, likes/dislikes, movement patterns, and attitudes do humans and animals share?

5. Explain that it is possible to learn a great deal about human behavior by observing animals. Understanding how animals think, behave, and feel has been studied not only by veterinarians and psychologists, but also by artists and actors. Frequently, we compare ourselves to animals. Have you ever described someone as "mousy" or as "timid as a rabbit"? Can you think of people's actions that have animal attributes? Invite students to discuss famous people who remind them of animals. Then begin the following improvisation.

6. In pairs, students repeat their pantomimes, as human beings using language. The leader travels from group to group helping participants to transform animal behavior into human behavior.

7. Share these short scenes, and subsequently reflect on them through questioning:
    - Was the tricking clear?
    - Could you feel animal characteristics in the human role?
    - How did the human roles make you feel?
    - Which human role was your favorite?
    - Does nationality or race change the behavior of animals?

Extended Activities:

- Listen to Saen Sans' *Carnival of Animals* with the class. Plan a movement session in which participants playing animals create their own carnival.
- Tell the story of Noah and the flood and devise the ritual of the animals boarding the ark. Using simple instruments (drums, recorders, cymbals) and animal sounds made by the students, create original marching music to accompany the boarding ritual.

Anansi the Spider

Goal:

To acknowledge the universality of the trickster role as a shared denominator of diverse cultural narratives.

Materials:

1. Large space without chairs.
2. Large drawing of a spider.
3. Various colors of flow pens for the group.

Theatre Game Warm-ups:

1. Divide the class into pairs, "A" and "B." Give two coins to each "A" group, telling them to balance one coin in the palm of each hand with arms fully extended. "A" faces "B," who will try to steal the coins without touching the partner. "A" is told to distract "B" by moving arms without closing fingers over the coins. The partners try to trick each other. Reverse roles.

2. In pairs, designate "A" and "B." "A" takes a simple object (ring, scarf, pen, pin, etc.) in one hand and faces "B." "A" verbally transforms the insignificant object into something of great value or beauty, enticing "B" to steal it. "B" tries to distract "A" through verbal tricks to steal the object. Reverse roles.

Drama Activity:

Storytelling in pairs. Seat students on the floor in pairs, "A" and "B," asking them to think of some trick or bit of mischief they have played or that was played upon them. After the pairs share their stories, form a circle and have "A" tell "B"s story. Remind students that the listener may add details or clarify situations. When several pairs have shared, combine two pairs and ask each group of four to select one story for the next activity.

Small group work. After selection, students improvise the sequence of events, assigning roles the way Anansi assigned them when he told his story in *The Mischief Makers.* Explain that participants are to improvise both action and dialogue and that they may have a narrator or storyteller if they wish.

Enactment of stories: role-play. Share these improvisations as a festival of pranks and tricks. To conclude, ask the group to reflect on the nature of the tricks. The following questions can be useful:

- How were some tricks similar? Dissimilar?
- Why were they fun?
- How did those who were tricked feel?
- What methods of tricking were used?
- Do you think tricks are the same for people of all nationalities?

Role on Wall. Explain that there are numerous Anansi stories that originated in Africa and later spread to Jamaica and even to Australia. Pre-draw a line-figure of a "friendly" spider and display it. Distribute flow pens and ask students to write words and phrases that characterize the spider's behavior and personality. It may be necessary to ask questions that increase the flow of ideas.

Reflection. To conclude, seat the class in a semi-circle around the drawing and read back their various ideas. Reflectively inquire if they think all races have these same characteristics.

Extended Activities:

1. Read (or preferably tell) the class the following adaptation.

"An Anansi Story from the West Indies"

Many years ago the Tiger was the king of the Forest. Every one knew that. In the evenings, around the fire, all the animals gathered to talk and laugh.

"Who's the strongest among us?" the Snake asked.

"Tiger, of course," replied the Dog. "When Tiger whispers, the trees listen; when he is angry, the trees tremble."

"And who is the weakest among us?" Snake wondered.

"Anansi, of course," shouted the Dog. "When he whispers, no one listens. When he shouts, everyone laughs."

Not long after this conversation, Tiger and Anansi happened to meet in a clearing in the forest. Anansi bowed low but the Tiger just looked at him.

"Good morning, Tiger," Anansi said. "I have a favor to ask."

"And what is it, Anansi?" the Tiger replied.

"We all know that you are the strongest among us. That is why so many things are named after you: Tiger lilies, Tiger moths, Tiger this and Tiger that. But nothing bears my name. NOTHING. Tiger, I ask that something be called after the weakest among us so that everybody will know my name, too."

"Well," thought the Tiger, "What would you like to bear your name?"

"Stories," the Spider instantly replied. "The stories we tell in the evenings, the stories about all the animals."

"Oh, no." Tiger shook his head. "I like those stories, too. They must be known as Tiger stories, not Anansi stories." Then he thought he would play a trick on Anansi so that all the animals would laugh at him and he would not bother the Tiger again. "Very well, I'll let the stories be named after you, if you do what I ask."

"I'll do anything," Anansi assured him.

"It's easy, really. Just bring Mr. Snake to me, but he must be alive and well."

"Tiger, I'll do exactly as you ask."

Then a great burst of laughter exploded throughout the forest because all the animals had been listening. And Tiger laughed loudest of them all, for how could a spider catch a snake? And as Anansi went home to make a plan to do this, he heard everyone laughing all along the way.

His first idea was to make a noose which would tighten as Mr. Snake crawled through. But when he tried this plan it did not work because the snake simply kept crawling—right through. His next scheme was to fill a deep hole with bananas that he knew Mr. Snake loved. But instead of falling into the hole as Anansi had hoped, Mr. Snake wrapped his tail around a tree trunk and lowered himself down to the bananas, ate them all, then lifted himself up and went on his merry way. Anansi was angry because he lost both the bananas and the snake.

Time was running out and none of his plans had worked. What could he do?

Then suddenly Mr. Snake came along and called to Anansi. "I'm angry with you, Anansi. For several days now, you have been trying to capture me."

"But you're too clever for me," Anansi replied. "All I wanted to do is prove that you are the longest animal in the forest. That's all." "But of course, I am. Just look at me." And at that, he began stretching himself to prove the point.

"Oh, you're long, all right. But not as long as this bamboo branch."

"Of course I am. Even longer. Put that bamboo branch down beside me and I'll show you."

Anansi did this, and stood, shaking his head. "No, Snake, you're not as long as this bamboo branch. Sorry."

Well, Mr. Snake could not bear to hear this and insisted that Anansi tie his tail to one end of the branch, which the spider promptly did. "Now if I stretch and stretch and s-t-r-e-t-c-h, you'll see I am longer. Tie me around the middle so I can't slip back."

Anansi was happy to oblige his request and Mr. Snake continued to stretch longer and longer along the bamboo branch. And just as he got to the end, Anansi tied his head.

Well, there he was, all tied up and ready to be delivered to the Tiger who, when he saw this strange sight, was truly amazed. This time there was no laughing from the other animals. As the Tiger accepted the Snake and unbound him, he said, "Anansi has proved not to be so weak, after all." And all the other animals applauded his cleverness.

Still surprised, the Tiger declared that no longer should they call them Tiger stories but Anansi stories, and from that day to this, this is what we call them.

Story Theatre

1. Analyze this story with the students by asking such questions as:
   - Why did the Tiger try to trick Anansi?
   - How did Anansi succeed in tricking the Snake?
   - Why was the Snake tricked by Anansi?
   - How is this Anansi similar to the Spider in *The Mischief Makers?*
2. Explain that a play has a beginning, middle, and end. Ask students what action occurred in each section. Write these in sequence on the board. Review the actions establishing for each unit:
   a) The roles required (who).
   b) The location (where).
   c) The action (what).
   d) The motivations (why).
3. Post these units of action on the board or wall like a scenario so students can refer to them.
4. Explain that while the format of story theatre may require a master narrator who introduces actions, it also is possible for the characters themselves to set the scene verbally, to describe their actions and feelings as they enact character. List the roles; students then select the role they wish to play. Leaders may find it helpful to play the narrator's role to ensure a fluidity of action.
5. Improvise each unit (beginning, middle, and end), reminding students to refer to the posted scenario, if necessary. Repeat improvisations, adding character detail and focusing the action. Change casts for subsequent improvisations offering more student opportunities to participate.

Glossary of Some Common Dramatic Terms

Many of the following terms will not be part of an elementary school child's vocabulary, but in the event that they come up in class discussion after seeing a play, the teacher will have brief definitions to share at his or her discretion.

Act. To perform or play a role; a division of a drama.

Actor. A person who performs in a play, who assumes the role of a character.

Adaptation. A play based on a story or novel rather than being an original plot.

Amateur. A person who engages in an art or a sport for love of it rather than for a livelihood.

Backstage. The area behind the stage, not visible to the audience.

Border lights. Overhead lighting at the front of the stage.

Box office. The office where tickets are sold, located either in or in front of the lobby.

Choreographer. A person who designs and directs a dance.

Choreography. The design for a dance; the written representation of the steps of dancing.

Climax. The highest point of interest, usually near the end of the play.

Comedy. A play that ends satisfactorily for the hero or heroine; it is entertaining and usually lively, as opposed to a tragedy.

Community theatre. Theatre organized and run by persons living in the community; actors generally perform for the enjoyment of the experience rather than as a profession.

Cue. The signal for an actor to speak or perform an action; usually a line spoken by another actor.

Curtain call. The return of the entire cast to the stage after the end of a performance, when the actors acknowledge applause.

Dénouement. The final unraveling of the plot of a play; the solution or outcome.

Dialogue. The lines of the play spoken by the actors.

Director. The person in charge; the one who gives directions to the actors and assumes ultimate responsibility for the production.

Double cast. To prepare two casts for a play, both of which will play the same number of performances.

Downstage. The front of the stage; the area nearest the audience.

Dramatist. Another name for a playwright.

Dramatization. The creation of a play from a story or poem.

Dramaturge. Assist the director and observe rehearsals.

Dress rehearsal. The final rehearsal or rehearsals of a play, when costumes are worn and all stage effects are completed.

Epilogue. A short scene or speech at the end of the play; not often found in modern plays.

Footlights. The row of lights across the front of the stage, on a level with the actors' feet.

Hero. The central male character in a play; a man distinguished for valor.

Heroine. The central female character in a play.

The house. The auditorium or seating area of a theatre.

Houselights. The auditorium lights, turned off or dimmed when the performance starts.

Intermission. A recess or temporary stopping of action, usually about halfway through a play.

Lines. The dialogue or words spoken by the actors.

Lobby. The foyer or hall at the front of a theatre.

Mounting. The scenery and costumes used to dress the production.

Musical. A theatrical production characterized by music, songs, dances, and often spectacular settings and costumes.

Performance. A representation before spectators; an entertainment.

Playwright. A person who writes plays.

Plot. The story.

Production. The total theatrical product, including the play, the acting, the direction, scenery, costumes, lighting, and special effects.

Professional theatre. Theatre in which actors and all other employees earn their living.

Prologue. An introduction to a play, usually spoken by one of the actors; occasionally employed in plays for children to orient the audience to the piece.

Prompter. The person who watches the script backstage during the performance of a play; he or she gives the lines to the actors if they forget.

Scenery. The large pieces (flats, backdrops, furniture, and so on) that are placed on the stage to represent the location.

Script. The manuscript or form in which the play is written; it contains the dialogue, stage directions, and time and place of each act and scene.

Side coaching. Encouraging and prompting actors from the sidelines.

Soliloquy. Lines in a play spoken by one character alone on the stage, in which his or her thoughts are revealed.

Sponsor. A person or an organization engaging a theatrical company.

Spotlight. A strong beam of light used to illuminate a particular person or area of the stage.

Stage manager. The person in charge backstage; he or she helps the director during rehearsals and then takes charge backstage when the play is given.

Straight play. A drama without music or dance.

Subplot. A plot subordinate to the principal plot.

Tableau or tableaux. A picture or scene composed of silent, motionless actors, which suggests a situation and characters involved in it. A popular device for all age levels to stimulate the imagination; often called "statues."

Theme. A topic or subject developed in a play; the subject on which the plot is based.

Thrust stage. A stage or platform that extends into the auditorium, with the audience seated on three sides.

Touring company. A company of actors who take their show on the road, as opposed to a resident company.

Tragedy. A play that ends with the defeat or death of the main character; it is based on a serious theme or conflict, as opposed to a comedy.

Understudy. The actor who learns the part of another actor playing a major role; he or she is ready to go onstage in the unexpected absence of the original actor.

Upstage. The rear of the stage; the area farthest from the audience.

Villain. A character who commits a crime; the opponent of the hero or heroine.

Wings. The side areas of the stage, out of view of the audience; the area where the actors wait for their entrances.

Selected Bibliography

Creative Drama

AVITAL, SAMUEL. *Mime and Beyond: The Silent Outcry*. Studio City, CA: Players Press, 1990. Exercises and selected writings from contemporary mimes; geared toward the older student and the young professional actor. There is also valuable material for the teacher who is particularly interested in developing skill in this art form.

———. *Mime Workbook*. Studio City, CA: Players Press, 1995. Material appropriate for beginning and intermediate students.

BOOTH, DAVID. *Story Drama*. York, ME: Stenhouse, 1998. The author uses story as a basis for drama activities, suited to grades K-8.

BRUNER, JEROME. *Actual Minds, Possible Worlds*. Cambridge, MA: Harvard University Press, 1986. An excellent and well-known book with particular emphasis on the adult in play interaction. Pertinent to the interests of the drama teacher and the classroom teacher.

BURGER, ISABEL B. *Creative Drama in Religious Education*. Wilton, CT: Morehouse-Barlow, 1976. One of the few books on the use of creative dramatics in religious education. Burger's years of successful teaching make this a practical and authoritative text for leaders in this field.

CARUSO, SANDRA, AND SUSAN KOSOFF. *The Young Actor's Book of Improvisation*. Westport, CT: Heinemann, 1998. Divided into two volumes, arranged so that teachers can select activities most appropriate to the age of the students. Selections range from fairy tales to contemporary literature.

CHEIFETZ, DAN. *Theatre in My Head*. Boston: Little, Brown, 1971. Describes an experimental workshop in creative drama conducted by the author in an inner-city New York church. As he reports his successes and failures, Cheifetz communicates the need to look *into,* not merely *at,* the child.

CRESCI, MAUREEN MCCURRY. *Creative Dramatics for Children*. Glenview, IL: Good Year Books, 1989. A practical resource book for young children. Group imagery and movement and relaxation chapters are particularly effective.

CSIKSZENTMIHALYI, MIHALY. *Changing the World: A Framework for the Study of Creativity*. Westport, CT: Praeger, 1994. A new work by a well-known scholar in the areas of play, psychology, and education. Applicable to classes in drama and education.

FOX, MEM. *Teaching Drama to Young Children*. Portsmouth, NH: Heinemann, 1987. A simple, highly readable, and sensible book for the teacher of the very young. It is one of the few in the field addressed to the needs and interests of this level.

FURMAN, LOU. *Creative Drama Handbook and Role Play Guide.* Denver: Pioneer Drama Service, 1990. An excellent handbook for teachers and leaders of creative drama in community centers and camps. It is brief but not superficial, clear and succinct in style. What distinguishes it from other texts in the field is the emphasis on role play. Recommended.

GOODWILLIE, BARBARA. *Breaking Through: Drama Strategies for Ten's to Fifteen's.* Charlottesville, VA: New Plays, 1986. Simply written with humor and sympathy. Highly recommended for teachers of upper grades and junior high school students.

HAYES, JENNIFER, AND DOROTHY SCHINDEL. *Pioneer Journeys: Drama in Museum Education.* Charlottesville, VA: New Plays, 1994. The first book of its kind, a *must* for drama and classroom teachers interested in the wealth of ideas to be found in the local museum. It is practical, imaginative, and accessible.

HEINIG, RUTH. *Creative Drama for Kindergarten Through Grade 3.* Englewood Cliffs, NJ: Prentice Hall, 1987.

——. *Creative Drama Resource Book for Grades 4 through 6.* Englewood Cliffs, N.J.: Prentice Hall, 1987. These two books are addressed to the classroom teacher who has no background in drama but is interested in using it. Practical and clearly written by an experienced and respected leader in the field.

——. *Creative Drama for the Classroom Teacher,* 4th ed. Englewood Cliffs, NJ: Prentice Hall, 1993. The latest version of a textbook originally written by two experienced teachers. Pantomime, improvisation, songs, and games are among the activities suggested. They are arranged to guide the classroom teacher through simple to more advanced techniques, and each chapter has suggestions and assignments for the college student.

——. *Improvisation with Favorite Tales.* Portsmouth, NH: Heinemann, 1992. This book goes beyond the story line with suggestions for exploring character and themes in the narrative. A practical and imaginative text for the classroom teacher.

HODGSON, JOHN, AND ERNEST RICHARDS. *Improvisation.* New York: Grove Press, 1979. Not directed exclusively to work with children. The aim is to use two elements from everyday life: spontaneous response to unexpected situations and the employment of this response in controlled conditions. Exercises are given.

JOHANSEN, MILA. *Theatre Games for Drama Teachers, Classroom Teachers, and Directors.* Studio City, CA: Players Press, 1994. Although there are several popular books on theatre games, this one seems particularly appropriate for the classroom and the nonprofessional group.

KASE-COOPER, JUDITH. *The Creative Drama Book: Three Approaches.* New Orleans: Anchorage Press, 1988. The author gives three approaches to the subject of creative drama in a book that is different from all the other texts in the field. Written by an experienced and well-known leader, it should be of interest to specialists and generalists. Recommended reading for persons working in schools, recreation programs, and therapeutic settings.

KEINER, LENORE. *The Creative Classroom.* Westport, CT: Heinemann, 1993. Offers simple strategies for stimulating creativity in grades K-6. Simply and clearly written, the text is accessible to the beginner as well as useful to the experienced teacher.

KEYSELL, PAT. *Mime Themes and Motifs.* Boston: Plays, 1980. This little paperback is divided into three parts. The first deals with beginning activities for children from five to seven; the second, with development for seven- to nine-year-olds; and the third, application for those from nine to twelve. Starting with real objects, the author progresses to mime. She works for awareness of size, weight, shape, and the use of space. Although the material is organized according to age levels, it also follows a logical progression from simple to complicated and is therefore useful on any level.

KRAUS, JOANNA HALPERT. *Sound and Motion Stories.* Charlottesville, VA: New Plays, 1971. Describes how sounds and actions can be used to capture attention to stimulate the imagination of younger children. The reader can learn from the author's suggestions on how to use other material in this way. Not a textbook, but recommended for special education teachers.

LEE, ALISON. *A Handbook of Creative Dance and Drama.* Westport, CT: Heinemann, 1992. One of the few books that focuses on dance and drama for the elementary classroom. An audiotape of the music and sounds for exercises in the book is also available.

McCASLIN, NELLIE, ed. *Children and Drama.* 3rd ed. Studio City, CA: Players Press, 1999. A collection of essays on creative drama written by twenty experts in the field. A variety of viewpoints and methodologies are represented. Of greater interest to the experienced teacher than to the beginner.

——. *Creative Drama in the Intermediate Grades.* Studio City, CA: Players Press, 1987.

——. *Creative Drama in the Primary Grades.* Studio City, CA: Players Press, 1987. Two books on creative drama, written specifically for the classroom teacher. Theory and lesson plans are combined with scope and sequence of objectives in mind.

MERRION, MARGARET, AND JANET RUBIN. *Creative Approaches to Elementary Education.* Westport, CT: Heinemann, 1996. Contains activities and exercises that combine creative drama and music with different areas of the curriculum. Designed for elementary schools.

NOBLEMAN, ROBERTA. *Fifty Projects for Creative Dramatics.* Charlottesville, VA: New Plays, 1986. An excellent source for activities that can be used by classroom teachers and recreation leaders. All activities have been tried out and used successfully by the author, an experienced teacher.

——. *Using Creative Drama Outside the Classroom.* Charlottesville, VA: New Plays, 1974. Describes how creative drama can be taught successfully in nontraditional spaces and places. As valuable for the teacher as for the leader in community and camp situations.

PEREIRA, NANCY. *Creative Dramatics in the Library.* Charlottesville, VA: New Plays, 1974. Offers suggestions for starting points, games, use of time and space, and handling of groups, visual aids, and culminating activities. Although the content is not substantially different from other books on the subject, the neighborhood library is a nontraditional location for dramatic activities.

POLSKY, MILTON. *Let's Improvise!* New York: Applause, 1998. A popular book filled with short and lively suggestions for improvisations. The book can be used in class and in after-school interest groups.

——. *Improvisation Workshop Handbook.* Studio City: Players Press, 2001. The author shares a wealth of suggestions for improvisation from his own years of experience in classrooms on every level. He places particular emphasis on teamwork for both artistic and social goals.

ROSENBERG, HELANE. *Creative Drama and Imagination: Transforming Ideas into Action.* New York: Holt, Rinehart, and Winston, 1987. The subtitle describes the thrust of this book by a well-known author. Beginning with a brief history of the field, she goes into imagery, the Rutgers method, drama structures, and "starters." The book was several years in the making and should be of interest to teachers and drama leaders.

SALISBURY, BARBARA. *Theatre Arts in the Elementary School.* 2 vols.: K–3, 4–6. 2nd. ed. New Orleans: Anchorage Press, 1994. Designed for the classroom teacher who is required to teach creative drama along with the other arts but has had little or no preparation for it. In each book the guidelines are clear, and the exercises and activities are practical and on the level for which it was intended. Each is a most useful and simple text by an expert in the field.

SCHWARTZ, DOROTHY, AND DOROTHY ALDRICH, eds. *Give Them Roots and Wings,* 2nd ed. New Orleans: Anchorage Press, 1987. A guide to drama in the elementary school, prepared by leaders in the field and edited by Dorothy Schwartz and Dorothy Aldrich as co-chairs of a project for the Children's Theatre Association. Published in workbook form, it offers the classroom teacher goals and dramatic activities with checklists for rating children's development. Usable and attractively illustrated.

SIKS, GERALDINE BRAIN. *Drama with Children,* 2nd ed. New York: Harper & Row, 1983. This book by a well-known creative drama leader and author of other texts in the field is of interest to the more experienced teacher or graduate student. It is divided into three parts: the philosophy of drama, the teaching of drama, and individual experiences and uses of drama. In this edition the author expands on what she calls the "process-concept structure approach." Includes a selected bibliography and a few short plays.

SLADE, PETER. *Child Drama.* London: University of London Press, 1954. Written by an expert in children's dramatics in England, this landmark text presents a philosophy and way of working. It is detailed and informative and should be of interest to all leaders and teachers of creative dramatics. The author takes an unequivocal stand against using children in public performances.

——. *An Introduction to Child Drama.* London: Hodder and Stoughton, 1976. All the fundamental principles of Slade's methods are here. Children, if unhampered by adult imposition, can find self-expression and reach toward full human development. The book is simply written, short, and to the point. Highly recommended for the beginner.

SPOLIN, VIOLA. *Improvisation for the Theatre: A Handbook of Technical and Directing Techniques.* Evanston, IL: Northwestern University Press, 1963. A comprehensive handbook of teaching and directing techniques, not specifically designed for use with children but nevertheless appropriate and useful to the more experienced teacher. Contains a variety of exercises and theatre games.

——. *Theatre Games for the Classroom.* Evanston, IL: Northwestern University Press, 1987. An adaptation of Spolin's popular handbook for adult actors, *Improvisation for the Theatre.* This book, however, is written to meet the needs of the classroom teacher who is required to teach drama and knows little about it or how to present it to children.

STERNBERG, PATRICIA, AND ANTONINA GARCIA. *Sociodrama: Who's in Your Shoes?* Westport, CT: Praeger, 1994. A timely text on a subject of particular interest to teachers and leaders of drama programs. The authors are well known and highly respected in a field about which little has been written for the classroom teacher.

STRAUSS, JOYCE. *Imagine That! Exploring Make-Believe.* New York: Human Sciences Press, 1985. Less well known than most creative drama books, but contains some good material that leaders should find useful. The title gives an idea of the spirit that prevails.

SWARTZ, LARRY. *Dramathemes: A Practical Guide for Teaching Drama.* Portsmouth, NH: Heinemann, 1995. This recently revised textbook uses literary themes to structure dramatic activity. It covers humor, mystery, folklore, animal stories, the past and future, and multiculturalism. An excellent resource.

SWORTZELL, LOWELL. *Cinderella: The World's Favorite Fairy Tale,* Charlottesville: New Plays, Inc., 1995. Three plays from three different cultures.

VAN ALLSBURG, CHRIS. *The Mysteries of Harris Burdick.* Boston: Houghton Mifflin, 1984. An excellent book for work on improvision. Photographs of paintings with evocative captions challenge the imagination.

WAKE YOUR WISHES UP! Wolf Trap Institute for Early Learning Through the Arts. Vienna, VA: U.S. Department of Health and Human Services, 1985. A creative drama handbook developed by experts in the field for teachers of preschool-age children. Much of the material could be used on upper levels. A good resource from a strong program.

WARD, WINIFRED. *Playmaking with Children.* New York: Appleton-Century-Crofts, 1957. A landmark textbook by a distinguished leader. It is arranged both as to age levels and use, including dramatics in school, recreation, religious education, and therapy. Highly readable; valuable both for the beginning and the experienced teacher.

——. *Stories to Dramatize*. New Orleans: Anchorage Press, 1986. A collection with a rich variety of stories and some poems for use in school and recreation groups. Arranged for children on various age levels (from six to fourteen); contains material that the author tested and found rewarding in her many years of teaching.

WATTS, IRENE N. *Making Stories*. Portsmouth, NH: Heinemann, 1992. The author offers encouragement to students in making up and dramatizing original stories. Ideas come from newspapers, objects, letters, folk tales, people, and problems.

WAY, BRIAN. *Development Through Drama*. Atlantic Highlands, NJ: Humanities Press, 1990. The development of the whole child is the topic of this book, directed particularly to teachers of older children. Many practical exercises in improvisational drama are included. Highly recommended.

WILDER, ROSILYN. *A Space Where Anything Can Happen: Creative Drama in the Middle School*. Charlottesville, VA: New Plays, 1977. The author brings a wealth of experience to this book, directed to the teacher of older children. Challenges, projects, descriptions of her own classes and students, discipline, and clear guidelines for leading modern youngsters in creative work are the most valuable aspects.

Play

BARRAGER, PAMELA. *Spiritual Understanding through Creative Drama*. Valley Forge, PA: Judson Press, 1981. The author's specialization in religious drama gives her the background necessary for the approach used in this book. Recommended particularly for teachers in parochial schools and religious education programs.

BETTELHEIM, BRUNO. *The Uses of Enchantment: The Meaning and Importance of Fairy Tales*. New York: Knopf, 1976. This landmark book validated the fairy tale, thus giving teachers of younger children the confidence to use these popular, age-old stories in drama classes. Children love them, and teachers can see their value psychologically as well as dramatically.

BLATNER, ADAM, AND ALLEE BLATNER. *The Art of Play: Helping Adults Reclaim Imagination and Spontaneity*, rev. ed. New York: Brunner/Mazel, 1997. An excellent book for parents, teachers, and community program leaders in the arts. Written by specialists, it is readable and interesting. Recommended to both the experienced and inexperienced teacher.

GARVEY, CATHERINE. *Play*. Cambridge, MA: Harvard University Press, 1990. A recent book on play, written by a respected scholar and recommended to teachers and others interested in and responsible for children.

GROOS, KARL. *The Play of Animals*. New York: Arno Press, 1976. This classic was first published in 1898. Groos is still considered an important scholar and scientist. This book provides a detailed and comprehensive classification of the play of animals from an instinctive point of view. Recommended for teachers who are particularly interested in the phenomenon of play.

HARTLEY, RUTH, LAWRENCE FRANK, AND ROBERT GOLDENSON. *The Complete Book of Children's Play*. New York: Cromwell, 1975. A book of particular interest to teachers of younger children. Readable and clear, it has held its place in the forefront of textbooks on child behavior.

HENIG, RUTH BEALL. *Improvisation with Favorite Tales*. Portsmouth, NH: Heinemann, 1992. An experienced creative drama specialist offers valuable help to inexperienced teachers in the use of literature for improvisation. Recommended.

HUIZINGA, JOHAN. *Homo Ludens: A Study of the Play Element in Culture.* Boston: Beacon Press, 1950. A classic text for those interested in psychology, philosophy, and drama. A must for creative drama leaders, who will see the relationship of play to all aspects of life and as necessary for full human development.

JOHNSON, JAMES E., JAMES F. CHRISTIE, AND THOMAS D. YAWKEY. *Play and Early Childhood Development,* 2nd ed. New York: Longman, 1998. Highly praised as a practical guide to the study of play in child development. Personality development, use of materials, observation, and many other topics are included.

KIEFF, JUDITH E., AND RENEE M. CABERGUE. *Playful Learning and Teaching.* Boston: Allyn and Bacon, 2000. This is a valuable resource and a reader-friendly book for teachers. The authors show the relationship of play to learning and how it can be integrated into the preschool and primary school programs.

KOSTE, VIRGINIA GLASGOW. *Dramatic Play in Childhood: Rehearsal for Life.* Portsmouth, NH: Heinemann, 1995. A delightful collection of observations made by the author in the study of the dramatic play of young children. In keeping with the spirit of her study, she deliberately eschews scholarly writing. Highly recommended for teachers of the young, but enjoyable reading for everyone.

LOWENFELD, MARGARET. *Play in Childhood.* New York: Cambridge University Press, 1991. A classic book written more than a hundred years ago by an American educator, aimed at the teacher and highly readable. Still good; recommended.

MEARNS, HUGHES. *Creative Power: The Education of Youth in the Creative Arts,* 2nd rev. ed. New York: Dover, 1958. An inspiring book written during the height of the progressive education movement. Out of print for a number of years, it was reprinted nearly forty years ago and is to be found on the reading lists of all teachers of the arts. Simple and sound.

NACHMANOVITCH, STEPHEN. *Free Play: Art.* New York: Putnam, 1990. *Free Play* is that exceptional book which combines philosophy and practical guidance to make use of our resources of creativity and play. An excellent resource for artists and teachers of every age level who use improvisation as a technique.

OPIE, IONA, AND PETER OPIE. *I Saw Esau.* Cambridge, MA: Candlewick Press, 1992. The most recent book by well-known writers about the traditional culture of childhood. Not a textbook, not literature, but deserving of recognition, with illustrations by Maurice Sendak.

PIAGET, JEAN. *Plays, Dreams, and Imitations in Childhood.* New York: Norton, 1962. Probably our most respected and best-known educator, Piaget describes the value of play and of imitation in the development of the human being. His concept of five developmental stages gives teachers of creative drama more than a grid; it helps us understand the materials to use and the responses to expect at each stage.

SCHECHNER, RICHARD, AND MADY SCHUMAN. *Ritual, Play, and Performance.* New York: Seabury Press, 1976. Richard Schechner's interest in ritual has led him into an analysis of play and its relationship to theatre. Schechner is one of the best-known analysts of the subject. Recommended to teachers of older and adult students.

SINGER, J. L. *The Child's World of Make-Believe: Experimental Studies of Imaginative Play.* New York: Academic Press, 1973. Written by a well-known expert in the field, this work speaks to teachers and therapists.

THISTLE, LOUISE. *Dramatizing Mother Goose: Introducing Students to Classic Literature Through Drama.* North Stratford, NH: Smith and Kraus, 1997. Described as "the teacher's guide to play acting in the classroom," this book is designed for preschool and primary grades. The author uses improvisation to develop children's language skills and an appreciation of literature, then develops the lines of nursery rhymes into plays. A good book by an experienced teacher.

TORRANCE, PAUL. *Encouraging Creativity in the Classroom.* Dubuque, IA: Brown, 1970. Torrance is a well-known name among educators. He writes with clarity and enthusiasm as he describes his research into the subject. Still recommended reading.

VYGOTSKY, LEV. "The Role of Play in Development." *Mind in Society.* Cambridge, MA: Harvard University Press, 1978. The author believes education to be a combination of imitation and instruction. Imitation and play are necessary to effective communication and social development.

Theatre for Children

BEDARD, ROGER, ed. *Spotlight on the Child.* Westport, CT: Greenwood Press, 1990. Essays by authorities in the field of children's theatre. Pioneering theatres and persons responsible for them are included in this different approach to the subject.

BREEN, ROBERT. *Chamber Theatre.* Evanston, IL: Caxton, 1986. The originator of chamber theatre describes the technique clearly and simply. Although it is not practiced widely, chamber theatre is still a good way of handling literary material that is not written in dramatic form.

CHAPMAN, GERALD. *Teaching Young Playwrights.* Portsmouth, NH: Heinemann, 1991. An important book by the organizer of the Young Playwrights Festival, and an essential guide for teachers interested in helping students write plays. The author describes his method, which includes improvisation, individual and collaborative writing, and the analysis of this process.

COREY, ORLIN. *Theatre for Children—Kids' Stuff or Theatre?* Anchorage, KY: Anchorage Press, 1974. A short collection of essays by an author who knows the field well and writes with honesty and conviction.

DAVIS, JED, AND MARY JANE EVANS. *Theatre for Children and Youth,* rev. ed. New Orleans: Anchorage Press, 1987. Written by two lifelong practitioners of theatre for children. A handsome text-book, covering all major areas of the subject.

GOLDBERG, MOSES. *Children's Theatre: A Philosophy and a Method.* Englewood Cliffs, NJ: Prentice Hall, 1974. One of the best books on the subject. Written by a professional children's theatre producer with years of experience behind him, it is an invaluable college text that is now out of print but still available.

HEALY, DATY. *Dress the Show: A Basic Costume Book.* Charlottesville, VA: New Plays, 1976. An excellent resource for the classroom teacher working on a limited budget with limited time. A practical, simple book, for teachers faced with costuming a play, illustrated by the author.

KORTY, CAROL. *Writing Your Own Plays: Creating, Adapting, Improvising.* New York: Scribner, 1986. An excellent guide for young people writing original plays.

LEVY, JONATHAN. *A Theatre of the Imagination.* Charolottesville, VA: New Plays, 1986. A splendid collection of essays on children's theater.

McCASLIN, NELLIE. *Children's Theatre in the United States: A History,* 2nd ed. Studio City, CA: Players Press, 1997. The only history of the children's theatre movement in this country. Written twenty-five years after the first edition, this book brings the material up to date.

——. *Historical Guide to Children's Theatre in America.* Westport, CT.: Greenwood Press, 1987. A reference book designed for library use. It contains information on children's theatre and profiles all known children's theatres past and present that have been in existence for at least five years and have given at least fifty performances a year.

——. *Shows on a Shoestring: A Simple Guide to Amateur Productions.* Charlottesville, VA: New Plays, 1989. This book falls somewhere between creative drama and children's theatre. It offers suggestions to older children about preparing shows of various kinds for fun, street fairs, community events, and so on. Short plays, mime, fashion shows, pet shows, puppet shows, and clowning are included.

WAY, BRIAN. *Audience Participation: Theatre for Young People.* Boston: Baker's Plays, 1981. The only thorough book on the subject. It lists goals and values and describes in detail the method devised by the author.

WHITTON, PAT HALE, ed. *Participation Theatre for Young Audiences.* Charlottesville, VA: New Plays, 1972. A collection of articles by directors who have used audience participation.

WOOD, DAVID, AND JANET GRANT. *Theatre for Children: A Guide to Writing, Adapting, Directing, and Acting.* London: Faber and Faber, 1997. This is the first book on children's theatre to be published in nearly two decades and is well worth the consideration of instructors dealing with this branch of theatre. It is practical and clearly written by experienced leaders in the field.

Drama-in-Education

BISSINGER, KRISTEN, AND NANCY RENFRO. *Leap into Learning: Curriculum Taught Through Creative Dramatics and Dance.* Photographs by Anne Jackson. Charlottesville, VA: New Plays, 1990. A recent book written by a teacher of dance and a puppeteer. Highly recommended for teachers in the elementary grades.

BOAL, AUGUSTO. *Games for Actors and Non-Actors.* London: Routledge, 1992. A popular book by the Brazilian theatre director, in which theatre is used to confront social problems as well as educate the actor. Both this book and Boal's earlier *Theatre of the Oppressed* are widely used on the high school and college level.

BOLTON, GARVIN. *Acting in Classroom Drama.* Portland: Calendar Islands Publishers, 1992. A book by a well-known educator, highly recommended for drama teachers in upper schools.

——. *Drama as Education: An Argument for Placing Drama at the Centre of the Curriculum.* London: Longman, 1984. A theoretical and practical book by one of England's most respected leaders.

——. *Towards a Theory of Drama in Education.* London: Longman, 1979. A theoretical treatment of the subject, written by one of England's outstanding drama educators. Of greatest interest to the specialist or the experienced classroom teacher.

BOOTH, DAVID, AND ALISTAIR MARTIN-SMITH. *Re-Cognizing Richard Courtney: Selected Writings on Drama and Education.* Markham, Ontario: Pembroke. 1988. A valuable collection of the writings of Richard Courtney, arguably the most prolific scholar in the field. An excellent resource for graduate students working in areas across the curriculum.

CAMPBELL, LINDA, BRUCE CAMPBELL, AND DEE DICKINSON. *Teaching and Learning Through Multiple Intelligences.* Needham Heights, MA: Allyn and Bacon, 1996. Another textbook on multiple intelligences, a subject that has intrigued American teachers since the publication of Howard Gardner's *Frames of Mind* in 1983.

CECIL, NANCY LEE, AND PHYLLIS LAURITZEN. *Literacy and the Arts for the Integrated Classroom.* White Plains, NY: Longman, 1994. A short, clear, and practical book of equal interest and value to both the field of education and that of the arts.

CHARTERS, JILL, AND ANNE GATELY. *Drama Anytime.* Portsmouth, NH: Heinemann, 1986. *Drama Anytime* explores the place of drama in the primary curriculum and provides guidelines for planning a variety of activities in movement, role play, improvisation, and performance. A practical short handbook for the classroom teacher.

COURTNEY, RICHARD. *Play, Drama and Thought: The Intellectual Background to Education,* 3rd ed. New York: Drama Book Specialists, 1974. Many useful sections in this publication are directed toward the philosophy and practice of drama in the school.

CULLUM, ALBERT. *Aesop in the Afternoon.* New York: Citation, 1972. A most usable collection of Aesop's fables, which can be played creatively by children of all ages.

——. *Shake Hands with Shakespeare: Eight Plays for Elementary Schools.* New York: Citation, 1968. Eight of Shakespeare's plays, adapted for children. The results are filled with action and are relatively simple to produce. They do require time to prepare but could also be improvised, if desired. The value of using Shakespeare is the richness of the language, a further recommendation for this text.

DAVIES, GEOFF. *Practical Primary Drama.* London: Heinemann, 1985. A short, useful text for the generalist. It contains suggestions on how to prepare and conduct drama sessions, particularly in schools where space and time are limited. Ideas for lessons are included.

FRASER, DIANE LYNCH. *Playdancing.* Princeton: Princeton Book Company, 1991. A small volume filled with detailed lesson plans to be incorporated into the general curriculum. Includes suggestions for open-ended questions to encourage creativity.

——. *A Model Drama/Theatre Curriculum: Philosophy, Goals, and Objectives.* New Orleans: Anchorage Press. 1996. This brief spiral-bound publication offers guidance to teachers developing programs based on the individual needs of the learners (K–12). It provides a rationale for educating students in the theatre arts and ways of building a series of sequential learning experiences.

GANGI, JANE. *Encountering Children's Literature: An Arts Approach.* Boston: Allyn and Bacon, 2004. If a teacher could have only one book, this one would provide the educational philosophy, the material, and the resources needed. A readable and comprehensive text and bibliographies.

GOLDBERG, MERRYL. *Arts and Learning: An Integrated Approach to Teaching and Learning in Multicultural and Multilingual Settings.* New York: Longman, Inc., 1997. A must-read text for teachers in the elementary grades. The author believes that the arts should not be kept separate from education in other areas, although she agrees that learning about the arts is important. Discussion and description of lessons are given equal treatment in all art forms.

GREEN, HARRIET H., AND SUE MARTIN. *Sprouts.* Carthage, IL: Good Apple, 1981. An amply illustrated collection of ideas for use with younger children. Highly recommended.

HALE, PATRICIA, AND TRISH LINDBERG. *Children's Writings: Process to Performance.* Charlottesville, VA: New Plays, 1997. Different from the other books on playwriting by children. These authors encourage writing of all kinds: poems, stories, plays, anecdotes. The style is lively, the ideas are fresh, and the text is easy to follow. Highly recommended to elementary school teachers.

HALL, MARY ANN, AND PAT HALE. *Capture Them with Magic.* Charlottesville, VA: New Plays, 1982. A wonderful and useful collection of ideas to help kindergarten and primary school teachers enliven classes in language arts and science, encourage reading, and improve self-esteem. Described by the authors as "real life" lessons, the suggestions deal with the magic of everyday experiences and activities.

HASEMAN, BRAD, AND JOHN O'TOOLE. *Dramawise.* Richmond, Victoria: Heinemann Educational Books Australia, 1987. An extremely helpful and clear how-to book on understanding the construction and writing of a play with young people.

HEATHCOTE, DOROTHY, AND GAVIN BOLTON. *Drama for Learning.* Portsmouth, NH: Heinemann, 1995. "The mantle of the expert" is explained in the presentation of problems, which students and teachers explore using knowledge of their own and the discoveries they make along the way.

JACKSON, TONY. *Learning Through Theatre: New Perspectives on Theatre in Education.* London: Routledge, 1993. Revised and updated to take account of recent developments in the methods and practice of TIE, with chapters written by experts in the field.

KASE-COOPER, JUDITH. *Children's Theatre: Creative Drama and Learning.* Lanham, MD: University Press of America, 1986.

——. *Creative Drama in a Developmental Context.* Lanham, MD: University Press of America, 1985.

——. *Drama as a Meaning Maker.* Lanham, MD: University Press of America, 1989. These three books contain the papers and responses generated by symposia sponsored by the Children's Theatre Association of America (now the American Alliance for Theatre and Education). Multiculturalism is one of the themes presented in the third book.

KORTY, CAROL. *Writing Your Own Plays: Creating, Adapting, Improvising.* New York: Scribners, 1986. A well-known children's playwright shares her experience with both beginners and classroom teachers who seek help. Still an excellent resource.

LANDALF, HELEN. *Moving the Earth: Teaching Earth Science Through Movement for Grades 3–6.* Lyme, NH: Smith and Kraus, 1997. A simple but carefully organized textbook for the classroom teacher to use in teaching science topics, with extended activities involving art forms. Music and movement enrich the learning.

LANDY, ROBERT J. *A Handbook of Educational Drama and Theatre.* Westport, CT: Greenwood Press, 1982. A book based on New York University's Sunrise Semester, in which the various uses of drama and theatre currently found in schools and communities are described. The author describes interviews with experts in all the fields covered.

MCCASLIN, NELLIE. *Children and Drama,* 3rd ed. Studio City, CA: Players Press, 1999. The third edition of a collection of essays written by leaders in England, Canada, Australia, and the United States. It is appropriate in either drama-in-education or theatre for young people.

MEARNS, HUGHES. *Creative Power: The Education of Youth in the Creative Arts,* 2nd rev. ed. New York: Dover, 1958. This classic textbook by a gifted educator offers a philosophy of education in the creative arts, along with techniques with which to implement it. Long out of print, it was republished in paperback at the instigation of the Children's Theatre Association of America, a strong supporter of Mearns's views.

MOFFETT, JAMES. *Student-Centered Language Arts, K–13,* 4th ed. Portsmouth, NH: Boynton/Cook, 1991. The latest edition of a book originally written by two well-known educators; an argument for the use of drama in language learning and comprehension.

NEELANDS, JONATHAN. *Beginning Drama: 11–14.* Portland: Calendar Islands, 1998. A good choice for teachers of middle school and high school drama.

——. *Making Sense of Drama.* London: Heinemann, 1985. A good resource for teachers of all grades. Shows how drama can enhance all subject areas across the curriculum. Recommended.

OLSTER, FREDI, AND RICK HAMILTON. *Discovering Shakespeare (A Midsummer Night's Dream, Romeo and Juliet,* and *The Taming of the Shrew).* Three Workbooks for Students and Teachers. North Stratford, NH: Smith and Kraus, 1995. Three separate workbooks appropriate for grade 7 and up. Information on stage directions and a translation into the vernacular make the plays accessible to children and useful to teachers.

O'NEILL, CECILY. *Drama Worlds: A Framework for Process Drama.* Portsmouth, NH: Heinemann, 1995. Explains and examines what O'Neill calls "process drama." She includes examples of her approach, showing strategies. Clear and accessible; highly recommended to classroom teachers.

O'NEILL, CECILY, AND ALAN LAMBERT. *Drama Structures: A Practical Handbook for Teachers.* London: Heinemann, 1982. The subtitle describes the book's intent, which is how to teach drama in the classroom. Structures show how to take themes and use them in small group work and how to build drama across the curriculum. An excellent textbook for college students planning to teach.

PIAGET, JEAN. *Play, Dreams, and Imitation in Childhood.* New York: Norton, 1962. A study of child development in terms of systematic and representative imitation, the structure and symbolism of games and dreams, and the movement from sensory-motor schema to conceptual schema. A landmark book.

POLSKY, MILTON. *You Can Write a Play.* New York: Applause, 2002. Another useful text on helping young people write plays. Both he and Korty (*Writing Your Own Play*) bring years of experience writing and teaching.

SAXTON, JULIANA, AND NORA MORGAN. *Teaching Drama.* Portsmouth, NH: Heinemann, 1987. The authors are experienced teachers who write from the standpoint of education in which drama is used as an effective tool. Highly recommended as a drama-in-education resource.

——. *Teaching, Questioning, and Learning.* London: Routledge, 1991. A welcome new book by the authors of *Teaching Drama.* Useful and accessible to students and teachers of drama.

SHORT, KATHY G., JEAN SCHROEDER, JULIE LAIRD, GLORIA KAUFFMAN, MARGARET J. FERGUSON, AND KATHLEEN MARIE CRAWFORD. *Learning Together Through Inquiry.* York, ME: Stenhouse, 1996. An accessible text for teachers who have been exploring processes in both the language arts and other areas of the curriculum. It is the story of the way in which six teachers worked together in their classrooms. A unique textbook.

STABLER, TOM. *Drama in Primary Schools* (Schools Council Drama 5–11 Project). London: Macmillan, 1978. Report on a one-year study of forty schools in England, including preschool, junior high, and secondary levels.

STEWIG, JOHN WARREN. *Informal Drama in the Elementary Language Arts Program.* New York: Teachers College Press, 1983. This textbook focuses on the value of drama in the development of language skills. The author deals with the various ways in which the classroom teacher can use movement and improvisation and can evaluate sessions in terms of the language arts. Of greatest value to the generalist or the classroom teacher.

——. *Teaching Language Arts in Early Childhood.* New York: Holt, Rinehart, and Winston, 1980. A textbook on language arts by a specialist in the field, stressing drama for its value in teaching English. The author shares his enthusiasm with readers.

STEWIG, JOHN W., AND CAROL BUEGE. *Dramatizing Literature in Whole Language Classrooms,* 2nd ed. New York: Teacher's College Press, 1994. Of use to teachers with a background in creative drama.

SWARTZ, LARRY. *Dramathemes.* Portsmouth, NH: Heinemann, 1995. Lessons that show the teacher how to use drama throughout the elementary school curriculum.

TAYLOR, PHILIP. *Applied Theatre.* Portsmouth: Heinemann, 2003. The clearest definition that I know of theatre as a medium. The subtitle, *Creating Transformative Encounters in the Community,* is explained with case studies in language university students can understand.

——. *Red Coats and Patriots: Reflective Practice in Drama and Social Studies,* 1999. Taylor describes the way in which drama can be used to bring history to life. Excellent for teachers of upper grades.

WAGNER, BETTY JANE. *Dorothy Heathcote: Drama as a Learning Medium.* Portland, ME: Calendar Islands, 1999. The author has done a masterful job of describing the methods of this distinguished English drama teacher. Wagner explains how Heathcote finds material, helps children build an imagined situation, and leads them to see and feel the elements of human experience. Most important, she shows how the learning takes place. It is apparent from this book why Heathcote has so great a following among elementary school teachers.

——. *Educational Drama and Language Arts: What Reseach Shows*. Westport, CT: Heinemann, 1998. Considered the first overview of the major research in the field. Presents recent research that shows the effect of drama on thinking, oral language, reading, and writing.

Puppetry and Masks

ALKEMA, CHESTER J. *Mask Making*. New York: Sterling, 1981. Beautiful illustrations, in both black and white and color, of a variety of masks made from a variety of materials, ranging from simple paper bags to elaborately decorated masks.

BOYLAN, ELEANOR. *Puppet Plays for Special Days*. Charlottesville, VA: New Plays, 1976. This delightful collection of short plays is helpful to classroom teachers and community leaders engaged in puppetry. Focuses on the play rather than on methods of construction.

CHAMPLIN, CONNIE. *Puppetry and Creative Drama in Storytelling*. Austin, TX: Nancy Renfro Studios, 1980. The Renfro Studios are known for work in puppetry. The book covers other uses of puppets, for example, as aids to storytelling and in therapy for children with special problems. Highly recommended, especially for teachers of younger children.

CHAMPLIN, JOHN, AND CONNIE BROOKS. *Puppets and the Mentally Retarded Student*. Austin, TX: Nancy Renfro Studios, 1980. The focus is on developing literary comprehension in the child who is developmentally disabled. Shows how to adapt books for telling stories, and offers special techniques for using puppets in programs at the K–6 levels.

COLE, NANCY. *Puppet Theatre in Performance: Everything You Need to Know About How to Produce Puppet Plays*. New York: Morrow, 1978. What distinguishes this book is its emphasis on performance. Whereas many books on puppetry offer detailed instructions for making puppets, Cole gives ideas and clear directions for handling puppets. An unusually good book for advanced as well as older puppeteers.

ENGLER, LARRY, AND CAROL FIJON. *Making Puppets Come Alive: How to Learn and Teach Hand Puppetry*. Mineola, NY: Dover, 1996. It is a joy to know that this excellent book on puppetry is again available and in paperback. One of the best I have seen, and most accessible to the beginner.

FONG, KUANG-YU, AND STEPHEN KAPLIN. *Theatre on a Tabletop*. Charlottesville: New Plays, Inc., 2003. This is the first and only text on puppetry for small stages and a valuable resource for teachers on all levels and in community centers. Clear directions are given for making and manipulating the puppets in this unique art form. Derived from the toy theatre of the late nineteenth century, it is a useful and inexpensive tool for both puppeteers and teachers.

FREERICKS, MARY, AND JOYCE SEGAL. *Creative Puppets in the Classroom*. Charlottesville, VA: New Plays, 1979. This book gives instruction for using puppets in the curriculum. Its focus on inexpensive materials and simple techniques add to its value for the teacher.

HUNT, TAMARA, AND NANCY RENFRO. *Puppetry in Early Childhood Education*. Austin, TX: Nancy Renfro Studios, 1982. One of the most comprehensive books on the subject. Teachers, librarians, and recreation leaders will find it enormously helpful. Highly recommended.

NOBLEMAN, ROBERTA. *Mime and Masks*. Charlottesville, VA: New Plays, 1979. The performing and visual arts meet as a gifted teacher brings two areas together in this book: mime, which is an actor's tool, and the mask, used for dramatic projection.

RENFRO, NANCY *Puppetry and the Art of Story Creation*. Austin, TX: Nancy Renfro Studios, 1979. A guide to story creating with simple puppet ideas. There is a special section on puppetry for the disabled.

ROLFE, BARI. *Behind the Mask*. Oakland, CA: Personabooks, 1977. One of the few books on the mask. Recommended for teachers and students looking for material on masks.

Ross, Laura. *Hand Puppets: How to Make and Move Them.* New York: Holt, Rinehart, and Winston, 1989. A clearly illustrated book that describes four basic kinds of puppets. A list of materials supplements the directions.

Schmidt, Hans J., and Karl J. Schmidt. *Learning with Puppets.* Chicago: Dramatic Publishing Co., 1980. A guide to making and using puppets in the elementary school. Stresses acquisition of academic and social skills, as well as artistic expression.

Sims, Judy. *Puppets for Dreaming and Scheming.* Walnut Creek, CA: Early Stages, 1978. A source book for those using puppetry in the elementary classroom. Especially well suited to the needs of teachers of younger children; includes many ideas and simple, clear directions.

Movement and Dance

Barlin, Anne Lief. *Hello, Toes: Movement Games for Children.* Pennington, NJ: Princeton Book Co., 1989. A collection of creative movement ideas for children age one to five. Although the activities are written for one-on-one, adult-child play, they can easily be adapted to groups.

Blatt, Gloria T., and Jean Cunningham. *It's Your Move: Expressive Movement Activities for the Language Arts Class.* New York: Teachers College Press, 1981. The authors' aim is the integration of expressive movement and the language arts. Lessons in movement help teach language and literature.

Canner, Norma, and Harriet Klebanoff. *And a Time to Dance,* 2nd ed. Boston: Beacon Press, 1975. A simply written, sensitively illustrated book that explains and encourages the reader, showing how to involve children in creative dance. It also shows what can be done with children who are developmentally disabled.

Carr, Rachel. *See and Be: Yoga and Creative Movement for Children.* Englewood Cliffs, NJ: Prentice Hall, 1980. This beautifully illustrated book shows parents and teachers ways of helping preschool-age children to develop self-awareness and confidence through yoga and creative movement.

Dorian, Margery. *Ethnic Stories for Children to Dance.* San Mateo, CA: BBB Associates, 1978. This second book by a co-author of *Telling Stories Through Movement* includes stories from around the world with suggestions for rhythmic accompaniment on drums and other instruments. Years of experience as a dancer and teacher of dance give the author knowledge and insight. A valuable addition to the resources available to teachers in lower grades.

Dorian, Margery, and Frances Gulland. *Telling Stories Through Movement.* Belmont, CA: Fearon, 1974. An invaluable little book for creative drama teachers working with young children. The authors bring a rich background in dance, education, and drama to the task, and the result is practical and clear. Creative movement and rhythms are used to tell stories from many lands.

Grant, Jane Miller. *Shake, Rattle and Learn.* York, ME: Stenhouse, 1995. The text is based on students' natural love of movement and is filled with an abundance of practical classroom tested activities. Appropriate for K–6.

King, Nancy. *The Actor and His Space.* New York: Drama Book Specialists, 1971. Explains the importance of movement in an actor's training. Many exercises are given. It is probably less useful to the elementary and secondary school teacher than the author's other book, *Giving Form to Feeling,* but it is good material nevertheless.

——. *Giving Form to Feeling.* New York: Drama Book Specialists, 1975. A sound and useful handbook with many exercises and ideas. Although the author states that it is a book of beginnings, it is not necessarily written for the beginner; the actor, dancer, and teacher on any level will find help in expressing ideas and feelings through movement, rhythm, sounds, and words.

——. *A Movement Approach to Acting.* Englewood Cliffs, NJ: Prentice Hall, 1981. A text that goes from breathing and body awareness exercises to circus skills, stage combat, and nonverbal elements of drama. Written by an experienced teacher; highly recommended.

LANDALF, HELEN. *Moving Is Relating.* North Stratford, NH: Smith and Kraus, 1997. The author stresses developing interpersonal skills through movement. Chapters include topics such as emotions, maintaining personal boundaries, trust, and collaboration. Lessons are followed by questions for class discussion and ideas for further learning. The author is well known for her several books on movement and her workshop appearances.

LANDALF, HELEN, AND PAMELA GERKE. *Movement Stories for Children Ages 3–6.* North Stratford, NH: Smith and Kraus, 1996. The authors, professional dance and theatre educators, have created a valuable book for teachers. Imaginative but easy to use, this book should be welcomed by classroom teachers as well as specialists.

LEE, ALISON. *A Handbook of Creative Dance and Drama.* Portsmouth, NH: Heinemann, 1992. A collection of exercises and ideas to guide teachers of grades K–6, written by a teacher experienced in dance and drama.

MONTANARO, TONY. *Mime Spoken Here.* Gardiner, ME: Melnicove, 1995. A practical and entertaining book by a well-known mime who draws on his own years of performance and teaching.

ROWEN, BETTY. *Learning Through Movement: Activities for the Preschool and Elementary Grades.* New York: Teachers College Press, 1982. Describes how to use the child's natural movement for the teaching of language, science, numbers, and social studies. Lists of literature and recordings add to its value as a reference book.

SLADE, PETER. *Natural Dance: Developmental Movement and Guided Action.* London: Hodder and Stoughton, 1977. Particularly recommended for the teacher of creative drama. Slade discusses "natural dance," or dance that is improvised, as opposed to formal dance techniques. The book deals with all ages, levels of experience, and levels of ability; the therapeutic aspects of dance are also included.

Choral Speaking

GULLAN, MARJORIE. *The Speech Choir.* New York: Harper & Row, 1937.

RASMUSSEN, CARRIE. *Let's Say Poetry Together and Have Fun.* Minneapolis: Burgess, 1962.

These two books appeared during the time when there was great interest in choral speech. They are both excellent and recommended for any age level but particularly for use in the elementary classroom. Although the technique is not used widely today, some teachers like it and need help in arranging groups and practicing reading or speaking together. Both books have practical value.

Storytelling

BARTON, BOB. *Telling Stories Your Way.* Portland: Stenhouse, 2000. A good text for the beginning storyteller and teacher.

BARTON, BOB, AND DAVID BOOTH. *Stories in the Classroom.* Portsmouth, NH: Heinemann, 1990. Two experienced teachers and storytellers use folk tales, poetry, novels, and picture books to enrich the curriculum. Highly recommended.

Booth, David, and Bob Barton. *Story Works*. Portland: Stenhouse, 2002. Veteran teachers explain the value of stories in helping young people organize their thoughts and emotions in language learning. Excellent resource for all levels.

Bosma, Bette. *Fairy Tales, Fables, Legends, and Myths: Using Folk Literature in Your Classroom*. New York: Teachers College Press, 1992. The content is good, and the activities are practical and useful for the elementary school.

Coles, Robert. *The Call of Stories: Teaching and the Moral Imagination*. Boston: Houghton Mifflin, 1989. An important resource for teachers by a well-known author of books on education and the arts.

Cooper, Pamela, and Rives Collins. *The Power of Story: Teaching Through Storytelling*. Scottsdale, AZ: Gorsuch and Scarisbrick, 1997. A second edition of *Look What Happened to Frog*. Although more inclusive than the first edition, it retains the enthusiasm and charm of the original text. Highly recommended.

Creswell, Jeff. *Creating Worlds, Constructing Meaning: The Scottish Storyline Method*. Westport, CT: Heinemann, 1997. The first book of its kind to be published in the United States. The author offers a revolutionary method for teaching content, integrating the curriculum, and engaging students. It uses the power of story to teach skills and concepts. Examples are included.

Gillard, Marni. *Storyteller, Storyteacher*. York, ME: Stenhouse, 1995. The author is an experienced storyteller who has held listeners from preschool through college spellbound with a wide range of stories and has elicited their stories in return. In this book she shares both her skill and the lessons she has learned about teaching and telling. An excellent resource for all levels.

Greene, Ellin. *Storytelling: Art and Technique,* 3rd ed. New York: Bowker, 1996. An excellent book. With the renewed interest in this form of oral communication, this text is welcome.

Harrison, Annette. *Easy to Tell Stories for Young Children*. Jonesborough, TN: National Storytelling Press, 1992. Twelve folk tales and fables to be used by teachers of young children, with good ideas for participation and dramatization.

Jensen, Richard A. *Thinking in Story*. Lima, OH: CSS Publishing Co., 1993. An interesting book on storytelling and religion; philosophical rather than practical. Of greatest value to the teacher of religion or church school staff.

King, Nancy. *Storymaking and Drama*. Portsmouth, NH: Heinemann, 1994. The book falls into several categories, all useful to the drama teacher, the classroom teacher, the librarian, and the teacher of storytelling and creative writing. It is both practical and inspiring.

McGuire, Jack. *Creative Storytelling: Choosing, Inventing, and Sharing Tales for Children*. New York: McGraw-Hill, 1984. A book that teachers will find of great value. The author covers all the important areas in a clear and helpful manner.

Pellowski, Anne. *The World of Storytelling: A Practical Guide to the Origins, Development, and Applications of Storytelling*. New York: Wilson, 1990. The title states the content of a book written for both teachers and storytellers.

Pitzele, Peter. *Our Father's Wells*. San Francisco: HarperCollins, 1996. Although this book is written for the purpose of offering religious stories, it is of value for storytellers of all faiths and for all occasions.

Sawyer, Ruth. *The Way of the Storyteller*. New York: Viking, 1976. Probably the best known of the books in the field, *The Way of the Storyteller* still takes its place at the top of the list. Available in most libraries after nearly forty years.

Schram, Pinninah. *Jewish Stories One Generation Tells Another*. Jonesborough, TN: National Storytelling Press, 1987. A book by a professional storyteller with a particular emphasis. Of value to all persons interested in the art of telling stories.

Readers Theatre

Coger, Leslie, and Melvin White. *Readers Theatre Handbook: A Dramatic Approach to Literature,* 3rd ed. Chicago: Scott, Foresman, 1982. An excellent handbook on this technique, written by experts in the field. Directed toward the adult reader; equally useful to the high school teacher or to any teacher interested in trying this concept of theatre.

Lippert, Margaret H. *Read Aloud Anthology.* New York: Macmillan/McGraw-Hill, 1993. Although this is a practical text on the art of readers theatre, it is basically an anthology.

Maclay, Joanna Hawkins. *Readers Theatre: Toward a Grammar of Practice.* New York: Random House, 1971. An excellent book that covers a definition of readers theatre, gives a selection of material, and also describes performance techniques. Most useful to teachers of upper grades.

Porter, Steven, ed. *New Works for Readers Theatre.* Studio City, CA: Players Press, 1994. A useful and welcome addition to this form of theatre. Useful for older players.

Sloyer, Shirlee Epstein. *Readers Theatre: Story Dramatization in the Classroom.* Champaign, IL: National Council of Teachers of English, 1981. An excellent book for teachers of junior and senior high school students. It offers good ideas and a clear description of a technique that appeals to students and gives good training in voice and diction as well as appreciation of literary material.

Drama for the Special Student

Blatner, Adam. *Acting-In: Practical Applications of Psychodramatic Methods,* 3rd ed. New York: Springer, 1996. This book is well known in psychological circles but is readable and practical for the classroom teacher as well. Recommended for all age levels.

Booth, David, and Alistair Martin-Smith, eds. *Recognizing Richard Courtney.* London: Kingsley, 1991. The editors have selected writings on drama and theatre from the prodigious amount of work of one of the foremost writers and scholars in the fields of drama, theatre, education, and therapy.

Duggan, Mary, and Roger Grainger. *Imagination, Identification, and Catharsis in Theatre and Therapy.* London: Kingsley, 1997. The authors argue that the same psychological mechanisms in theatre operate in drama therapy: it is the theatricality of therapy that is healing.

Emunah, Renee. *Acting for Real.* Bristol, PA: Brunner/Mazel, 1997. Although this book is written for drama therapists, it provides an integrative framework for the practice of drama therapy and for that reason is recommended to teachers with some background and interest in the field. The author is a leading practitioner and founder of Beyond Analysis, a theatre company for former psychiatric patients.

———. *Acting for Real: Drama Therapy—Process, Technique, and Performance.* New York: Brunner/Mazel, 1994. The subtitle explains the content of this book by a leading pioneer in the field. It is an up-to-date text for the therapist and special education teacher.

Gersie, Alida, and Nancy King. *Storymaking in Education and Therapy.* London: Kingsley, 1990. Source materials and ideas for teachers and therapists by two well-known authors. Storytelling and myths offer guidance and inspiration.

Jennings, Sue. *Creative Drama in Groupwork.* London: Winslow Press, 1986. A book by a well-known drama therapist. Simply written and easily understood by the nonspecialist.

———, ed. *Dramatherapy: Theory and Practice for Teachers and Clinicians,* 3rd ed. New York: Routledge, 1997. The value of this book lies in its theoretical content. Not a textbook for classroom teachers, it is recommended for college students preparing to teach.

——. *Introduction to Drama Therapy: Theatre and Healing.* London: Kingsley, 1998. This new book by a well-known practitioner is welcomed for its optimistic approach and accessibility.

——. *Remedial Drama: A Handbook for Teachers and Therapists.* New York: Theatre Arts, 1974. The message in this book is that the experience of drama can enrich everyone's life, whether one is developmentally or physically disabled or socially disadvantaged. For non-specialists. It is clear and easy to read and will help the teacher to work with the therapist.

JONES, PHIL. *Drama as Therapy: Theatre as Living.* New York: Routledge, 1996. As the title suggests, this book is for students working in the field of drama therapy.

LANDY, ROBERT J. *Drama Therapy: Concepts, Theories, and Practices,* 2nd ed. Springfield, IL: Thomas, 1994. One of the few books on drama therapy for students preparing to work in this new field. Readable and sound, by a leader with a background in drama, education, and therapy.

——. *Essays in Drama Therapy: The Double Life.* London: Kingsley, 1996. This book combines new material with some of the author's best-known work. The essays give an account of his growth and development as a leader in the field.

——. *Persona and Performance: The Meaning of Role in Drama, Therapy, and Everyday Life.* New York: Guilford, 1993. An absorbing text best suited to the teacher of special education.

LONG, GREG, AND CHRIS BERBERICK. *All Children are Special.* Portland: Stenhouse, 1995. A book for nonspecialists who want information and help in creating inclusive classrooms.

MCINTYRE, BARBARA. *Informal Dramatics: A Language Arts Activity for the Special Child.* Pittsburgh: Stanwix, 1963. Still a useful guide for special education teachers. It was one of the first books in the field.

MITCHELL, STEVE. *Dramatherapy, Clinical Studies.* London: Kingsley, 1996. A collection of perspectives accompanied by case studies. Highly praised by users and reviewers.

PEARSON, JENNY. *Discovering the Self Through Drama and Movement: The Sesame Approach.* London: Kingsley, 1996. A welcome addition to the literature in the field by a staff member of the well-known Sesame program.

PIAGET, JEAN. *Play, Dreams, and Imitation in Childhood.* New York: Norton, 1962. Recommended for students of drama therapy and teachers of education as well as theatre.

PORTNER, ELAINE S., ed., updated by Robert J. Landy, Roberta Zito, and Renee Emunah. *Drama Therapy in Print: A Bibliography.* New York: National Association for Drama Therapy Publications, 1986. This publication is a valuable resource prepared by three of the best known drama therapists in the country.

RIEF, SANDRA F. *How to Reach and Teach ADD/ADHD Children.* West Nyack, NY: Center for Applied Research in Education, 1993. This book clearly states the problems and identifies ADD and ADHD students. Storytelling, visualization, use of the imagination, and listening skills are among the topics covered in language accessible to the nonspecialist.

RESSLER, PAULA. *Dramatic Changes.* Portsmouth: Heinemann, 2000. This text discusses sexual orientation and gender. Good for high school teachers and students and leaders in community center theatre programs.

SCHATTNER, GERTRUDE, AND RICHARD COURTNEY, eds. *Drama in Therapy.* 2 vols. New York: Drama Book Specialists, 1981. The editors have collected and assembled two volumes of essays written by a large group of experts in a variety of specialized areas. Of interest and value to teacher and student, as well as to specialist and generalist in drama education.

STERNBERG, PATRICIA. *Theatre for Conflict Resolution.* Portsmouth, NH: Heinemann, 1998. A welcome addition to both special education and multicultural education in the arts. The author brings a background in theatre, therapy, and education to readers who may be teachers or students. It is practical in offering activities and exercises and concludes with essays from theatre directors who use conflict resolution in their work. Highly recommended.

STRIMLING, ARTHUR. *Roots and Branches, Creating Intergenerational Theatre*. Portsmouth: Heinemann, 2004. An excellent description of intergenerational theatre: What it is and how to do it. The author addresses the problem and conflicts between youth and age. Suggestions are given for devising, adapting, and presenting material dealing with these relationships and for discussing these relationships with the audience afterward.

WETHERED, AUDREY G. *Drama and Movement in Therapy*, 2nd ed. Philadelphia: Kingsley, 1993. The therapeutic use of movement, mime, and drama is covered in this short text. Useful to both nonspecialist and specialist.

WILDER, ROSILYN. *Come, Step into My Life (Youth and Elders Inter-act)*. Charlottesville, VA: New Plays, 1995. A unique guide to intergenerational work, enhanced with anecdotes from the author's years in the field. It aims to give both generations a sense of the future and an awareness of their connectedness.

Multiculturalism

ARNOW, JAN. *Teaching Peace: How to Raise Children to Live in Harmony—Without Fear, Without Prejudice, Without Violence*. New York: Berkley, 1995. Teachers need to develop skills in order to help children understand the results of prejudice and oppression based on race, disability, class, and gender.

BANKS, JAMES A. *Educating Citizens in a Multicultural Society*. New York: Teachers College Press, 1997.

BERLINER, DAVID C., AND BRUCE J. BIDDLE. *The Manufactured Crisis: Myths, Fraud, and the Attack on America's Public Schools*. Reading, MA: Addison Wesley, 1995. A political publication which, however, offers recommendations to teachers regarding what the authors perceive to be the real concerns of children.

CASTRO, ELENA, AND LINDA MANUELITO. *Multicultural Education*. Portsmouth, NH: Heinemann, 1991. Two teachers working in bilingual schools show how they use culture and community to construct a curriculum that respects children and their experiences.

COHEN, LIBBY G., AND LORAINE J. SPENCINER. *Assessment of Children and Youth*. New York: Longman, 1998. A highly recommended new textbook recognizing the changing composition of American society and the need to educate children in new ways. Presents a balance between the traditional and the new techniques of assessment. Supplemented with an instructor's manual and other resources.

COSSA, EMBER, GROVER, AND HAZELWOOD. *Acting Out: The Workbook. A Guide to the Development and Presentation of Issue-Oriented, Audience-Interactive, Improvisational Theatre*. Washington, DC: Accelerated Development, 1996. This is a practical text for leaders interested in social issues with audience participation.

DAY, FRANCES ANN. *Multicultural Voices in Contemporary Literature*. Portsmouth, NH: Heinemann, 1994. Although a reference work, this is an excellent collection of ideas to stimulate cultural sensitivity. From it teachers can find material for reading, writing, and dramatization.

DE ANDA, DIANE. *The Ice Dove and Other Stories*. Houston, TX: Arte Publico Press, 1997. A collection of stories about children struggling with their Hispanic identity. It is particularly important for the rapidly growing Hispanic minority in this country. Contains excellent material for dramatization.

DELPIT, LISA. *Other People's Children*. New York: New Press, 1995. The author recommends theatre as a way of introducing African American children to language.

DENTLER, ROBERT A., AND ANNE L. HAFNER. *Hosting Newcomers: Structuring Educational Opportunities for Immigrant Children*. New York: Teachers College Press, 1997.

ELLIS, ROGER. *Multicultural Theatre: Scenes and Monologues from New Hispanic, Asian, and African American Plays.* Colorado Springs: Meriwether, 1996. Recommended by the committee on multiculturalism of the AHTE. A useful material in studying other cultures.

GRADY, SHARON. *Drama and Diversity: A Pluralistic Perspective for Educational Theatre.* Portsmouth: Heinemann, 2000. A new text for all teachers but of particular value to the drama teacher and community theatre leader.

HALE, JANICE. *Unbank the Fire.* Baltimore: Johns Hopkins Press, 1994. The author of the highly acclaimed book *Black Children, Their Roots and Wings* offers a book on ways of reaching African American children through storytelling. This book fits several categories in this bibliography.

HAYES, JENNIFER FELL, AND DOROTHY NAPP SCHINDEL. *Pioneer Journeys: Drama in Museum Education.* Charlottesville: New Plays, Inc., 1995. An excellent resource for the classroom teacher. Could fit into several categories as the authors tell how trips to all kinds of museums can illuminate and enhance learning.

KING, JOYCE E., ETTA R. HOLLINS, AND WARREN C. HAYMAN. *Preparing Teachers for Cultural Diversity.* New York: Teachers College Press, 1997. Both of the above books were written to meet the needs of teachers of immigrant children in American classrooms.

KUZMESKUS, JUNE. *We Teach Them All.* York, ME: Stenhouse, 1996. A collection of stories, poems, and personal anecdotes by teachers from schools across Massachusetts, where diversity is considered an advantage rather than a problem in schools. Each teacher explains his or her strategies to increase the effectiveness of teaching and learning.

LA BELLE, THOMAS, AND CHRISTOPHER R. WARD. *Multiculturalism and Education: Diversity and Its Impact on Schools and Society.* Albany: State University of New York, 1994. Multiculturalism is a social and political condition that effects education as it affects society.

LANG, GREG, AND CHRIS PERBERICH. *All Children Are Special.* York, ME: Stenhouse, 1995. This book fits in this category or in special education; the authors discuss special needs which can be either cultural or physical and intellectual. Practical information and confidence building for the young teacher.

NAJERA, RICK. *The Pain of the Macho and Other Plays.* Houston: Arte Publico Press, 1997. A collection designed for high school or even upper elementary grades. It deals with ethnic issues, particularly the male experience in Hispanic society.

O'NEILL, CECILY. *Dreamseekers: Creative Approach to the African American Heritage.* Westport, CT: Heinemann, 1997. O'Neill offers teachers relevant themes and models. Multicultural prose, poetry, and drama are also included.

OXFORD UNIVERSITY PRESS 1997 MULTICULTURAL BOOKS FOR CHILDREN AND YOUNG ADULTS CATALOGUE. Includes the multivolume *The Young Oxford History of African Americans, The Oxford Companion to African American Literature, The Mexican American Family Album, The Irish American Family Album,* works by Langston Hughes, and folklore.

RUBIN, JANET. *Teaching about the Holocaust through Drama.* Charlottesville: New Plays, Inc., 2003. A unique and valuable book for both classroom and drama teacher, religious education and community center leader. Readable and recommended for the generalist anywhere.

SAMWAY, KATHERINE DAVIES, AND GAIL WHANG. *Literature Study Circles in a Multicultural Classroom.* York, ME: Stenhouse, 1995. A practical book for teachers who want to move beyond curriculum-centered to learning-centered teaching. Applicable to language arts courses.

SIKUNDER SYLVIA, AND BARBARA DUMOULIN. *Celebrating Our Cultures.* York, ME: Stenhouse Publishers, 1998. Language arts activities for classroom teachers. Includes background information, holiday stories, ideas for study of many cultures of the world.

Related Fields

Aesthetics

ARTS EDUCATION FOR THE 21ST CENTURY AMERICAN ECONOMY. A conference report prepared for the American Council on the Arts. Documents the proceedings at the ACA conference in Louisville, Kentucky, in 1994. Available from the ACA office, New York.

BALFE, JUDITH H., AND JONI CHERBO HEINE, eds. *Arts Education beyond the Classroom.* New York: American Council on the Arts, 1987. Recommended for teachers interested in finding community resources outside the school that will supplement or enhance the classroom experience.

COMING TO OUR SENSES: THE SIGNIFICANCE OF THE ARTS FOR AMERICAN EDUCATION. Panel Report, David Rockefeller, Jr., chair. New York: McGraw-Hill, 1977.

COURTNEY, RICHARD. *Drama and Feeling: An Aesthetic Theory.* Downsville, Ontario: McGill-Queens University Press, 1994. A well-known and respected scholar examines the role of drama from children's play through ritual and creative drama to theatre. Recommended for college and university students of education, drama, and aesthetics.

EDMAN, IRWIN. *Arts and the Man.* New York: New American Library, 1950. Written by a well-known philosopher almost sixty years ago, this is still an important text on aesthetic education. Recommended to college students.

FOWLER, CHARLES. *Can We Rescue the Arts for America's Children? Coming to Our Senses Ten Years Later.* New York: American Council for the Arts, 1987. A response to the 1977 book *Coming to Our Senses: The Significance of the Arts for American Education.* The author takes a look at the goals of arts education and how far we have gone toward reaching them. His findings are disappointing; the outlook appears less bright now than at the time the original research was done.

GARDNER, HOWARD. *Art, Mind, and Brain: A Cognitive Approach to Creativity.* New York: Basic Books, 1982. The author, a Harvard Medical School professor, draws together two areas, cognitive and affective, in a study of human development and learning. A brilliant study, but of greater interest to the specialist than to the generalist.

——. *Frames of Mind: The Theory of Multiple Intelligences.* New York: Basic Books, 1993. Gardner offers a theory that explores the interests and abilities of different students, and in so doing he validates the capacity of some students to respond particularly to the arts.

GREENE, MAXINE. *Landscapes of Learning.* New York: Teachers College Press, 1978. An earlier book by a distinguished American philosopher but still timely and thought provoking for teachers and university students.

LANGER, SUSANNE. *Problems of Art: Ten Philosophical Lectures.* New York: Scribner, 1957. Although written more than forty years ago, still good and of interest. Langer is a well-known philosopher, highly regarded among artists and students of aesthetics.

LEVY, JONATHAN. *Practical Education for the Unimaginable.* Charlottesville: New Plays, Inc., 2003. A collection of essays on the place of the theatre in the liberal arts. Interesting perspectives and style. For teachers and graduate students.

LINDERMAN, EARL W., AND DONALD W. HABERHOLZ. *Artworks for Elementary Teachers: Developing Artistic and Perceptual Awareness.* Dubuque, IA: Brown, 1990. One of the best books for both the specialist and the generalist. Written simply by two master teachers, it gives guidance and confidence to teachers of all the arts, not just teachers of the visual arts.

MCLAUGHLIN, JOHN, ed. *A Guide to National and State Arts Education Services.* New York: American Council on the Arts, 1987.

——. *Toward a New Era in Arts Education: The Interlochen Symposium.* New York: American Council on the Arts, 1988. These two books present both a picture of arts education today and ideas on how it can be upgraded and enhanced in the future. The author, a former teacher, is knowledgeable and sensitive to the problems of the American educator.

NATIONAL STANDARDS FOR ARTS EDUCATION. Developed by the Consortium of National Arts Education Associations. Reston, VA: Music Educators National Conference, 1994. This is a long-awaited guide to study of the arts on all levels, K–12. Charts for each art form list goals and show what teachers should cover to build skills and appreciation.

Media and Music

CONCANNON, TOM. *Using Media for Creative Teaching.* Charlottesville, VA: New Plays, 1980. A textbook for today's classroom: a media specialist explains how skills can be developed through the use of camera, videotape, tape recorders, and even the human body. Includes methods and specific suggestions for using media in the curriculum areas in grades K–8.

LIST, LYNNE K. *Music, Art, and Drama Experiences for the Elementary Curriculum.* New York: Teachers College Press, 1982. This book differs from most in that it focuses on all the arts, showing how they can stimulate learning and enhance teaching. Games and projects are described, as well as suggestions for using them with children who have special problems and needs.

Circus Arts

BURGESS, HOVEY. *Circus Techniques.* New York: Drama Book Specialists, 1989. A comprehensive book for teachers by a master teacher of circus arts at New York University. Includes a series of structured lessons.

CROWTHER, CAROL. *Clowns and Clowning.* London: Macdonald Educational, 1978. A book for children. Includes a history of clowning, with many suggestions for activities.

SWORTZELL, LOWELL. *Here Come the Clowns: A Cavalcade of Comedy from Antiquity to the Present.* New York: Viking, 1978. An excellent book for young people; it has interesting material for all ages.

Anthologies of Children's Literature

ARBUTHNOT, MAY HILL, ed. *The Arbuthnot Anthology of Children's Literature,* 4th ed. Glenview, IL: Scott, Foresman, 1976. This anthology contains the three classic Arbuthnot texts for children's literature: *Time for Fairy Tales, Time for Poetry, and Time for True Tales and Almost True.* Not all the stories and poems lend themselves to dramatization, but many of the poems can be used for choral speaking.

——. *Children's Books Too Good to Miss,* 7th ed. Cleveland: Press of Case Western Reserve University, 1980. A treasury of materials for the elementary school classroom. Poetry, stories, biography, and study guides and explanations of literary and other items make this a useful and authoritative source.

BUTLER, FRANCELIA, ed. *Sharing Literature with Children: A Thematic Anthology.* New York: Longman, 1977. This well-known anthology is divided into sections in a unique way: "Toys and Games," "Fools," "Masks and Shadows," "Sex Roles," and "Circles." The editor has included material for all age levels, providing a rich source of stories for the teacher to tell, read aloud, and use in creative playing.

CIARDI, JOHN. *I Met a Man.* Boston: Houghton Mifflin, 1961. Amusing verses for children, written by a well-known American poet. Useful for both creative drama and choral speaking.

——. *The Man Who Sang the Sillies.* Philadelphia: Lippincott, 1961. Another collection of amusing verse for both younger and older children.

COLE, WILLIAM, ed. *Poem Stew.* New York: Harper & Row, 1981. Fun for children, this collection has more than fifty poems for reading and dramatic enactment.

CULLINAN, BERNICE, AND LEE GALDA. *Literature and the Child,* 4th ed. New York: Harcourt Brace Jovanovich, 1998. A new book by two well-known educators. Useful for the drama teacher as well as the classroom teacher.

DAY, FRANCES ANN. *Multicultural Voices in Contemporary Literature.* Portsmouth, NH: Heinemann, 1995. A resource for teachers and librarians. Objectives include cultural sensitivity, reading, creative writing, and possibilities for drama in the classroom. The works of thirty-nine authors and illustrators from a wide variety of cultural backgrounds encourage students to learn more about others in the community.

DE LA MARE, WALTER, ed. *Come Hither: A Collection of Rhymes and Poems for the Young of All Ages.* New York: Avenel, 1990. This collection of more than five hundred traditional poems, with notes, is interesting to children of all ages.

DONELSON, KENNETH, AND AILEEN PACE NILSEN. *Literature for Today's Young Adults,* 5th ed. White Plains, NY: Longman, 1997. Although the age level discussed by the authors is higher than many teachers of creative drama are concerned with, the areas covered and the principles that apply are right on target for today. The concern for literature that reflects the diversity of our society is only one example of the authors' recognition of the changing scene.

FARJEON, ELEANOR. *Eleanor Farjeon's Poems for Children.* Philadelphia: Lippincott, 1951. Some of these favorite poems by a well-known poet are good for dramatization, and many are suitable for choral speaking.

FISHER, AILEEN. *Out in the Dark and Daylight.* New York: Harper & Row, 1980. Selections from Fisher's books are compiled in a varied collection that is representative of her work.

FITZGERALD, BURDETTE, ed. *World Tales for Creative Dramatics and Storytelling.* Englewood Cliffs, NJ: Prentice-Hall, 1962. A splendid collection of folk tales from around the world, many of which are little known.

GEORGIOU, CONSTANTINE. *Children and Their Literature.* Englewood Cliffs, NJ: Prentice Hall, 1969. An excellent resource for teachers of all grades. This book treats the history and criticism of children's literature. Includes extensive lists of stories for primary, intermediate, and upper grades. Recent books by the same author include the highly praised *Wait and See, Whitey and Whiskers and Food, The Clock, The Nest,* and *Prosperpina, the Duck That Came to School,* all published by Harvey House; and *Rani, Queen of the Jungle,* published by Prentice Hall.

HARRIS, V. J., ed. *Teaching Multicultural Literature in Grades K–8.* Norwood, MA: Christopher-Gordon, 1992. A valuable addition to the list of books recognizing our multicultural resources.

HUCK, C. S., S. HEPLER, AND J. HICKMAN. *Children's Literature in the Elementary School,* 4th ed. New York: Holt, Rinehart, and Winston, 1987. A popular and practical textbook for the classroom teacher and the drama specialist in the elementary school.

JENNINGS, COLEMAN A., AND AURAND HARRIS, eds. *Plays Children Love.* Garden City, NY: Doubleday, 1981. An excellent collection of plays edited by two of our best-qualified practitioners, a child-drama specialist and a leading children's playwright. In the first part are plays for children to enjoy as spectators; in the second part are plays for older children to perform. The latter are shorter, making them suitable for children to memorize and produce.

KASE, ROBERT, ed. *Stories for Creative Acting.* New York: French, 1961. Although compiled in 1961, this selection is well worth having in the library, for it includes stories used and recommended by leading creative drama teachers. Many of them would be included today if another such book were assembled. The editor is a leading figure in the field who still devotes much time to drama/theatre, now working with senior adults.

LEAR, EDWARD. *A Book of Nonsense.* New York: Knopf, 1992. This collection of the poet's amusing limericks is always fun and good for all ages.

LINDGREN, M., ed. *The Multicolored Mirror: Cultural Substance in Literature for Children and Young Adults.* Fort Atkins, WI: Highsmith Press, 1991. Another addition to the growing list of literature from many cultures.

LUCKENS, REBECCA J., AND RUTH K. G. CLINE. *A Critical Handbook of Literature for Young Adults.* New York: HarperCollins, 1994. Of particular value for teachers of English in junior and senior high schools and for librarians and media specialists. Literature for this age level is evaluated according to character development, theme, conflict and style. Modern in point of view; highly readable and a useful resource.

——. *A Critical Handbook of Children's Literature,* 5th ed. New York: HarperCollins, 1995. A comprehensive and valuable book for teachers in the primary grades. It does not provide reading lists but rather offers criteria for selecting, evaluating, and sharing good literature with children. The author discusses fiction and nonfiction, including the following genres: realism, fantasy, mystery, and folk and fairy tales.

MAYER, MERCER. *A Poison Tree and Other Poems.* New York: Scribner, 1977. For intermediate grades, these verses express children's feelings—anger, sadness, wishes—as well as less serious themes.

McCORD, DAVID. *One at a Time.* Boston: Little, Brown, 1977. A collection of the poet's most popular work. Most useful to teachers of intermediate grades.

MOORE, LILLIAN. *See My Lovely Poison Ivy.* New York: Atheneum, 1975. Short verses with appeal for children in grades 3–6. Light and amusing.

MORTON, MIRIAM, ed. *A Harvest of Russian Children's Literature.* Berkeley: University of California Press, 1967. In this comprehensive collection of prose and poetry, the editor has included material for ages five to seven, eight to eleven, twelve to fifteen, and young adults. She has translated some material from the Russian, told some of the folk tales in her own words, and written introductions to each section. A wealth of material for the classroom teacher as well as for the specialist.

NADELMAN, PERRY. *The Pleasures of Children's Literature,* 2nd ed. White Plains, NY: Longman, 1996. A basic text for use in both undergraduate and graduate courses in education and literature. The author's main purposes are to provide the adult with strategies and to suggest that children can be taught to understand these same contexts and strategies. Modern and comprehensive in its range.

OPIE, IONA, AND PETER OPIE, eds. *The Oxford Book of Children's Verse.* New York: Oxford University Press, 1994. A wealth of material, some of which is suitable for choral speaking and creative drama.

PRELUTSKY, JACK. *The New Kid on the Block.* New York: Greenwillow Books, 1984. These modern, childlike verses with a sense of humor can be enjoyed by children in lower and middle grades. Good for both creative drama classes and choral speaking.

——, ed. *The Random House Book of Poetry for Children.* New York: Random House, 1984. A collection of more than five hundred poems with more than four hundred illustrations; a valuable addition to the library of books for creative playing. Amusing verse, witty rhymes, and serious poetry are all included in a source book for teachers and creative drama leaders of children of all ages.

ROTHLEIN, LIZ, AND ANITA MEYER MEINBACH. *Legacies: Using Children's Literature in the Classroom.* New York: HarperCollins, 1996. Directed to all adults who are interested in introducing children to literature, although primarily designed as a college textbook for students planning to teach in grades K–8. Comprehensive in scope; rich in suggestions for activities that deepen the understanding of literature. Creative drama, the other arts, and creative writing are suggested as particularly effective. Highly recommended.

RUDMAN, MASHA KABAKOW. *Children's Literature: An Issues Approach,* 3rd ed. White Plains, NY: Longman, 1995. A resource guide offering practical suggestions for using books to help children confront personal and societal concerns. A highly recommended resource for issue-based literature. The book examines literature for children from kindergarten age through junior high school. It is divided into three parts, including family, life cycle, and society. It deals with such topics as adoption, divorce, family constellations, sexuality, aging, death, gender, heritage, special needs, and war and peace.

——, ed. *Children's Literature: Resources for the Classroom.* Norwood, MA: Christopher-Gordon, 1993. A recent addition to the field, introducing new resources and materials for the modern classroom.

RUSSELL, DAVID L. *Literature for Children,* 3rd ed. White Plains, NY: Longman, 1997. A modern, thoughtful book for college students preparing to teach children. The author organized the material according to contexts and kinds of literature and includes lists of books for children and recommended reading for the adult student.

SALDANA, JOHNNY. *Drama of Color: Improvisation with Multiethnic Folklore.* Portsmouth, NY: Heinemann, 1995. A practical and long-needed book for teachers of drama and literature. Unlike many books and plays previously available, it focuses on the oral traditions of selected groups (Hispanics, Native Americans, Asians and Pacific Islanders, and Africans and African Americans) rather than on folklore. The author acknowledges omissions.

STEVENSON, ROBERT LOUIS. *A Child's Garden of Verses.* New York: Simon and Schuster, 1999. These familiar verses are still interesting to children and good to use for both creative drama and choral speaking.

SUTHERLAND, ZENA. *Children and Books,* 9th ed. White Plains, NY: Longman, 1997. A book in its ninth edition is likely to be useful and of high quality. Illustrated throughout, its more than seven hundred pages include chapters on all aspects of children's literature, genres, methodology, and techniques that can be used in introducing children to literature and issues. There is a separate instructor's manual.

SWORTZELL, LOWELL. *Around the World in Twenty-One Plays.* New York: Applause, 1996. An excellent and quite different anthology of plays suitable for the child audience, some of which could be performed by the children themselves. The author has selected works from a variety of countries and periods. One of the best collections around.

VIORST, JUDITH. *If I Were in Charge of the World and Other Poems for Children and Their Parents.* New York: Atheneum, 1981. The poet gives a variety of children's most secret thoughts, worries, and wishes in this collection. Perceptive and humorous.

WARD, WINIFRED, ed. *Stories to Dramatize.* New Orleans: Anchorage Press, 1986. A rich collection of stories and poems from the author's years of experience as a creative drama teacher. It is arranged for players of various ages and contains material both classical and contemporary.

Annotated Bibliographies of Children's Literature

KIMMEL, MARGARET MARY, AND ELIZABETH SEGEL. *For Reading Out Loud!* New York: Dell, 1983. This book shows adults how to enrich children's lives and stimulate their interest by reading aloud to them. The authors explain why it is important to start early and how to do it successfully. The most valuable part of the book is a bibliography in which almost 150 books are described in detail. A long list of titles aids the teacher (or parent) in finding material for all age levels and interests.

TRELEASE, JIM. *The Read-Aloud Handbook,* 4th ed. New York: Penguin Books, 1995. The author tells how reading aloud awakens the listener's imagination, improves language arts, and opens doors to a new world of entertainment. An annotated list includes more than 300 fairy tales, short stories, poems, and novels that the author describes in detail, with suggested age and grade levels.

Suggested Music for Creative Drama

The following mood music is suggested for creative drama. It is listed in categories implying different moods and conditions. Many leaders find music a great asset in freeing children and inducing creative movement. All the selections are well known and available. This is by no means an exhaustive list, and many teachers will have ideas of their own.

It is suggested that children first listen to the music and then either move to it or talk about the feelings it suggests. It often is a good idea to play a piece a second or even a third time before attempting to do anything with it.

Music Suggesting Activity

Beethoven, Ludwig van	Sonata op. 10, no. 2 [fourth movement]
Bizet, Georges	March and Impromptu from *Jeux d'enfants*
Chopin, Frédéric	Mazurka in B-flat
Copland, Aaron	"Rodeo"
Gershwin, George	*An American in Paris*
Grainger, Percy	"Country Gardens"
Mendelssohn, Felix	Tarantella from *Songs without Words*, op. 102, no. 3
Paganini, Niccolò	"Perpetual Motion"
Prokofiev, Sergei	Symphony no. 1 in D [fourth movement]
Rimsky-Korsakov, Nicolai	"Flight of the Bumble Bee"
Sousa, John Philip	Marches
Strauss, Johann, Jr.	"Thunder and Lightning, Galop"
Wagner, Richard	"Spinning Song" from *The Flying Dutchman*

Music Suggesting Animals, Birds, and Insects

Dvořák, Antonin	"Legend no. 7"
Grieg, Edvard	"Little Bird"
	"Papillon [Butterfly]"

Respighi, Ottorino	*The Birds*
Rimsky-Korsakov, Nicolai	"Flight of the Bumble Bee"
Saint-Saëns, Camille	*Carnival of the Animals*
Schumann, Robert	*Papillons*
Stravinsky, Igor	Suite from *The Firebird*

Ballads and Folk Songs

Many well-known ballads and folk songs are appropriate for creative drama.

Environmental Music

Britten, Benjamin	"4 Sea Interludes" from *Peter Grimes*
Copland, Aaron	*Appalachian Spring*
Debussy, Claude	*La Mer [The Sea]*
Delius, Frederick	"Summer Night on the River"
Mendelssohn, Felix	*Fingal's Cave* Overture
Respighi, Ottorino	*The Fountains of Rome*
Smetana, Bedřich	"The Moldau" from *My Fatherland*
Strauss, Johann, Jr.	"Blue Danube" Waltz

Happy Music

Dvořák, Antonin	Slavonic Dances
Grainger, Percy	*Country Gardens*
Mozart, Wolfgang Amadeus	Serenade in G (*Eine Kleine Nachtmusik*)
	Symphony no. 40 in G Minor [first movement]
Nicolai, Otto	Overture to *Merry Wives of Windsor*
Offenbach, Jacques	*Gaité Parisienne*
Rossini, Gioacchino	*La Boutique Fantastique*
Scarlatti, Domenico	harpsichord sonatas
Schumann, Robert	*Carnaval*
Telemann, Georg Philipp	*Don Quixote*
	Concerto for Flute

Lullabies

Brahms, Johannes	"Lullaby"
Godard, Benjamin Louis Paul	"Berceuse" from *Jocelyn*
Gottschalk, Louis Moreau	"Berceuse"
Grieg, Edvard	"Cradle Song" from *Peer Gynt*
Khatchaturian, Aram	"Lullaby" from *Gayne*

Military Music

| Chopin, Frédéric | "Military" Polonaise |
| Elgar, Edward | *Pomp and Circumstance* marches |

Sousa, John Philip	any marches
Suppé, Franz von	*Light Cavalry* Overture
Tchaikovsky, Peter Ilyich	*1812* Overture

Music Suggesting Mystery

Dukas, Paul	*The Sorcerer's Apprentice*
Grieg, Edvard	"Abduction of the Bride" from *Peer Gynt*
	"March of the Dwarfs" from *Huldigungsmarsch*
	"The Hall of the Mountain King" from *Peer Gynt*
Mussorgsky, Modest	*Night on Bald Mountain*
	Songs and Dances of Death
Saint-Saëns, Camille	"Danse Macabre"
Schubert, Franz	"The Erlking"
Sibelius, Jean	*The Swan of Tuonela*
Strauss, Richard	*Death and Transfiguration*

Romantic Music

Beethoven, Ludwig van	Sonata no. 23 for Piano (*Appassionata*)
Brahms, Johannes	"Valse"
Liszt, Franz	"Liebestraum [Love Dream]"
Mendelssohn, Felix	*Songs without Words* op. 38, no. 2
	Songs without Words op. 102, no. 1
Paderewski, Ignace	"Love Song"
Rubinstein, Anton	"Melody"
Tchaikovsky, Peter Ilyich	Overture to *Romeo and Juliet*
	Symphony no. 5 [selections]
Wagner, Richard	Prelude to *Tristan and Isolde*

Music Suggesting the Seasons

Beethoven, Ludwig van	Sonata op. 24, no. 5 for Violin and Piano (*Spring*)
	Sonata op. 27, no. 2 (*Moonlight*)
	Symphony no. 6 (*Pastoral*)
Debussy, Claude	"Claire de Lune"
Delius, Frederick	"Summer Night on the River"
Grieg, Edvard	"Morning Mood"
	"To the Spring" from *Lyric Pieces*
Grofé, Ferde	*Grand Canyon* Suite
Mendelssohn, Felix	Melody in F ("Spring Song")
Prokofiev, Sergei	"In Autumn"
	Summer Day Suite
Ravel, Maurice	*Daphnis and Chloe*
Rossini, Gioacchino	"The Storm" from the Overture to *William Tell*
Sibelius, Jean	"Night Ride and Sunrise"
Vivaldi, Antonio	"Spring" from *The Four Seasons*

Serene Music

Bach, Johann Sebastian	Cantata no. 147 ("Sheep May Safely Graze")
Barber, Samuel	"Adagio for Strings" from Quartet for Strings op. 11
Bizet, Georges	*L'Arlésienne* [third movement]
Debussy, Claude	*Afternoon of a Faun*
Mendelssohn, Felix	*Songs without Words* op. 102, no. 6
	A Midsummer Night's Dream
Schubert, Franz	Quintet in A Major for Piano and Strings (*Trout*)
Schumann, Robert	*Traumerei*

Music Suggesting Strong Movement

Beethoven, Ludwig van	Sonata op. 27, no. 2 (*Moonlight* [third movement])
Falla, Manuel de	"Ritual Fire Dance" from *El Amor Brujo*
Holst, Gustav	"Mars" from *The Planets*
Khatchaturian, Aram	"Saber Dance" from *Gayne*
Prokofiev, Sergei	*Scythian* Suite [selections]
Shostakovich, Dmitri	Symphony no. 5 [fourth movement]
Tchaikovsky, Peter Ilyich	"Marche Slav"
	Symphony no. 4
The Vangelis	"Chariots of Fire"

Music Suggesting Toys and Puppets

Bratton, John	"Teddy Bears' Picnic"
Coates, Eric	*Cinderella*
	The Three Bears
Debussy, Claude	*Children's Corner*
Delibes, Léo	*Coppelia*
Elgar, Edward	*Nursery* Suite
	The Wand of Youth Suites nos. 1 and 2
Herbert, Victor	"March of the Toys" from *Babes in Toyland*
Humperdinck, Engelbert	*Hansel and Gretel*
Jessel, Leon	"Parade of the Tin Soldiers"
	"Tubby the Tuba"
Joplin, Scott	Ragtime "drags"
Kleinsinger, George	"Peewee the Piccolo"
Mozart, Leopold	"Toy Symphony" from Cassation for Orchestra and Toys in G
Pierné, Gabriel	"March of the Little Lead Soldiers"
Prokofiev, Sergei	*Cinderella*
	The Love for Three Oranges
	Peter and the Wolf
Ravel, Maurice	*Mother Goose*
Rossini, Gioacchino	*La Cenerentola*
Tchaikovsky, Peter Ilyich	*The Nutcracker*
	The Sleeping Beauty
	Swan Lake

Whimsical Music

Grieg, Edvard	*Humoresque*
Mozart, Leopold	"Toy Symphony" from Cassation for Orchestra and Toys in G
Ponchielli, Amilcare	"Dance of the Hours" from *La Gioconda*
Strauss, Richard	*Till Eulenspiegel*
Tchaikovsky, Peter Ilyich	*Humoresque*

Some popular music, including jazz, ragtime, rock, country, and show tunes, is appropriate and popular with young people. Because what is popular and available today may not be tomorrow, no specific pieces are listed here.

Film and Videotape

ANIMAL FILMS FOR HUMANE EDUCATION. New York: Argus Archives, Dept. AF-4, 228 East 49th Street, New York, NY 10017. There are 136 entries in this new and expanded version of the earlier Argus Archives collection. Includes reviews, discussion techniques, and suggestions about how to integrate humane education with other subjects in the curriculum. Many of the films are excellent for creative drama, stimulating original work and raising consciousness of this area in urban children.

BERGGREN, LOIS, AND VERY SPECIAL ARTS, MASSACHUSETTS. *The Great Escape.* 50 Sippiwissett Road, Falmouth, MA 02540. A National Education Association award-winning teacher-training videotape showing children who are multiply disabled at the Kennedy Memorial Hospital School. The creator of the film is an artist-teacher dedicated to making the folk traditions accessible to low-income, minority, and disabled children. Las Posadas, a bilingual Mexican American Children's Theatre Festival, which she founded, celebrated its fifth year in 1987, at which time this film was introduced.

COLLINS, RIVES. *Creative Drama and Improvisation.* Insight Media, 2162 Broadway, New York, 10024. *Creative Dramatics: The First Steps.* 29 min. color, sound. Northwestern Film Library, 614 Davis Street, Evanston, IL 60201. A vintage film that demonstrates the teaching of creative dramatics to a group of fourth-grade children. Guided by an experienced teacher, the group moves from faltering first steps to the creation of a drama.

CREATIVITY: A WAY OF LEARNING. 11 min. color, sound. NEA Distribution Center, Academic Bldg., Saw Mill Rd., West Haven, CT 06516. This film explores creativity, how it is related to life in and out of school, and how it can be encouraged.

DOROTHY HEATHCOTE TALKS TO TEACHERS: PART I. 30 min. color. Northwestern University Film Library, 1735 Benson Avenue, Evanston, IL 60201.

DOROTHY HEATHCOTE TALKS TO TEACHERS: PART II. 32 min. color. Northwestern University Film Library, 1735 Benson Avenue, Evanston, IL 60201. Both films show a master teacher at work as she explains her method of teaching subject areas through drama.

DRAMA WITH THE KINDERGARTEN (videotape presentation). 1987. Arizona State University, Tempe, AZ. Jennifer Akridge introduces this color videotape of creative drama classes taught by Lin Wright, Donald Doyle, and Johnny Saldana. Three approaches to creative drama are shown, documenting the first year's work in a seven-year longitudinal study of drama with and theatre for children.

EVERYMAN IN THE STREETS. 30 min. color. Channel 13 NET (New York), 304 West 58th Street, New York, NY 10019. An old but still interesting film on the uses of creative drama.

FEIL, EDWARD, producer. *Aurand Harris Demonstrating Playwrighting with Children.* 1983. 24 min. color (¾″ U-MATIC; ½″ VHS; ½″ BETA). Distributed by Edward Feil Production, 4614 Prospect Avenue, Cleveland, OH 44103. A children's playwright demonstrates how to teach playwriting to a class of fifth and sixth graders. The lesson is interspersed with Harris's discussion of what he is doing and how playwriting strengthens writing.

GAY, ELIZABETH. "Gert Schattner's Drama Sessions for Short-Term In-Patients." Videotape and report of the methods of a founder of drama therapy in the United States. Ph.D. dissertation, New York University, 1986.

IDEAS AND ME. 17 min. color. Dallas Theatre Center, 3636 Turtle Creek Boulevard, Dallas, TX 75200. In this film children participate in the various aspects of creative drama.

MULTICULTURAL EDUCATION. 30 min. (purchase or rental). Portsmouth, NH: Heinemann, 1995. This award-winning video shows how two teachers from bilingual and multicultural schools built a curriculum, using both school and community.

ONE OF A KIND. 58 min. color, sound. Phoenix Films, Inc., 470 Park Avenue South, New York, NY 10016. Intended for audiences of all ages, this powerful film deals with the relationship between a child and a troubled mother. Through participation in a traveling puppet show, the child is able to express her anguish and needs. The film can be used effectively for classes in special education, psychology, creative drama, and language arts.

PLAYING: PRETENDING SPONTANEOUS DRAMA WITH CHILDREN. 20 min. b/w. Community Services Department, Pittsburgh Child Guidance Center, 201 De Soto Street, Pittsburgh, PA 15213. This film, by Eleanor C. Irwin, describes a number of different forms of spontaneous drama with primary- and elementary-age children. Activities showing creative movement, puppetry, role playing and improvisation are demonstrated. Discussion includes the nature of creativity, the developmental roots of drama, the importance of impulse control as well as expression, the individuality of children and their fantasies, and the value of dramatic play for children in both cognitive and affective learning.

STATUES HARDLY EVER SMILE. 25 min. color. Brooklyn Museum, Eastern Parkway and Washington Avenue, Brooklyn, NY 11238. This film shows work done at the museum. Although several years old, it is unique in content, form, and approach to creative drama.

TAKE 3. 70 min. 16-mm, color, sound. National Audio-Visual Aids Library, Paxton Place, Gipsy Road, London SE27 9SR. This English film describes the work of three drama teachers and is intended to provoke thought and raise questions about the nature of drama, assessment, and evaluation.

THREE LOOMS WAITING. 52 min. color. BBC Production. Distributed by Time-Life Films, Inc., 43 W. 16th Street, New York, NY 10016. This film shows Dorothy Heathcote, one of the leading British teachers of creative drama, working with a group of children. An excellent demonstration of her method.

WHY MAN CREATES. 25 min. color. Pyramid Films, P.O. Box 1048, Santa Monica, CA 90406. A popular film to be shown more than once. It inquires into the human need to create in an unusual way.

Selected Web Sites

Theatre for Young Audiences

Seattle Children's Theatre: http://www.sct.org
The Children's Theatre Company (Minneapolis): http://www.childrenstheatre.org

Stage One: The Louisville Children's Theatre: http://www.stageone.org
Creative Arts Team (NYU): http://www.nyu.edu/gallatin/creativearts
NYU's Program in Educational Theatre: http://www.nyu.edu/education/music/edtheatre
A.A.T.E. (Arizona State University): http://www.aate.com
Alaska Theatre of Youth: http://www.aty.org
Annenberg Center: http://www.upenn.edu/fm/map/annenc.html
Denver Center Theatre Academy: http://www.artstozoo.org/denvercenter/edu/academy.html
Honolulu Theatre for Youth: http://alaike.lcc.hawaii.edu/openstudio/hty
The John F. Kennedy Center for the Performing Arts: http://www.kennedy-center.org
The Seattle Repertory Theatre: http://www.seattlerep.org
Sundance Theatre: http://www.sundance.org/theatre.html
Theatreworks/USA: http://www.theatreworksusa.org
Nashville Children's Theatre: http://www.nct-dragonsite.org

Puppetry

The Puppetry Home Page: http://www.sagecraft.com/puppetry
The Puppeteers of America, Inc: http://www.puppeteers.org
The Center for Puppetry Arts: http://www.puppet.org
UNIMA (USA): http://www.unima-usa.org
University of Connecticut Puppet Arts Program:
    http://www.sfa.uconn.edu/Drama/Puppetry/HOMEPAGE.HTML

Dance

American Ballet Theatre: http://www.abt.org
New York City Ballet: http://www.nycballet.com
Alvin Ailey American Dance Theatre: http://www.arts-online.com/ailey.htm
Pittsburgh Dance Council: http://www.dancecouncil.org
Merce Cunningham: http://www.merce.org
Paul Taylor Dance Company: http://www.ptdc.org
San Francisco Ballet: http://www.sfballet.org

Universities

Arizona State University: http://www.asu.edu
Brigham Young University: http://www.byu.edu
California State University at Northridge: http://www.csun.edu
Eastern Michigan University: http://www.emich.edu
Emerson College: http://www.emerson.edu
Hunter College of the City University of New York: http://www.hunter.cuny.edu
New York University: http://www.nyu.edu
Northwestern University: http://www.nwu.edu
Ohio State University: http://www.osu.edu
University of Hawaii at Manoa: http://www.uhm.hawaii.edu
University of Kansas: http://www.ukans.edu
University of Northern Iowa: http://www.uni.edu
University of South Florida: http://www.usf.edu

University of Texas at Austin: http://www.utexas.edu
University of Utah: http://www.utah.edu
University of Wisconsin-Madison: http://www.wisc.edu

Drama Therapy

New York University Drama Therapy: http://www.nyu.edu/education/music/drama/dramther.html
California Institute of Integral Studies: http://www.ciis.edu
Gallaudet University: http://www.gallaudet.edu

Acknowledgments

From National Standards for Arts Education. Copyright ©1994 by Music Educators National Conference. Used by permission. The complete National Arts Standards and additional materials relating to the Standards are available from Music Educators National Conference, 1806 Robert Fulton Drive, Reston, VA 22091.

Maya Angelou: "Workers' Sons." By permission of Random House.

Dorothy Baruch: "Merry-Go-Round." Permission granted by Bertha Klausner International Literary Agency, Inc.

Margaret Wise Brown: "The Little Scarecrow Boy" from Fun and Frolic. Published by D. C. Heath, copyright 1955. Reprinted with permission.

Sinead de Valera: "Jack and His Animals" in Irish Fairy Tales. Published by C. J. Fallon Educational Publishers, Dublin, Ireland, 1973.

Anne Fessenden:"Height of a Season." Printed by permission of the author.

Alice Ellison: "Sing a Song of Seasons." Copyright ©1964 by Alice Ellison. From Children's Literature for Dramatization: An Anthology by Geraldine Brain Siks. Reprinted by permission of Alice Ellison.

Langston Hughes: "The Negro Speaks of Rivers." Copyright 1926 by Alfred A. Knopf, Inc., and renewed 1954 by Langston Hughes. Reprinted from Selected Poems of Langston Hughes by permission of the publisher.

James Weldon Johnson: "The Creation" from God's Trombones. Copyright 1927 The Viking Press, Inc., renewed ©1955 by Grace Nail Johnson. Used by permission of Viking Penguin, a division of Penguin Books USA, Inc.

Penny Jones: The Story of Noah's Ark. Reprinted by permission of the author.

Kitty Kirby: "Bimi." Copyright © by Kitty Kirby. By permission of the author.

Ann B. Klotz: "Threads." Reprinted by permission of the author.

Carol Korty: Mr. Hare Takes Mr. Leopard for a Ride and Plays from African Folk Tales. Copyright ©1969, 1975 by Carol Korty. All performance rights are restricted. No performance, professional or amateur, may be given without written permission, in advance, of Players Press, Inc., P.O. Box 1132, Studio City, CA 91614-0132, U.S.A.

Joanna H. Kraus: "The Night the Elephants Marched on New York" from Seven Sound and Motion Pictures. Reprinted by permission of New Plays, Inc., Bethel, Conn.

Judith Martin. *The Bird and the Girl*. Copyright ©2003 by Judith Martin. Text and art used by permission of the author.

Lucy Sprague Mitchell: "Jump or Jiggle" from Another Here and Now Storybook. Copyright ©1937 by E. P. Dutton & Co., Inc. Renewed 1965 by Lucy Sprague Mitchell. Reprinted by permission of the publisher, E. P. Dutton & Co., Inc.

Julia Morris. *Study Guide*. Printed by Permission of the author.

News Plays Inc.: "Galileo Study Guide"

J. Paget-Fredericks: "Imaginings" from Green Pipes, MacMillan, 1929.

Shirley Pugh: "Rimouski" from In One Basket. Copyright ©1972 by Shirley Pugh. Reprinted by permission of Anchorage Press of New Orleans.

J. Barrie Shepherd: "Definition" from The Moveable Feast. Published by The Sheepfold Press, copyright 1990. Reprinted with permission.

Geraldine Brain Siks: "Halloween" from Children's Literature for Dramatization: An Anthology. Copyright ©1964 by Geraldine Brain Siks. Reprinted by permission of Harper & Row, Publishers, Inc.

Shel Silverstein: "Yuck" and "Danny O'Dare." Copyright ©1996 by Shel Silverstein. Used by permission of HarperCollins Publishers.

Nancy Swortzell. *Study Guide*. Permission of the author.

R. Rex Stephenson: "Jack and the Haunted House." Reprinted by permission of the author.

Yoshiki Uchida: "The Wise Old Woman" from The Sea of Gold and Other Tales. Copyright ©1965 by Yoshiki Uchida. Reprinted by permission of Charles Scribner's Sons.

Index

449